# Nationalising femininity

'La donna e mobile', *Time and Tide*, 16 October 1943, p. 841

# Nationalising femininity

Culture, sexuality and British cinema
in the Second World War

edited by
CHRISTINE GLEDHILL and GILLIAN SWANSON

## Manchester University Press
Manchester and New York

distributed exclusively in the USA and Canada by St. Martin's Press

*Published by* Manchester University Press
Oxford Road, Manchester M13 9NR, UK
*and* Room 400, 175 Fifth Avenue, New York, NY 10010, USA

*Distributed exclusively in the USA and Canada*
*by* St. Martin's Press, Inc., 175 Fifth Avenue, New York, NY 10010, USA

*British Library Cataloguing-in-Publication Data*
A catalogue record for this book is available from the British Library

*Library of Congress Cataloging-in-Publication Data*
Nationalising femininity : culture, sexuality, and British cinema in the Second World War /
    edited by Christine Gledhill and Gillian Swanson.
        p.        cm.
    Includes bibliographical references and index.
    ISBN 0–7190–4259–3
    1. Women—Great Britain—History—20th century.   2. Women in war—Great Britain—
History—20th century.   3. Women in motion pictures—Great Britain—History—20th
century.   4. World War, 1939–1945—Women—Great Britain.   5. Motion pictures—Great
Britain—History—20th century.   6. Femininity (Psychology)   I. Gledhill, Christine.
II. Swanson, Gillian.
HQ1593.N37   1996
305.42′0941′09044—dc20                                                                                  95–39218

ISBN 0 7190 4259 3 *hardback*

First published in 1996
00 99 98 97 96        10 9 8 7 6 5 4 3 2 1

Typeset in Minion with Tekton
by Northern Phototypesetting Co Ltd, Bolton

Printed in Great Britain
by Biddles Ltd, Guildford and King's Lynn

# Contents

CONTENTS

# Figures

# Notes on the contributors

ROSALIND BRUNT teaches media studies and women's studies at Sheffield Hallam University. She is currently involved in a research project studying women, media culture and the city.

CHRISTINE GERAGHTY is a lecturer in media and communications at Goldsmith's College, University of London. She has written extensively on both film and television, is the author of *Women and Soap Opera* (Polity Press, 1991) and is currently working on a study of post-war British cinema.

CHRISTINE GLEDHILL is principal lecturer in media and cultural studies at Staffordshire University. She has written widely on melodrama and feminist film theory and is editor of *Home Is Where the Heart Is: Studies in Melodrama and the Woman's Film* (British Film Institute, 1987) and *Stardom: Industry of Desire* (Routledge, 1991). Her next project is a monograph on 1920s British cinema.

SUE HARPER teaches cultural history at the University of Portsmouth. She has written widely on British cinema. Her book, *Picturing the Past: The Rise and Fall of the British Costume Film*, was published by the British Film Institute in 1994.

DELIA JARRETT-MACAULEY teaches at Birkbeck College, London University. She has written a biography of Una Marson and is editor of *Reconstructing Womanhood, Reconstructing Feminism* (Routledge, forthcoming 1996).

PAT KIRKHAM is Professor of Design History and Cultural Studies at De Montfort University, Leicester. She has written widely on design, gender and film, is co-editor of *A View From the Interior: Women and Design* (Women's Press, 1989; reprinted 1995), *You Tarzan: Masculinity, Movies and Men* and *Me Jane: Masculinity, Movies and Women* (Lawrence and Wishart, 1993 and 1995). She is currently working on body shape and dress in the 1940s and 1950s. *The Gendered Object* edited by Pat Kirkham will be published by Manchester University Press, mid-1996.

ANNETTE KUHN is reader in film and television studies at the University of Glasgow, and director of the research project, 'Cinema culture in 1930s Britain'.

ANTONIA LANT, author of *Blackout: Reinventing Women for Wartime British Cinema* (Princeton University Press, 1991), teaches cinema studies at New York University. She is now writing on orientalism in early cinema and is co-editing a sourcebook with Ingrid Pariz entitled *Woman's Writings on the Cinema: The First Fifty Years*.

JOY LEMAN is senior lecturer in media studies in the Media School, London College of

Printing. She has contributed to various volumes including John Corner's *Popular Television in Britain* (British Film Institute, 1991). Her current research interests include a comparative study of post-war television in Britain and France.

MELINDA MASH teaches women's studies at Middlesex University. She is co-editor of *Travellers' Tales: Narratives of Home and Displacement* (Routledge, 1994) and *Futurenatural: Nature, Science, Culture* (Routledge, forthcoming).

ALISON ORAM teaches women's history and social history at Sheffield Hallam University. Her research interests include the history of feminism, women teachers, spinsters and lesbian history. She has recently published a book with Manchester University Press on women teachers' politicisation as feminists in the period 1900–39, *Women Teachers and Feminist Politics*.

TESSA PERKINS trained and worked as a stage manager, worked as a secretary, read sociology as a mature student, is raising children, taught sociology, researched women's part-time employment, has written about stereotypes, Doris Day and other matters, and is now principal lecturer in communication studies at Sheffield Hallam University, teaching popular culture, television fictions, feminist film theory, media studies and cultural theory.

CAROL SMART teaches sociology and women's studies at the University of Leeds. She is author of *Feminism and the Power of Law* (Routledge, 1989) and *Law, Crime and Sexuality: Essays in Feminism* (Sage, 1995), and she is editor of *Regulating Womanhood* (Routledge, 1992). She teaches courses on sexuality and the body and is currently doing further research on divorce and relationship breakdown.

PENNY SUMMERFIELD is Professor of Women's History at Lancaster University. She is author of *Women Workers in the Second World War* (Routledge, 1989) and co-author of *Out of the Cage: Women's Experiences in Two World Wars* (Pandora, 1987). She has also published numerous articles on women, war and social change, and on gender, class and schooling in the twentieth century.

GILLIAN SWANSON is lecturer in cultural studies and women's studies in the Faculty of Humanities, Griffith University, Brisbane. She writes on gender and culture, is an advisory editor of *Screen* and is working on a study of sexual pathology in post-war Britain (Routledge, forthcoming).

JANET THUMIM lectures in film and television at the University of Bristol Department of Drama: Theatre, Film, Television. She is the author of *Celluloid Sisters: Women and Popular Cinema* (Macmillan, 1992) and co-editor, with Pat Kirkham, of *You Tarzan: Masculinity, Movies and Men* (Lawrence and Wishart, 1993) and *Me Jane: Masculinity, Movies and Women* (Lawrence and Wishart, 1995).

JANICE WINSHIP is a lecturer in media studies at the University of Sussex and author of *Inside Women's Magazines* (Pandora, 1984).

[x]

# Acknowledgements

This book has been a long time in the making – ten years from the time of our first resolve to follow up our jointly authored article on women in World War Two films – and many people have helped bring it to fruition. Our sense of the need for an interdisciplinary approach to the question of how the conditions of wartime influenced women's lives during the Second World War and its aftermath took us on a circuitous route as we identified contributors for the various components of this study. We thank all the women who we approached during this process of gestation, either for contributions or advice, and also those who acted as anonymous readers.

We are indebted to the women who agreed to contribute to a book which in most cases led them into new research directions, and required a certain amount of faith in the logic of our interdisciplinary combinations. They have been prompt and patient, generous in their willingness to submit to an editorial process which, because of our geographical separation, has had more stages than most, and exceptionally good-willed in their responses to our comments and suggestions. We hope the final product lives up to their expectations.

We owe grateful thanks to Dorothy Sheridan and Joy Eldridge at Mass Observation Archive for help with access and advice. And we must also thank Katharine Reeve, formerly our Editor at Manchester University Press, who had the vision to take on this book and who respected our commitment to the final form in which it appears.

We should also acknowledge support, both institutional and personal, in writing our own chapters. The fax machines at our two Universities – Staffordshire University, UK and Griffith University, Brisbane, Australia – ran hot as chapters spat out each end and were returned, yet the administrative staff who faced the pile of paper each morning were a model of equilibrium and efficiency. Our institutions provided research funds or teaching relief, three years of international postage bills, opportunities to try out our own contributions in Research Forums and at Conferences, and above all colleagueal environments which sharpened our ideas. Our families remained supportive despite our preoccupation with the minutia of wartime conditions. Colin Mercer's advice and intelligence, testy humour and book loans were given with the same generosity and rock solid reliability as they always are and Tara stayed her hunger until long dinner-time phone calls were over. Matthew and Luke were forgiving about late returns from the fax machine and tolerated the parade of black and white films across the video monitor. We thank all of these direct and indirect contributors, supporters and enthusiasts.

# Introduction

## CHRISTINE GLEDHILL and GILLIAN SWANSON

This collection of essays is about women, the home front and cultural representation during the Second World War. While offering a special study of the role of film in the refashioning of femininity for a wartime 'home front', this book seeks to situate cinema at the intersection of social policy and representation. Thus the volume's three-part structure focuses on, respectively, social policy and regulation concerning women, cultural practices which address femininity and the family, and the representation of gender and sexuality in wartime British cinema. The question of the relation of British cinema and women is thereby situated within the wider circulation of discourses, images and narratives between official policy-making, social practices, cultural events, fashion, magazines, broadcasting and films. Such representations provided the means by which it was possible to imagine the working woman without disrupting the image of woman as homemaker. At the same time, stresses and strains appear in magazines, radio programmes, advertisements and films as traditional images attempt to accommodate new social demands made on women. Thus 'reading' the significance of wartime representations of women requires a wide familiarity with their surrounding cultural context. For example, the social concept of 'empty shell marriages' circulated through public debates and government policy on divorce animates the representation of the loveless arranged marriage in *The Man in Grey* and gives the historical fantasy of that film a contemporary meaning for 1940s audiences which is lost on today's audiences unless put back into touch with discourses circulating at the time. In this respect the book documents a diversity of discourses, practices and representations in which we can trace the frameworks which shaped and responded to the necessary social changes of the time while maintaining as far as possible a sense of stability and continuity for a war-torn society.

Among the range of discourses and media which addressed women during the war and which are discussed in this book, the cinema holds a special place because it commanded huge and regular audiences, day and night, and became the focus of a concerted effort to realise a sense of national unity and identity. But since cinema is a medium which synthesises a wide range of art, entertainment and informational forms and is given to adaptation from other sources, it is always unwise to look for the significance of films in isolation from other cultural practices. This is even more true in the case of British cinema in the Second World War, which was impelled to justify its claim on scarce resources by a calculation of the audience's wartime needs and by reference to the extraordinary conditions being endured. It was necessary to find cinematic forms capable of reconciling the contradictory demands of government propaganda, the box office, audiences, film-makers and critics; to develop an address capable of winning audience recognition across class, gender, age, region and ethnicity; and to tap into historically specific circumstances and dilemmas – whether through realism *or* fantasy, for even 'escape' indirectly acknowledges that which must be escaped from. A full analysis of the war's film production, then, cannot be made without reference to governmental controls and production conditions, to audience expectations and critics' exhortations, and to the social and cultural materials out of which cinema's documentary and fictional worlds were constructed. For these reasons we were led to construct this anthology as an interdisciplinary investigation, which gathers together research drawing on history, sociology, cultural and media analysis, and women's studies.

Over the past two decades the Second World War has become a popular focus for a stream of publications, films, documentaries and television series. It is used as either a repository of nostalgia for lost national greatness or, alternatively, as a site of revisionary inquiry, investigating and challenging the official histories or popular representations of the war. One of the 'assumed truths' of the Second World War is that it involved a radical change in the organisation of the domestic sphere and women's roles. For some commentators at the time, such changes appeared as *the* measure of the effects of the war.[1] Feminist historians, however, have shown how changes in women's lives were couched in temporary terms: 'for the duration only', in the now familiar phrase. In addition, some have argued that any benefits accruing to women during the war were equally dramatically reversed after the war's end. This rather too neat move from change to containment, however, risks constructing the Second World War in terms of an extraordinary set of 'mould breaking' conditions and events, entirely distinct from the pre-war or the post-war period. In contrast to accounts which see the feminist platforms of the 1960s–1980s emerging largely in reaction to a prior period of constraint and repression, a more detailed picture of the history of gender from the 1930s to the 1950s is essential to understand the significance of the war period for gender relations and feminist debates in the second half of the twentieth century. This anthology, then, revisits the Second World War to investigate the processes of social and cultural gender change in a specific historical context.

This book asks questions about the reconstruction of femininity in wartime in relation to questions of women's place in the pre-war 1930s and in the period of national reconstruction in the late 1940s and 1950s. The picture this wider context provides immediately puts the claim that war conditions initiated change into a different perspective. Many transformations in women's lives attributed to the war were in fact already in progress in the 1930s. In particular, as the chapters show, women's roles as mothers, wives and workers were already under debate, while, for example, changes in fashion, housework, consumption patterns, or stars popular at the box office signalled redefinitions of femininity emerging in the 1930s which are generally attributed to the war. Equally, while the war made breaks in continuity more visible, established routines and conventions of gender were maintained, for example the retention of glamour and pre-war fashion in the face of utility clothing or uniforms. In other words, as well as shifts from traditional to new gender definitions and roles, there were also *convergences* between meanings and practices emerging in the 1930s and the conditions of war. The war can be seen as both a catalyst for changes already in the making and an incitement to energies directed towards preserving traditional gender differences.

Signs of – or hopes for – a return to earlier models of femininity are found in the post-war reconstruction of women's roles. Nevertheless, just as a sharp division did not exist between wartime and the pre-war period, so it proved impossible simply to erase the new demands made on and by women as a consequence of wartime upheavals. In fact, Janice Winship and Alison Oram show that war conditions and government policies led to modernising *as well as* conservative trends in post-war Britain. From this perspective, the seemingly traditionalist 1950s emerges as a period marked by contradictions between the lasting effects of these changes and the earlier project of readjustment for which planning began from 1942. The history of gender in this period, then, suggests that the new social conditions of wartime were more uneven, contradictory and complex in their short and long-term effects than has often been assumed.

Divergences of meaning exist within, as well as between, historical periods, as those who focus on the experiences and testimonies of women from different classes, regions or national cultures show. In fact, co-editing this book from opposite ends of the world highlighted for us the differences of perspective that derive from different national locations. Thus not only do

Australia and Britain commemorate the fiftieth anniversary of the war's ending according to different events and dates, but for Australia, close to the Asian-Pacific military theatre, the threat of Japanese invasion was contemplated in terms which inspired fears for racial – rather than national – identity. This fear entailed a markedly different experience of war for Australian women: for example, the 'Brisbane Line' placed parts of the Northern Territory and Northern Queensland outside the protection of the military, marking them as areas to be left undefended. This signalled to the women living there that they and their families were to be discarded and thereby severely dislocated the connection between nation and home. However, despite the historical specificity of conditions and experiences within national boundaries, correspondences in gendered meanings generated by the war can be found across different national contexts. Thus total mobilisation in Australia produced many gendered changes which paralleled those in Britain and elsewhere, while despite the absence of formal conscription in the United States, the image of woman was still mobilised in national propaganda campaigns and wartime fictions.[2] These differences and commonalities suggest the interest of this volume to an international readership.

The high profile of gender issues in the Second World War presented a new challenge for a range of government and social agencies whose role it was to mobilise women: the need to address women as part of a national community pulling together in the interests of Britain at war. This need to prepare a gendered population for huge changes in social and personal life, and the reciprocal need to define women's place in the war effort in terms which did not undermine established gender distinctions and conventions, provided the framework for making new wartime policies. This involved developing a repertoire of national images capable of uniting diverse groups in the war effort and thereby mobilising a new relation between gender and nation. In the class and gender encounters dramatised in British wartime cinema, social and sexual boundaries represent divisions but also meeting points, allowing exchange and the potential for new meanings and identities. Pulling together also implied women pulling together with men – often literally – as women joined men on their 'turf' in factories, in the military and emergency services. But this conscription of women threw traditional gender roles into confusion as 'joining' men also meant replacing men, and invading a sphere traditionally outside the province of women. Such a disruption was modified in various ways, including an address to the 'genderless citizen',[3] a rhetoric of 'equality' which assumed women could do what men did,[4] and the development of a *distinctive* address to women, maintaining gender as a crucial marker of one's place in the national community. That these alternatives, amongst others, were not finally resolved is evident in the points of tension and incompatibility emerging in the changing parameters and meanings of femininity.

The focus on gendered change in the specific circumstances of the British home front demands a historical approach which attends to a diversity of practices and source materials. This is reflected in the range of topics addressed in this anthology, from women's industrial labour and government legislation, to strategies for living everyday life in wartime, to cartoons, advertisements, articles, radio programmes and films. Our enterprise also demands attention to the definitions of work, sexuality or home assumed by government policy, trade union demands or domestic arrangements. Thus the historical analysis of gender inevitably engages with the analysis of cultural discourses and representations, as gender definitions are reframed and new identities negotiated.

Representations of women in British 'home front' films emphasise female roles and domestic concerns. The centrality of 'woman' as a sign capable of securing the identity of nation as 'home' sits uneasily with policies conscripting women into war work and the governmental address to 'mobile women', as well as with the increase in women's political activism which Alison Oram charts as a feature of wartime debates. Thus we find competing definitions of woman as the term itself becomes 'mobile'. This increased attention to women's concerns in British wartime cultural life is not simply a 'reflection' of transformations taking place in the social fabric, but a sign of the difficulty involved in engineering new gender definitions and representations within the parameters of existing and slowly evolving cultural traditions.

If public attention is turned to women's issues and domestic organisation in a new way, the historian is also directed to women's experiences and the minutiae of everyday life as the place where government legislation, the pronouncements of policy-makers and social or psychological investigators and media representations take their effects, are negotiated, resisted or ignored. For this reason this book does not seek to reproduce the official image of women in wartime, nor to show women simply as objects of government policy but to explore the relationship between the official framing of women's lives and the ways they found to participate as agents, endeavouring to shape their own histories and thereby national life. This is a far more difficult terrain to track than government legislation or social policy. While some contributors draw on the archives of Mass Observation or the Wartime Social Survey, they also warn that the agendas of these organisations were influenced by the objectives of government and do not necessarily derive from the perspectives of women, nor could they represent the views of all women. Letters, diaries and women's political journalism offer alternative sources, and are being published in increasing quantities. Fashion, fandom and audience responses carry further traces of the ways in which women responded and made sense of their circumstances and options, as well as providing clues to their identifications and fantasies. Such material is vital to a historical investigation that seeks to track the twists and turns of the social changes promoted and contained through governmental agencies and media representations and the negotiations involved in and resistances encountered in the attempt.

The cinema offers an exemplary site for such historical 'tracking'. Despite rising seat prices, the cinema audience reached its all-time peak of 31.4 million a week by 1946. According to Angus Calder, three-quarters of the adult population were cinema-goers, a third attending once or more a week.[5] Although increasingly a source of middle-class interest and debate, the cinema drew larger numbers of women, young people and people from the lower middle or working classes than many of the other media.[6] Jeffrey Richards argues the importance of British wartime cinema in producing and sustaining a 'national persona' characterised by class unity.[7] In addition to its role as an arm of propaganda spanning documentary, newsreel and feature film, the cinema was a major source of entertainment and communal experience for women whose husbands were away in the forces or who had themselves joined the women's services or been directed to work in factories away from home. Guy Morgan's account of British cinemas in wartime, *Red Roses Every Night*, claims that the nightly queues forming in Leicester Square for *Gone With the Wind* (1939) where it played continuously throughout the war became *the* symbol of London's solidity.[8] It should be noted that this monument is constructed around an American film, for the dominance of Hollywood on British screens is a significant factor in debates amongst government ministries, film industry leaders, critics and audiences, about whether a national cinema was needed and what kind of cinema it should be for 'these times'. This makes the cinema doubly interesting as a site of cultural construction. The search for a specifically national style and subject matter which could also address *women* as part of the national community raises questions about not only the relation of gender to nation but also the particularity of British femininity as distinct from Hollywood models of glamour and sexuality.

The book's three sections, focusing respectively on social policies, cultural practices and cinema, reflect in part these different disciplinary concerns and the materials they take for analysis. But more importantly, their concerns intersect as social policies and cultural representations feed each other, giving greater depth to our understanding of, for example, the significance in wartime films of listening to the radio, of fashion and set design, or of narratives of sexual temptation. The divisions between sections, then, reflect disciplinary emphases and orientations or identify particular objects and processes under investigation rather than hard-and-fast distinctions.

Moreover, the conjuncture in this volume of different approaches and materials sets up a dialogue across the disciplines which is essential to any investigation of gender and femininity. Interchange is also encouraged between the different functions performed by these essays. While longer, more wide-ranging contributions map out general issues and frameworks, shorter ones provide specific case studies, or, in the cinema section, textual analyses of particular films.

As already noted, one of the distinctive features of the Second World War consequent on the high profile given to women's roles on the home front is that the particularity of women's lives became a matter of national importance. Antonia Lant's 'Prologue' to the volume explores the concerted political and cultural campaign to align these two terms – femininity and nationality – normally seen as distinct and incompatible. Thus she reveals the imbrication of government legislation and social policies concerning women with cultural discourses and media representations which sought to mobilise women for the national good while needing to contain the tensions opened up in traditional definitions of the feminine – attempting for example to retain the symbol of woman as mother and wife and to ward off the threat of independent female sexuality.

Part One, 'Mobile women: change and regulation', takes as its focus legislation and policies which sought to mobilise women for the war effort while at the same time seeking to frame that mobilisation in terms that would retain the conventional roles and meanings associated with women. The chapters by Penny Summerfield and Carol Smart bring into focus connections between governmental legislation, social policy and cultural representation. Penny Summerfield examines how women's increased involvement in industrial labour was reconciled with the important figure of the housewife as a 'cornerstone' of British national life in her discussion of the implications of mobilisation for women, while Carol Smart looks at law reform debates for their responses to changing patterns of marriage and divorce during and after the war, exploring the material pressures against sexual infidelity for women and the facilitation of divorce for serving men returning to 'empty shell marriages'. In Gillian Swanson's essay we see just how deeply official attention penetrated to the heart of everyday and personal life as the application of the psychological sciences to questions of morale focused on women's sexual behaviour and consumption patterns, while Alison Oram's investigation of women's political activism explores the debates and struggles through which women sought to define and shape their own lives and the outcomes of the war.

While the essays in Part One focus on the broad contours of social policies and the representational discourses through which they were framed, Part Two, 'Fashioning the national self: cultural practices and representations', comprises a series of more local case studies. In this section we see the attempt of the cultural industries to produce a specific address to women, for example Joy Leman's account of the struggle of a woman producer in the BBC to win a slot for a broad-based women's radio programme or the growth in prestige of women's magazines as they gave advice to women on managing their 'war selves' and solicited their contribution to post-war planning, which Janice Winship explores through the example of *Woman's Own*. Delia Jarrett-Macauley examines another area of specialist BBC programming which drew on the skills of a Jamaican woman broadcaster to negotiate the challenge to British imperialism by the colonies in their demand to contribute on equal terms to a war supposedly waged for democracy against totalitarianism and racism. This essay introduces the virtually unrepresented and undiscussed intersection of nationality and ethnicity in the politics and culture of the home front, although Antonia Lant's concluding analysis of *I See a Dark Stranger* (1946) opens up the problematic construction of a British national femininity in relation to the kingdoms, and Ireland in particular. Critical here are the parallels and differences in maternal imagery that can be drawn between woman as unifier of the home front, the black broadcaster Una Marson's maternal function for the West Indian community and forces, and Britain's assumed role as 'mother country' of the Empire. Rosalind Brunt's examination of the role of the royal family as constructed by British Pathé News stresses the function in the royal image of an idealised family, centred on a fairytale queen and her two little princesses, as a means of binding the nation and Empire through a common fantasy of family. The importance of dress which Rosalind Brunt notes in the image of this familial paradise is taken up by Pat Kirkham in an analysis which explores the role of dress in the practices of femininity by moving between the fashion industry, magazine features and advertisements, and the everyday practices, skills and desires of women themselves in fashioning a more diverse form of wartime femininity than is often recognised.

Part Three, 'Nationalising femininity: the case of British cinema', explores the concentrated intersection of government, culture and personal life, taking cinema as a site where issues of femininity, sexuality and nation are vividly dramatised. Annette Kuhn examines the representation of femininity in 1930s British cinema through the genres, fan magazines and stars popular at the time, and like many of the preceding essays she locates the end of that decade – citing in this case 1937 and the particular popularity of Deanna Durbin then emerging in Britain – as a moment when a shift towards a more modern, outgoing yet respectable femininity can be discerned. Sue Harper introduces wartime film production by charting the quarrels between ministries, cultural institutions, critics and the film industry about the kind of cinema required for the national emergency and the impact these different perspectives had on the representation of women in films of different genres and made by different studios. Christine Gledhill pursues these issues by exploring in particular the intersection of documentary, melodrama and romance in two major genres of the period, the home front film and Gainsborough melodrama. The problematic relation of femininity and nation introduced by Antonia Lant is directly addressed by Christine Geraghty, who in a case study of three films dealing with the problem of national allegiance explores the differences in narrative strategies these films employ according to whether the double agent at the centre of the plot is male or female. Janet Thumim examines the problems of reconstructing audience responses in a study that moves between the audience addressed in and by the film, critical reviews and the practices of women's wartime film-going. In a case study of two post-war films, Melinda Mash shows how the contradictory post-war discourses of 'austerity' and 'affluence' shape and determine the fate of some of the alternative femininities glimpsed during wartime production. Tessa Perkins concludes the volume in an examination of the negotiations and tensions involved in the post-war reconstruction of gender relations and how these were played out in films of the late 1940s.

The range of responses which women may have had to film during wartime is hinted at by the diversity of interpretations collected here. For example, different dimensions of an important wartime film, *Millions Like Us* (1943), are drawn out by Sue Harper, Christine Gledhill and Janet Thumim: the need for personal sacrifice so that the home front could be strengthened; an ambivalent depiction of the pleasures and constraints of domestic and marital relations and motherhood; the acknowledgement of women's need to manage diverging commitments to family and work; the image of a population capable of forming solidarities that cross class and gender boundaries; and the complex of reactions called up to exhortations towards personal sacrifice by female spectators identifying with the grief suffered by the heroine in her bereavement.

While most discussions of cinema make reference to fiction films rather than documentary, the marked rise that we noted in documentary films taking as their themes 'female subjects' during the war, and their equally sudden disappearance after the war,[9] supports the contention that the everyday lives of women became a central focus in the management of a nation at war, just as those forms of information signalled to women a new set of responsibilities, options and forms of public presence. While the medium of photodocumentation, including such publications as *Picture Post*, is also referred to amongst other sources by some contributors, clearly the documentary media would warrant a separate study.

Our cover image, a painting by Dame Laura Knight, *Ruby Loftus Screw-*

*ing a Breech Ring* (1941), reminds us of the work of women working in the traditional rather than popular arts. The distinction between high and mass culture is an arbitrary one, particularly in respect of women's literary production which has always borne an ambiguous relation to established canons. For example, the bestselling fiction *Mrs Miniver*, published just after the war began, collected the entries of a regular column first written for *The Times* in the late 1930s. According to Valerie Grove, introducing the recent Virago re-issue, Jan Struther had been asked to write about 'an ordinary sort of woman who leads an ordinary sort of life' because the Court Page was 'full of woodpeckers and stoats'.[10] In this literary source, we find a feminine sensibility at work, registering amidst the minutiae of the daily tasks of organising domestic and personal life, the backwash of social change. Like many women writers popular with their generation and later forgotten, she is credited with a political impact far outstripping the critical recognition of her work: President Franklin D. Roosevelt told Jan Struther that *Mrs Miniver* had hastened America's entry into the war and Winston Churchill is said to have declared that *Mrs Miniver* had done more for the Allies than a flotilla of battleships.[11] In the upper-middle-class but liberal and responsible Mrs Miniver we find the prototype for a range of specifically British and class-bound femininities exemplified, for instance, in the poems of Patience Strong or in the characterisations of Celia Johnson. It is the crossover between Mrs Miniver and her character played by Celia Johnson in *Brief Encounter* (1945) which Janice Winship uses to exemplify the tenor of emotional restraint adopted by women's magazines.

This collection, while analysing the determining policies, legislation and definitions circulated by government and social institutions, also highlights the agency of women as trade union or political activists, as broadcasters and writers in women's magazines, and in the prosecution of everyday life, as workers, readers, film fans, consumers, or fashion experts. Related to this is their presence in the film industry as stars, representing a crossover point between the performer and the image which is circulated in a number of ways through the media as material for the activity of fans. Here is a rich field of investigation inviting exploration of the competing femininities on offer, for example in the popularity of such diverse star personae and actresses as the solidly middle-class Celia Johnson, Phyllis Calvert, Patricia Roc, the arriviste femininity represented by Margaret Lockwood, or the working-class duo who rose to fame in the war years, Gert and Daisy, touched on by Sue Harper. This highly popular pair of comediennes brings into view a major feature of wartime culture: comedy, both radio and film, for the neglect of which official bodies such as the Ministry of Information (MoI) were roundly berated,[12] but which has for different reasons been the subject of only minimal attention by critics and feminists alike. In this respect, as Sue Harper's essay suggests, the critical canon of films valorised as the 'golden age' of British cinema falls closely into line with the preferred genres of the MoI literati and quality press critics, which is now being challenged and enlarged.

Finally, as several contributors observe, the gendered social changes brought about by the war all focus on women and more extensive change would necessarily have involved a transformation in the identities and roles of men and masculinity. Many wartime and post-war discourses were concerned to manoeuvre women into positions that would shore up a masculinity that was itself undergoing transition, challenge and sometimes damage. While considerable work is underway elsewhere on the construction of masculinity, the specific interrelationship between masculine roles and definitions in wartime culture demands fuller analysis. The domestication of the home front, its apparent feminisation, and the frequently 'neurotic' representations of masculinity offered in wartime films, open up new perspectives on the workings of sexual difference.

This brings us back to the purpose of this volume. It has not been its intention to provide a definitive and conclusive account of the period and its culture. What the essays gathered here teach is that neither nationality nor sexual identity are pre-given, coherent or fixed, but are constantly in the process of production and negotiation. Additionally, a close historical focus of the kind used in these essays, rather than providing a unified picture of sweeping change during and after the war, warns against attempting a too general account of the effects of government intentions, industrial objectives or social propaganda. Rather than attempting a definitive history, this volume unearths from a diversity of sources and documents, both official and the more randomly collected recordings of lived experience, a complex of social and institutional policies, practices and representations. It is on the multiple, sometimes mutually reinforcing, at other times argumentative, nature of these discourses that the essays focus, showing the ways they influenced the changing shape of domesticity, leisure and work and the shifting place of women within them.

### Notes

1 See Antonia Lant in this volume.
2 For a useful overview of the effects of wartime mobilisation on women's lives, see Kay Saunders and Geoffrey Bolton, 'Girdled for war: women's mobilisations in World War Two', in Kay Saunders and Ray Evans (eds), *Gender Relations in Australia: Domination and Negotiation* (Sydney, Harcourt Brace Jovanovich, 1992); for an account of the influence of war on Australian women's experiences and memories, see Kate Darian-Smith, 'War stories: remembering the Australian home front during the Second World War', in Kate Darian-Smith and Paula Hamilton (eds),

*Memory and History in Twentieth Century Australia* (Melbourne, Oxford University Press, 1994); and for discussion of the representation of gender in the war, see Marilyn Lake, 'Female desires: the meaning of World War II', *Australian Historical Studies*, Vol. 24 No. 5 (1990), and 'The desire for a yank: sexual relations between Australian women and American servicemen during World War 2', in Patricia Grimshaw, Ruth Fincher and Marion Campbell (eds), *Studies in Gender: Essays in Honour of Norma Grieve* (Melbourne, University of Melbourne, 1993).

3  Denise Riley discusses an official attempt made by Sir Stafford Cripps in 1943 to address national problems through a genderless notion of the citizen, in 'The Free Mothers: pronatalism and working mothers in industry at the end of the last war in Britain', *History Workshop Journal*, No. 11 (1981).

4  See Alison Oram in this volume.

5  Angus Calder, *The People's War: Britain, 1939–1945* (London, Granada, 1982), pp. 423–4.

6  Jeffrey Richards and Dorothy Sheridan note that the average weekly audience rose from 19 million in 1939 to 31.4 million in 1946, the peak year of attendance in British cinema history, in *Mass-Observation at the Movies* (London, Routledge and Kegan Paul, 1987), p. 112. They also suggest that for 'the vast army of female war workers' the cinema was as important to morale as the pint of beer (p. 12).

7  Jeffrey Richards, 'National identity in British wartime films', in Philip Taylor (ed.), *Britain and the Cinema in the Second World War* (London, Macmillan, 1988).

8  Guy Morgan, *Red Roses Every Night: An Account of London Cinemas Under Fire* (London, Quality Press, 1948), p. 77.

9  This is evident in the chronological list of film synopses in the invaluable collection by Frances Thorpe and Nicholas Pronay, *British Official Films in the Second World War* (Oxford, Clio Press, 1980).

10  Valerie Grove, 'Introduction' to Jan Struthers, *Mrs Miniver* (London, Virago, 1989), p. x.

11  *Ibid.*; Alison Light, *Forever England: Femininity, Literature and Conservatism Between the Wars* (London and New York, Routledge, 1991).

12  Anthony Aldgate and Jeffrey Richards argue that the MoI Films Division's anxiety about Britain's image abroad led to the neglect of comedy and humour in the service of morale; see Aldgate and Richards, *Britain Can Take It: The British Cinema in the Second World War* (Oxford, Blackwell, 1983), pp. 26–7.

# 1

## Prologue: mobile femininity[1]

### ANTONIA LANT

The Second World War forced the question of nationality into every crevice of public and private life. Objects, acts, and people were sifted into their national categories: alien, enemy, neutral, naturalised, Allied. Emergency legislations brought conscription, blacking out, rationing, and transformed the cultural sphere; cinema and theatre, radio and magazines, official pamphlets and posters, cartoons and advertisements were all caught up in discussion of the national.[2] As familiar daily routines disappeared, surviving ones acquired a peculiar, symbolic glow: rearing a champion marrow became an act of patriotism; sighting an orange a precious glimpse of peace. Domestic life lurched from the epitome of the ordinary to the quintessence of the extraordinary.

Mobilisation was to 'inculcate in every citizen the maximum feeling of responsibility as part of the actual defense of the community'.[3] A sense of participation was needed all around, regardless of a person's sex, age, or distance from the front. The front was in fact to be everywhere, a home front, shaping everyone's domestic decisions. However, uniformly alert and knowing subjects of the realm were not so easily conjured up. There were Britain's subdivisions into England, Wales, Scotland, Northern Ireland; its relation to the colonies (or Empire); its regional differences; its class stratifications in every zone. Its political boundary did not (and does not) coincide with the island's physical border, notably in the case of Northern Ireland. Additional differences within Britain had accrued, and audibly, during the pre-war influx of European refugees, and then with the arrival of European forces after the war's outbreak, and the GI 'invasion' of 1942–43. The spectre of further disunity loomed as homes were broken up, families disbanded, and children evacuated in the face of 'total war,' its official title. From the start of war until the end of 1945 there were some 34,750,000 changes of address in

England and Wales in a civilian population of about 38 million. People moved in such numbers as to provoke the slur, 'a nation of migrants'.[4] How could the notion of common purpose overshadow these divisions?

There was an urgent need to stem the perceived fracturing of Britain, at least in terms of official rhetoric and symbols, so that the idea of national unity could emerge. But national identity is not a natural, timeless essence, on tap and waiting to be revealed. Rather, as an intermittent, combinatory form, developed when familiar boundaries are contested, it had to be actively built up in Britain by comparison with other national identities (German, Russian, or American), in order to demonstrate that, despite (and often because of) the internal differences of the nation – of class, of gender, and so on – the most important divide was between Britain and Germany, between democracy and fascism. However, in developing such comparisons there still remained the management of internal divisions in relation to an external picture of unity. This was particularly tricky when it came to mobilising women. How were women to be part of total war, part of the nation's unity, both at the level of work, and in cultural representation? That is the question for this essay.

The Second World War generated a very complicated and contradictory interaction of femininity and nationhood, whose traces linger in the voices of memory, in official surveys, in images, in diaries, in textual fictions, and elsewhere. The conceptual relations of the two identities, femininity and nationhood, will be charted here by reference to specific images chosen from different points of wartime life: from the relatively conservative magazine *Punch* with a middle-class readership; the feminist leaning *Time and Tide* weekly; the manufacturer's advertisement tinged with war guilt; and films, particularly *I See a Dark Stranger* (1946) made as the war was ending by the independent Two Cities team, Frank Launder and Sidney Gilliat. By looking to the evidence of cartoons, advertising, and cinema in this way we learn that war had to reshape the landscape of gender as it sought out national character. These materials represent fascinating sites of ideological work as the process of nationalising femininity got underway. We can conclude that the struggle for national security entailed a struggle over gender definitions, for the female body and female image challenged national coherence in a graphic literalisation of sexual politics, forcing a multitude of redefinitions of what womanhood, manhood, and nationhood might be.

With the passing of the British National Services Act (2 September 1939), men aged 19–41 had become liable for conscription, but women's contribution was still voluntary. However, from November 1940 onwards Labour MP Ernest Bevin described the urgent need for women's 'employment and training', and on 10 December 1941 the controversial National Service Act (No. 2) became law, marking the first call-up ever of British women, and adding men in their forties to the pool. By 5 March 1942 almost all British single women aged 20–31 could be conscripted, a form of legislation never introduced in the United States and only implemented in Germany as a last ditch effort in 1945. Drafting women came to symbolise national specificity; as the proud male voice-over in *Desert Victory* (1943) put it, 'In no country are women so thoroughly organised for war'.

However, implementing female conscription did not run smoothly. First of all, the Ministry of Labour's unfortunate classifications of 'mobile' and 'immobile' to designate women who could be moved to work anywhere in the country (mobile), or who had to work locally because they had dependants or were married (immobile), conveyed and fuelled no end of consternation and jokes about the dependability of women in war. When asked by the Ministry of Information to make a film about domestic war Launder and Gilliat used the mobile woman's story, but Gilliat recalled that while they were 'very impressed with the fate … of the conscripted woman, the mobile woman', they could not call their film that because it was 'such a silly title'; their embarrassment points to the difficulty of both naming and representing wartime female experience – instead they chose the title *Millions Like Us*.[5] One area of Britain – the Isle of Man – went its own way with respect to the draft, refusing to extend the National Services Act (No. 2) to cover its populace. The Manx parliament insisted that under Manx law no women could be required to fight, and that men in their forties were also exempt. Cultural perception of the island as literally one of men perfectly coincided with, and indeed seemed to inform, the Tynwald's political slant. (For other reasons, relating to the memory of the partition of Ireland during the First World War, Northern Ireland also provided volunteers rather than draftees.)

Despite these imperfections female recruitment symbolised the ideal that every individual would count towards the body politic, nourishing the goal of coherent national union, of pulling together across lines of difference. As a wartime history put it, 'The mobilization of labor eventually became a swing over from man-power to woman-power … It was as though with the passing of the National Service Act No. 2, the country at last realized we were in for total war'.[6] The writers, actors, and film-makers Leslie Howard, J. B. Priestley, Frank Launder and Sidney Gilliat all proclaimed that the phenomenon of the mobile woman was for them the paradigm of war: her story crystallised the unique character of the crisis.[7] However, at another level recruitment sapped the idea of nation from within; mass mobilisation undermined traditional notions of civil stability in which the sexes had clearly defined roles and in which a woman's place was at home. Women could no longer be counted on to be at home – indeed they were now required by law not to be. The idea of home could hardly function as a synecdoche for national unity (as it had in earlier wars) when it now

[ 15 ]

contained no family, few women, fewer men, and was physically being destroyed.

A study of the iconography of home, and other references to home as a metaphor for nation in wartime, forms a useful approach to understanding the relationship of femininity to nationhood. In the case of film, however, the analysis of home must note that most movies screened in Britain before and during the Second World War were made outside the nation, in the United States. Partly in response to this imported cinema, Britain developed a category of home-produced feature films now labelled the home front genre. Documentary and instructional film-making also mushroomed, mixing into the style of feature films to make Britain the most filmed nation ever during the 1940s, according to Penelope Houston. The home front feature film was always set during the war and repeatedly used the same visual motifs – the raid, the recruitment poster, the blackout, the image of urban destruction and its complement, rural rejuvenation – and narrative tropes, such as deferred romantic union and frequent romantic partings. The latter contributed to a sense of imperfect closure within the films, consonant with the ideological promotion of 'making do' on the part of the mobilised citizen. Determinedly banal, quotidian locations were filmed with a restrained acting and camera style, save for those moments during a raid. Corner shops, bomb sites, front door steps, and station platforms provided the films' typical settings, while parlours, pubs, and spartan dance halls, lit by lonely, revolving mirrored globes, added a modicum of lustre to the austere wartime environment. The resulting 'new school of realism' became a generic marker of Britishness against the spectacular Hollywood film, and so also participated in the construction of national identity.[8]

Government memoranda on the filming of bomb sites are significant in this discussion since such images collided with the idea of home as a shorthand for the nation. As might be expected, officials worried about the potentially demoralising impact of reproducing urban destruction. As Nicholas Pronay and Jeremy Croft show, at the height of the Blitz the chief censor required that each panning shot 'start from an undamaged building … conclude on an undamaged building and … not linger over damaged buildings'.[9] However, the need for audience recognition loosened 1930s censorship regulations generally and overwhelmed these specific panning rules in the service of increased realism. British films abound with bomb site scenes as an almost compulsory element of their iconography. Such scenes contributed to claims for the greater relevance of 'social realism' as opposed to Hollywood glamour since it was Britain that was experiencing the front line. Late war films such as *Waterloo Road* (1944), *A Canterbury Tale* (1944) and *Perfect Strangers* (1945) contained particularly potent images of urban devastation, which perhaps reminded spectators of the post-war effort of reconstruction to come – the need to rebuild the nation's house.

Material destruction is paralleled in British home front films by incomplete or irregular families whose absent components are left unexplained: absence is simply a condition of war. These absences also trouble the chain of meaning that would produce the idea of nation out of the home – the metonymic linkage from woman to mother, to family, home, and finally to nation in a sequence that might promise to emphasise homogeneity, sliding over class and regional diversity. As a solution, home front films produced makeshift pseudo-families, diverse groups of characters united through the Navy, RAF or Auxiliary Territorial Service (ATS), through their journeying on a train together, through beer-drinking in the local saloon, or through co-operating as a 'working village', as in *Great Day* (1945). The key narrative location for such films was as often a training camp, a factory, a village, or a city, as a home itself. These sites demanded different social structures, more communal than those of the traditional home, and so serving the national interest better. Dancing in aircraft hangars, pub scenes, listening to the radio, fighting alongside one another, harvesting, and other group activities endlessly recurred, collectively symbolising team strength and the overcoming of class, sex, and regional difference in the face of possible defeat.

But as actual homes disintegrated, legislation ensured the home's continued existence, at least in daily vocabulary. The notion of a home front, borrowed from the First World War, was commandeered again. In peacetime 'home' had meant everything from not-foreign, not-a-colony, to a house, family, fireside, or England itself, but in the 1939 crisis it needed to stand for the defended nation. A new ministry was created, the Ministry of Home Security, responsible for planning and supervising Air Raid Precaution (ARP) services, with the Home Secretary at its head. The Home Guard, Home Intelligence Unit and BBC Home Service (a radio station) were all instituted in the first year of war. In all these instances 'home' is virtually interchangeable with the word 'national'. The power of the wireless to suggest national cohesion accounts in part for the large number of communal radio-listening scenes in home front films. Images of families clustering around radio sets perfectly encapsulated the notion of the home front: small units of patriotism, resourceful, bound by familiarity and linked by the radio, armed with a pencil and ready to act when required.

With ideas of family and home under duress, a refashioning of the semiotics of sexual difference was inevitable, in which the stereotype of the mobile woman played a key role.[10] 'Mobile' had both literal and metaphorical meanings. Women were actually being shipped out of the home, while the category 'woman' was also on the move, elusive, constantly having to be resighted through wartime imagery and tales. An extremely literal example

[ 17 ]

of this occurs in the opening, over-the-shoulder shots of *The Gentle Sex* (1943) when Leslie Howard, director and narrator of the film, is seen in silhouette on a gantry above Victoria Station, a mass of potential female recruits swarming beneath his gaze on the platforms below.[11]

Priestley described female conscription as an 'intricate' task: a question of finding as many immobile women as possible to release mobile ones, since by 1943 the latter were in 'rapidly dwindling supply'. He explained that it was far more difficult to 'mobilise' women than men, because women were not 'free' and could not 'be moved about in the casual fashion that will do for the male'; transplanting and training them was a 'highly complicated and difficult task'.[12] It was so difficult, he added, that most countries had historically refused the challenge even if 'desperately in need of manpower'. He referred to the German wartime woman's role as mother rather than fighter.

The precariousness of this new femininity is highlighted in a cartoon which probes the perceived incompatibility between innate femininity and the waging of war, and in the process produces a very contradictory image (see frontispiece).[13] A single woman sits passively on a park bench, her arms folded. A couple cuddle in the distance. She wears a long, enveloping Victorian dress edged with the slogan 'Victory'. Three Allied leaders court her: Churchill with chocolates, and Stalin and Roosevelt with bouquets of flowers. Seduction is their method, not business-like bargaining or official recruitment. Churchill has abandoned his attributes of hat, cane, and briefcase to concentrate on the task, but the woman seems as yet unmoved. The first contradiction is that she is a personification of victory, an allegorical female figure, but needs to be approached by particular men equipped with all too material bribes.

In the foreground Hitler clutches a large handkerchief and cries out in a bold operatic gesture as if delivering 'La donna è mobile', Verdi's famous 1851 aria from *Rigoletto* and the cartoon's caption. In *Rigoletto* the melody is first sung by the Duke of Mantua as he laments the fickleness of women; in the cartoon Hitler does the same. He bemoans that things are not going his way, for he now knows, as Priestley promised, that those nations which woo and organise their women will win. The cartoon was published in 1943 in *Time and Tide*, a magazine begun as a feminist political weekly in 1920 spurred by the struggle for women's suffrage. This suggests why the centrality of women's contribution is stressed as compared with representations more typical of *Punch* in which women's new roles show up chiefly as anxiety-producing jokes. Here the female figure has great potential power, both in being the focus of the highest male attention (which was indeed the case), and in the implied possible consequences if she remains stubborn. However, in rewriting 'mobile woman' as 'la donna è mobile', and in reducing her actions to allegory, Hitler (and the cartoon) sets up a tension around her role. At one level, the image and caption poke holes in the government's classification system of mobility. At another, the Italian phrase, invoking the stereotype of woman as flighty and undependable, produces her not as a vital participant but as a stationary sign of victory, swayed by seduction, flowers, and confectionery. The suggestion can be that women are always susceptible; what if Hitler had offered chocolates? Would British women have joined the enemy? This image of a woman surrounded by four military leaders is a clear attempt to nationalise femininity. But because no one version of femininity can be secured through it, it is exemplary of the general mobility of wartime femininity, and of the difficulty of harmonising woman and nation in the crisis.

The expression 'La donna mobile' (sic) crops up elsewhere in wartime representation. In *Waterloo Road*, as two men beyond conscription years chat with an American GI in the local pub, Tom Mason, pigeon fancier and family lodger looks across the bar towards a furtive couple, Ted and Tilly. He nurses his pint sighing, 'If you ask me the youngsters are having the toughest time in this war.' The GI casually replies 'What war? I ain't found it yet.' Just then a uniformed woman walks past. 'La donna mobile' enunciates Mason carefully, following her with his eyes. 'What's that?' asks the GI. 'Italian!' 'What's it mean?' his neighbour repeats. 'What's it mean? It means women is [sic] mobile.' 'Who said that? Mr Bevan?' Mason ends the exchange exploding: 'Females are a problem all round. Blooming crossword puzzle. Give me pigeons every time. Not so blinking whimsical.' He raises homing pigeons who find their way back to the East End even after he evacuates them as train freight. By contrast, the homing instincts of mobile women are, by legal definition, in suspension.

One way of coping with the dissonance resulting from shifting women's primary place of work from the home to the barracks or factory was to generate just such new slogans of femininity which might encompass the contradictions. Homi K. Bhabha theorises that the stereotype has precisely this capacity, for it 'is a form of knowledge and identification that vacillates between what is always 'in place', already known, and something that must be anxiously repeated'.[14] In the case of the mobile woman two contradictory reputations coexist: the reliable, invaluable war-worker on whom victory depends, and the capricious, whimsical companion and potential collaborator who distracts male attention. Saying 'La donna mobile' vacillates between traditional notions of femininity and the evidence of historical women.

As might already be apparent, during the war women encountered impossibly incompatible representations of themselves: from being inessential to national identity, to being central to it, to threatening it; from being patient wives to mobile women; from being painted ladies to military beauties. In the early war, before it was apparent how dire the labour shortage would become, female images of non-participation were possible. In a Clarks shoes advertisement of 1940 the female consumer is reassured that 'It would really be a bore, if every woman went to war'.[15] The trope of the waiting woman who is also a happy consumer became unthinkable, even traitorous after Ernest Bevin's mid-war female recruitment drive. But another stereotype, of the sexy woman as a national risk, flourished throughout the war. In the poster 'Keep Mum, She's not so Dumb', female sexuality disguises female intelligence as a young woman in a transparent, breast-revealing dress eavesdrops on the military men who surround her. This message is repeated in another poster, 'Don't Tell Aunty and Uncle' which warns against giving strategic secrets to anyone, even your relatives, but especially not to a young, apparently naked woman. In a venereal disease (VD) poster female sexuality again threatens national security: here a feminised skull sports a pink hat decorated with vaginal flowers while the slogan reads, 'The "easy" girlfriend spreads Syphilis and Gonorrhoea, which unless properly treated may result in blindness, insanity, paralysis, premature death'.[16] In all three representations women are a danger to the nation: at worst they constitute an internal enemy.

This range of femininities would seem to counteract the national interest, both by inciting female anger, and by sending contradictory messages about appropriate roles for women. How these items nevertheless came to coexist despite the crisis (even as a result of it) is illuminated through a foundational premise of feminist theory. The power of gender rests on the notion that social, economic, and political inequalities between men and women are made to seem natural in being aligned with biological sex. The biological division legitimates others: culture vs. nature, intellect vs. intuition, activity vs. passivity, and so on. Woman then becomes a kind of cultural dumping ground, as Judith Williamson puts it – the main vehicle for the representation of difference and otherness within mass culture.[17] This system buckled under the weight of the Second World War when the primary meaning of the opposition 'them' and 'us' shifted from referring to the two sides of gender – the battle between the sexes – to the two sides of war, the battle of nations. 'Woman versus man' collided with 'enemy versus allied'. Thus women were always suspect in wartime through the barely avoidable substitution women=enemy, men=allied, despite representational efforts to circumvent the inference. While British wartime propaganda demanded patriotism in women, the message that women, especially young single women, were natural collaborators was never far below the surface.

Extreme images of VD women and Clarks consumers raise the question of how women as a social group made sense of governmental discourses on femininity. Occasionally advertisements can give us a clue, since they needed to recognise the difficult lived experience of women in order to snag their customer; in their style and language are traces of women's efforts and frustrations as the rhetoric of wartime calls on their national duty. Jeyes Fluid acknowledges the contradictory demands war makes upon the female consumer in order to reach her: 'Are you leading a double-life? Are you doing national service as well as looking after your home?' says the caption. 'Jeyes Fluid will protect you ... A supply of Jeyes Fluid should be an essential part of both your domestic and your A.R.P. arrangements.'[18] The advertisement shows a woman's body split in half vertically, dressed as a nurse on the left, holding Jeyes, and dressed with an apron on the right, wiping a dish, but using the same product, according to the copy. A promotion for Rinso juggles the same issues, entirely losing sight of the woman at home in its image, and acknowledging that she is only intermittently there in its text.[19] It claims: 'Holder of riveting record is also Model Housewife' (see Figure 1). She manages to excel at the two roles by washing the 'Rinso no-boil way' which saves her an hour and a half, and also saves fuel. Patriotism is infused into the purchase of Rinso, while the appeal is made through a glimpse of the conflicts women experienced. The myth is that Rinso will bridge the gap.

The syndrome of the double life was not specific to war, and has if anything become more burdensome in the 1990s, but the war both induced its acknowledgement and changed its meaning. Instead of the labour of home being invisible vis-à-vis waged and public work, shifting women into a patriotic category gave equal representational weight to domestic labour, nursing, or riveting. In such advertisements women were invited to view themselves as split, and to understand this as a symptom of patriotism. One outcome of nationalising femininity was thus to generate a fleet of citizens whose chief identity was that of doubleness – of having a dual role, one traditional, private and of the past, the other new, public and of the crisis. Further, the split person identity was almost always a feminine war-supportive attribute, even if its combinations required a masculine performance, comparing boiling to riveting in the case of Rinso.

All investigation of wartime femininity must reckon with the practical constraints on its continued existence, particularly on its props of dress and make-up (in whose absence women became very ingenious, as Pat Kirkham writes). Clothes were put on points rationing from June 1941 to reduce demand and free garment workers for more urgent tasks; in 1942 the Civilian Clothing Order introduced 'utility' garments (alongside utility furniture and other economy measures) to control prices, to ensure access to basic clothing, and to conserve resources. The result was a subtle uniforming of the nation with its own powerful effect in figuring national unity. Utility clothing eventually accounted for four-fifths of all clothes produced in Britain.[20] Even couturiers Norman Hartnell and Hardy Amies designed suits that, while developing pre-war trends, also echoed women's forces uniforms in their cut, their thrifty use of fabric, and their standardised look.

Conscription affected clothing in a further way, by requiring women to don overalls and uniforms. This challenged old habits of viewing femininity as incapable of cohesion, rationality, and public dependability, and thus as easily distinguishable from masculinity, a challenge registered in some wartime cartoons which showed 'Wrens' getting tattoos, or the chaotic rumpus of the women's uniform supply shop. In *Punch* there were a series of caricatures, especially about the Women's Land Army, from which we can infer a male fear that the adoption of uniforms or overalls by women might actually diminish sexual difference.[21] If women and men looked similar, were they not indeed similar? Legislating women's dress by equiping them with practical uniforms in order to unify them might have the power to disguise, alter, or even reconstruct their real selves; the male power attached to a mililtary uniform might permanently empower a female wearer. A Fougasse cartoon reassured readers that the sexes really were their pre-war selves, away from war, even on account of the uniform[22] (see Figure 2)

The question raised by these cartoons was, 'What was the effect of the uniform on the "real" woman underneath?' It might signal psychological, social, or political changes in gender roles. It was for this reason that the War Office was so concerned about losing the *physical* definitions of femininity – the curving hips. It announced that serving women 'must be corseted, and corseted correctly' and commissioned corset designs from Frederick Berlei which would 'preserve the feminine line, and at the same time be practical under a uniform'.[23] A *Picture Post* report on the results showed 'fashion experts' scrutinising a wartime corset as they legislated womanliness. This aspect of patriarchal discourse intersects interestingly with a similar concern over the visibility and decoration of the female figure in contemporary British cinema. At both sites many voices expressed the view that glamour should be taken down a notch or two in the interests of patriotism, but also that the possible consequences might be very dismaying, and ultimately not in the national interest. On the screen the step away from glamour was simultaneously understood as a step away from Hollywood and nearer a national film style. Glamour was in no sense absent from the British screen, and was eagerly consumed there, especially in the form of Gainsborough melodramas, but in home front films it had at least to be diegetically noted and was often shown to be causing consternation to characters. In *Love Story* (1944), for example, set in wartime, Lissa is played by Margaret Lockwood who had recently flamboyantly performed in the very successful costume melodrama *The Man in Grey* (1943). However, in *Love Story* her femininity

# Holder of Riveting Record is also Model Housewife

## DOES ALL OWN WASHING

MRS. Edna Smith holds the record in a Midlands factory for helping to complete the entire riveting of an aircraft's wings. This blonde bombshell works a 9½-hour day, earns good money and "loves the job." She's a model housewife, too, says it's easy to fit in cooking and cleaning if you plan things out. Washing, for instance, she does the Rinso no-boil way because it saves an hour and a half on the boiling method. Clothes come clean with a 12-minute soak in hot-tap water and Rinso. Extra-dirty places are first damped and a little dry Rinso smoothed in. This method saves lighting the copper so it saves fuel, too. Many housewives on war jobs do their wash the Rinso way.

1    Rinso advertisement, *Picture Post*, 24 January 1942

is presented as excessive in the context of reigning austerity conditions, even though the manager of the hotel where she is staying has asked her to dress for dinner because 'it's good for morale'. She shocks two young female dinner guests with her slinky, low-cut black attire: 'Fancy dressing like that, and in wartime', exclaims one of them at Lissa's entrance. 'Oh stop bleating' retorts the other, 'There are plenty of men to go round.'

While the generation of glamour via the screen had potentially anti-national connotations, the government protected actual toiletries and make-up despite the shortages. Since the late eighteenth century's 'Great Masculine Renunciation' in which 'man abandoned his claim to be beautiful', lipsticks and other cosmetics have been key markers of sexual difference – at least when applied to women.[24] A lack of lipstick, rouges, and vanishing cream were reported early in the conflict but special efforts were made to maintain a supply since ministers deemed cosmetics 'essential to female morale', again indicating an official preference for a stable, traditional femininity in imagining national health and strength in wartime.[25] In 1942 the Board of Trade considered prohibiting the most inessential cosmetics but decided against it on the same grounds, introducing instead a stricter Order which disallowed the sale of scarce materials in toilet preparations such as the solvent in nail varnish.[26] But evasion was rife throughout the industry. Creams were accredited with medicinal properties, and doctors were quoted to medicalise products to avoid the Order; advertisements and labels made clear to women that the products were really 'cosmetics in disguise'.[27]

While understanding making-up as a positive female pleasure, these governmental policies also surely saw it as essential to male morale: making-up secured, through difference, masculine identity. The baroque structure of wartime cosmetics legislation is testament to the powerful cultural place the tiny potions held. By the end of 1943 regulation of the production and sale of toiletries was described as 'one of the most complicated of the controls over manufacture and supply that had been evolved within the Board of Trade'.[28] Cosmetics had acquired a strategic importance worthy of legal protection, even as the (directly contradictory) stereotype of the painted lady as lethal for fighting men persisted in official posters and films.

Many wartime texts betrayed a fear of the consequences of de-emphasising female appearance, recognising at some level that the validation of women's social role on the basis of other criteria – those reserved for men – would erode the logic of the gendered divide. A *Picture Post* column on 'Shelter life', written as if seen by a 'Martian', describes the 'strangest sight in London – strangest scene of all our time'.[29] The article reflects on the fate of the nuclear family during the Blitz: 'Here all one's life is public. Privacy, so highly cherished by Britons, is gone … Here nothing is intimate. One talks, eats, sleeps, lives, with a hundred, a thousand others' (see Figure 3). The strangest sight is of a young woman making-up in an underground passageway, ignoring the bodies collected around her. Applying her macquillage, she represents metonymically all those other lost private activities. But this one must be shown, must be photographed, despite the Blitz; for wearing make-up was and is one of the most culturally embedded signifiers of femininity. This woman with her mirror reassures us that femininity *is* innate, in that even in total war a woman is compelled to do her face.

The contradictory status of feminine glamour was solved by some advertisers in their suggestion that legible femininity was an integral part of

*When John Smith gets away on leave—*       *a subtle change takes place :*

*the same is true of his sister Joan—*       *only rather different.*

2  Fougasse cartoon 'Joan and John', *Punch*, 2 September 1942, p. 183

national service. Slogans such as 'Hair Beauty – is a Duty Too!', 'Beauty Answers the Call ...', 'Instant Beauty for Women in Wartime', and Potter and Moore's Powder-Cream makes her 'ready for action', urge women to buy products because the survival of femininity is a patriotic sign of strength and perseverance.[30] Elsewhere military terminology papers over the difficulties: Kemt hairspray is said to induce 'Regimental Curl', for instance, as well as a 'crisp new war-time hair-style'.[31] In two such advertisements, for Palmolive and Evan Williams, comparative vignettes of women in uniform appear alongside naked women, thereby minimising excessive glamorisation of the body by keeping the war in sight (and also showing women ways to enjoy glamour *with* war).

Many advertisements walk the tightrope between being unpatriotic by suggesting that women should be thinking about their looks rather than war, and being war affirmative at the risk of undermining both the need for their product and the category of traditional womanhood altogether. A symptom of this tension lies in the frequent reference to 'natural beauty'. This look emerged through comparison with an imaginary type of pre-war womanhood, a sort of artificial American cinematic female. According to this rhetoric, natural beauty certainly required effort and maintenance, but this had to be invisible in contrast to American glamour. A quasi-medical advertisement for Crookes' Lacto-Calamine powder-based 'skin food' out-lines the parameters of 'natural beauty' quite clearly, and is fascinating in the precise ways it articulates the challenge to glamorised beauty during war. Despite the artificial lighting which illuminates the image of a half-naked woman, and the poppies in her hair, the caption for this product implies that this is the woman's natural state: 'Whither beauty? Beauty's at the cross-roads. Many young women now have less time for make-up, and more occa-sions when they would rather not look made up at all.' The reasons why women might rather 'not look made up at all' suggest those cultural associ-ations of female glamour with national liability, and further, with the idea that single women or women separated from their husbands should avoid looking made-up in order to avoid new sexual encounters, since these also shadow the nation's integrity – loyalty to one man as loyalty to one nation. The overall message is that looking unmade-up is the appropriate wartime appearance. A nineteen-year-old student nurse interviewed for J. P. Mayer's commissioned survey of British cinema-goers was certainly caught up in these new and complex definitions of femininity. She stated: 'I always used to imagine that Hollywood hairstyles, clothes, and make-up were well out of my reach, but since the advent of natural beauty has arrived, it has become apparent to me that the rest are only appendages to produce the desired effect'.[32] American film standards of femininity – a remoter possibility than ever in wartime – now seem to her unappealing because the effort needed to attain them has been thrown into relief by the crisis; the effort has become too apparent, and inappropriate.

The suspect political valence of glamour inevitably challenged recruitment poster design since these had to make women's war jobs attractive, encourage women to identify with the poster image, and hence enlist. The fate of an ATS poster is instructive: it was withdrawn and changed on the grounds that its female image was too glamorous. The replacement image was based on a photograph rather than a painting, and contemporary Eric Newton used the phrase 'a slightly Russianised young lady' to express the

3    'Here all one's life is public', *Picture Post*, 16 December 1939

new character of womanhood thus produced.[33] The initial withdrawal suggests that the War Office was wary of using stylised female images to speak to real women of national need. These might send the (not entirely incorrect) message that the services were a route to glamour under wartime circumstances and that the War Office rated this achievement over other kinds of effort. On the other hand, there was the risk that a female audience would not recognise itself in what had now become a relatively unattainable femininity.

Comparisons of different national populations of women was generally an important element in building official wartime womanhood, another aspect of nationalising femininity. As an article in *Woman and Beauty* asked, 'Are you equal to two German women?' The invocation of the Soviet Union as source of alternative, mobilised femininity was quite widespread. Soviet women were offered for emulation in a poster which read, 'Cover Your Hair for Safety: Your Russian Sister Does!' A simple headscarf was knotted at the nape of the woman's neck, with a hammer and sickle decorating the larger scarf on which her whole image was drawn.[34] The idea of Soviet women as unglamorous counterbalanced the aura of the American screen goddess in this discussion. Notions of Soviet femininity came at least in part from the showing of Soviet films in England, and perhaps the *Herald Tribune*'s comment on *Brief Encounter* (1945) as 'between Hollywood and Moscow in style and quality' should be understood in reference to this femininity, as much as to other aspects of its style.[35] Knowledge of Soviet women's wartime experience boosted their association with despecularity.[36] The Soviet Union was the only nation to make more extensive use of female labour during the Second World War than Britain; Soviet women saw combat and fired weaponry unlike their British counterparts. They were trained as snipers and fighter pilots (dubbed the Night Witches by the Germans) and one of the most successful snipers toured Allied territory, the model for the visiting 'Lady Sniper' in the British film *Tawny Pipit* (1944). Lieutenant Bocolova, as she is called there, is the most successfully gynandromorphic figure of the entire home front film genre. She is the 'brave and beautiful representative of our gallant Russian ally' according to the character Colonel Barrington, has killed over a hundred 'Hitlerites', and can sling the colonel's telescopic rifle effortlessly over her shoulder. Her combination of strength and attractiveness, sustained for just a few minutes on the screen, tantalises the local Land Army girl who ponders: 'I want to see what she's got that I haven't'. It is a comparison female audience members are also asked to make.

Launder and Gilliat's *I See a Dark Stranger* (1946) offers a peculiarly complex instance of the kind of interaction of nationality and femininity that wartime forced into being and so forms here a conclusion to my essay.

It tells of an Irish woman's collaboration in a German spy network with links across England, Ireland, France, and the Isle of Man. It thus takes on Ireland's choice of neutrality during the war as well as the general independence of Manx policy. Inheriting her father's fervent nationalism, Bridie Quilty (Deborah Kerr) initially resolves to join the Irish Republican Army and avenge the wrongs done to Ireland at British hands since Cromwell's day. She channels her anti-British ardour into aiding a German agent, embroiling herself in vandalism, strategic seduction, killings, manhunts, disposing of unwanted bodies, forgery, and other vagaries of film espionage. Finally realising the error of her ways, she burns the crucial D-Day landings information which she was to help leak to the Nazis, and which she had earlier discovered hidden in the Manx Parliament. As the film ends, Bridie's threatening status as a single Irish woman has been only partially diffused: she marries David Baynes (Trevor Howard), both English and a Cromwell scholar to boot, who during the course of the film has been on sick leave trying to complete his Cambridge thesis on Cromwell's military strategies. However, her Irish nationality remains a sore. She refuses to spend her honeymoon in the Cromwell Arms and the film's last shot shows her stomping off into the English night, suitcase in hand.

In 1946 collaboration was a narrative subject which perfectly thematised the war's wreckage of weakened, shifted, or destroyed boundaries, between nations as well as between the sexes. Launder and Gilliat's choice of a neutral female collaborator as their central character invites scrutiny of a political structure that positions Irish neutrality and wartime femininity as unstable and unpredictable in equal measure. Here Irish identity and womanhood are interrogated and compared, entwined in a tale of political espionage, trading identities across a sheet of 'ideological ice', as one contemporary named it.[37] By using each to signify the other, the film brings into sharp focus the ideological ground rule that the active female figure constitutes a threat to the nation, a 'one woman invasion', or a menace which has to be neutralised, to use Baynes's words (to which Bridie retorts, 'I was born neutralised').[38] Bridie's relation to nationhood, her place as a hostile outsider vis-à-vis Britain, works as a synecdoche for barely concealed ambivalences towards women's general role in wartime. It is the shared fate of women and Ireland, in a neutral yet suspect place, entitled to autonomy yet not to be politically embraced, that Launder and Gilliat pinpoint when they personify Ireland as a female collaborator in their film, for Ireland too loomed as an internal enemy for Britain on account of her decision to remain neutral throughout the war.

What I See a Dark Stranger articulates so vividly is that in wartime the alignment of woman with nation is never simple: it needs to be reasserted, restated, in fact overstated. A woman will always be beyond, outside, on the edge of the national boundary, until she has been joined to the nation, labelled, classified, readmitted, through the re-establishment of strict gender differences. *I See a Dark Stranger* highlights this difficulty by mounting a plot in which the double resolution of national and gendered identity can never occur, adding the spice of the Isle of Man to the mix for good measure. While the film forecloses on female independence, it necessarily leaves the vexed question of Irish nationhood raw and unhealed at the end, an outcome that can be seen as demobilising nationhood and reconstructing gender for the post-war world.

Bridie carries that which escapes the category nation, that which is other to it and excluded from it: the designations enemy, foreigner and, crucially, neutral subject. It is the latter position which makes her especially dangerous, for in her neutrality she is free-floating. The film's plot slides across these registers, searching for a place to rest, shifting Bridie from neutral to enemy in the realm of nationality, and, in the realm of gender, mapping a system in which a woman is a neuter until proven otherwise by men, in this case through marriage. This logic by which a woman cannot belong to a nation without first being authorised by a male was one shared until recently by British immigration laws. The asymmetrical arrangement claimed man's natural state as a citizen and woman's dependence on it. As the many other examples I have presented suggest, the precarious relations between femininity and citizenship had to be brought to the surface during the war in an effort to promote a unity of gendered citizenship, while at the same time the attempt to maintain sexual difference continued, needed as an old sign of stability. It was the tension between these two impulses that gave women mobility even within the boundaries of a nationalised wartime femininity.[39]

### Notes

1  Much of this essay is taken from Antonia Lant, *Blackout: Reinventing Women for Wartime British Cinema* (Princeton, Princeton University Press, 1991), and 'The Female Spy: Gender, Nationality, and War in *I See a Dark Stranger*', in Robert Sklar and Charles Musser (eds), *Resisting Images: Essays on Cinema and History* (Philadelphia, Temple University Press, 1990), pp. 173–99. See both texts for elaboration of many of the points presented. I would like to thank Christine Gledhill for her assistance in reworking these versions here.

2  Television was shut down from 1 September 1939 to 7 June 1946.

3  Eric Biddle, *The Mobilization of the Home Front: The British Experience and Its Significance for the United States* (Chicago, Public Service Administration Press, 1942), p. 26. Biddle is writing of lessons the United States might learn from British policy.

4  Sheila Ferguson and Hilde Fitzgerald, *Studies in the Social Services* (London, HMSO, 1954), p. 100.

5  Geoff Brown, *Launder and Gilliat* (London, British Film Institute, 1977), p. 108.

6  Anonymous, *Ourselves in Wartime: An Illustrated Survey of the Home Front in the*

*Second World War* (London, Odhams Press, 1944), pp. 31–2.

7 Brown, *Launder and Gilliat*, p. 108; Ronald Howard, *In Search of My Father: A Portrait of Leslie Howard* (London, Kimber Press, 1981), p. 125; J. B. Priestley, *British Women Go To War* (London, Collins, 1943).

8 Roger Manvell, 'Recent films', *Britain Today*, May 1945, p. 36. See further discussion of these issues in Lant, *Blackout*, chapter 1.

9 Nicholas Pronay and Jeremy Croft, 'British film censorship and propaganda policy during the Second World War', in James Curran and Vincent Porter (eds), *British Cinema History* (London, Weidenfeld and Nicolson, 1983), p. 149, citing Public Record Office, INF 1/178, A, 13 September 1940.

10 Another aspect of this refashioning, the metaphorical attachment of women to land and men to the air, is discussed in Lant, *Blackout*, pp. 50–6.

11 See Lant, *Blackout*, chapter 2 for an extensive discussion of this film.

12 Priestley, *British Women Go to War*, pp. 14, 19, and 20.

13 *Time and Tide*, 16 October 1943, p. 841.

14 Homi K. Bhabha, 'The Other Question . . . the Stereotype and Colonial Discourse', *Screen*, Vol. 24 No. 6 (November/December 1983), p. 18.

15 Clarks Shoes, *Picture Post*, 17 February 1940, p. 3.

16 Reginald Mount, anti-VD poster, 1943–44 illustrated in Joseph Darracott and Belinda Loftus, *Second World War Posters* (London, Imperial War Museum, 1972), and in Lant, *Blackout*, p. 78.

17 Judith Williamson, 'Woman is an Island: Femininity and Colonization', in Tania Modleski (ed.), *Studies in Entertainment: Critical Approaches to Mass Culture* (Bloomington and Indianapolis, Indiana University Press, 1986), p. 101.

18 Jeyes Fluid, *Picture Post*, 6 July 1940.

19 Rinso, *Picture Post*, 24 January 1942.

20 Angus Calder, *The People's War: Britain, 1939–1945* (London, Granada, 1982), p. 323.

21 See 'And a hundred acres of arable', *Punch*, 13 August 1943, p. 139; and 'Tattooing', *Everybody's Weekly*, 9 January 1943.

22 Fougasse, *Punch*, 2 September 1942, p. 183.

23 Anonymous, 'Wartime corsets', *Picture Post*, Vol. 6–7, 2 March 1940, p. 26.

24 See J. C. Flugel, *The Psychology of Clothes* (London, Hogarth Press, 1930), p. 119. The phrase refers to the radical simplification and increased uniformity of male dress with the onset of industrialisation. Flugel is quoted in Kaja Silverman, *The Acoustic Mirror: The Female Voice in Psychoanalysis and the Cinema* (Bloomington, Indiana University Press, 1988), pp. 24–5.

25 Calder, *The People's War*, p. 321.

26 E. L. Hargreaves and M. M. Gowing, *The History of the Second World War: Civil Industry and Trade* (London, HMSO, 1952), p. 533.

27 *Ibid.*, p. 533.

28 *Ibid.*, p. 531.

29 Anonymous, 'Shelter life', *Picture Post*, 26 October 1940, p. 9.

30 'Hair Beauty is a Duty Too', *Picture Post*, 16 December 1939; 'Beauty answers the call', *Picture Post*, 18 April 1942; 'Potter and Moore's Powder-Cream', *Picture Post*, 19 October 1940.

31 'Would You Like this Regimental Curl', *Picture Post*, 2 March 1940.

32 J. P. Mayer, *British Cinemas and Their Audiences: Sociological Studies* (London, Dobson, 1948), p. 58.

33 Darracott and Loftus, *Second World War Posters*, p. 65.

34 *Ibid.*

35 *Herald Tribune*, 15 September 1946.

36 'Despecularity' is a cine-psychoanaltyic term which derives from film theory. 'Specularity' links the idea of the mirror image through which the child first takes on human identity to the notion of the screen spectacle. Since the mirror image is often metaphorically speaking the mother's face and woman is traditionally central to the screen spectacle, the effort to produce representations of historical (rather than symbolic) women involves a degree of *de*specularisation. This involves a certain 'deglamorisation' of the female form but that term does not suggest the attempt to separate the female representation from the symbolic, patriarchal function of the image which is involved in the notion of 'despecularisation'. Pat Kirkham in fact challenges the notion that uniform was seen as incompatible with glamour either by the fashion magazines or by women themselves, although the discourses and practices of fashion have different goals from those which bear on cinematic representation where the female image often serves a symbolic function and moreover comes under pressure from other cultural and social discourses which find female sexuality dangerous and threatening.

37 *Spectator*, 12 July 1946.

38 *Irish Independent*, 12 August 1846, p. 2.

39 Until recently foreign women married to British men could take up British citizenship on entering the country, but foreign men acquiring British wives could not do likewise; her citizenship lacked the power to naturalise a man while his could naturalise a woman. In the newest legislation, under a general tightening of immigration law, British men can no longer give nationality to their foreign wives.

# Part one

## Mobile women: change and regulation

**4**   'There is surely something of the Stalingrad spirit about this heroic British working-class mother …', from J. B. Priestley, *British Women Go To War*, 1943

# 2

## 'The girl that makes the thing that drills the hole that holds the spring ...': discourses of women and work in the Second World War

### PENNY SUMMERFIELD

Feminist work on the Second World War in Britain has established that 1939–45 was a period when assumptions about and perceptions of gender roles and boundaries were profoundly disturbed.[1] Some historians emphasise the material base for this disturbance: the pull of the labour shortage on women normally occupied in 'women's work' or in their homes, and their appearance in occupations and roles defined in terms of the war effort; the tensions between this pull and the conventional demand for their labour in a reproductive, servicing role in the home.[2] Others have examined the ideological dimensions to the disturbance of gender roles, expressed in policy and rhetoric concerning women, and in representations of women in government propaganda and popular culture.[3]

The questions they have pursued include how change was justified, whether it was advocated or lamented, whether it was depicted as permanent or temporary, how women were represented in relation to war. The war effort did not only imply work, in industry, agriculture and the army. It also involved attitudes. It was important for the government that wartime arrangements contributed to good morale, that they elicited a willingness to co-operate and to 'make an effort', rather than creating indifference, obstruction and defeatism. As a result, war focused special attention both on the steps taken to alter gender relations in material ways, and on representations of gender. Parallel to the tension embedded in official policy towards women,[4] another existed between creating representations of women fully participating in the war effort, and perpetuating images of enduring feminine characteristics: sweethearts and wives, housewives and mothers.

The purpose of this chapter is to explore the wartime discourse of the woman war worker within this problematic. The focus is on the woman at the heart of the tension, the married woman, who represented the feminine norm. The labour power of single women was more easily tapped for the demands of the wartime emergency, and their behaviour in the labour market was considered to be conditioned by the prospect of marriage. In wartime the fate of the norm to which they were expected ultimately to conform was an uncertain and important matter. As Gledhill and Swanson have argued, the housewife occupied a strategic position as a symbol of the family, the community and the nation.[5]

Vera Brittain encapsulated the problem when she wrote in 1941 of the dominant image of the housewife in peacetime as 'the cornerstone of that family unity which is the moral foundation of English life'. She expressed the view (from a pacifist perspective) that, as a result of the insatiable demand for workers which war created, this image was 'one of the first casualties of modern war'.[6] Brittain's understanding of the contribution of the housewife to the English 'moral foundation' explains why, even though she was a feminist, she wrote in tones of regret about sacrificing the role to the war effort. She saw the housewife as the emotional centre of the family, especially vulnerable in war which was destructive of all human bonds, a lesson she had learnt bitterly in the First World War: 'War takes the dearest human relations and tramples them ruthlessly into the dust. It has no concern for love and marriage, for maternity and childhood'.[7] Furthermore Brittain the pacifist (unlike other feminists at the time and since) could not regard wartime opportunities for paid work in a positive light. She felt that the 'non-essential' occupations from which women were being drawn between 1939 and 1941, including housewifery, were 'those trades and professions which create the beauty, the grace and the culture of civilized living'. In contrast war work was geared to 'inflicting death and perpetrating destruction'.[8]

Brittain was writing from within a minority tradition of dissent. This paper explores dominant wartime discourses concerning war work in order to evaluate her view of the housewife as a 'casualty'. It will consider the extent to which the housewife's image was preserved, what kinds of deviation from it were allowed and in what ways it was reinstated at the end of the war.

The mobilisation policy of the British government is an appropriate initial site of study, since it had enormous potential either to cement women's position as the cornerstone of the family, or to dislodge them from that position. The development and effects of the policy of mobilising women for war have been discussed elsewhere.[9] In what follows I shall highlight the implications of the policy for the housewife: did it preserve her conventional role or encourage her to deviate from it?

In the first phase of the war, the British government displayed considerable reluctance to direct any women into the war effort. Even though Ernest Bevin acquired powers of direction over every member of the population soon after his appointment as Minister of Labour and National Service in May 1940, he did not apply them to women until March 1941. Ostensibly Bevin preferred the voluntary principle: women would join the war effort of their own free will. But just as it was assumed from the outset that such a method of recruitment would not produce sufficient male labour, so by 1941 it was clear that the numbers of women required for the war effort could not be obtained by relying on volunteering alone. The gendered application of the voluntary principle in the first eighteen months of the war indicates the reluctance of the government to disturb the position of women in family life, as well as its relative confidence that the removal of men en masse into the forces would not so dangerously undermine the family. The first steps to apply compulsion to women reveal the government's special nervousness about the position of the housewife.

In March 1941 the government decided that all women aged eighteen to forty-five should 'register' at their local employment exchange, that is they should report their current paid work and household responsibilities. The government's starting point was that all women, married and single, could be expected to be available for paid work for the war effort. However, it assumed that domestic responsibilities might make some housewives less available than others. This turned conventional assumptions about the availability of married women for paid work inside out. The Anomalies Act of 1931 limiting the payment of unemployment benefit, for example, had placed all married women in the category 'not genuinely seeking work' because they were considered to be fully occupied at home (notwithstanding involvement in paid work prior to becoming unemployed).[10] In the wartime circumstances of labour shortage the government was keen to identify every woman who could be considered available for war work. It needed to deconstruct the housewife into a number of sub-categories, defined by degree of household responsibility and informed by judgements about the implications of these responsibilities for a woman's availability for work. The Ministry of Labour and National Service delegated this job to its Women's Consultative Committee, which drew up an inventory of domestic work that constituted grounds for exemption from compulsory participation in war work.

The Committee was quick to decide that maternal responsibility was an immovable cornerstone as far as state direction into work was concerned. Mothers of children under school-leaving-age (fourteen) living at home were not subject to any of the regulations governing the mobilisation of women: the registration and direction process described above; 'call-up' into the armed forces, industry or civil defence under the National Service (No. 2) Act of December 1941; or the Control of Engagement Order of January 1942, which required women to obtain paid work only through employment exchanges so that the state could keep track of their labour power.

The exemption of mothers from compulsory war work was uncontroversial. But the Women's Consultative Committee debated at length which other groups should be placed in the 'Household R' category of women exempt from direction because of domestic responsibilities. A 'household' was defined in male terms: it consisted of one or more persons such as 'father, husband or brother' other than the woman herself.[11] These exemptions applied to single as well as married women. Celia, in the film *Millions Like Us*, could have avoided her call-up on the grounds that she had to look after her widowed father, though she did not choose to do so. Even women who employed paid help to look after a masculine household of this sort were exempt. But not all married women had men at home: five million men were in the forces in 1944.[12] The Committee decided there was no reason why they should not be directed into war work locally, though it drew the line at sending them away from home, even if they were the wives of servicemen whose home leaves were likely to be infrequent. In considering the liability for war service of this group, the Committee made explicit the patriarchal definition of home with which it was working. A serviceman's wife who had moved away from 'his' home to one of her own was liable to direction, unless the new home was that of his or her parents or was near where he was stationed.[13]

Official sensitivity was for the feelings of husbands in the forces rather than wives. Servicemen were assumed to want their wives to be available when they were on leave and to be providing 'as much of a home as, in the circumstances, is possible' when they were posted.[14] They were also assumed not to want their wives placed in danger by being made to work in a location that might be a target for enemy attack.[15] On this basis young married women who had no children were exempt from being called up alongside single women in the same age group, under the National Service (No. 2) Act of December 1941, though ironically in total war no one was spared the danger of air attack or invasion. And servicemen's wives received such small state allowances that those with no other support had to do paid work anyway if they were not to live in poverty. But underlying the decision to refrain from requiring wives to be 'mobile', was deference to the suspicions of servicemen that call-up might involve other kinds of dangers: it might offer wives opportunities for illicit liaisons.[16]

To sum up, the implications of the mobilisation regulations were that mothers and wives were not to be sacrificed to the labour shortage, so long as they conformed to male-defined norms. In contrast to Vera Brittain's observation in 1941, government mobilisation policy proclaimed that the housewife was not to be one of war's first casualties.

Wives and mothers were not, however, left entirely alone. There was a powerful tension between the construction of the mother as non-worker and the wartime social reality of extreme labour shortages. In spite of the principle of exempting mothers from any sort of compulsory call-up, the government encouraged them in various ways to join the workforce voluntarily. Local Ministry of Labour officials were permitted to write to mothers of two to fourteen-year-olds in 1942 encouraging them to take part-time work, and by 1943 the government was providing nursery places for approximately one-quarter of the under-five-year-old children of women war workers.[17] Nursery policy was, however, contested ground. The government stepped back from making collective wartime arrangements for the care of the other three-quarters of the eligible group, recommending (in the name of the war effort) that working mothers find their own private minders. Nursery places were not created for these children of women war workers primarily because of the preference of the authorities concerned (especially the Ministry of Health) that under-school-age children should be looked after by their mothers in their own homes, even in wartime.

In spite of the enduring hesitancy of the government about dislodging the housewife from the home, there were some regulatory encroachments on her inviolability. In 1943 the Ministry of Labour extended the upper age limit for the registration and potential direction of women from forty-five to fifty. And it decided that women throughout the registration age groups (now eighteen to fifty) who reported domestic work that exempted them from direction into full-time work could be directed into local part-time work, the first time such work had been officially sanctioned. In taking this step, the Ministry cast apologetic glances in the direction of 'the morale of male workers in industry'.[18] It even organised outwork schemes, to take war work to the homes of 'immobile' women (who could not be directed to work away from home). Women did jobs like sorting small parts and cleaning instrument covers in their front rooms.[19]

However, as Margaret Allen argues, one solution to the barrier to recruitment presented by 'Household R' was never officially advocated: that of requiring men to share housework. 'The official conception of the breaking down, or at least temporary relaxation, of the sexual division of labour for the war effort, was a one-sided one'.[20] This was the case even though ten million adult men were not in the services but in civilian employment.[21] Women could be prosecuted for avoiding work in 'men's jobs' for the war effort if they did not come within one of the exemption categories, but men were given no encouragement to take a share of 'women's work' in the home.

In spite of the demands of the war effort, the feminine identification of the job of running a home remained undented.

This review of the regulations controlling the mobilisation of women for war work indicates strongly that the wartime government regarded women as the key to the stability of the gendered family. Married men called up into the forces might be absent for years. The government's response was to compensate for any disturbance to the family this caused through the payment of the serviceman's wife's allowance, the official guarantee of men's economic contribution as breadwinners. Women's presence in the family was, in contrast, crucial – for symbolic as well as material reasons. But in acute tension with this set of imperatives was the urgent need for women to participate in the labour force (a dilemma experienced also in the United States and Nazi Germany).[22] The state had to draw on women's labour power, families were financially better off if mothers worked, and wartime nurseries proved that substitutes for their reproductive labour in the home were possible. But official modifications of women's roles as wives and mothers must be limited. Mobilisation policy placed women at the interface of two conflicting versions of patriotism: on the one hand, the demands of the national war effort for more workers implied the sacrifice of conventional domestic arrangements and gender roles within them; on the other, national stability and morale required the continuation of family forms based on women's conventional roles.

Producers of official propaganda dodged this dilemma by separating the woman worker and the housewife. They concentrated on the young, single woman, the 'girl' of popular parlance, as the ideal recruit. Ministry of Information posters depicted her in patriotic wartime roles like uniformed jeep driver in the Auxiliary Territorial Service, jodhpur-wearing tender of cart-horses in the Women's Land Army, or overall-clad factory worker beckoning 'Women of Britain' into the war factories. Mothers and housewives were shown in domestic settings, wearing high-heels and broad-shouldered coats or frilly pinafores. They were urged to 'make do and mend', the symbol of the economical maintenance of a healthy wartime population, well fed and clothed within the constraints of wartime shortages.

But the two groups, women workers and housewives, in fact overlapped. In 1943, 43 per cent of all women in paid work were married, in contrast to 16 per cent in 1931. Advertisers capitalised on the market that working wives constituted, seeking ways of linking consumption with patriotism. Editors of women's magazines, the trade journals of the housewife, adapted to war circumstances by advising women on how to cope with wartime pressures. Both advertisers and editors reversed the directives of a century of official sources which had deplored the low standards of housekeeping and mothering among women who did paid work. This was epitomised, for example, by Lord Shaftesbury's statement, in support of a bill to ban women from working underground in the mines in 1842, that working wives 'poison the waters of life at the very fountain'. Such a view was perpetuated in tirades against married women workers throughout the nineteenth and early twentieth centuries, in particular during the First World War, for causing high levels of infant mortality and driving their husbands to drink because of their comfortless homes.[23]

Now, in contrast, women were urged to do their housework less well in order that they could participate more effectively in the war effort. A few examples will stand for many. Pre-war advertisements like those for Rinso, one of the first washing powders, stressed the improved quality of housework, compared with that of other housewives, that their products could achieve. The time saved was for personal use. 'I put brilliant clothes out on the line to dry hours ahead of my neighbours – thanks to Rinso! Now the rest of the morning's mine' said 1938's Rinso housewife. Wartime Rinso advertisements emphasised the saving of time and energy in the national interest: 'Me boil clothes? Not likely! I've got to be at the factory by two!' said 1943's housewife/war worker.[24] Editorials in *Woman's Own* kept up a stream of advice to women on how to cut down on housework. It could be done collectively or shared; for instance by women cooking for several households instead of one, and by mothers of small children mending and cleaning for women in war work. Breast-feeding could be sacrificed to the war effort, and spring cleaning could be reduced to the minimum compatible with health. Lady Reading allegedly urged members of the Women's Voluntary Service to skimp on their housework and care of their husbands in order to throw themselves into war work.[25] *Woman's Own* backed her up: 'House-pride is no longer the virtue it was. Carry on in comradeship with the women who have put it in their pockets to make munitions, work on the land, hold down a man's job ... do anything in your capacity to the utmost of your power to hasten victory.'[26]

How are we to understand this apparent justification of the abandonment of the high standards of domestic maintenance which women had been expected to uphold for so long? It was closely linked with the temporariness of the war emergency, and implied that housewives should go back to normal when victory had been won. Indeed, the special advocacy of wartime deviation effectively reinforced the peacetime norm: departure from it was justified in terms of the wartime emergency and patriotism, not of permanent and desirable changes in women's approach to housework. This was reinforced after the war, as it became evident that domestic tasks were to resume their priority in women's lives in comparison to paid work or any other activity.

Contemporary images of women war workers also emphasised

deviance from normal gender roles in a way that was special and exceptional. The idea that women were crossing gender boundaries into men's working environments was a pervasive motif of verbal and visual representations of women workers. For example, advertisers made extensive use of depictions of women in uniform or suitable dress for industrial work, particularly the overall and the boiler suit, in contrast to the almost exclusively domestic settings used before the war. They inserted into their advertising copy salutations to the woman war worker which emphasised the unusualness of her wartime role:

> In every sort of war time task that women can do – and in a great many that women were never expected to do – the women of Britain are scoring triumph after triumph. The services, munitions, the land, transport, hospitals and canteens all bear witness to their skill and their courage. Bovril applauds their achievements.[27]

At the same time, the need to preserve some aspects of the peacetime norms was emphasised. As Pat Kirkham outlines in her chapter, advertisers and magazine editors advised women that they should maintain their femininity in these settings as a matter of morale. For example L'Onglex nail varnish depicted beautifully manicured hands reaching for the insignia of each of the women's services in turn in a series of advertisements. O'Do Ro No robustly warned women to 'Stop the rot!' of underarm perspiration: 'However hard you work, however thick your uniform, O'Do Ro No will give you complete protection'.[28] The makers of Bourjois beauty preparations summed up the line on work appearance taken by cosmetic and clothing manufacturers during the war: 'Being careful about her clothes, her skin, her hair, her hands, helps a woman to feel a match for all the hard work and worry in the world'. They claimed that 'The practical men who run our war industries know it too. In at least one Government Ordnance Factory, a special book of beauty hints is issued to women workers'.[29]

The stress on the special steps needed to protect and enhance femininity in the war context emphasised both that women were crossing into masculine territory and that this was exceptional and temporary. Commentators who celebrated women's wartime participation communicated the same idea in official and semi-official publications. Their stress on the heroism of women's war participation contributed to the construction of the war effort as masculine, and their reassurances to their readers that the individual women they described had not in fact deserted femininity emphasised the limited and temporary nature of that participation.

For example, the author and journalist J. B. Priestley wrote the text of a book of large colour plates of women war workers, *British Women Go to*

*War*, published in 1943. He told his readers that 'the finest aircraft in the world – Spitfires, Hurricanes, Beaufighters, and Lancasters, Halifaxes and Sterlings – have been largely produced by a mass of women workers, who not long ago were shop assistants, housemaids, hairdressers, clerks, chorus girls, dressmakers, and the like'. But Priestley later reassured them, 'Women do not stop being women because they have started work in a factory or may be doing a job formerly done by a man'.[30] Yet he delighted in playing upon the tension he had set up, between the potentially masculinising effects of war work and the contrasting 'feminine' qualities required by women's conventional female roles. The muscular strength demanded by war work versus feminine gentleness was a favourite opposition. For example 'Margaret' operated a power-saw, which 'calls for such a degree of physical strength that men are reserved from the Forces for this particular job. But Margaret, as that splendid forearm amply suggests, happens to be exceptionally strong ... Let us hope that Margaret marries a slight, charming, rather invalidish sort of young man, who calls out her deepest maternal instincts'.[31] Priestley's playful commentary sets up a frisson of anticipation that the post-war world might be destabilised by a new breed of exceptionally strong young women. It harks back to the fearful delight which Arthur Munby and other Victorian patriarchs took in working-class women who flouted feminine conventions due to the size and strength they developed through heavy work.[32] In the 1860s as in the 1940s, the potential problem of exceptional female strength could be contained and resolved only by marriage and the release of maternal feeling.

Peggy Scott, who published a number of books on women's wartime roles, was keener than Priestley to emphasise that the masculinising effects of war work went no deeper than the uniform.[33] She defined war work as work done by 'Women in Slacks, their dress symbolical of their task – a Man's Job'. But in her account women did men's work with their femininity unscathed, in spite of having to put on masculine garb. 'Mrs Gregory is quite unlike a butcher except for the blue-and-white-striped apron that she wears over her white coat. She has soft brown eyes and a gentle face. She looks more like a children's nurse than a butcher but she served in a shop before the war and she was sent by the Ministry of Labour to assist the butcher in Peckham'.[34]

While Scott emphasised the motherliness of the married woman war worker, whose masculine uniform thinly disguised her true nature, Priestley represented the working wife as a larger than life heroine whose features of strength and stoicism were an essential part of her identity as a wife and mother. Describing Mrs C who soldered engine lamps on the railways, he commented:

surely there is something of the Stalingrad spirit about this heroic British working-class mother, who with a large young family to support, a home destroyed by the blitz, and a man's job added to all her maternal responsibilities, has more than fulfilled every possible obligation and has successfully defied all challenging circumstances as Stalingrad successfully defied the full fury of the Nazi hordes.[35]

The prioritising in this account of domestic and maternal responsibilities means that this woman's paid work could be nothing other than a temporary exception to her normal, proper role of wife and mother, taken on as an additional civic 'obligation' rather than for reasons of personal preference or economic need. Unlike the single 'Margaret' whose patriotic wartime expression of strength menaced conventional understandings of femininity, the war called forth from 'Mrs C' the capacity to respond patriotically to 'challenging circumstances' from within the maternal frame of reference, a point emphasised by the positioning of a plate showing Mrs C surrounded by her six children on the page facing the picture of Mrs C at work (see Figure 4, p. 33).

The popular representations reviewed here contributed to a powerful construction of war work as 'men's work'. Dilution policy, that is the arrangements under which the numbers of skilled and semi-skilled workers were expanded by the inclusion of those who were less skilled, did the same thing. Deals were struck between most trade unions and employers' organisations early in the war. These were known as relaxation agreements because they relaxed pre-war practices controlling the employment of women. The trade unions looked to the agreements to protect male workers from being undercut by women employed at lower rates. The wages of women allowed to do men's work were supposed to rise in stages till, at the end of thirty-two weeks in engineering, they were the same as men's, as long as the women dilutees could do the work 'without additional supervision or assistance'. The unions intended the agreements to make it impossible for employers to use women to do the same work as men at lower rates of pay, which might have tempted them to keep women on after the war. The agreements stated that women could be employed in classes of work regarded as 'men's work' only if they were regarded as temporary. They were there 'to meet war-time emergencies' and were expected to leave when the emergency had passed.[36] The agreements did not apply to 'women's work'. As this suggests, they were predicated on the idea that it was unproblematic to differentiate 'men's work' from 'women's work'. The exemption of 'women's work' emphasised its marginality to 'war work'.

The temporary nature of women's participation in the war effort, as well as the masculinity of the work involved in that 'effort', was thus inscribed in the terms on which women were employed in war work. In practice, and ironically given the depictions of women flocking into men's work, only a tiny number of women appear to have obtained jobs in civilian industry labelled 'skilled'. Attempts to identify the 'degree of skill possessed by women war workers'[37] are confounded by the socially constructed character of the concept of skill. The label conferred political power and privileged status as well as economic benefits, and was closely guarded by male workers and contested by employers. An official historian wrote in 1957 that in 1942–44 only 15 per cent of women dilutees were classified as unskilled, while most were in the 'skilled and semi-skilled' categories. But 'many were employed as semi-skilled workers and only a very small proportion in the highly skilled grades'.[38] Few qualified for the male rate of pay. A US government representative observed: 'Much of the work undertaken by women since [the start of] the war was formerly classified as women's work in certain plants or certain sections of an industry, and lower rates were the rule for women on women's work'.[39] The official historian thought that this applied to 75 per cent of the women in engineering in 1942.[40]

Government training policy has been seen as preparing women for men's work in the skilled categories. However, this was contested ground. Male trainees were prepared for work in engineering and metal manufacture classified as semi-skilled (like fitting, machine operating, instrument making, sheet metal working, welding and draughtsmanship) from which they might be promoted when in work. In 1941 when women were first admitted to government training centres they took the same courses as men. Employers, however, were unenthusiastic about taking on women trained even to semi-skilled levels, because they would require a higher rate than it was customary to pay to women, and because their presence might upset men in the works. The government was forced to respond by reducing the length of training courses for women from sixteen to eight or four weeks, and concentrating mainly on preparing them for 'demi-semi-skilled' work like machine minding, routine fitting and assembly.[41] The temporary nature even of this level of training, however, is demonstrated by the rapid reduction in the numbers of women receiving formal training in the last two years of the war. At the beginning of 1944 over 4,000 women were being trained each month compared with around 3,000 men. At the end of 1945 the number had dwindled to a mere thirty-five compared with nearly 5,000 men.[42] The opportunities for women to exchange technical skills suitable for war jobs for those suitable for peace, in the way that men were doing, was severely constrained. Opportunities for women after the war lay mainly in areas conventionally defined as suitable for women, for which training was either considered unnecessary or was predefined as feminine, as in the case of hairdressing, nursing or teaching.

The category of 'women's work' (in which over six million women were employed before the war) posed a problem for those wishing to protect 'men's work' from encroachment during the war. A clause of the relaxation agreements stated that their terms were not applicable to 'women workers engaged on work commonly performed by women in the Industry'. This clause gave rise to lengthy wrangles between employers' representatives and trade unionists about which work was 'women's work', with employers wishing to claim that any work that came within women's competence was 'commonly performed by women', a move which gave them the advantage of paying women less, and if it suited them keeping them on in such work after the war. Trade unionists were keen to argue that as little work as possible was women's work, so as to preserve men's prior right to work and its remuneration at the male rate of pay. Trade unionists therefore appear during the war to be arguing for gender equality. For example, union representatives in the Midlands argued for any work which women did in the motor and aircraft sector (such as sweeping up the factory floor, core-making, lathe operating or fork-lift truck driving) to be classified as men's work, and for women to receive equal pay for such work.[43] But at the end of the war they showed a more unfriendly face, putting into action the temporary clause so that women in such jobs would be the first to be made redundant and would make way for returning servicemen. Some were more temporary than others. Married (immobile) women were released before single (mobile) women.[44] Government policy-makers assumed that wives wanted to 'return home' urgently; that husbands wanted the same thing; that a wife's sustenance by the breadwinner's wage was part of the return to normality; that home and family needed to be restored by their full-time presence.

The relaxation agreements were known to and operated by a relatively small group, principally of men, in industry. Though the number of women trade union members and shop stewards did increase during the war, male unionists persistently represented women as abnormal trade union members. They were described as not being interested in wages and the process of collective bargaining, like male trade unionists, but as more concerned with welfare issues (ventilation, toilets, canteens) which were not 'real' trade union matters.[45] Women were not allowed to join the Amalgamated Engineering Union, the main organisation of skilled and semi-skilled men in the industry, until 1943. They were then given special white, temporary membership cards, eloquently expressing their eccentric position.

The social construction of the woman war worker in the relaxation agreements was of the woman who stepped into 'men's work' during the war on a temporary basis. A woman dilutee did a man's job in his absence, and was supposed to return it to him without protest when he came back from military service. Although this was embodied in documents and practices

available to a minority, it was popularised by authors like Scott and Priestley in wartime literature and (as other contributions to this volume explore)
it spilled over into media like radio, cinema, the press and popular song.
Whatever her age, the woman dilutee was 'the girl that makes the thing that
drills the hole that holds the spring / That drives the rod that turns the knob
that works the thing-emmy-bob'. In other words she did not really know
what she was doing, but her work was strategically vital, in the short-term:
'it's the girl that makes the thing that holds the oil that oils the ring / That
works the thing-emmy-bob THAT'S GOING TO WIN THE WAR'.[46] Scott
and Priestley represented her fate at the end of the war in a way that supported the social norms codified in the relaxation agreements, and ignored
the concurrent expansion of employment in the area of 'women's work'. This
latter trend was not of interest since by definition women's work could not
be war work.

Scott and Priestley celebrated the revelations of women's competence in
their 'men's jobs'. But even though both acknowledged that war created
potential for change in the labour market, they concluded that there was no
permanent threat to the gender order. Priestley wrote in general terms of
women's part in post-war social reconstruction. Scott referred more disrup-
tively to the possibilities perceived by wartime feminists for war to open up
new, long-term opportunities for women, writing of women being aware
that 'they were capable of greater things than tradition put into their hands'
and of war altering 'these social and sex balances which years of convention
had established'. But she was nevertheless adamant that women would want
to go back home after the war, expressing herself within the dilution paradigm: 'when the war is over the job will not be so much her concern as the
home. The majority of the girls are looking forward to running homes of
their own, not to running a man's job for him'.[47]  Scott

This was the dominant message of literature about women and paid
work in the post-war world. Both Mass Observation, the independent
public opinion research organisation, and the Wartime Social Survey, a government research body, published surveys about women working after the
war in 1944. They concurred that, in the words of Mass Observation, 'The
most general opinion seems to be that women will want to go back home, or
take up the jobs which were usually considered suitable for women before
the war, while awaiting marriage'.[48] The data collected and quoted by both
organisations in fact revealed women's ambivalence. Buried within the
Wartime Social Survey's figures were some startling findings which contra-
dicted the confident assumption that everything would return to 'normal'.
Only 36 per cent of married women and 7 per cent of single women did *not*
want to go on in paid work after the war. The rest either definitely wanted
to, or were undecided, answering 'if possible' or 'may have to'. Two-thirds of

the small percentage of single women who did not want to go on working gave 'getting married' as the reason, and less than a tenth of the 36 per cent of married women said they wanted to have a family. But blithely disregarding these tiny proportions, the nationally proclaimed and approved reasons for women withdrawing from the labour market at the end of the war were getting married and having a family.[49]

The high marriage rate in 1945 and the post-war baby boom in 1947 appeared to confirm that women's main aim was to go home and settle down after the disruption of war.[50] Yet the WSS had found in 1943 that more married women with children than without wanted to go on in paid work, particularly in the age group thirty-five to forty-four, and (most surprising of all) while many single women were expecting to move out of engineering, over 70 per cent of the married women in engineering who wished to do paid work after the war wanted to go on working in that sector.[51] The survey did not explore the feelings of married and single women about engineering, specifically, as an area of work. But it made certain assumptions about them. It commented on the 'conservatism' of married women who were suspected of not wanting to leave their masculine area of work for feminine reasons: 'because a change of job often necessitates a change of shopping habits and home routine'.[52] The expectations of both married and single women that they would stay in engineering were lower than for other industries (except transport), a point which the survey report emphasised, in keeping with its 'back to normal' approach. But the dramatic difference was for single rather than married women: across all industry, 68 per cent of single women wished to continue in their war jobs (as opposed to 77 per cent of married women); in engineering only 52 per cent of single women wished to carry on working (71 per cent of married women). The survey report interpreted this as a rejection by single women of the masculinising effects of the work: 'among single women, at least, and in relation to other jobs, Engineering is still not regarded as a woman's job'.[53]

In general the expectations of job continuity expressed by women who were asked about their post-war work intentions in 1943 may not have been realised. A follow-up survey to the 1944 investigation in 1948 reported that there had been the expected decrease in the number of women in paid work after the war. But it was not the case that marriage and motherhood were barriers to work. The report commented, 'There is no difference between the overall proportion of married, single and widowed women employed in 1943 and 1947'.[54] The main change was that more married women workers were in the older age groups (over thirty-five). There had also been much movement between industries. The biggest drop was in the proportion of all employed women who worked in engineering. But this did not mean that there had been a complete reversal of the wartime increase in the number and proportion of women working in engineering. Research by the economist C. E. V. Leser, published in 1952, showed that even though it was no longer the case in 1948/50 that one-third of engineering workers were women, as they had been in 1943, the proportion of women in the engineering workforce was double what it had been in 1939 (21 per cent compared with 10 per cent). The trend was also characteristic of other manufacturing industries, service industries like transport and distribution, and government. Leser commented that it meant 'not so much that women took men's jobs as that women-employing sections of the industries concerned gained at the expense of men-employing sections'.[55] These sectors (in a wide variety of manufacturing, in the service industries and in clerical work) were characterised by relatively low pay and, increasingly, part-time work.

Indeed there was plenty of work available for women after the war. The 1948 survey accompanied 'a campaign to stimulate the recruitment of women to industry',[56] undertaken in order to boost production for the export trade. There was also a demand for teachers and nurses. The campaigns focused on the recruitment of married women. Post-war 're-mobilisation', like wartime mobilisation, represented this recruitment as a temporary measure to help with a crisis, and now gave special emphasis to the idea that women would *not* do 'jobs usually done by men'. Mothers of children under two were emphatically excluded from the appeals.[57]

In 1951 30 per cent of all adult women did full-time paid work and 5 per cent did part-time, which was on a rising trend. The figures for 1961 were 32 per cent full-time, and 9 per cent part-time.[58] Married women formed an increasing proportion of the women in the post-war labour force: 43 per cent in 1951, 52 per cent in 1959. They came particularly from the older age groups.[59]

Peggy Scott had resolved the apparent contradiction between her 1944 observation that women became aware of new capabilities during the war, and that they would want to return home after it, by focusing on changes in the lives and expectations of older married women. 'Emancipation from drudgery, from individual isolation, is most likely to come through to them. They have found freedom by working part-time outside the home and earning their own money'.[60] The post-war demographic and employment trends appear to have confirmed both her prediction and the neglected wartime indicators of women's new patterns of participation: the huge expansion of married women in the workforce, particularly in part-time work, and the redistribution upwards of women across the age groups. But whatever women might actually be saying and doing, the path to post-war reconstruction, predicated on full male employment and wifely dependence, needed to be paved with reassuring statements about women's preference for life as the cornerstone of the British family.

The trends in the employment of women, particularly married women, and the rhetoric of their 'return to the home' at the end of the war, were in mutual opposition. But this was consistent with the duality at the heart of their treatment during the war. To recapitulate, government mobilisation policy showed a determination not to allow wives and mothers to be 'casualties' of the war effort by being compelled to leave their homes and do war work. Yet economic necessity, government propaganda and magazine addresses to women urged them to do so. These promptings, however, emphasised that the reprieve under which the housewife might move from her crucial position in the family was temporary. Femininity could be sacrificed in the shape of unmade beds, and it could be concealed by overalls and uniforms, and even by muscular strength and independence. Women could enter male work in civilian industry and in the forces, the heroic territories in which the instruments of death and destruction were manufactured and used. But representations of these female transgressions emphasised their status as patriotic exceptionalities, for the duration only. The continuing salience of femininity urged upon women, their temporary status as dilutees or servicewomen, the inaccessibility of truly 'skilled' status, and above all the dominance of the domestic norms of marriage and motherhood at the end of the war, appeared to contain and resolve any instabilities that war had set up. Yet the housewife was not to be entirely contained. Even if she did not do paid work when her children were young, and even if she did it part-time, in 'woman-employing sectors' at relatively low rates of pay and solely to boost the family income,[61] she was never after the Second World War debarred from paid work in the way she had been before, despite a strongly marginalising rhetoric. While she remained central to the family, during the war there had been a redefinition of what that meant: the housewife was now a financial as well as a moral, material and emotional cornerstone.

## Notes

1 Margaret Higgonet *et al.*, *Behind the Lines: Gender and the Two World Wars* (New Haven, Yale University Press, 1987); Denise Riley, *War in the Nursery: Theories of the Child and Mother* (London, Virago, 1983); Penny Summerfield, *Women Workers in the Second World War: Production and Patriarchy in Conflict* (London, Routledge, 1989).

2 Summerfield, *Women Workers in the Second World War*; M. Allen, 'The domestic ideal and the mobilisation of woman power in World War II', *Women's Studies International Forum*, Vol. 6 No. 4 (1983), pp. 401–12; H. L. Smith, *War and Social Change: British Society in the Second World War* (Manchester, Manchester University Press, 1986).

3 Christine Gledhill and Gillian Swanson, 'Gender and sexuality in Second World War Films – a feminist approach', in G. Hurd (ed.), *National Fictions* (London, British Film Institute, 1984); Riley, *War in the Nursery*; Antonia Lant, *Blackout:*

*Reinventing Femininity for Wartime Cinema* (Princeton, Princeton University Press, 1991).

4  Summerfield, *Women Workers in the Second World War*.

5  Gledhill and Swanson, 'Gender and sexuality'.

6  Vera Brittain, *England's Hour: An Autobiography 1939–1941* (London, Futura, 1981), p. 137.

7  *Ibid.*, pp. 60–1.

8  *Ibid.*, p. 132.

9  Summerfield, *Women Workers in the Second World War*, Allen, 'The domestic ideal'.

10  Jane Lewis, *Women in England 1870–1950: Sexual Divisions and Social Change* (Sussex, Wheatsheaf, 1984), p. 190.

11  Public Records Office (PRO) Lab 26/130 1941.

12  Ministry of Labour and National Service, *Report for the Years 1939–1946*, Cmd 7225, 1947, appendix 8.

13  Summerfield, *Women Workers in the Second World War*, pp. 46–8.

14  PRO Lab 26/130 1941.

15  PRO Cab 65/20 1941.

16  PRO Lab 26/63 1942.

17  Summerfield, *Women Workers in the Second World War*, p. 84.

18  PRO Lab 8/623 1942.

19  Summerfield, *Women Workers in the Second World War*, pp. 142–3.

20  Allen, 'The domestic ideal', p. 407.

21  Ministry of Labour and National Service, 1947, appendix 8.

22  See L. J. Rupp, *Mobilizing Women for War: German and American Propaganda 1939–1945* (Princeton, Princeton University Press, 1978); R. Bridenthal *et al.*, *When Biology Became Destiny: Women in Weimar and Nazi Germany* (New York, Monthly Review Press, 1984).

23  Ivy Pinchbeck, *Women Workers and the Industrial Revolution* (London, Routledge, 1930), p. 262; Gail Braybon, *Women Workers in the First World War* (London, Routledge, 1989), pp. 22ff and chapter 5.

24  *My Weekly*, 5 February 1938; *Picture Post*, 1943, quoted in Riley, *War in the Nursery*, p. 129.

25  A. C. H. Smith with E. Immirzi and T. Blackwell, *Paper Voices: The Popular Press and Social Change 1935–1965* (London, Chatto and Windus, 1975), pp. 113–14.

26  *Woman's Own*, 20 March 1942, quoted in Allen, 'The domestic ideal', pp. 403–4.

27  *Woman's Friend*, 15 January 1943.

28  *Woman*, 12 June 1943.

29  *My Weekly*, 12 June 1943.

30  J. B. Priestley, *British Women Go To War* (London, Collins, 1943), p. 55.

31  *Ibid.*, p. 35.

32  L. Stanley, *The Diaries of Hannah Culwick* (London, Virago, 1984).

33  P. Scott, *British Women in War* (London, Hutchinson, 1940), and *They Made Invasion Possible* (London, Hutchinson, 1944).

34  Scott, *They Made Invasion Possible*, pp. 7, 132.

35  Priestley, *British Women Go To War*, p. 38.

36  P. Inman, *Labour in the Munitions Industry* (London, HMSO, 1957), pp. 441–2.

37  *Ibid.*, p. 78.

38  *Ibid.*, pp. 78–80.

39  J. M. Hooks, *British Policies and Methods of Employing Women in Wartime* (Washington, US Government, 1944), p. 29.

40  Inman, *Labour in the Munitions Industry*, p. 374.
41  Penny Summerfield, 'The patriarchal discourse of human capital: training women for war work 1939–1945', *Journal of Gender Studies*, Vol. 2 No. 2 (1993).
42  PRO Lab 18/169; PRO Lab 18/170.
43  MRC MSS, 66/1/1/2 1940 and 66/1/1/6 1942.
44  Ministry of Labour and National Service, 1947, p. 139.
45  R. Croucher, *Engineers at War* (London, Merlin, 1982), pp. 261ff.
46  Arthur Askey, 'Thing-emmy-bob', HMV BD989; M. Leitch, *Great Songs of World War II* (London, Wise, 1975), p. 58.
47  Scott, *They Made Invasion Possible*, pp. 7–8.
48  Mass-Observation, *The Journey Home: A Mass-Observation Report on the Problems of Demobilisation* (London, John Murray, 1944), p. 66.
49  Wartime Social Survey, 'Women at work: the attitudes of working women towards post-war employment and some related problems', by Geoffrey Thomas (London, Central Office of Information, 1944), pp. 12–13.
50  Smith, *War and Social Change*, p. 225.
51  Wartime Social Survey, 'Women at work', pp. 12–15.
52  *Ibid.*, p. 15.
53  *Ibid.*, pp. 14–15.
54  Social Survey, 'Women and industry: an inquiry into the problem of recruiting women to industry carried out for the Ministry of Labour and National Service', by Geoffrey Thomas (London, Central Office of Information, 1948), p. 7. Some recent oral history studies explore how women looking back on their war work regard its gendering, and what factors influenced their decisions about whether to continue with it or look for other work. See, for example, G. Braybon and P. Summerfield, *Out of the Cage: Women's Experiences in the Two World Wars* (London, Pandora, 1987); D. Sheridan, 'Ambivalent memories: women and the 1939–1945 war in Britain', *Oral History*, Vol. 18 No. 1 (1990); Summerfield, 'The patriarchal discourse of human capital'. Discussion of this data would require a separate chapter.
55  C. E. V. Leser, 'Men and women in industry', *Economic Journal* (1952).
56  Social Survey, 'Women and industry', p. 1.
57  For example, Cmd 7046, 1947.
58  H. Joshi, 'The changing form of women's economic dependency', in H. Joshi (ed.), *The Changing Population of Britain* (Oxford, Blackwell, 1989), p. 158.
59  G. Routh, *Occupation and Pay in Great Britain 1906–1960* (Cambridge, Cambridge University Press, 1965), p. 47.
60  Scott, *They Made Invasion Possible*, p. 147.
61  J. H. Smith, 'Managers and married women workers', *British Journal of Sociology*, Vol. 12 (1961), pp. 12–22.

# 3

## 'Bombs don't discriminate!' Women's political activism in the Second World War

### ALISON ORAM

In July 1942, the Women's Freedom League expressed the hope that 'out of women's enormous contributions to the war effort there would come greater recognition of their status as equal citizens with men'.[1] Historians have begun to discuss some aspects of women's wartime political activities, including their role in party politics and Parliament, in the trade unions and in campaigns for equal pay.[2] The changing shape of the women's movement itself has been little explored, however, and this chapter will map out one approach to wartime feminist politics.

While some historians contest the notion that the war fundamentally changed women's material position, others point out important shifts in contemporary understandings of masculinity, femininity, and gender relations. The main contention of this chapter is that contradictory discourses of gender in wartime stimulated a variety of feminist campaigns and enabled new demands (and reworkings of old ones) to enter the public arena. It has been suggested that feminism occurs in the gap between the idea of 'woman' and the reality of 'women', when women cease to recognise themselves in current constructions of femininity and begin to blame the social structure rather than their own individual failings.[4] The Second World War disrupted existing gender codes considerably and produced huge tensions in representations of gender, in the meanings attached to women's place in the national struggle, and in relations between women and men. While clear distinctions between femininity and masculinity were maintained, this contestation also opened up space for the political articulation of women's concerns, grievances and difficulties in wartime and their hopes for the future. The war stimulated diverse elements of feminism, including the equal rights tradition as well as that championing women's interests as housewives and mothers.

The war presented an opportunity for the women's movement to reconcile deep differences which had emerged in the interwar years when feminist activism had fragmented into a number of single issue campaigns, none notably successful. Feminist political philosophy in the 1920s was divided between those who advocated equal rights between women and men (and therefore downplayed gender difference) and those who reasserted women's particular needs based on their role as mothers (which consequently emphasised feminine difference). While this polarity can be over-emphasised, it did pose a real crisis in the unity of the women's movement.[6] The personnel and preoccupations of wartime feminism were directly related to this history, and explicit attempts were made to address and overcome these divisions, especially in the insistence on the importance of women's increased political participation and the plurality that this implied.

An important role was taken by a major wartime feminist coordinating group, the Women's Publicity Planning Association (WPPA), which will be discussed here as a case study. The WPPA, set up by representatives from existing women's organisations, was led by Margery Corbett-Ashby and Rebecca Sieff, with the aim of increasing the flow of information and views between women's groups both nationally and internationally.[7] Wartime paper shortage prevented the WPPA from setting up its own journal, but it was able to take over the existing *International Women's News* from 1940, in order to 'enable women to make their work known to others as an encouragement and rouse all women to a sense of individual and collective responsibility in the planning of a new world'. The WPPA united both old and newly active feminists, describing itself as 'the logical development of the work of progressive women during fifty years' and acted as an umbrella group and mouthpiece for the whole range of wartime women's issues.[8]

### Equality or difference?

Changing wartime understandings of gender relations revitalised feminist activity around claims based both on 'equal rights' *and* on women's 'difference'.[9] During the Second World War women were treated as citizens who owed certain 'masculine' responsibilities towards the state; they were called up into the auxiliary defence services and conscripted into industry as workers for the war effort.[10] Despite the representation of this participation as temporary and ideologically restricted, a rhetoric of equal contribution and equal sacrifice was attached to women's new roles, and this allowed an opportunity for new 'equal rights' desires to be voiced, and old ones to be put more forcefully and effectively. This did not come out of the blue. The issue of equal pay, for example, had already begun to resurface in the mid to late 1930s, and a major Commons debate on the issue was provoked by Ellen Wilkinson MP in 1936.[11]

At the same time, the war also emphasised gender *difference* very powerfully. Men went off to the battlefield, while women maintained the home front. Although in reality women's traditional sphere of influence, the home, was undermined by the war, the connection between femininity and family life was strengthened as an iconic representation of the future for which the nation was fighting. During the war, social issues typically gendered as feminine, such as evacuation, housing and welfare, were pushed higher up the political agenda, and this fostered the reworking of the idea (already existing in different forms much earlier in the century) of a complementary feminine citizenship for women, in which they contributed to the wider community through their roles as mothers and carers. Discussions in the early 1940s which anticipated post-war reconstruction and a return to social stability were presented as having particular resonance for women, and these issues were enthusiastically taken on by feminists in an attempt to acquire greater status for the housewife and mother.[12]

This ambivalence between 'equality' and 'difference' was represented in the pages of the *International Women's News* (*IWN*). What kind of woman did they speak for, the war worker or the housewife? Although these distinctions were in some respects heightened in wartime, the active feminists writing for the *IWN* made genuine efforts to unite them, considering that both roles were important and recognising that the worker and the mother could be the same woman. In the early years of the war there was enthusiastic reporting of the new types of work which women were undertaking or could aspire to. But at the same time there was discussion of evacuation problems, and from 1941 a series entitled 'After the war' raised reconstruction topics such as education and childcare. By 1944 and 1945 discussion of post-war society had expanded, and alongside fears about the falling birthrate, concern was also expressed about future wage levels and training for women workers.

### Equal participation: equal pay and compensation

The wartime rhetoric of women's full citizenship and equal participation in the war effort was very strong. Women became subject to registration and conscription into the services and war industries such as engineering and munitions in a similar (though not identical) way to men. Women worked in a much wider range of occupations than they had done previously, including some skilled processes previously designated men's work. However spurious this equivalence was if closely analysed (women's industrial

[ 55 ]

earnings were on average 53 per cent of men's, for instance), it was widely assumed to exist at the time, and could therefore be used as a powerful political discourse for equality.[13] This approach was particularly used by feminists to argue for improvements in women's employment position and in the campaign for equal compensation for war injuries.

The *IWN* called on the government to 'Conscript the women' on the grounds that 'This is total war and we are all in it'.[14] The *IWN* was enthusiastic about the introduction of conscription in April 1941, believing it marked a realisation of the seriousness of the crisis, and a 'recognition of the potential value of women's services to the State'.[15] But this emphasis on the needs of the nation, and women's contribution to it, was soon modified by an articulation of the needs of the mother and her children. A leading article on the 'Woman-power debate' reiterated criticism of earlier government mishandling of women's voluntary response and found fault with the idea of 'minders' for children rather than proper nurseries. The *IWN* also expressed concern about the protection of home life, and warned against separating mothers from their young children unnecessarily. The writer called for greater provision of part-time work for women; this and the nursery question remained unresolved and continued to cause friction between organised women and government ministries for several years of the war.[16]

In practice, women's place in the war industries was complicated and variable but rarely equal. As many women moved into new types of work previously the preserve of men, and received higher pay than before, they were in a more 'masculine' position at work. One effect was a tremendous expansion of women's trade union membership. But male-dominated trade unions were an ambivalent political vehicle for women. Even though trade unions were increasingly interested in recruiting women members, their main concern was often to preserve the better jobs and higher rates of pay for men at the end of the war.[17] On the other hand it has been shown that in those instances where women were directly represented by women shop stewards they developed a close concern with workplace politics. Trained to do men's work to release men for the military, but paid at a lower rate despite union agreements, women workers did occasionally take industrial action to stake their claim for equal pay during the war. Penny Summerfield suggests that the Hillington equal pay strike in 1943 marked the beginning of greater activity on this issue by women workers through their trade unions.[18]

Feminists soon recognised and protested against the unequal conditions under which women's war work was carried out. In December 1941 the *IWN* complained about the government's weakness and inefficiency in using women's labour for wartime industry, citing poor training and the indifference of the male workers. It criticised the failure of some trade unions (particularly in engineering) to insist on the application of the equal pay principle as narrow short-sightedness and unreasoned prejudice.[19] The position taken by many women's groups was that if women were to be conscripted for the auxiliary services, civil defence, or industrial work, they should receive equal pay with men doing similar work, and enjoy the same terms and conditions.[20] Following a 1942 speech made by Ernest Bevin, the Minister of Labour, paying tribute to the women who entered wartime industry and looking forward to their place in the post-war world, the *IWN* demanded that positive changes in women's position should be made straight away – material change was wanted, not just lip service.

> The skilled trade unions do not yet admit women to membership; the higher ranks of the administration and of industry are still closed to them, in fact if not in theory ... Whenever it is a question of pay, bonus, compensation – and nowhere more markedly than in undertakings run or controlled by the State – the tradition of cheap labour persists.[21]

Feminists made the same call for equality in practice, not just in rhetoric, in the campaign for equal compensation for war injuries. This was a flagrant gendered contradiction. Women were compulsorily mobilised for war duties as full and implicitly equal citizens, but if injured their weekly compensation payments and pensions were well below the rates for men. After the *IWN* had condemned the differentiation in the rates of compensation paid to women and men injured in air raids in January 1941, the National Federation of Business and Professional Women called a meeting and sent a deputation to the Ministry of Pensions.[22] The Six Point Group identified unequal civil compensation rates as the most glaring example of old prejudices still apparent despite the glowing tributes paid to women and their service in the national emergency.[23]

In July 1941 the WPPA ran a special issue of *IWN* on equal compensation. The leading article, 'Bombs don't discriminate', argued that 'the home front [is] a real military front'. Civilians would suffer death and injury as well as servicemen. 'In this we are all equal. Will the Ministry and the Government recognise that equality?' 'Women are expected to perform equal duties and to face equal danger of disablement, yet they are offered unequal compensation if injured. Can this be justified?'[24]

The campaign gathered momentum and continued for three and a half years, with meetings in many towns and cities, petitions, lobbying of ministers and debates in Parliament. The group of thirteen women MPs acted (cross-party as they had previously on wartime women's issues) as the focus for the campaign.[25] Equal compensation was the subject of the first wartime popular political demonstration in Trafalgar Square in September 1941. The leading organisations involved were longstanding associations of professional women and feminist groups.[26] The question of equal compensation was brought into prominence again in the autumn of 1942 by a government order making fire-watching compulsory for women.

> Full equality? Well, hardly! As far as the running of the risk is concerned, the equality is unimpeachable. But what happens if the risk becomes a fact, if, in carrying out their duties, women fire guards are injured? At that point equality ceases. The allowances for injury are 35/- for men and 28/- for women ... No other explanation of this discrimination can be offered, except that women are still considered by our rulers to be of less worth than men.

This view was not shared by the public, however; opinion surveys showed that 84 per cent of those questioned were in favour of equal rates.[27]

When the campaign was finally won (and it is often cited as the only clear feminist victory of the Second World War years) it was welcomed by feminists not only as a victory for the principle of equality but also as an example of unity among all women's organisations, one which overrode party divisions among women MPs, and as 'democracy in action'. The women's fight was linked to the aims of the war itself. '[I]t is even more significant as an example of the way democracy can be made to work and achieve its ends ... It provides a lesson which ordinary men and women will take to heart, that so long as a people remains free in spirit ... there are ways and means of making our wishes effective, and of affirming our faith in democracy.'[28]

### Femininity and feminism: the housewife and the war

In contrast to peacetime, domesticity became a public issue during the war.[29] Rather than being a private place, the home was now part of the war effort and the housewife was asked – and in some instances compelled – to 'do her bit' by collecting salvage, conserving food or billeting evacuees and service personnel. Women could make special demands on the basis of their specific skills and qualities. A deputation of foster mothers, organised by the Married Women's Association, 'told Miss Horsburgh [the Minister of Health] in unequivocal terms the impossibility of feeding, housing, nursing, washing and caring for the children and their clothes on the present meagre allowances'. They also asked for a further sum for the housewife's labour.[30]

Feminists made the argument that women's skills in the private sphere should be put to use in the national effort. An *IWN* article in June 1941, 'Use the women', complained that women had not been given real responsibility in relation to home front concerns.

> We hope we shall not be accused of an outworn feminism if we say that the richest source of unused intelligence and capacity is to be found among the women of this country ... Is there, in any department where the practical experience of

women should be exploited to the utmost – in food, housing, billeting, health – is there a single woman who has been given real responsibility? ... Our home front reproduces on a gigantic scale the problems of a disorganised household. In any sensible family the woman would take charge and get things put right.[31]

The war did create a larger arena for women's voluntary activity, a traditionally acceptable female public role, but though some women gained positions of considerable responsibility in this way, they continued to be under-represented on government committees.[32]

Halfway through the war, the emphasis shifted towards reconstruction and the new post-war world. National debates about children's education after the war, the social importance of motherhood, the looming 'problem of population', housing and the creation of a welfare state were engaged in with tremendous energy. During these discussions, women were primarily considered as housewives and mothers, albeit of a new post-war breed. A consensus developed – among feminists as well as others – that the housewife was to be considered as a citizen in her own right, though one of a different and complementary type to the male breadwinner. In a 1943 Commons debate Mrs Cazalet Keir MP suggested that the home would continue to be the centre, but never the boundary of a woman's life. 'After the war the vast majority of women who return home will want to spend some of their time on citizenship.' She suggested, as did others in this period, that new services like British Restaurants and school meals would continue into peacetime, and release the housewife for both leisure and public service.[33]

Some quite prescriptive and traditional arguments for more status for women in the home were presented on the wide-ranging pages of the *IWN*. Dorothy Paterson wrote in 1943 that child-bearing and rearing should be the first purpose of women. 'Many women have splendid intellects. They are women's brains, not men's, and they are different. Let women have confidence in that. As individuals, they must first be the mothers of the race and accept the training of young children, which is a responsible duty and a great privilege. The want of home influence is tragically affecting the young.' Women should aim to raise 'the status and moral significance of the mother, irrespective of her class, to at least the same level as her business and professional sister'. She believed that society 'should approve most of those women who, irrespective of class or capability, rear fine families, and should equally disapprove of those who can, and selfishly do not, have children'.[34]

This concern about the birth-rate, juvenile neglect and crime was echoed in a more liberal article by Anne Hawkins in 1945, 'Mother or housewife'. She wrote, 'During at least the early years the key to the family and emotional situation is the mother'. She discussed the difficulties of working-class mothers which could be partly addressed by better housing, home helps, laundries, and day nurseries. 'The truth is that motherhood is an important and exacting job in itself and not a branch of the housework.' Good mothering, she argued, depended on leisure for mothers, 'and also, I think, on a recognised status for the mother as such, not primarily as "housewife"'. The status of the mother was partly improved by paying her family allowances, but 'it might be supplemented by some sort of guardian benefit by which the State acknowledged the value of her work in bearing and rearing her children'. This type of argument echoed the earlier demand of 1920s feminists for the endowment of motherhood, and similarly explored the ways in which women might be given an independent income by the state in return for their duties and responsibilities as mothers.[35] However these discussions of state help for mothers became inseparable from the broader terrain of pronatalism and the more radical of the feminist suggestions did not outlive the war.[36]

### Uniting the women's movement

At times, the WPPA through the pages of the *IWN* explicitly addressed the nature of contemporary feminist politics and attempted to develop a women's movement that would be more broadly based and overcome the divisions between equal rights campaigners and home-making women. This was evident in a pair of articles published in July 1941, which criticised the failings of the interwar women's movement, particularly its narrow focus on equality. The first, 'The rise and fall of the women's movement', was written by Katherine Bompas, who identified herself as 'one who has worked in the women's movement all her life [and] cared for it passionately'. Bompas had edited the *IWN* for a number of years, when it had been the organ of the International Alliance for Suffrage and Equal Citizenship, and continued as editor into the 1940s. After describing the nineteenth- and early twentieth-century women's movement, she wrote of how interwar women's organisations, whether social groups such as Women's Institutes or employment-based groups, fought shy of feminism:

> it sounded old fashioned, anti-man or something odd ... The remnant of the feminist movement went along on its old lines, rigidly limited to the demand for equality with men, and refusing to deal with the bewildering variety of problems that face women in practical ways inside her home as a wife and mother in an age when being a wife and mother is not very often, and perhaps never ought to be, a full-time and life-time job ... they got further and further away from the mass of women.

She called for a fusion of all the theoretical, practical and social movements for women which could change with the times and adapt to new problems.[37]

Though even more antagonistic to equal rights feminism, the second article, 'Should the women's movement be re-created?' by Rebecca Sieff, also called for a renewal of the women's movement, as well as making a strong argument for 'difference' feminism. She was particularly critical of the trend towards educating girls in the same way as boys. This system had driven women into the existing professions, without them bringing fresh initiative or outlook. These successful career women had been too occupied and self-satisfied to bother about the more general problems concerning their sex. More women's organisations had grown up, but they tended towards insularity and resisted political discussion, she wrote. She called for 'the proper participation of women in the responsible direction of the war effort in every possible field, especially in the fields of social reconstruction and education. From it should flow a movement associating the women of all the democracies in the desire to participate actively in the planning and creation of the post-war world.'[38]

The wartime feminist coalition was struggling to unite these varied approaches to women's issues, and revealed an interesting mixture of commitment to equality issues and attacks on equal rights feminism. Attempts to re-orientate the movement towards feminine difference and the woman at home can be seen in the later campaign for the Equal Citizenship (Blanket) Bill, which combined legal rights for women as workers and women in the family.

### The Equal Citizenship (Blanket) Bill

Work on this Bill began in mid-1943, following the victory on equal compensation. Feminists believed that with similar efforts they could probably remedy other inequalities bit by bit, but that it would be a great saving of effort to work for a blanket Bill to remove all existing sex discrimination in law, and prevent future legislation discriminating on the grounds of sex or marriage.[39] The Equal Citizenship (Blanket) Bill was strongly informed by equality principles, and made similar arguments for women's equal citizenship on the basis of their equal participation in the war as had earlier campaigns. It aimed to give women 'a fair field and no favour' in public life and employment. But it also took on board, in a number of different ways, the position of the housewife. It would amend the married women's property laws. A recent case which ruled that a husband legally owned his wife's savings from the housekeeping and profits from lodgers had 'aroused indignation among the usually inarticulate mass of women working in the home, amounting to a minor revolution'.[40] It was also intended that the Bill would prevent sex discrimination in the new social security arrangements. 'Social Security, on which so many hopes are set, will be of little use to women if

[ 61 ]

they are expected to live on less than men need. Sir William Beveridge recommended the same allowances for men and women but allowed less for housewives than for other persons.'[41]

At a meeting to inaugurate the campaign, attention was also drawn to the Bill's relevance to the current concern about a wife's loss of nationality on marriage to a foreigner. Interestingly the Bill did not include any provision for the endowment of motherhood, and as a Bill concerned with outlawing sex discrimination it would also abolish protective legislation for women, which had been a key issue for 'difference' feminists in the 1920s.

Feminists referred scathingly to government promises to women:

> It may seem surprising that, in the fifth year of the war to defeat the evils of fascism, there should have been the need for a large meeting in London to demand for women equality of citizenship ... And while the demands on the skill, energy and devotion of the women of Britain increase from day to day, we are assured that, after the war, we shall be able to work out our own salvation in the homes of the future which 'they' are going to provide. Is this completely convincing?[42]

But while it was relatively easy to draft anti-discrimination laws to apply to the public sphere, it was much more difficult to legislate a satisfactory basis for women's position in the family. An article published at the end of 1943 identified financial arrangements and property rights as the key concern. 'The marriage relationship is ... often [spoilt] because a wife is not paid, and cannot get her husband to discuss money matters, or give her her money regularly so that she knows where she is.' It described how husbands used their financial power over wives in a number of ways. 'The time has clearly come for a wife's legal and economic position to be put on a more satisfactory basis. Sir William Beveridge suggests that man and wife should be considered members of a team. As such the wife certainly has the right to participate in the income of the team.' The Equal Citizenship (Blanket) Bill would not be a remedy for this, since marriage laws came under common law not statute, yet it was difficult to find a framework to give wives the legal right to a specific share of the household income, whether through the courts, or an enforceable pre-nuptial agreement.[43]

This article is interesting since it shows the difficulties faced by feminists in trying to develop the idea of equal citizenship. If this was claimed on the basis of equal service to the state (such as defence work or other employment), not all women could be included. On the other hand, marriage roles were so highly gender-differentiated that it was impossible to establish equal status for the housewife out of a relationship in which women were dependent upon men. Work on the Equal Citizenship (Blanket) Bill continued to try to develop demands on behalf of mothers and housewives alongside professional and women workers, but the campaign lost momentum with the death of one of its key figures, Dorothy Evans, in 1944. Rather than changing women's position in marriage, the post-war 'patriarchal welfare state' reinforced it by recognising women primarily as dependants on a male breadwinner rather than as independent citizens or workers in their own right.[44]

### Women, feminism and political participation

One constant and striking preoccupation of the WPPA and the *IWN* throughout the war was the relationship of women to the wider political process. It was recognised that one failing of the interwar women's movement had been its inability to mobilise more than a small minority of women around women's issues. The stress on women's political participation was also a way of uniting (or displacing) the differences within feminist politics into a more pluralist vision within which equal rights, women's family interests and other positions could be represented and addressed politically. In the *IWN* debates, a variety of wartime discourses were cleverly linked, including women's citizenship and equal participation, the need for greater political representation for women, and the battle between democracy and fascism.

The central premise of the war – that it was being fought to defend democracy – inspired the feminist fight for women's improved political participation. The negative effects of fascism and totalitarianism on women's independence and freedom were emphasised in an early leading article on 'The Nazi way with women'. '[N]o part of the community is so immediately affected by the Nazi encroachment as women.' In Nazi-occupied France:

> *No girl may any longer study Latin or Mathematics in French schools* ... The first move of the invading Nazi forces has in every case been to drive back women into the twilight of affairs from which they have so recently emerged ... To render the women powerless is to cut by one half a nation's resistance to conquest, for in the final analysis the women are the custodians of the nation's morale.[45]

The argument being made here was that the status of women was an indicator of a nation's freedom and superior politics, both in their actual social freedom, and also symbolically as moral guardians of the nation's fibre. This discussion echoed the warnings of interwar feminists such as Winifred Holtby, who had linked the rise of fascism to anti-feminism in the 1930s.[46]

Women in Britain were liberated in their democratic freedoms. 'We women in England may loathe war and long to end it. We may be feeling the strain of these months in the front line ... We have the will to carry on because we are determined to avoid the fate of the women of Germany. We have the inspiration which comes from freedom to help in the building of a more just social order.[47] However, in this context, the shortcomings and omissions of British politics in relation to women could also be criticised. '[I]t was mere lip-service to talk about a "true democracy" while fifty per cent of the adult citizens neglected to take an intelligent interest in affairs.'[48] The paper recognised some of the reasons for women's political apathy, including old traditions and powerful social pressures; it noted that many obstacles, some deliberate, were put in women's way.[49]

In some ways the war added to these practical and psychological barriers to women's political activity. The extra burdens of war work and the greater difficulty of housework under rationing gave women less free time and may also have contributed to the low morale found among women by contemporary surveys.[50] Travel restrictions inhibited women more than men, it was found, and made holding any kind of political meetings and conferences difficult. But the war also stimulated women's political engagement, and increased knowledge not only about the progress of the war, but also about issues of reconstruction in post-war Britain. Mass Observation found in 1941 that women took considerably more interest in the news and in politics than they had done before the war, though it was still very much less than men's.[51]

To redress the lack of women's voices in national politics, wartime feminists put their emphasis on promoting more women candidates for Parliament and local councils. In 1940, the Six Point Group called for an adequate number of women candidates when the next General Election was held, and regarded it as of the utmost importance that 'the present ridiculously low proportion' of women MPs should be increased in the first post-war Parliament.[52] Edith Summerskill MP wrote that democratic institutions and methods would remain broadly the same after the war. But:

> Are we going to surrender our equal part in the war for an unequal part in the peace ... are we willing to have [affairs] managed so predominantly by men, with all that that has meant in terms of unequal status and unequal rights? ... let us make up our minds now that we want an equal share. It is a claim that no honest democrat can deny, but it is a claim that will not be granted merely for the asking.[53]

The Women for Westminster movement, launched by the WPPA in 1942, aimed to consolidate the wartime practice of women MPs working together in women's interests and to assist women to stand for all parties. '[T]he programmes of the various Parties are full of gaps in matters concerning the economic interests of women and the welfare of children.' The prejudice within each of the political parties against women candidates and the tendency to give them hopeless seats was condemned.[54]

But in making the argument for more women MPs, emphasis was also put on women's gender-specific contribution to post-war reconstruction. Women 'are profoundly anxious to help to rebuild the post-war world. Much of the work of reconstruction will lie in fields in which women are particularly interested, both as women and as citizens of a democracy – housing, town planning, education, feeding and welfare services.'[55] This rhetoric called on women to use their political power to protect their interests and improve their status on the basis of their equal part in the war and proven abilities, but also in terms of a new form of citizenship for the housewife, in which she would be more actively engaged in the community, and contribute in terms of her particular aptitudes and fields of expertise. 'Reconstruction after the last war gave us a manmade world. Are women content that once again the new social order shall be shaped almost entirely by men?'[56]

### Conclusion

Wartime shifts in gender discourses re-energised the women's movement, precipitated more women into active feminist politics and enabled new demands to be made of the government and voiced in public debate. An important attempt was made to reconcile the diverse approaches within the movement and combine activism on behalf of the working woman alongside that of the housewife and mother.

The 'new social order' after the Second World War established a wider notion of social citizenship centred around the welfare state. Feminists were striving to achieve a complex ideal of citizenship and political participation for women, which included a claim for equality in the public sphere together with greater recognition of and support for women's particular contribution to the state as mothers. But the subtleties and ambiguities of these contradictory discourses were difficult to maintain in the context of pronatalism and a welfare state which, while rhetorically elevating women's role as mothers and wives, reinscribed them as dependants on a male breadwinner. With the conclusion of hostilities, women's war effort could more clearly be seen as temporary and as 'really' men's work, and so the argument for equality on the basis of equal participation lost purchase, although equal pay was strongly pressed in Parliament and a royal commission on the question set up.

The post-war women's movement did continue the attempt to integrate issues of employment and family life. Feminists in the 1940s and 1950s made considerable efforts to square the belief in the psychological importance of full-time motherhood with the conviction that women's employment skills should not be wasted, by developing the idea of women's 'two roles'.[57] The new meanings attached to equality issues in wartime continued to give impetus and success to post-war battles. Despite the blocking of equal pay for teachers in 1944, and the equivocal conclusions of the 1944–46 Royal Commission on Equal Pay, the campaign for equal pay expanded dramatically in the later 1940s and 1950s and was won for civil servants and teachers in 1955.[58] The wartime attempt by feminists to unite equal rights with a politics of the private sphere continued to resonate in the following decades and forms an important link with the Women's Liberation Movement of the late 1960s.

## Notes

I would like to thank Anna Clark and Alison Twells for their helpful comments on drafts of this chapter, and Christine Gledhill for her useful editorial suggestions.

1 *International Women's News* (*IWN*), Vol. 36 No. 10, July 1942, pp. 187–8. The Women's Freedom League had been founded in 1907 to campaign for women's suffrage.

2 P. Brookes, *Women at Westminster: An Account of Women in the British Parliament 1918–1966* (London, Peter Davies, 1967), pp. 130–46; M. Pugh, *Women and the Women's Movement in Britain 1914–1959* (London, Macmillan, 1992), chapter 9; P. Summerfield, *Women Workers in the Second World War* (London, Croom Helm, 1984); H. Smith, 'The problem of "equal pay for equal work" in Great Britain during World War II', *Journal of Modern History*, Vol. 53 No. 4 (December 1981), pp. 652–72.

3 Summerfield, *Women Workers*; M. Higonnet *et al.* (eds), *Behind the Lines: Gender and the Two World Wars* (London, Yale University Press, 1987).

4 D. Riley, *'Am I That Name?'* (London, Macmillan, 1988), pp. 1–5; R. R. Pierson, 'Experience, difference, dominance and voice in the writing of Canadian women's history', in K. Offen, R. R. Pierson and J. Rendall (eds), *Writing Women's History: International Perspectives* (London, Macmillan, 1991). Contradictory pressures seem to have been a stimulus to the articulation of feminist politics in very different historical periods. See P. Levine, *Feminist Lives in Victorian England* (Oxford, Blackwell, 1990), pp. 16–17; V. Randall, *Women and Politics* (London, Macmillan Education, 1987), p. 222; R. W. Connell, *Gender and Power* (Cambridge, Polity Press, 1987), p. 271.

5 C. Gledhill and G. Swanson, 'Gender and sexuality in Second World War films', in G. Hurd, *National Fictions* (London, British Film Institute, 1984); A. Lant, *Blackout: Reinventing Women for Wartime British Cinema* (Princeton, Princeton University Press, 1991); D. Parkin, 'Women in the armed services, 1940–5', in R. Samuel (ed.), *Patriotism: The Making and Unmaking of British National Identity, Vol. 2: Minorities and Outsiders* (London, Routledge, 1989), pp. 158–70; Summerfield, *Women Workers*, and see her chapter in this volume; 'Introduction' to Higonnet, *Behind the Lines*.

6 H. Smith, 'British feminism in the 1920s', in H. Smith (ed.), *British Feminism in the Twentieth Century* (Aldershot, Edward Elgar, 1990); J. Lewis, *Women in England*

*1870–1950* (Sussex, Wheatsheaf Books, 1984), pp. 102–6.

7  The WPPA was formed as a result of a meeting in December 1939 (Introduction to the records of the WPPA, Fawcett Library). Margery Corbett-Ashby was an important figure in interwar British and international feminism, and was particularly involved in the National Union of Societies for Equal Citizenship, the Townswomen's Guilds and the International Woman Suffrage Alliance. See J. Alberti, *Beyond Suffrage: Feminists in War and Peace, 1914–28* (London, Macmillan, 1989). Rebecca Sieff, of the Sieff retailing family (Marks and Spencer), was involved in the women's movement only during the war years; her later political activity was in the Zionist movement (I am grateful to David Doughan of the Fawcett Library for this information). The WPPA also published a book by Vera Douie, *The Lesser Half* (London, WPPA, 1943), which discussed the unequal position of women in the Second World War.

8  *IWN*, Vol. 35 No. 1, October–November 1940. The monthly *IWN* was formerly the paper of the International Alliance of Women for Suffrage and Equal Citizenship. Other feminist groups which continued to be active throughout the war included the Six Point Group, The Women's Freedom League, The National Union of Women Teachers and the British Federation of Business and Professional Women.

9  Though historians have suggested that the war stimulated the women's movement, some kinds of women's politics, most obviously pacifism, suffered from government censorship and harassment. See Pugh, *Women's Movement*, pp. 275–6; H. Smith, 'The effect of the war on the status of women', in H. Smith (ed.), *War and Social Change: British Society in the Second World War* (Manchester, Manchester University Press, 1986), p. 223; Brookes, *Women at Westminster*, p. 130. For wartime censorship see V. Brittain, *Testament of Experience* (London, Virago, 1978), chapters 7 and 8; A. M. Pierotti, *The Story of the National Union of Women Teachers* (London, NUWT, 1963), p. 49.

10  See Summerfield, this volume; Pugh, *Women's Movement*, p. 264; A. Phillips, *Democracy and Difference* (Cambridge, Polity Press, 1993), p. 107; C. Pateman, 'The patriarchal welfare state', in C. Pateman, *The Disorder of Women* (Cambridge, Polity Press, 1989), pp. 185–6.

11  This debate and vote in favour of equal pay (subsequently reversed on a motion of confidence) was on equal pay in the civil service. *Hansard*, 1 April and 6 April 1936. Equal pay also began to reappear as an issue for the teachers' associations at this time.

12  D. Morgan and M. Evans, *The Battle for Britain: Citizenship and Ideology in the Second World War* (London, Routledge, 1993), pp. 71–9; Summerfield, *Women Workers*, chapters 4 and 5; D. Riley, 'The Free Mothers: pronatalism and working mothers in industry at the end of the last war in Britain', *History Workshop Journal*, No. 11 (1981), pp. 59–118; Phillips, *Democracy and Difference*, p. 107; Pateman, *Disorder of Women*, p. 11.

13  Smith, 'The status of women', pp. 211–17; Summerfield, *Women Workers*, pp. 151–2, 170.

14  *IWN*, Vol. 35 No. 5, March 1941, p. 81.

15  *IWN*, Vol. 35 No. 6, April 1941, p. 101.

16  In some areas, groups of housewives as well as Labour Party women and women trade union leaders put pressure on government during 1941–42 for greater provision of day nurseries to allow mothers to work. *IWN*, Vol. 35 No. 7, May 1941, p. 121. For other calls for more part-time work see *IWN*, Vol. 35 No. 7, May 1941, p. 122; Vol. 36 No. 3, December 1941, p. 42; Vol. 36 No. 10, July 1942, p. 188.

17 Summerfield, *Women Workers*, pp. 158–9, 170; Higgonet *et al.*, *Behind the Lines*, p. 10; *IWN*, Vol. 35 No. 7, May 1941, p. 122; Vol. 36 No. 3, December 1941, p. 41.

18 Summerfield, *Women Workers*, pp. 157–8, 171–3. Also see Smith, 'Equal pay for equal work', pp. 663–5.

19 *IWN*, Vol. 36 No. 3, December 1941, p. 42.

20 See for example: *IWN*, Vol. 35 No. 8, June 1941; Vol. 35 No. 10, August–September 1941, p. 202; Vol. 36, No. 4, January 1942, p. 79; Vol. 36 No. 10, July 1942, p. 188; Vol. 37 No. 12, September 1943, p. 169.

21 *IWN*, Vol. 36 No. 12, September 1942, p. 206.

22 *IWN*, Vol. 35 No. 5, March 1941, p. 81. Women's groups had protested against this legislation since 1939, but the organised campaign took off in 1941. Smith, 'Equal pay for equal work', pp. 655, 661.

23 *IWN*, Vol. 35 No. 6, April 1941, p. 119.

24 *IWN*, Vol. 35 No. 9, July 1941, pp. 161, 163–5. Unequal rates were defended in the Commons on the grounds of women's average lower wages than men. But feminists pointed out that many women workers would get more for an industrial accident under the Workman's Compensation Act.

25 Brookes, *Women at Westminster*, pp. 130, 138–9.

26 *IWN*, Vol. 35 No. 9, July 1941, p. 165; Vol. 35 No. 10, August–September 1941, p. 202; Vol. 36 No. 1, October 1941, p. 5; Vol. 36 No. 4, p. 79.

27 *IWN*, Vol. 36 No. 12, September 1942, pp. 205–6.

28 *IWN*, Vol. 37 No. 8, May 1943; Smith, 'Equal pay for equal work', p. 663.

29 Summerfield, *Women Workers*, p. 185.

30 *IWN*, Vol. 36 No. 4, January 1942, p. 79.

31 *IWN*, Vol. 35 No. 8, June 1941, p. 142.

32 Women's voluntary activity in wartime is still inadequately researched, but see Mass Observation File Reports, January 1940, No. 26; M. Stott, *Organisation Woman: The Story of the National Union of Townswomen's Guilds* (London, Heinemann, 1978), chapter 3; R. Minns, *Bombers and Mash: The Domestic Front 1939–45* (London, Virago, 1980), chapter 5; Pugh, *Women's Movement*, p. 268. For feminist complaints about under-representation see for example *IWN*, Vol. 36 No. 10, July 1942, p. 187.

33 *IWN*, Vol. 37 No. 12, September 1943, p. 170.

34 *IWN*, Vol. 37 No. 9, June 1943, p. 133.

35 *IWN*, Vol. 39 No. 9, June 1945, pp. 102–4. Other writers attacked the artificial boundary made for women between marriage and a career. *IWN*, Vol. 39 No. 11, August 1945, pp. 123–4. For family allowances see H. Land, 'The introduction of family allowances: an act of historic justice?', in C. Ungerson (ed.), *Women and Social Policy: A Reader* (London, Macmillan, 1985), pp. 9–29.

36 D. Riley, *War in the Nursery: Theories of the Child and Mother* (London, Virago, 1983), pp. 171–8.

37 *IWN*, Vol. 35 No. 9, July 1941, pp. 166–7. Bompas was also a member of the Women's Freedom League, and the co-author, with Elizabeth Abbott, of a 1943 pamphlet criticising the Beveridge Report.

38 *IWN*, Vol. 35 No. 9, July 1941, pp. 167–8.

39 *IWN*, Vol. 37 No. 9, June 1943, p. 131. And see Smith, 'The status of women', pp. 224–5.

40 See the chapter by Carol Smart in this volume.

41 *IWN*, Vol. 37 No. 11, August 1943, pp. 165–6. For discussion of contemporary feminist criticism of the Beveridge proposals see J. Lewis, 'Dealing with dependency: state practices and social realities, 1870–1945', in J. Lewis (ed.), *Women's Welfare,*

*Women's Rights* (London, Croom Helm, 1989), pp. 19–20, 30; Smith, 'The status of women', p. 223; Pierotti, *The NUWT*, p. 51.

42  *IWN*, Vol. 38 No. 1, October 1943, p. 3.

43  *IWN*, Vol. 38 No. 3, December 1943, pp. 27–8.

44  *IWN*, Vol. 38 No. 6, March 1944, p. 69; Vol. 38 No. 10, July 1944, p. 117; Vol. 39 No. 1, October 1944, pp. 5–6; Six Point Group, *Dorothy Evans and the Six Point Group* (London, Six Point Group, 1945); Pateman, 'The patriarchal welfare state'.

45  *IWN*, Vol. 35 No. 2, November–December 1940, p. 21. Emphasis in original.

46  W. Holtby, *Women* (London, John Lane The Bodley Head, 1934), chapter 4; 'Black words for women only' (1934) and 'Shall I order a black blouse?' (1934), reprinted in P. Berry and A. Bishop (eds), *Testament of a Generation: The Journalism of Vera Brittain and Winifred Holtby* (London, Virago, 1985), pp. 84–6, 170–3.

47  *IWN*, Vol. 35 No. 2, November–December 1940, p. 22.

48  *IWN*, Vol. 35 No. 1, October–November 1940, p. 1.

49  *IWN*, Vol. 36 No. 10, July 1942, p. 174. For comment on women's lack of political influence also see an article by Tom Harrisson for Mass Observation, prepared in 1942 for the *Daily Express*. Mass Observation File Reports, June 1942, No. 1316–7.

50  Mass Observation File Reports, October 1941, No. 919, pp. 11–12; No. 919, p. 13; Pugh, *Women's Movement*, pp. 266–7.

51  Mass Observation File Reports, October 1941, No. 919, p. 14.

52  *IWN*, Vol. 35 No. 6, April 1941, p. 119.

53  *IWN*, Vol. 36 No. 5, February 1942, pp. 83–4.

54  *IWN*, Vol. 36 No. 7, April 1942, pp. 125–6.

55  *IWN*, Vol. 36 No. 5, February 1942, pp. 83–4.

56  *IWN*, Vol. 36 No 7, April 1942, pp. 125–6.

57  J. Lewis, *Women in Britain since 1945* (Oxford, Basil Blackwell, 1992), pp. 16–26; J. Lewis, 'Myrdal, Klein, women's two roles and postwar feminism 1945–1960', in Smith (ed.), *British Feminism*.

58  In 1944 the House of Commons voted in favour of an amendment to the Education Bill to give equal pay to teachers, but this was subsequently overturned on a vote of confidence. Equal pay for teachers and civil servants was phased in between 1955 and 1961. For discussion of the Royal Commission on Equal Pay 1944–46 see Summerfield, *Women Workers*, pp. 174–8, 189; E. Wilson, *Only Halfway to Paradise: Women in Postwar Britain: 1945–1968* (London, Tavistock, 1980), pp. 45–7; Lewis, *Women in Britain since 1945*, pp. 79–80.

# 4

## 'So much money and so little to spend it on': morale, consumption and sexuality[1]

GILLIAN SWANSON

### Altered conditions

The Second World War was crucial to the post-war project of modernising femininity, especially in the enhanced attention paid to familial and sexual relations. The altered relations of home, work and family life occasioned by war and post-war reconstruction challenged nineteenth-century models of sexual difference which relied on the motif of separate spheres to define distinctive and complementary masculine and feminine natures.

Traditional concepts of femininity were also challenged by the increasing recognition of non-familial sexual cultures in wartime and post-war Britain. The rise in illegitimate births, the incidence of venereal diseases and divorce brought the concept of a maternal femininity that was passive, chaste, unworldly and tied to domestic life under pressure, for it provided a static image, unresponsive to the contemporary conditions of women's lives. In this chapter, I will look at the ways in which altered conditions of family life in Britain during the Second World War gave a greater visibility to sexual behaviour, especially that of women.

As the public mode of address to women in the Second World War recognised their ability to move between spheres formerly considered separate, relations between public and private were being remade in proposals for national regeneration and reconstruction. The publication of the Beveridge Report in 1942 instigated a shift in welfare and social management strategies towards supporting married women and mothers, in contrast to previous systems which provided 'relief' for those women who fell outside the norms of family life.[2] The report thereby consolidated the regulation of patterns of private life as a project for defining British national character, while it simultaneously assumed the need to govern the problems of 'normal' individuals, marriages and families and the patterns of their every-day life. The argument that every individual and family should be the target of this programme drew on an expanded rhetoric of 'democracy'. Presented as a mark of British humanitarianism, the concept of democracy proposed a model of educated consensus in opposition to the imperatives of 'dicta-torship'. As a Ministry of Information memorandum indicated in 1941, 'The principles of Democracy do not simply affect our political system ... They are reflected in our family life, in our attitude to children, to marriage, to all personal relationships ... They are woven inextricably in the texture of our daily life.'[3] Newly visible patterns of private life came to define an 'ordinary', intimate, familial Britain (or more usually England) whose common habits were testimony to unity and stability.

The regularising of female sexuality played a part in this process: as the psychiatric management of morale addressed familial, marital and sexual relations as part of a social domain, sexual behaviour and the management of private life became a matter of national definition. Nikolas Rose argues that the psychological sciences provide techniques which make individual differences and capacities visible.[4] During wartime they offered a taxonomy delineating different sectors of the population and their everyday habits and patterns of living for the purposes of managing morale. The sexual was given a central place in definitions of national character. The delineation of sexual differences and appropriate forms of sexual behaviour helped to instate a newly modernised British national character, formed from the altered con-ditions of war.

The question of women's morale, their devotion to the war effort and their contribution to the nation's future in post-war Britain became funda-mentally linked to the issue of the effect of the war on their sexual behaviour and its implications for the reconstruction of national character. In particu-lar the management of new sexual cultures – and their connection to leisure, entertainment and consumption – identified women as the prime object of this modernising process.

### Managing morale

Richard Titmuss, in his official history of the Second World War, proposes that the concern with morale was its defining feature: 'the subject of morale among the civilian population – and not merely the fighting part of it – was being considered long before anyone believed that war was certain'.[5] The change occurred in response to the new threat of civilian air attack: as early as 1924, an inquiry of the Committee of Imperial Defence warned of the dis-astrous 'moral' effect of civilian air attack in a future war.[6] Preparations for war throughout the 1930s, based on a greatly exaggerated calculation of the extent of bombing of mainland Britain, assumed a much more extensive psychological impact on the civilian population than occurred: a report submitted by a committee of leading psychiatrists to the Ministry of Health suggested that psychiatric casualties could exceed physical casualties by three to one.[7] In the expectation that civilians' lack of military training and discipline rendered them particularly vulnerable, the spectre of mental collapse and resulting civilian disorder gave an urgency to preparations for a wave of 'neurotic casualties'.[8] Effectively, the forecasts of an outbreak of mass hysterical neurosis meant that emergency services were designed predominantly around a psychological rather than a physical imperative: the avoidance of civilian disorder rather than civilian safety.[9]

The outcome of such concern with regulating the population's mental health was a greater interest in gauging the psyche of the civilian:[10] as Nikolas Rose has argued, 'winning the war was to require a concerted attempt to *understand* and *govern* the subjectivity of the citizen'.[11] The interest in civilian mental health, notwithstanding the fact that there were many men involved in the home front too, led to a new attention to women and the effects of war on female subjectivity. As government became concerned with the possible failure of civilian morale, women and family life became an object of inquiry, research and propaganda.[12] 'Never before, in the history of warfare, had there been so much study and so many plans which were concerned with the protection and *welfare of the women and children of the nation*'.[13] That neither the degree of bombing, nor the envisaged neurotic collapse on the home front, would transpire was clear by 1940. Even preparations for mass evacuations on the basis of panic flights from the cities had not been rewarded: rather, many mothers had recalled their children and propaganda urged them to reconsider. However, the government was made aware of the antipathy to 'morale propaganda' designed to prevent panic, and by 1941 this strategy was abandoned by the Ministry of Information in favour of a more 'unambitious' programme of information, explanation and education.[14] Civilian morale could not be sustained by the 'glory' of dangers associated with military aims, for civilian risks were taken 'in order that some quite unromantic task should be carried out by the end of a given day'.[15] Thus it became clear that despite a continual adjustment of the routines, habits and environment that formed the texture of certainty, it was the maintenance of the features of normal life in the face of new conditions and experiences that would sustain the civilian population. Such an acknowledgement is embodied in Titmuss's retrospective observation that 'it was not altogether unremarkable that people who were dug out of the ruins of their homes first asked, not for food or safety, but for their false teeth'.[16]

The shift to measures for 'maintaining and fortifying psychological

5    Early propaganda campaigns, including 'Mightier yet!', were popularly
     disparaged as irrelevant to the demands of recreating everyday routines

health' rather than dealing with widespread neurotic collapse allowed psychologists to argue that 'normal' individuals could be encouraged to use 'the
simpler aspects of making life livable in war' as a means towards generating
their own psychological discipline.[17] It was this 'strong inner discipline'
which, it was argued, defined the British people, in contrast to the Germans
who had to have discipline 'enforced … by authority from without'.[18] As
inner discipline was presumed to be greater amongst those who were

responsible not only for themselves but also for their dependants,[19] it became necessary to understand the dynamics of family relations and commitments – the 'everyday emotions' – to maximise the ordinary citizen's ability to withstand situations of stress and danger.

Although leading psychiatrists had been appointed for the selection, training and treatment of military forces, psychiatric methods initially received little official recognition in the civilian context, provoking a plaintive call upon the government to take the lead in co-ordinating a unique opportunity to study pathological states.[20] But although the Ministry of Information was not disposed to consult psychiatrists in the development of propaganda,[21] the psychiatric paradigm had nevertheless infiltrated understandings of 'the subjectivity of the citizen' and how morale could be maintained, and was being deployed by other ministries involved in the dissemination of information and the organisation of resources and personnel, as well as providing the basis for the activities of the voluntary organisations.[22] Thus psychological studies of family, marriage and parenting conducted through the 1930s informed the monitoring of civilian morale.[23] Claims concerning the centrality of the relationship between mother and child to emotional well-being and the capacity for self-discipline and responsibility, and the deleterious effects of its disruption, gained new emphasis during the war.[24] With the division of families already in place as an emergency measure, the effects of evacuation, correlated early on with an increase in recorded cases of delinquency,[25] became a particularly important feature of the study of morale and war neurosis. In fact it was observed that 'The most prevalent and the most marked symptom of psychological disturbance among the civilian population during the war was not panic or hysteria, but bed-wetting'.[26]

Treating the disturbances of 'national character' as it would diagnose and treat the neurotic individual[27] and moulding a subjectivity that could sustain the disruptions of war, the psychological sciences also contributed to questions of post-war reconstruction, helping to shape programmes for rebuilding a new, modern and stable British psyche.[28] Questions about how British character could adapt to new post-war conditions and their new moral problems therefore become defined in psycho-medical terms: as the Chief Medical Officer at the Ministry of Health stated, 'medicine ... needed to treat the "sick society" as well as the "sick person"'.[29] How then were women drawn into the field of investigation established by the psychologisation of morale, becoming visible both as individuals and as members of the national community in the regulation of British character?

### The cottager's wife: women and morale

Edward Glover, President of the British Psycho-Analytical Society during the war[30] and Director of the Institute for the Study and Treatment of Delinquency, had argued the application of psychoanalytic models of individual pathology to social problems in the early 1930s.[31] His broadcasts for the BBC in 1940,[32] published the same year in a Penguin Special entitled *The Psychology of Fear and Courage*, specify the character of British national life in order to promote 'steadiness of purpose' and 'solidarity between the various groups within the state'. He argues that to maintain morale, the population should be trained to exert control over mental stress, anxieties and 'primitive fears characteristic of the thought of children and of savages' which are stirred up from dormancy by war. One of the key themes in this publication is the importance of overcoming the natural instincts and Glover expounds a 'form of war work that can be undertaken by every civilian, irrespective of age, sex or class. He can at least keep his head.'[33] Fear, doubt and suspicion in their healthy manifestation may be 'common sense', a manifestation of the 'natural instinct of self-preservation', according to Glover, but the cultivation of various forms of 'self-discipline' is necessary to ensure that they do not remain unchecked and erode morale.[34]

Woman is given a particular place in Glover's picture of the unity of purpose, distilling many assumptions implicit in other psychological texts.[35] His account is indicative of the contemporary focus on preserving continuity in the minutiae of domestic patterns.[36] For woman appears as a 'cottager's wife', devoted above all to the simplicity of family life and local routines. Her patriotism is drawn from an archaic yet somewhat suburban pastoralism that stands for the 'inarticulate' devotions of all Britons.

> A cottager's wife may tell you that it simply isn't 'good enough' to have her cups and saucers smashed by Hitler. We know that behind this statement there is not only a passionate resentment of interference but a deep devotion to her family. We know, too, that behind this family devotion there exists a deep attachment to all the simple things that go to make up her picture of England – meadows and cowslips, grazing cattle, the children's cricket pitch on the village green, the church steeple that holds guard over the market square, the local omnibus service, the cinema, the garden fence over which she can gossip or the inn-parlour in which her man can air his opinions or grouse to his heart's content. For to her this is what civilisation means. These quiet and often secret devotions are the basis of *our morale*.[37]

As Glover argues that women's devotions to family constitute a cornerstone of civilisation and form the basis of British morale, he also proposes that the emotional fervour of love of country derives from love of family.[38] Glover contrasts this familial version of 'England' to the Nazi's dependence on a 'mechanistic' concept of state.[39] Elsewhere, Samuel Igra wrote that the 'secret vice' of the Germans was their derogation of the feminine and downgrading of the maternal.[40] The distinctiveness of the British, it was claimed, was their valuation of a domestic femininity.

Glover's argument that 'sex differences' should be acknowledged in the management of morale derives from his view that the devotion of women to family is the basis of male morale. But this is simultaneously the feature that renders her problematic, for 'once the women are demoralised the end is near':

> The real danger about women's morale is that the war may widen the breach between the family and the State ... [W]omen ... react to their *family* as if it were their country. They see the power of the enemy directed against *their* husbands, *their* children, *their* houses and furniture ... this could result in a determination to defend the family and let the country go hang.[41]

Women are fundamentally to be defined in relation to the family and furniture, but this connection should be made as a *national* affiliation, not a personal one.[42] For this reason, those women who are not wives are at special risk: single women, deprived of the ties of family love, are of particular concern in their adherence to the national effort. They are 'defenceless ... their morale tends to deteriorate' and, relapsing into 'phantasies of what they would do to Hitler', they become involved in 'shop counter skirmishes', being rude to the greengrocer instead.[43] Their other recourse is to an 'orgy of knitting. Failing such solace they are inclined to eat their hearts out'.[44]

Glover's approach, drawing on an alliance common at this time, implies both a psychoanalytic concept of repressed drives and an anthropological model which identifies certain groups as more susceptible to the disturbances of the instincts.[45] This configuration of psychological interests had emerged from the 1920s onwards, but the governmental imperative of maintaining morale in wartime Britain meant that women's instincts, their adherence to appropriate regimes of sexual discipline, and their role in promoting the healthy functioning of the socialised family, became a key area of public inquiry. What were the means for preserving that alliance of family to country which Glover suggests is so important to women's maintenance of morale on behalf of the community, and what were the signs of its disintegration?

### Managing the nerves

Assessments of women's constitutional weakness under stress were to be challenged by war experience – as was the assumption that civilian steadfastness was more at risk than that of fighting personnel – but still featured strongly in the early years of the war. Studies of the incidence of personnel discharged from the army on medical grounds[46] showed psychiatric disorders to be the most common reason, with anxiety neurosis (the form of reaction experienced by the 'otherwise healthy individual' to an abnormal stimulus) the major class of these disorders recorded. While the numbers per thousand of men and women discharged on medical grounds were almost exactly equal, female service personnel were more than twice as likely to be discharged on the grounds of anxiety neurosis and hysteria as men.[47] These rates may well reflect a greater disposition to diagnose such conditions in women rather than standing as proof of incidence, as the report speculates. Patterns of discharge, then, can be seen as one indication that women were perceived as particularly susceptible to psychiatric disorders and their complaints were defined as 'instabilities' according to psychological concepts of sexually differentiated patterns of 'war strain'. It is not a susceptibility confined to psychiatric observation of military personnel, either. For when Mass Observation reported on a notable instance of 'hysteria, terror, neurosis' in Coventry, it was women's behaviour – albeit of a type that seems somewhat unexceptional in the circumstances of twelve hours of saturation bombing – that stood as the visible sign of a severe display of broken morale. As the report described the scene: 'Women were seen to cry, to scream, to tremble all over, to faint in the street, to attack a fireman, and so on'.[48]

Hysteria represented not only the surfacing of those primitive instincts that suggested the collapse of social inhibitions but was also seen as indicating a constitutive psychological difference in women. While anxiety was seen as a response of the 'normally healthy' individual to the abnormal conditions of war, and situated in a class of psychopathic disorders deriving from masculine impotence, woman's maternal instincts were assumed to predispose her to develop hysteria. Hysterical behaviour, read as an exhibitionistic appeal to a mate, is understood as a natural response to frustrated motherhood, in contrast to a hysterical man for whom such symptoms simply show he 'is regressing to infancy'.[49] Hence the psychopathologies associated with women implicitly affirm both their greater dependency – as they rely on male intervention for their satisfaction of maternal desires – and their natural susceptibility to states regarded as regressive in adult men and hence defined as infantile, primitive and unsocialised. In addition, some writers associate hysterical reactions 'with a lower kind of social conscience … the greater the individual responsibility, the less likelihood of resort to primitive or at least socially inadequate reactions'.[50] While women's maternal instinct could provide the familial context that secured male morale, this could not lead to the 'inner discipline' of individual responses so characteristic of the superior form of British character. It was a fabric of external, domestic relations – as a context for the exercise of their devotion – which secured women's familial natures: once these were disturbed, patterns of female psychopathology made their instabilities more lethal.

Studies of war strain and morale helped the national effort on the home front to be defined in terms of a psychological war, identifying the training of women to maintain the equilibrium of everyday life under adverse conditions as a primary task. Magazines and poster campaigns stressed it was women who should not lose hope but remain constant, transmitting encouragement to those on the military front or to others waiting at home.[51] The notion of 'nerves' provided a way of discussing appropriate forms of female conduct. Magazine advertisements and articles suggested how women should function: keeping courage, keeping heart, fending off sexual temptations provided by other men, maintaining composure, patience, being understanding, standing firm. They must avoid succumbing to the selfishness of useless emotions: they must avoid brooding or depression, feeling hurt by men's 'lapses' with other women while away from home. Indulging themselves by confessing to sexual infidelities in letters was tantamount to acting as 'fifth columnists'. Women's magazines gave advice on withstanding the loneliness of evacuation, the grief of bereavement, the strains caused by men's altered behaviour while on leave, and especially rebuilding marriages. Women were thereby exhorted to absorb and manipulate psychological techniques to school the emotions, becoming agents of psychological management, not just its subjects. Self-management would enable women to manage the manifestation of nerves in those close to them as part of the job of maintaining their family during times of disruption. For example one article, 'In courage keep your heart', tells women their 'most honourable war work', for their family, lies in keeping their home 'a place from which they will go out with strong nerves and sound minds … from which all their lives they will draw strength'.[52]

The importance of this form of advice in psychological self-management lies in its ability to make the problems of war ordinary; the experience of nervous or emotional reaction becomes something familiar, to be incorporated into the disciplines necessary to morale. Above all, it is women's management of self – their commitment to a self*less*ness – which is crucial to male morale.[53] The psychological war women were to conduct on the home front is also one in which sexual continence is stressed, for frequently talk of nerves and 'moods' is about women's susceptibility to temptation or the consequences of sexual misconduct, making their adherence to marital and familial stability questionable.

### Managing consumption

The management of nerves was only one aspect of women's wartime duties, but one linked to national objectives through practices of consumption. From the appropriate techniques in household management and treatments for 'war worry' or 'blitz dreams' to personal hygiene, the appropriate techniques of consumption became a means to, and a sign of, emotional and mental health. Wartime disciplines demanded of women that they devoted themselves to family survival through prudent and efficient consumption: it also required that they did so in full recognition of national constraints and of the need to sustain the whole community in times of shortage. In the rhetoric of reciprocity between national and community welfare and that of the individual and the family, a tension arises as the consumer must 'manage' consumption within changing conditions, constantly adapting to new objectives, new supplies, new policies. The consuming individual became the point of coherence in a dialogue between public and private interests, those of nation and family. Accordingly, a psychiatric analysis of the housewife's mentality was targeted by propaganda, as the Ministry of Health's psychiatric medical inspector's statement that 'the housewife, seeking food, has to acquire some of the attributes of the primitive hunter' makes clear.[54] The motivation of the female consumer was seen as an *instinct*, thereby placed on a level with those innate selfish drives for corporeal satisfactions which constitute the sexual instincts. To bring it in line with a social aim, it needed to be disciplined, socialised. To effect this, the Ministry of Food appealed as much to personal investment as it did to communal aims: in its *Tips for Healthy Living*, Sandra the 'wallflower' turns to eating lettuce, 'after which, a radiant figure bursting with vitality, she is seen in the final panel besieged by importunate admirers'.[55] In their address to the consuming woman, then, the Ministry presumed that she was driven by sexual aims as much as by national objectives. From that perspective, therefore, rationing and the points system, although (or perhaps, because) they made housekeeping 'complicated', established 'an excellent school of social discipline' which would moderate the female consumer's instincts.[56]

Thus the less 'socialised' drives towards consumption were channelled into more familial directions, towards community cohesion as opposed to the satisfactions of individual pleasures. Ironically, however, it was a concern with managing the forms of female consumption directed towards the satisfaction of individual pleasures – particularly new forms of entertainment and leisure – that resulted in new ways of defining a modern post-war femininity. Here the psychological sciences' attention to female sexuality permitted a connection to be made to consumption, providing a means of refashioning and modernising femininity. The address to these new women had to acknowledge options and aspirations crafted from the fracturing of traditional domestic routes characteristic of their mothers. However, managing these new tastes confronted the difficulty of managing the sexual instincts stimulated by the altered conditions of war: hence defining women's sexual disciplines was the central feature of producing well-regulated modern femininity.

## Psychopathology, war and national character: a problem of the sexual

While the question of women's morale was sexualised in wartime Britain, George Ryley Scott claimed in *Sex Problems and Dangers in Wartime*: 'The sexual excitatory effect of war is known to every student of psycho-pathological problems ... Woman, granted a new-born partial freedom simultaneously with the means of avoiding the consequences of illicit love, has become drunk on sex'.[57] For Scott, the chief of war's evils was the creation of amateur prostitutes as the 'disappearance of those barriers which in times of normalcy do so much to keep girls reasonably pure and respectable ... [meant] the girl, in the throes of sexual ecstasy for some passing "hero" ... gave herself to soldier or civilian'.[58] A key factor identified as favouring the spread of venereal diseases was that 'the nation's womanhood is now mobilised as never before; women have replaced men in a multitude of tasks and have been drafted away from the home'.[59]

As another psychological expert noted, war destabilises effective familial 'checks' on the sexual instincts of women:

> War has its own sex problems. Girls and women are inclined to be too lenient to men in uniform ... Then there is the problem of many young women in wartime whose husbands have to serve in the Forces. They are not only sex starved, but are open to the temptation of consorting with older men or those in reserved occupations. Again, thousands of girls have joined the Women's Services and are flung right out of the protection of the home almost into the arms of men stationed in the localities to which they are drafted.[60]

In Scott's view the psychopathologies of war were derived from abnormal conditions which caused the 'natural' sexual instinct to become perverted. In women, it was taken as a sign of demoralisation in both senses: sexual instability created by the 'smashing of ancient standards' in war brings misery, ruin, social upheaval. For women these 'dangerous potentialities' place them in a 'perilous position' as war is inevitably accompanied by 'a reversion to primeval savagery'.[61] Scott urged that the methods necessary to deal with these 'social problems' be identified urgently, in the interests of social and individual welfare.[62]

As the departure from the protection of the home put young women in the way of unknown dangers, their 'lapses' were also due to the seductive nature of the new opportunities to be seized. It was not the experience of work *per se*, as much as its ability to provide the financial and other means to participate in a more extensive social realm, that marked the mobile woman's new autonomy. In the debates over how women should manage themselves under these modern conditions, the focus naturally fell on those single women who could make most use of these freedoms in post-war Britain. In the eyes of many commentators, the availability of contraception

also marked young women's distinctively modern departure from traditional heterosexual patterns. Edward Griffith, a popular writer on sex education and marriage guidance, saw contraception offering women a
different form of 'equality' and demanding a new kind of moral attentive-
ness:

> owing to the discovery of modern contraceptive methods ... for the first time
> in the history of civilisation woman finds herself sexually independent of man
> ... By virtue of her new power, woman has the capacity to hurt man quite as
> much as man has hurt woman in the past. She can if she is not careful, disrupt
> his emotional life, destroy his respect for her, turn him into a cynic and hurt
> him profoundly. Thus she too has to readjust herself to these new values and
> learn again the meaning of love and the proper use of power.[63]

It was not only that new sexual relations must be approached with responsibility for the equilibrium between the sexes, but that the sexual was identified as a cornerstone of the individual's future well-being. A comment
typical of wartime sex guidance manuals advised young people that: 'Your
happiness, your ambition, your health and your reputation, not for a day,
but right into old age, are allied to your behaviour in youth, for sex is virtually the axis of our lives.'[64] As women and their sexual self-management came
into view as a national concern, models of sexual pathology – in particular
those that indicated a fracture in the continuity between the sexual and the
maternal in contemporary femininity – were used to define the features of
appropriate sexual behaviour. The sexual becomes the axis of a programme
to rebuild a new post-war femininity which would prevent delinquency
and the cultivation of anti-social tendencies in young people: hence the
working-class adolescent girl, potentially susceptible herself but requiring
urgent education in her capacity as a future mother and guardian of the
national character, was a prime object of research and discussion as well as
the target for campaigns of sexual management. Femininity – specifically
youthful femininity – became a key site for the redefinition of a modern
British national identity.

### Adolescent training and the problem of leisure

The working-class adolescent girl is drawn in this context as a composite of
the problems of female consumption and sexuality. With an immoderate
desire for tawdry leisure pursuits and a lack of education in sexual discipline,
she stands for a primitive and pathological femininity. Subject to environmental influences that allow her instincts to become perverted, she requires
advice, training and regulation to avoid 'conflicting' with the aim of social
health. The need to overcome the excitations provided by war is of particular concern as her family background leaves her without resources to avoid

unhealthy sexual inclinations and exposes her to influences likely to pervert the instincts: 'The father may be a ne'er-do-well, the mother a conspicuously incompetent housewife ... there is often present in both parents a temperamental instability which expresses itself in fecklessness, irresponsibility, improvidence and indiscipline in the home ... Illegitimacy and promiscuity are common.'[65] As it became necessary to specify the techniques of training such girls for a responsible, female citizenship in the post-war period, new kinds of femininity became visible.

In his wartime publication, *Young Citizen*, A. E. Morgan identifies the problem of managing the adolescent citizen, whose capacity for socially disciplined behaviour is still to be formed.[66] Unruly primitive instincts yet to be schooled allow boys and girls to be seduced by 'thrills': 'In general terms the adult is a social being while the child is essentially an egoist. The child is a rapidly growing young animal, full of energy and unharnessed desires ... while adults are in control and balanced, employing judgement and responsibility.'[67] In a turbulent stage between childhood and mating, adolescents must face the most potent force of 'the rising tide of sex desire',[68] the emotional volatility of which threatens the development of a socialised personality:

> It is a time of urgent enthusiams, elation and depression, affection, waywardness, faithfulness, faithlessness ... Personality is molten and according to its treatment in this plastic state it will be moulded into something beautiful or ugly, good or ill, perhaps irrevocably. If it undergoes no moulding pressure, if it has no directive discipline, it may spill out into an amorphous lump.[69]

According to Morgan, sexual indiscipline is a feature of the absence of 'moulding pressures' in altered conditions, not of a permanent state of altered morals. A pervasive problem is that wartime patterns of work and the shortage of commodities brings the adolescent 'so much money and so little to spend it on'.[70] Their propensity towards excessive consumption leads adolescents to disreputable pursuits like visiting funfairs, and for girls, drinking with soldiers. Morgan advocates disciplined pleasures, looking to the educative entertainments of youth organisations to take up a position in citizenship training for 'better Britons'.[71] Of these pursuits, he proposes housecraft as a suitable occupation for girls – knitting again becomes identified as an index of temperament, this time used towards its regulation as it combines 'economy with a laudable satisfaction of vanity' – and he claims mothercraft as the 'crown of domestic skill'.[72] These activities constitute an important process of disciplining the 'sex instinct' in a way which directs leisure pursuits towards eventual domesticity, instead of pursuing thrills and intoxicating excitements.[73]

The identification of youth organisations as an important means of cultivating appropriate leisure pursuits to discipline youthful instincts is of particular concern in the case of working-class adolescents and, in the case of girls, combats a distinctive *apathy*, an indifference to the war. This apathy derives from a combination of an inadequate homelife which fails to cultivate the higher values, disruptions brought by war to family life, and an early commencement of routine and stultifying employment. Pearl Jephcott, in her study *Girls Growing Up*, expresses concern for the future of these girls, posing the formation of appropriate attitudes, desires and subjectivities as an issue for national reconstruction:

> their fathers have gone away with the Forces, their schools have been broken up and scattered, they have seen the destruction of places which have been known to them all their lives, and some of them have been near to violent death themselves ... What future awaits this last set of girls and what experiences does the community ... intend to provide for them by the time [they reach sixteen]?[74]

Lady Baden-Powell, identifying the role of the Girl Guide movement as a 'training for democracy' in 1944, quotes her founder husband to define their aim as 'the education and development of character through *their individual enthusiasm from within*'.[75] The training of girls towards appropriate enthusiasms which are channelled towards a reconstructive future of national regeneration must therefore find a means of seizing their psyches before they have been addressed by corrupting forms of entertainment. Reading 'erotic bloods' and 'trash magazines' or going to the cinema, pub and dance hall, young people are at the mercy of the dangerous influence of an inauthentic commercial world and its trashy entertainments. As Jephcott bemoans the influence of popular entertainments and consumption – 'if the food is low-grade it is only too likely that the mental and spiritual quality of the consumer will be the same' – she aligns this 'effortless and irresponsible use of free time' with its stimulation of 'the sex instinct' at the most vulnerable age: these are the factors liable to pervert the 'lovely state of adolescence'.[76]

In these unexceptional arguments an alliance is noted between new sexual opportunities and the development of new forms of potentially corrupting leisure pursuits. As well as disciplining their consumption, the process of developing citizenship for adolescent girls is posed as a matter of psychological management and equilibrium: the struggle between cultivated and responsible domesticity and a primitive world of sexual licence and untrammelled desires.

### 'The social problem' in a new light

This response to the impact of war on women's sexual instincts looked for forms of training which would reconcile the relationship between the social and the sexual according to a new kind of reciprocity. The urgency of a need to 'balance' the two followed from the experience of war, which encouraged a form of selfishness, a living only for the present, was identified by Jephcott as a feature leading adolescents to irresponsible leisure tastes, but was also referred to in a more direct address to the psychology of sexual behaviour by Edward Griffith. Part of his critique of the effect of wartime conditions on the state of Britain's morality hinges on the *materialism* of individualistic, anti-social motivations: 'War, by encouraging a materialist outlook which pays little attention to the deeper values of life and often ignores the personality of those around us, merely accentuates selfishness ... materialism is the curse of this age.'[77] This materialism gave rise to certain 'unsatisfactory conditions in social morality' which included increasing divorce and separation; sexual relations outside marriage; illegitimacy and abortion; and the spread of venereal diseases.[78] However, Griffith and others in the post-war period departed from previous models which pathologised adolescent sexual awareness, instead developing a new way of incorporating the sexual into the agenda of modern citizenships.

Emotional and sexual life were to be properly channelled. Social activities should not be privileged to the *neglect* of the 'sex instinct', especially in women, who needed to exercise their emotions in order to develop a truly feminine personality.[79] Instead, 'sex experience' is given a place, but one that must be continually attended to, monitored, regulated:

> The vast majority of people cannot see that the problems of our sex lives affect the whole structure of our civilisation; that our attitude to sex colours the whole of our outlook on life ... If our attitude to sex is negative, our attitude to life is warped, and may even become callous, brutal and harmful ... If the war has done nothing else, it has presented *the social problem in a new light*.[80]

The development of a 'healthy attitude' to sex is vital to psychological well-being and carries implications beyond the individual. The negative consequences of 'avoiding' the sex instinct are overcome in the harmonious channelling of the sex instinct into socially worthwhile activities, while exhortations to 'chastity' are seen to thwart 'natural' inclinations too severely. Hence total chastity becomes psychologised as a form of repression with unhealthy consequences: 'a *certain amount* of sublimation is the answer ... A mind tortured by the clamorous urge can be eased by occupation with some hobby or study, which is *better than the direct attempt to repress*. This usually fails, as well as being harmful and unnatural.'[81]

## Marital relations and the democratic imperative:
## post-war femininities

In the post-war period, programmes of marital training and sex education were motivated as much by the need to address a generation of young women whose positioning had been altered by war and new post-war cultures as it was by the interest in maintaining the birth-rate. The reform of marital relations was influenced by two distinct trends: one emphasised the need for education for motherhood and the other foregrounded women's sexual pleasure as a part of marital life. The first was initiated by D. W. Winnicott. Winnicott's 1944 broadcasts on the minds of wartime mothers had emphasised that the superficial pleasures women indulged in while their children were evacuated – earning more money and having less domestic work, 'having a good time', going out, 'flirting' – were unable to compensate for the disruption of their maternal function.[82] Although John Bowlby's later concept of 'maternal deprivation' proposed full-time mothering as a need of the child, Winnicott emphasised the 'deprived *mother*'.[83] In his post-war writings, he brings the two components of the maternal relation, mother and child, together, proposing that an increase in the proportion of anti-social children was caused by war and the evacuation scheme: these anti-social individuals, he argues, are the result of an 'interference' with the relationship between mother and child. Anti-social individuals comprise an anti-democratic force: the remedy for such social dangers is 'the mother's tremendous contribution, *through her being devoted*'. [84] The channelling of women's familial devotion into an unbroken maternal relation thereby becomes elevated to a measure for safeguarding a democratic society, 'mature ... well-adjusted to its *healthy* individual members'.[85]

The tone of these ruminations seems antiquated in comparison to the recognition of the diverse features of female self-fashioning in the post-war period. However, this project clearly gained purchase, demonstrating a determination to remake motherhood in a form acceptable to those young women whose lives were shaped by new social and sexual experiences. The importance of women's sexual pleasure in marriage was as much a means whereby women's familial devotion was to be secured as it was a recognition of modern femininity. While women's sexual pleasure could contribute to family stability, marital happiness also became identified as an important component of an individual's emotional well-being,[86] and the sexual became an integral part of social management in ways that had only been hinted at prior to wartime. In 1962, G. M. Carstairs, in his Reith Lectures, would stress the importance of recognising newly modernised sexual cultures: 'This is a time when women are taking the lead in re-exploring their own nature, and, in so doing, modifying our concept of man's nature also ... *this has led to a series of personal readjustments in which probably every family in this island is to some extent involved.*[87] The conditions of war had allowed the sexual to become a central aspect of national definition and women's sexual identity in modern definitions of citizenship had become a necessary part of acknowledging and developing the 'changing patterns' of British character. In the twenty years following war, the alliance of psychological sciences with programmes of social management ensured that it would become a project conducted on a scale and at a level of intimacy commensurate with the management of wartime morale itself.

## Notes

1 I would like to thank Jenny Mahon, Michelle Jagoe, Bronwyn Hammond and Ben Worpole for their determination in tracking down the material on which this chapter is based, and the Office of Research and the Faculty of Humanities at Griffith University for making research funding available.

2 Martine Spensky sees this shift occurring between those Acts that came out of the Beveridge Report and those previous forms of provision which were initiated by the New Poor Law of 1934. See Spensky, 'Producers of legitimacy: homes for unmarried mothers in the 1950s', in Carol Smart (ed.), *Regulating Womanhood: Historical Essays on Marriage, Motherhood and Sexuality* (London and New York, Routledge, 1992), p. 105.

3 Williams, cited in Ian McLaine, *Ministry of Morale: Home Front Morale and the Ministry of Information in World War II* (London, George Allen & Unwin, 1979), p. 153.

4 Nikolas Rose, *Governing the Soul: The Shaping of the Private Self* (London and New York, Routledge, 1990), p. 19.

5 Richard M. Titmuss, *Problems of Social Policy* (London, HMSO and Longmans, Green & Co., 1950), p. 337.

6 *Ibid.*, p. 18.

7 *Ibid.*, pp. 3–21.

8 Eliot Slater and Moya Woodside, *Patterns of Marriage* (London, Cassel & Co., 1951), pp. 7–8; Melitta Schmideberg, 'Some observations on individual reactions to air raids', *International Journal of Psychoanalysis*, Vol. 23 (1942), p. 147.

9 For example, the first evacuation committee in 1931 proposed the need for avoiding 'a disorderly general fight', rather than keeping civilians away from areas likely to be bombed. Titmuss's account of the evacuation schemes describes them as 'simply and solely a military expedient, a counter-move to the enemy's objective of attacking and demoralising the civilian population', preventing chaos, confusion and panic resulting from an unplanned mass exodus (Titmuss, *Problems of Social Policy*, pp. 18–23).

10 Concerns that soldiers suffering from 'shell shock' were 'malingerers' in the First World War can be contrasted to concerns in the Second World War with civilian 'apathy', 'deep shelter mentality', anxiety neurosis and other mental disorders. Ironically, it was the later reassessments of shell shock and the greater circulation of its psychiatric definition as war neurosis that led to the deployment of models of psychiatry, psychology and psychoanalysis in understanding civilian responses to war experiences: from air raids, evacuation and propaganda, to rationing.

11 Rose, *Governing the Soul*, p. 21, my emphasis.

12 Mass Observation, noting the sanguine way in which working people met the national situation in the course of their investigations of public opinion in the run up to the war, observed that 'it was only when the international situation threatened to enter their homes, as gas, that a real mass response was apparent'. See Tom Harrisson and Charles Madge, *Britain, by Mass Observation* (London, Century Hutchinson, 1986), p. 217.

13 Titmuss, *Problems of Social Policy*, p. 17, my emphasis.

14 McLaine, *Ministry of Morale*, p. 240.

15 W. R. Bion, in Emanuel Miller (ed.), *The Neuroses in War* (London, Macmillan, 1940), pp. 184–5.

16 Titmuss, *Problems of Social Policy*, p. 350.

17 Bion, in Miller (ed.), *The Neuroses in War*, pp. 195–6.

18 R. D. Gillespie, *Psychological Effects of War on Citizen and Soldier* (New York, W. W. Norton & Co., 1942), p. 210.

19 *Ibid.*, p. 11.

20 For example, J. R. Rees of the Tavistock Clinic was appointed Director of Army Psychiatry in 1939. See G. Trist and H. Murray (eds), *The Social Engagement of Social Science: A Tavistock Anthology, Vol. 1: The Socio-Psychological Perspective* (Philadelphia, University of Pennsylvania Press, 1990); Edward Glover, 'Changes in psychic economy', *Lancet*, 23 March 1940.

21 Sue Harper makes this point in her chapter in this volume.

22 Although, as Rose (*Governing the Soul*) argues, psychologists did not make a major contribution to the government's management of morale, psychology did have a significant practical influence and an indirect input. For example, Gillespie (*Psychological Effects*) shows both the Ministry of Health and the voluntary organisations associated with the Mental Health Emergency Committee formed the basis of an extensive range of civilian services addressing the 'pathological problems of war' and gave 'advice to parents and lectures to ordinary citizens, ARP workers, and others' (p. 162). Other non-governmental measures for gauging morale, such as the Wartime Social Survey and Mass Observation, framed their research by reference to psychological models of the individual citizen and most of the popular manuals offering advice for post-war adjustments also adopted psychological explanations of behaviour and relationships (for example, Phoebe Bendit and Laurence J. Bendit, *Living Together Again*, London and Chesham, Gramol, 1946, pp. 81–2).

23 Studies in these areas were conducted across psychological sciences, revised forms of eugenics and sexology and drew on the application of anthropological methods in studies of home populations.

24 Denise Riley, *War in the Nursery: Theories of the Child and Mother* (London, Virago, 1983), pp. 80–109.

25 Delinquency peaked in 1941 and was a matter of investigation throughout the war. It is not certain whether this was due to an increase in delinquent behaviour or the coincidence of factors such as a greater interest in monitoring delinquency, the availability of psychiatric and medical mechanisms for recording and addressing the symptoms of adolescent 'maladjustment', and an emerging field in psychology which sought to study the effect of environmental factors on the development of the child.

26 Titmuss, *Problems of Social Policy*, p. 349.

27 Riley, *War in the Nursery*, p. 65.

28 Harry Hopkins, writing in 1964 about the effects of war experience on the remak-

ing of Britain, suggests that the psychiatrist was a familiar, routine figure in 'uniform from the outset' and popularly accepted, as is evident in the coining of the phrase 'trick cyclist' (*The New Look: A Social History of the Forties and Fifties in Britain*, London, Secker & Warburg, 1964, p. 198).

29  Hopkins, *The New Look*, p. 142.

30  Glover replaced Ernest Jones, who had moved to the country. He became influential in the emergence of a 'social psychiatry' which linked psychoanalysis, psychology and psychiatry to programmes of social and sexual management.

31  W. R. Bion used his argument to suggest that insights concerning individual psychopathology in military personnel could be applied to the community as a whole, to deal with 'rather different problems of a civilian population' (in Miller (ed.), *The Neuroses in War*, p. 184).

32  One of which, on rumour, was broadcast on *Calling all women* (see Joy Leman's chapter in this volume for a discussion of this programme).

33  Edward Glover, *The Psychology of Fear and Courage* (Harmondsworth, Penguin, 1940), p. 9.

34  *Ibid.*, pp. 19, 23, 66.

35  Gillespie, *Psychological Effects*; Miller (ed.), *The Neuroses in War*.

36  Despite the grandiose framing of the problem of neurosis, Glover's mechanisms frequently stress 'homely remedies' such as barley sugar for shock, and his suggestion for preparedness shows that psychoanalysis, while helping to understand the processes of neurosis, is not essential for its treatment: 'one precaution … deserves special attention. It is to have handy some form of ear-plug. Curious as it may seem, this is a form of mental treatment' (Glover, *The Psychology of Fear and Courage*, pp. 63–4).

37  Glover, *The Psychology of Fear and Courage*, p. 16, my emphasis.

38  'Love' of country is thereby distinguished from the 'instincts' of defence or self-preservation. It is modelled on the integrated, socialised individual, 'warm-blooded' and 'organised', as opposed to the instinctual basis of the state, described as an 'amorphous mass' (*ibid.*, pp. 121–2).

39  *Ibid.*, pp. 121–2.

40  Samuel Igra, *Germany's National Vice* (London, Quality Press, 1940).

41  Glover, *The Psychology of Fear and Courage*, p. 71–2.

42  Glover discusses women's resentment of their husbands' need to work overtime as a major feature of their response to war, while their morale can be seen in a 'blazing almost rebellious determination to have the husband's meal on the table whenever he comes in' (*The Psychology of Fear and Courage*, p. 73).

43  *Ibid.*, p. 75.

44  *Ibid.*, p. 77.

45  *Ibid.*, p. 1. This model of what was endangered by the stimulation of fear was echoed by Hugh Crichton-Miller's argument: 'the civilian has no really powerful check to the desire for self-preservation … which can take a form that is primitive … There is a real danger that he [the civilian] will seek, not security, but infantile security' (in Miller (ed.), *The Neuroses in War*, p. 185).

46  The prevalence of psychiatry in assessment, treatment and training was greatest in the army (Rose, *Governing the Soul*, p. 41).

47  *Statistical Report on the Health of the Army*, 1948, pp. 1–2. Women were recruited to the forces at a younger age than military men, and as the incidence of the most significant disorders increased with age, these figures are age-standardised (p. 10). (NB The report surveys only those below officer rank.)

48  Mass Observation report on Coventry, 19 November 1940, cited in McLaine, *Ministry of Morale*, p. 119.
49  Crichton-Miller in Miller (ed.), *The Neuroses in War*, p. 205.
50  Gillespie, *Psychological Effects*, p. 210.
51  As Janice Winship shows in her chapter in this volume, a close liaison was established between magazine editors and the war ministries. The following discussion here is dependent on the invaluable anthology of material from women's magazines in wartime, Jane Waller and Michael Vaughan-Rees, *Women in Wartime: The Role of Women's Magazines 1939–1945* (London, Macdonald Optima, 1987).
52  *Ibid.*, p. 14.
53  In 'Are you brave?', readers are asked 'Can you forego *self* at a time of dire need for the sake of community, nation, a brotherhood of nations defending their common liberties, the bulk of humanity?' (cited in *ibid.*, p. 350).
54  Hopkins, *The New Look*, p. 43.
55  *Ibid.*, p. 43.
56  *Ibid.*, p.47.
57  G. R. Scott, *Sex Problems and Dangers in Wartime: A Book of Practical Advice for Men and Women on the Fighting and Home Fronts* (London, T. Werner Laurie, 1940), p. 70.
58  *Ibid.*, p. 40.
59  Sydney M. Laird, *Venereal Disease in Britain* (Harmondsworth, Penguin, 1942), p. 34.
60  Rennie MacAndrew, *The Red Light: Intimate Hygiene for Men and Women* (The Wales Publishing Co., 1952), pp. 46–7.
61  Scott, *Sex Problems and Dangers*, pp. 71, 76.
62  *Ibid.*, p. x.
63  Edward F. Griffith, *Morals in the Melting Pot* (London, Methuen, 1948), p. 56.
64  MacAndrew, *The Red Light*, p. 50.
65  C. P. Blacker (ed.), *Problem Families: Five Inquiries* (London, Eugenics Society, 1952), p. 16.
66  This is an updated version of his research for a 1938 survey on behalf of the King George's Jubilee Trust.
67  A. E. Morgan, *Young Citizen* (Harmondsworth, Penguin, 1943, pp. 10–11.
68  *Ibid.*, p. 162.
69  *Ibid.*, p. 10. The similarity to Glover's concept of unorganised emotions as an amorphous mass, cited n. 20, is striking.
70  *Ibid.*, pp. 161–3.
71  *Ibid.*, p. 186. Earlier commentators had looked to boys' and girls' clubs to alleviate the problems of evacuation (Gillespie, *Psychological Effects*, p. 149).
72  Morgan, *Young Citizen*, pp. 93–4.
73  *Ibid.*, p. 158.
74  Pearl Jephcott, *Girls Growing Up* (London, Faber & Faber, 1942), p. 35.
75  Douglas Cooke (ed.), *Youth Organisations of Great Britain 1944–45* (London, Jordan & Sons, 1944), p. 94, my emphasis.
76  Jephcott, *Girls Growing Up*, pp. 111–13, 124–5.
77  Griffith, *Morals in the Melting Pot*, p. 74.
78  *Ibid.*, pp. 73–99.
79  *Ibid.*, pp. 180–1.
80  *Ibid.*, p. 73, my emphasis.
81  MacAndrew, *The Red Light*, p. 25, my emphasis.

82 Riley, *War in the Nursery*, pp. 89–90.
83 *Ibid.*, p. 89.
84 D. W. Winnicott, 'Thoughts on the meaning of the word democracy', *Human Relations*, No. 4, reproduced in Trist and Murray (eds), *The Social Engagement of Social Science*, p. 552, original emphasis.
85 *Ibid.*, p. 547, original emphasis.
86 Eustace Chesser, *Women: A Popular Edition of 'The Chesser Report'* (London, Jarrolds, 1958), pp. 146–9.
87 G. M. Carstairs, *This Island Now: The BBC Reith Lectures 1962* (Harmondsworth, Penguin, 1964), p. 72, my emphasis.

# 5

## Good wives and moral lives: marriage and divorce 1937–51

### CAROL SMART

In December 1945, a few months after the end of the Second World War, the film *Brief Encounter* was released. Written by Noel Coward and directed by David Lean, it was to become popular with female middle-class audiences and was critically received as an excellent example of British cinematic realism.[1] The film concerns a middle-class housewife, Laura Jesson, who meets by chance a doctor, Alec Harvey, at a railway station. The film establishes a strong sexual attraction between the two and they plan, hesitantly, an adulterous liaison. In the event Laura cannot go through with it, her duty to her husband and children outweighs the attraction of sexual adventure and the sordidness of the actual scenario overwhelms the romance of contemplated desire. She remains faithful, having been sorely tempted. She is left with a yearning, but with a materially intact marriage.

While I shall avoid any critical reading of this film, I wish to show how it occupies and represents a particular moment of transition in the history of marriage and divorce in post-war England. I want to suggest that it epitomises a kind of yearning, a moment when women were desirous of greater freedoms, but when social and material constraints on their lives were redoubled after the war.

When I first saw *Brief Encounter*, perhaps some ten years ago, it evoked two sets of responses. The first was an irritation which was probably entirely generated by a strident second wave feminist ideal that women should be able to explore their sexuality and should not be denied sexual pleasure. The second was derived from a sociological understanding of the misery and punitiveness of the divorce process for guilty wives (and also many innocent wives) before the major divorce reforms of the 1960s and 1970s. A knowledge of the conditions of divorce in the 1940s and 1950s makes it perfectly understandable why Laura did not leave Fred, or even risk the possibility of him divorcing her. It is the conjunction of these two strands, foregrounding both female sexual desire and the material responsibilities accorded to women, which suggests that the film marked a moment of transition. On the one hand the film identifies a sexual woman. Unlike her Victorian predecessors, a married woman in the 1940s could remain respectable whilst being sexually knowing and responsive to her husband. She knows what it is to desire and yet can retain her social respectability, at least until she commits adultery.[2] Indeed by the 1950s married women were expected and encouraged to be sexually responsive[3] and so the film needs to make no pretence that she wants something platonic whilst the man wants sex. In this respect she is a woman typical of the war era in that sex or the potential for sex is a part of her life, even if it is presumed that it will occur only within marriage. On the other hand, the film reminds us of the duties and expectations of motherhood and marriage. In the film, sexual fulfilment and maternal and matrimonial duty are posited as alternatives between which the woman must choose. In practice the war had changed marriage and it had certainly given married women the opportunity to have sexual experiences whilst their husbands were away. But it was the aim of public policy in the post-war revival period to return marriage to the pre-war ideal. It was hoped that the war was an exceptional moment and that things would return to normal once some of the wartime excesses and mistakes had been put right. The brief flirtation of Laura Jesson can be said to encapsulate these concerns.

### The pre-war ideal

The pre-war ideal was a post-war construction which specified a moment in history when it appeared that all was well with the institution of marriage. Feminists had, of course, been campaigning for changes in marriage laws and practices since the 1860s (and arguably earlier) and so there would neither have been consensus over this ideal nor ignorance about how marriage disadvantaged women.[4] Nevertheless, before the war, rates of divorce and illegitimacy had been considerably lower[5] and these figures were read as statistical indicators of the greater social stability that once prevailed.[6] There was therefore a political desire to ensure that former levels of stability were re-established and that the war should not create a new and unacceptable norm of family breakdown.

The statute which governed divorce and related matters until immediately before the war was the Supreme Court of Judicature (Consolidation) Act of 1925. This drew together existing legislation and extended the grounds under which women could be granted maintenance when separated. By 1925 women could divorce their husbands on the same grounds as husbands could divorce their wives, namely a single act of adultery.[7] The so-called one-third rule became established as the principle for deciding the amount of maintenance an innocent wife could receive.[8] Also in 1925, wives were given the same rights as husbands to apply for the guardianship of their legitimate children on divorce or separation. (Whilst a marriage was intact, the husband was still legally the sole guardian.) Then in 1937, shortly before the outbreak of hostilities, the Matrimonial Causes Act extended the grounds of divorce to include cruelty and wilful desertion for over three years. These statutory changes were productive of numerous trials in which the courts gradually laid down the case law on the meaning of cruelty, which had to be intentional, deliberate and aimed at the other spouse, and the meaning of desertion, which was extended to include constructive desertion (i.e. where one party 'forces' the other to leave the matrimonial home by their behaviour).

Whilst these changes opened slightly the door to divorce, there were important factors which still made it a difficult process with an uncertain outcome. Firstly, divorce could only be granted where a matrimonial fault was established, the burden of proof for this generally being the same as in criminal courts (i.e. beyond reasonable doubt). This meant that if a wife complained of violence she would have to offer medical evidence. If the ground was adultery, there would have to be a confession or proof (this latter requirement generated a great deal of work for so-called private enquiry agents in the 1940s and 1950s). Secondly there was no legal aid, and although there was a Poor Persons Committee which could lend assistance, in the main divorce was too expensive for working-class people to initiate.[9] The only solution for working-class marital distress was provided by the magistrates' courts, known then as the police courts, which could order a man to pay his wife and children maintenance and could grant a person a non-cohabitation order but which could not deal with property or divorce. The working classes were therefore allowed to separate but prior to the availability of legal aid, divorce and subsequent remarriage was outside their reach.

### The post-war problem

In 1946 the divorce rate reached a peak of 41,704 petitions, a level it was not to reach again until 1967. During this period, adultery remained a common ground for divorce but initially the new ground of desertion was used as frequently – or slightly more frequently – until 1957, when adultery again became the most usual route to divorce because it was the one most likely to succeed. As a ground for divorce, adultery was particularly attractive to a husband because in the process of divorcing a wife he could simultaneously sue the co-respondent for damages. (A wife could not sue her husband's lover in this way.)[10] In suing the co-respondent the husband might secure enough money to settle a certain amount on his wife or to pay for the maintenance of children. He would also recoup enough to pay for his wife's legal fees for which he remained responsible. A wife's adultery therefore had its bonuses for the husband. The only difficulty might be in proving that the offence had occurred, but if he could afford a divorce he could probably afford a private detective to follow his wife and to pay hotel porters and others to give evidence in court.

Traditionally, adultery was more difficult for wives to use and in some instances it could be easier for a wife to establish desertion than adultery because of the high levels of proof required.[11] Cruelty was the hardest ground to establish, mainly because the courts were determined that mere incompatibility, no matter how damaging it might be, should not be regarded as a matrimonial offence. This ground covered physical violence and even some forms of mental cruelty such as the refusal of a husband to make his wife pregnant. As long as a wife had witnesses to the violence or medical evidence as to the physical and/or mental damage she had endured, and as long as her husband's behaviour was knowing and deliberate, she could secure a divorce. The outcome of such divorces was always uncertain, however, and gradually couples learnt to avoid these potential legal pitfalls and to turn to adultery as a relatively simple solution.

In addition to being a 'peak' year for divorce,[12] 1946 was interesting in that it was the last year in which husbands were more likely to petition for divorce than wives. We should be cautious of a simple reading of this statistic however. It is unlikely that it indicates some kind of direct representation of men's and women's dissatisfactions with marriage. It may, for example, have reflected the effects of the introduction of legal aid after 1949 which meant that more women could afford divorce proceedings. It might also have reflected the way that during the war the armed forces would 'help' men in service to secure divorces if their wives had been unfaithful. There is clear evidence in the letters serving men wrote to their wives that getting a divorce was not always a financial problem for a man as it could be organised for him by the armed forces. Naturally this kind of help was not available to the women at home. The end of the hostilities and the demobbing of thousands of men meant that fewer would be able to use this avenue after 1946 and the anticipation of the removal of this institutional support might have led both to an unusually large number of petitions by men at the close of the war and a decline in petitions by them thereafter.

It is interesting to consider the armed forces' role in relation to divorce during the war. There is little research on this topic so my conclusions can only be speculative. However, it is well established that the concept of the home front was seen as a powerful motivating device in the war effort as men were encouraged to fight to protect their wives and children at home and the dream of returning to the domestic hearth was used as a significant force in maintaining morale. This image must have become somewhat tarnished, however, when men learnt that their wives were pregnant after they had spent two or three years in active service or in a prisoner of war camp. A number of cases reached the higher courts (and no doubt many more went to the magistrates' courts where they remained unreported) in which it was revealed that wives had written to husbands they had not seen for years to tell them they were expecting a child.[13] In these cases it seems that the authorities were prepared to intervene to facilitate divorces rather than ignoring the problem or taking the more usual 'official' position of placing obstacles in the way of divorce. In this way morale could be safeguarded and the women/wives who put it at risk quickly jettisoned. Thus serving men could be freed of the burden of returning to a disastrous marriage and the prospect of supporting children they knew were not their biological offspring.

In fact, these cases produced an interesting legal dilemma at the end of the war. The then Bastardy Laws under which women could apply for affiliation orders from the biological fathers of their illegitimate children did not extend to married women. This was because of the legal fiction that a married woman's children were always her husband's and thus legitimate. This legal presumption was put under severe strain when husbands were abroad for years and had obviously not seen their wives nor 'had connection' with them. Yet if a husband refused to pay maintenance for a child because it manifestly was not his, and if the wife could not get an affiliation order against the natural father because she was married, she faced exceptional hardship. It seems that a number of men who got married women pregnant did try to use the bastardy legislation to exempt themselves from paying anything towards the upkeep of their illegitimate offspring, and although the higher courts did reinterpret the legislation to allow married women to claim affiliation, these post-war events reveal how vulnerable women were if they transgressed their marriage vows.

It is in the documentary evidence referred to in these bastardy cases, especially where husbands submitted letters they had written to their wives, that we get a glimpse of the nature of marital relations during the war.[14] Not infrequently the couple had only spent a few months together, followed by years of separation. In some cases it was clear that their wives were already pregnant by other men before their marriages, and in at least one other a woman had sex with her husband before marriage and prior to his departure overseas, had his child, but resolutely refused to have sex with him again on his return.[15] These stories conjure up very hasty marriages between

[ 95 ]

virtual strangers, hardly the sensible and stolid version of matrimony which still permeated most public policy discussions of the institution. The conditions of marriage during and after the war were therefore far removed from the idealised situation longed for in official documents such as The Royal Commission on Marriage and Divorce.[16] As I shall discuss below, official policy seemed intent on ignoring the immense practical and personal difficulties of married life in favour of educating people to expect less whilst behaving more responsibly. Notwithstanding this official line, namely that couples should buckle down and get on with a bad job, concern was growing in some quarters over so-called 'empty shell' marriages in which these virtual strangers or quickly estranged couples came to find themselves locked for life.

## The battle over the empty shells

The war had created an immediate concern over immorality and sexual licence. As long as a single act of adultery was enough to terminate a marriage it was obvious that sexual infidelity would be regarded as a major threat to the stability of the institution. However, the availability of divorce on the grounds of a single act of adultery did not mean that every wronged spouse actually rushed to start divorce proceedings. On the contrary, there were powerful reasons for desisting from these legal measures, especially if you were a woman. The first was that divorce then was still regarded as shameful. Divorce, and even hearings in magistrates' courts, would entail a public airing of private matters and newspapers were not restricted from publishing salacious details. Indeed, until 1952, matrimonial cases in the magistrates' courts were heard alongside criminal matters, and all the details of such cases would make routine reportage in local newspapers.[17] In the divorce courts, the citing of the co-respondent would also mean that his reputation would be harmed and, if he were married, it would provide grounds for his wife to divorce him.

But there were other reasons why a woman, in particular, might not wish to divorce an adulterous husband. On divorce her status would change dramatically. She would have no rights to share in his pension nor to inherit from him on his death, and she would also lose the right to live in the matrimonial home (assuming she was not the legal owner which would be most unlikely in the 1940s and 1950s). If her husband had left her to live with another woman, as long as she remained married she would gain special rights in relation to the matrimonial home such that she could not be evicted.[18] Moreover her husband would be obliged (in theory anyway) to provide for her. If she had no desire to marry again, she had little to gain from a divorce.

It was the existence of these empty shell marriages and the problem of 'illicit' unions where new partners could not marry, thus producing illegitimate offspring,[19] which began to produce pressures for reform after the war. It was in this context that Mrs Eirene White introduced her Private Member's Bill in 1950. This Bill would have allowed a guilty party to start proceedings for divorce against the wishes of the innocent party as long as there had been a period of separation for seven years. Had it been successful, the Bill would thus have introduced a major shift in the basic principles of divorce. Constructed as they were on a notion of matrimonial fault, akin to a criminal offence, it was argued that to allow a guilty party to start proceedings would be to allow people to benefit from their own wrongdoing. This, it was feared, would irreparably undermine the institution of marriage.

There was, nonetheless, much support for Mrs White's Bill and the government sought to deflect this mounting pressure by announcing a Royal Commission on Marriage and Divorce in 1951.[20] Its remit was much wider than divorce alone and it was required to speculate on how to promote healthy, happy, married life. The Commission identified seven causes of marriage breakdown including practical problems such as a lack of housing (many couples had to start married life living with in-laws) and premature marriages, but also more nebulous factors like the complexity of modern life, a growth in 'divorce-mindedness' and the spread of education. The main factor, however, was claimed to be the social and economic emancipation of women. The commissioners felt that women were not prepared to put up with an inferior status in marriage and, although they felt this was right, they clearly regretted the changes that flowed from women's discontentment. Indeed they went so far as to suggest that if the divorce rate went on increasing (which it actually failed to do during the 1950s) then divorce should be abolished altogether. Ultimately the report insisted on retaining matrimonial fault as the basis of divorce and rejected the ideas in Mrs White's Bill. They feared that any move towards divorce by mutual consent or against the wishes of the innocent party would transform marriage into a purely private contract between individuals rather than being a contract between two individuals and the state. This was regarded as potentially disastrous for the nation and would have removed divorce from the sphere of public policy and morality.

The Royal Commission sat for four years and heard reams of evidence, but in the end recommended very few changes to the laws of divorce. Instead, they laid their emphasis on marriage guidance and education in married life in general. In this respect it mirrored the earlier Committee on Procedure in Matrimonial Causes which was chaired by Mr Justice Denning from 1946–47.[21] This committee had emphasised reconciliation and had argued that the basic cause of the breakdown of marriage was false ideas about married life. Whilst recognising certain material factors as contributing towards breakdown, it was felt that these had been caused by the war and, with a return to normal pre-war circumstances, they would be removed. They therefore concentrated solely on the emotional factors. It was this report which also insisted that the state should become involved in determining the future of the children of divorcing couples. It suggested that parents about to be divorced forfeited their right to decide on the future of their children because they had shown that they were not fulfilling their responsibilities. It therefore recommended that court welfare officers be involved and that the courts should make determinations on the care and control of children, rather than leaving it to parents. The impact of these recommendations was not really felt until the divorce law itself changed radically after 1969, but the Denning Report at least hinted at changes which would occur a quarter of a century later. As it was, during the 1940s and 1950s one might almost imagine that children did not exist because divorce cases were entirely consumed with discovering and proving matrimonial fault rather than paying attention to life after divorce.

From the end of the war until 1969 the law on divorce did not change substantially. There were some minor adjustments and reinterpretations made by judges (principally Mr Justice Denning, later to be Lord Justice Denning) but the fault-based nature of the law did not change. This meant that issues of maintenance, property, and the custody, care and control of children all tended to be overshadowed by the bigger question of who was to blame for the breakdown. The aim of public policy was to punish people for divorcing, rather than to assist them to make the transition from one marriage to another, or back to single life. In this context, therefore, it is appropriate to return to my earlier assertion that 1946 marked a significant moment as far as divorce was concerned and that *Brief Encounter* somehow symbolised the salient issues.

### *Brief Encounter*: what if she'd done it?

As I have discussed above, in 1946 divorce petitions filed by husbands far exceeded the number filed by wives. However, as the impact of the war declined, a pattern emerges where it is clear that it is increasingly wives who take the legal initiative to end marriages. Divorce therefore gradually ceased to be something husbands threatened wives with, and became the accepted way for women to leave men. After 1946 things were really never the same again and women were able to take the initiative.

Under the prevailing divorce legislation, the person who filed for divorce was broadly regarded as the 'innocent' party. This did not necessarily mean that the petitioner was blameless in a broader sense however. Indeed a wife-petitioner might have committed adultery but, because the husband already wanted a divorce and wanted to avoid scandal, he might have agreed to be the guilty party and arrange for evidence of *his* adultery with a woman paid for the occasion. This would mean that no co-respondent would be involved and the divorce could be fairly painless, while the wife would also get legal aid. The legal system therefore created various devious routes to divorce and, although the suit would fail if the courts suspected collusion, connivance or condonation, it is clear from evidence given to the Royal Commission, debates in the House of Commons and the number of cases dismissed on these grounds, that such practices were far from rare.

So what might have happened to Laura Jesson if she had committed adultery with Alec, himself a married man? Her husband, Fred, might have been generous, given her a divorce and even pretended to be the guilty party to save her reputation and protect the children from unpleasant publicity. On the other hand her fate might have been far worse.

If we imagine that she committed adultery on that fateful afternoon and that she either confessed this to her husband or he became suspicious and employed a private detective who established that she was having a liaison, what might have ensued? If Laura had been astute or fully aware of her legal position, her best course of action at the point of discovery would have been to get her husband into bed as quickly as possible. If, after his discovery of her adultery, Fred had had intercourse with Laura the law would have regarded this as condonation. He would, effectively, have reinstated her as his wife and so would not now be able to use the offence as a grounds for divorce. Laura would still be in a difficult position however. If she ever strayed from the straight and narrow of domestic duty again (such as failing to do the housework, starting to meet with other men, refusing to have intercourse with Fred) her new misconduct could be used to *revive* the old offence and Fred could start proceedings against her. Her bad behaviour would thus have hung over her like a sword of Damocles and relatively insignificant behaviour could become her undoing even years later.

Assuming Fred would not be enticed into bed Laura would have faced a major problem. If he were to storm out of the house to stay with relatives and leave her with the children but no money she might be forced to go to the magistrates' court in the first instance to try to get a maintenance order. She could not get one for herself since her adultery relieved Fred of the common law duty to support her, but she could get one for the children. In 1946 she would have found herself in a criminal court and her case heard alongside petty thefts and prostitution cases. The local newspapers would have been able to report the full details of the case. She might then have found that her domestic help refused to work for her any more and that it had become very difficult to find alternative help in a small community. Any employee would in any case be unsure of whether she could afford to pay their wages.

Laura's lawyer might, of course, have arranged a more private maintenance agreement and so her affairs would not have become public. But she could not have used the 'family solicitor' since he would be, in effect, Fred's lawyer. So Laura would have to find an alternative and he would in turn need to feel sure that Fred would ultimately pay his fees since Laura would have no income. However, Fred might have decided that he wanted some kind of revenge. He could refuse to start proceedings and she would be left as a married woman unable to form another legitimate relationship. If Laura then continued her relationship with Alec and became pregnant, their children would have been illegitimate. Moreover, if she did this, Fred would almost certainly have won the care and control of their children especially if they were over the age of seven years (i.e. no longer of tender years and in need of a mother's care). As Laura would not have been receiving maintenance for herself she would either have had to get a job or rely on Alec. Alec would have no legal duty to maintain her, so she would be entirely dependent upon his goodwill for her support. She might, of course, by this time, have become a less attractive proposition to him. Indeed he might find her reputation affecting his career as a doctor or he might have decided not to leave his wife. As he could not or would not marry her, he might cut his losses, go elsewhere or go home to his wife.

Fred might, of course, have agreed to divorce Laura. In this case Alec would be cited as co-respondent and his reputation would be affected and his wife might feel she had to start divorce proceedings against him. He might try to deny the adultery but, if he succeeded, Laura would not get her divorce. If he did not contest it, Laura might expect some kind of financial settlement for herself to be paid out of the damages that Alec would pay to Fred. If Fred was happy to let her have care and control of the children she would also get maintenance for them. However, Fred would retain the legal custody of the children, allowing him to make all the important decisions such as which school they went to, whether they could undergo medical treatment or go abroad, and so on. If Fred wanted custody, care and control himself, and Laura was unfortunate enough to find herself in front of certain judges in the 1940s, she would certainly have lost the children, even if she might have won them back on appeal.[22] She would also lose the matrimonial home unless she was the legal owner or legal joint owner. Whilst married, a husband had the duty to house a wife somewhere (although not necessarily in the original matrimonial home) but on divorce this duty dissolved. She would have had to hope for some kind of settlement and this would have been more likely if she had care and control of the children. Her housework and child-raising activities would not have counted towards a share in the house. Indeed, if she had any savings and these had been generated from money her husband had given her as housekeeping money she would have to return them *all* to him. Such money was regarded as a kind of loan for the duration of the marriage and was not seen as the wife's, nor even half hers, until 1964.[23]

Given this scenario Laura would have had little choice but to marry Alec, assuming he was still willing and legally available. If she did not she would have been regarded in virtually the same light as a prostitute. Middle-class divorcees who failed to remarry and who had been sexually deviant would find they were on few dinner party guest lists.

It is therefore perhaps not surprising that Laura went back to Fred rather than committing adultery with Alec. The surprise is perhaps that any middle-class women took the risk at all. Of course, the horrors of a potential divorce were not part of *Brief Encounter* itself. But the middle-class audience of women would have had an understanding of these unstated consequences. Indeed it is quite probable that the following the film gained reflected the extent to which it expressed a widely felt wish amongst such women for sexual adventure and perhaps sexual satisfaction. This moment in post-war history does in fact coincide with the 'rediscovery' of middle-class women's sexuality. The work of Eustace Chesser,[24] amongst others, had begun to problematise women's supposed natural frigidity and popular, accessible books were written about married women's capacity for sexual enjoyment and the need for men to pay more attention to the sexual needs of their wives. Various surveys on married life were also uncovering the sexual dissatisfactions of married women.[25]

Many of the women watching *Brief Encounter* in 1946 might have had sexual adventures during the war or they might have come to marriage with expectations about their sex lives which had not been fulfilled. Laura's powerful sexual yearnings would not in themselves have been automatically dismissed as an unnatural nymphomania or a kind of atavistic sluttishness entirely inappropriate to a respectable married woman.[26] Many of the audience may have been anticipating years more of boredom and lack of fulfilment without any possibility of escape. It would seem that husbands still had a great deal to learn about female sexuality in the 1940s since even as late as the 1970s married women were reporting little sexual or physical satisfaction in marriage.[27] Although married women were being gradually sexualised they, unlike married men, could do little about their sexual frustrations since the divorce courts did not recognise women's sexual misery as a ground for divorce.[28] *Brief Encounter* therefore operates to acknowledge this yearning but reinforces the sublimation of desire as duty. As the audience brought to their reading a knowledge of the consequences of Laura's temptation, their identification with her dilemma would be far more compelling than that of a modern audience, to whom it may appear coy and unlikely.[29]

The appearance of this film in 1946 is perhaps hardly surprising since these issues were such pressing ones. But the film was then interpreted by critics as a kind of moral tale in which, although the moral order might be questioned, the only good outcome was a return to the fold.[30] In this respect the film mirrored public policy. There was a sympathy over the disruptions caused by the war, indeed almost a tolerance, but this could not be allowed to set a new moral norm and thus it was necessary to close the chapter. Thus the Royal Commission on Marriage and Divorce closed any broad discussion of changes to divorce for almost two decades. It acknowledged that it was a good thing for women to question their status in marriage, as long as they did nothing to alter their behaviour. Meanwhile the new National Insurance system introduced by Beveridge ensured women's financial dependence on men and made marriage the main route into state benefits for women.[31] Campaigning groups were meeting with little success in improving the position of women: the Married Women's Association failed to improve women's financial status within marriage and the Six Point Group had not achieved legal, moral and social equality for women.[32] Women were in many senses trapped. Their dissatisfactions with marriage were increasing but divorce seemed to promise greater financial hardship, stigma and loss of status (unless remarriage was guaranteed). The women trapped in this situation have perhaps been dismissed by contemporary feminists as the generation who failed to continue the feminist struggle. These are the women who supposedly went back into the kitchen, who began to treat marriage as a career and who embraced a stultifying femininity and struggled to keep their men. Certainly many women's organisations focused their efforts on improving marriage rather than women's independence. But this vision underestimates the limited options available to women immediately after the war and the concerted attempts to re-domesticise women who had experienced certain freedoms during the war. I suggest that Laura Jesson was probably, in the borrowed words of Linda Gordon,[33] regarded as a hero of her own life. That is to say she realistically appraised her situation and got on with it, and this was exactly what the majority of women had to do. She was not a heroine in the sense of a woman who is put in danger but overcomes the moral trial, rather she is a woman who has the courage to face boredom and drudgery and knows the limitations of her situation. Her circumstances spoke to many middle-class women and in this address volumes are spoken about the tensions surrounding married life in the 1940s.

## Notes

1  S. Aspinall, 'Women, realism and reality in British films, 1943–53', in J. Curran and V. Porter (eds), *British Cinema History* (London, Weidenfeld and Nicolson, 1983).

2  Interestingly, Antonia Lant (*Blackout: Reinventing Femininity for Wartime Cinema*, Princeton, Princeton University Press, 1991) identifies this respectability in Laura's hat. She always wears this hat when she meets Alec and it is only removed as the possibility of a sexual intimacy becomes apparent. The removal of the hat is therefore associated with the loss of respectability.

3  E. Chesser, *Love and Marriage* (London, Pan, 1952).

4  L. Holcombe, *Wives and Property: Reform of the Married Women's Property Law in Nineteenth Century England* (Oxford, Martin Robertson, 1983).

5  D. Gill, *Illegitimacy, Sexuality and the Status of Women* (Oxford, Blackwell, 1977).

6  Lord Morton, *The Royal Commission on Marriage and Divorce*, Cmd 9678 (London, HMSO, 1956).

7  The Matrimonial Causes Act of 1923 had actually allowed women to divorce their husbands on the same grounds as husbands were allowed to divorce their wives. Before 1923 wives had to prove aggravated adultery, or adultery combined with some other offensive act such as rape or violence.

8  The one-third rule was a long-standing convention which entitled innocent wives to one-third of their husbands' income on divorce. They were not entitled to a share in property unless they were legal owners in their own right.

9  Colin Gibson ('The association between divorce and social class in England and Wales', *British Journal of Sociology*, Vol. 25 No. 1 (1974), pp. 79–93) argued that 'between the two world wars some 90,000 men and women sought, but were unable to obtain, a divorce because of their inability to meet the likely legal costs' (p. 79).

10  A husband's right to sue the co-respondent for damages arose from the common law premise that a husband had rights in the person of his wife. If another person deprived the husband of these rights the husband was entitled to compensation. This practice clearly demonstrated that the mere property status of a wife was still a legal reality in the 1940s and 1950s.

11  It was not enough, for example, for a husband to fall in love with another woman and spend most of his time with her. In *Cox v. Cox* (1952) 2 The Times Law Report 141, Lord Justice Denning argued that a wife could prove neither adultery nor cruelty in a case where her husband was constantly out with another woman and one in particular. Denning stated that the husband had formed an attachment for another girl, 'preferred her to his wife, and he was showing preference, as men do, and neglecting his wife'. This was not seen as amounting to cruelty, however.

12  Divorce petitions filed in England and Wales 1937–69

| Year | Filed by husband | Filed by wife | Total |
|------|-----------------|---------------|-------|
| 1937 | 2,765 | 2,985 | 5,750 |
| 1942 | 6,303 | 5,310 | 11,613 |
| 1944 | 10,154 | 8,236 | 18,390 |
| 1946 | 26,429 | 15,275 | 41,704 |
| 1948 | 18,456 | 18,619 | 37,075 |
| 1950 | 13,207 | 15,889 | 29,096 |
| 1952 | 14,705 | 19,065 | 33,770 |
| 1954 | 12,708 | 15,639 | 28,347 |
| 1956 | 12,538 | 15,215 | 27,753 |
| 1958 | 11,540 | 14,044 | 25,584 |
| 1960 | 12,109 | 15,761 | 27,870 |

*Source:* Civil Judicial Statistics, HMSO.

13  *Jones* v. *Evans* (1945) 1 All E R 19; *Hockaday* v. *Goodenough* (1945) 2 All E R 335.

14  See especially *Fearn* v. *Fearn* (1948) CA 1 All E R 459; and cases cited in note 13.

15  *Smith* v. *Smith* (1947) 2 All E R 741; *Chaplin* v. *Chaplin* (1948) 2 All E R 408 on being pregnant by another man at the time of marriage.

16  Morton, *The Royal Commission on Marriage and Divorce.*

17  By the 1950s it was seen as unsatisfactory to treat matrimonial matters as if they were the same as criminal matters and so separate courts were established. These were still part of the magistrates' jurisdiction but broadly followed the trend of creating separate courts for juveniles. As hearings concerning juveniles were held in private it was also thought that cases concerning family matters should be given the same protection.

18  During the 1950s Mr Justice Denning created what was called 'the deserted wives' equity' precisely to protect innocent wives against their husbands selling the matrimonial home over their heads. See C. Smart, *The Ties that Bind* (London, Routledge, 1984).

19  It should be remembered that illegitimacy in the 1940s and 1950s was a serious disadvantage to children and not a mere technicality. Moreover a later marriage of the parents would not legitimise the child if one of the parents was married to another person at the time of conception.

20  Morton, *The Royal Commission on Marriage and Divorce.*

21  Mr Justice Denning, *Report of the Committee on Procedure in Matrimonial Causes,* Cmd 7024 (London, HMSO, 1947).

22  For example, Mr Justice Wallington was known to hold the view that once a woman had committed adultery she would almost certainly do so again and that it was not in the moral interests of a child to be cared for by such a woman. See *Allen* v. *Allen* (1948) 2 All E R 413; *Willoughby* v. *Willoughby* CA (195) P 184.

23  Married Women's Property Act, 1964.

24  Chesser, *Love and Marriage.*

25  Eliot Slater and Moya Woodside, *Patterns of Marriage* (London, Cassel & Co., 1951).

26  Throughout the 1940s and 1950s judges were ready to condemn women who committed adultery. However, it seems that they were fairly broad-minded about what couples got up to in the bedroom during marriage. It was not assumed that a woman who wanted sex was deviant (although sexual frustration alone would not

give her a ground for divorce). Thus Lord Justice Merriman, in *Holborn* v. *Holborn* (1947) 1 All E R 32, pointed out that there were extremes in attitudes between different couples about what constituted normal sexual relations. What one person regarded as revolting or as inordinate demands would be regarded as perfectly acceptable by another.

27  G. Gorer, *Sex and Marriage in England Today* (London, Nelson, 1971).
28  In fact during the 1940s and 1950s it was very difficult for wives to get a divorce on the grounds of sexual deprivation. If a wife claimed that her husband refused to give her children she would have a much better claim than if she cited sexual frustration. Husbands, on the other hand, could cite sexual frustration as a form of mental cruelty.
29  With the possible exception of the re-reading of the film as a comment on the problems of requiting gay sexual love. See A. Medhurst, 'That special thrill: *Brief Encounter*, homosexuality and authorship', *Screen*, Vol. 32 No. 2, pp. 197–208.
30  J. Thumin, *Celluloid Sisters* (London, Macmillan, 1992); Lant, *Blackout.*
31  E. Wilson, *Women and the Welfare State* (London, Tavistock, 1977).
32  The Six Point Group was set up in 1933. Its aims were to achieve equality for women with men in areas of employment, politics, education and so forth. See J. Clarke, A. Cochrane and C. Smart, *Ideologies of Welfare* (London, Hutchinson, 1987).
33  Linda Gordon, *Heroes of Their Own Lives* (London, Virago, 1989).

# Part two

Fashioning the national self:
cultural practices and representations

W.R.N.S.  A.T.S.  W.A.A.F.

## here is your own show—

'Women at War', a magazine
for women in the three services,
begins in the Forces programme
on Monday. Here's all about it,
by Robert MacDermot.

SOME weeks ago I felt that
we in the BBC were not doing
as much as we should for the
women's uniformed services. For
a long time now we have been
broadcasting 'Ack-Ack Beer-Beer';
we have lately started a magazine
for the Merchant Navy, 'The
Blue Peter', and we hope shortly to
begin another magazine for the
Royal Navy. But for the W.R.N.S.,

**6**    'WRNS, ATS, WAAF, here is your own show', *Radio Times*, 3 October 1941

# 6

## 'Pulling our weight in the call-up of women': class and gender in British radio in the Second World War

JOY LEMAN

> I am not satisfied that we are making all the use we can of the power we possess of reaching and influencing women at the present time … On questions practical, moral, ethical, that are arising as direct or indirect results of the call-up of women, I do not feel we are pulling our weight. This is serious as I believe that no single factor is at the present moment more important for the war effort than getting the call-up of women to run efficiently and happily.[1]

This statement by Janet Quigley, a woman producer at the BBC, which clearly identifies radio as a mechanism for propaganda in the Second World War, was in some ways unremarkable for the period. What is remarkable, however, is the suggestion that the BBC had failed to recognise the potential of broadcasting to communicate with a substantial part of the population in Britain at this crucial historical moment. Whilst, for the purposes of the war effort, women are classified here as a significant part of the population – an achievement in itself, in the male dominated world of the authorities in wartime Britain – the implied category of social class is still deeply buried. In the debates which followed, concerning the extent to which the BBC should address the majority of women directly, discourses of both gender and class can be detected.

Janet Quigley as a mere producer was questioning the judgement of those above her in the hierarchy. This led to a series of debates whose concerns were both ideological and bureaucratic. The tone was restrained. However, there was much at stake, including the effectiveness of radio in the war effort, and the extent to which women as war workers in industry could be acknowledged and incorporated into the radio discourse without disrupting dominant assumptions of class, femininity and the family.

These debates represent another part of the wider conflict of perspective within the authority structures of Britain in the Second World War which tends to be obscured by myths of unity in both nation and BBC – the mythological wartime 'voice of the nation'. The way in which the argument was conducted indicates how the requirements of broadcasting inevitably challenged earlier ideological assumptions of class and gender deeply ingrained in those controlling the medium of radio. Whilst my research encompasses the wider field of broadcasting for women during the Second World War, I shall discuss here the documents and context of a specific policy debate, and its relevance to one particular programme series, *Women at War*.

In the pre-war period of rapid expansion in radio, the majority of broadcasts addressed the generality of listeners with a strong invocation of the popular BBC image of the family at the hearth, with the father as the leading listener. This was a middle-class, nuclear family, which by the late 1930s constituted a minority of the listening public.

The conditions of wartime changed this image of the homogeneous audience. It became necessary to target specific segments of audience, not for commercial exploitation as in the 1990s, but for more explicit political manipulation. Whilst superficially the 'war effort' and attempts to sustain morale were the reasons for this widened address, there were other issues which shaped the timing and content of broadcasts. For example, some programmes addressing women were, at strategic stages of the war, intended to encourage more women to volunteer for military service or to work in industry. Unsurprisingly, a constant underlying theme was the pivotal role of the family as representing a stable society and a controlling mechanism for the dominant social order. This became a preoccupation of government and BBC policy-makers, even in the depths of wartime planning for peacetime.

A focus on the family and domestic concerns had from the outset of broadcasting typified the few programmes directed towards women.[2] During the 1930s there were short broadcast slots consisting of 'household hints' and shopping news. But these were effectively publicity for the Empire Marketing Board and were didactic and patronising in tone. Food programmes continued during wartime in a different form, including the extremely popular *Kitchen Front*, which regularly featured the working-class voices of comediennes Gert and Daisy and Mrs Buggins.

As with so many aspects of wartime policy which have historically been presented as well prepared and inevitable, the reality of BBC wartime policy concerning the majority of women listeners is far from being a smooth-seamed garment. It is more a story of internal conflict and pressure from below to widen the address to the female audience eventually leading to a more inclusive approach in the tone and content of programmes. The BBC had to be cajoled by its own producers into dealing with the more prominent role which the government was demanding of women in wartime.

In the early part of the war very little programming was aimed specifically at women. This was in spite of a survey by Mass Observation which showed that there had been a 15 per cent increase in radio listening by women since the start of the war – partly due to the fact that more women stayed at home after dark because of the blackout restrictions. The Draft Scheme for Broadcasting drawn up by the Home Morale Emergency Committee of the Ministry of Information in May 1940 makes only passing reference to women, stressing nevertheless the importance of a 'spirit of neighbourliness' and citizen participation.

By 1941 the Ministry of Information had to find ways of incorporating more women into the war effort. The government tried to deal with the acute shortage of labour in industry and the services by the compulsory conscription of women in certain age groups. Since all the communications media in Britain were expected to contribute to the achievement of MOI policies, the BBC needed to develop more effective methods of communicating with a wider female audience. This brought with it the necessity for change at the BBC, both in the predominance of upper-class voices and south-east English accents and in a redefinition of women's interests in the shaping of new programmes.

*Women at War* was launched in October 1941 as part of this BBC response. The new series, broadcast on Monday evenings at 8.15–9.00 p.m., adopted a magazine format, containing a range of regular slots including interviews, beautycare, comedy, music and games. The fact that it focused primarily on women in the military services soon became a matter of internal BBC debate. Letters of protest from 'land-girls' and nurses prompted the producer, Janet Quigley, to request permission to broaden the programme to include women in all areas of war work. Initially, this was resisted by programme controllers.

Nevertheless, internal correspondence on the format of *Women at War* suggests that different perceptions of gender and class were forcing themselves onto the media agenda out of the material and political contingencies of war. The assumptions of broadcasters were being challenged both by the logistical demands of the war effort and by the demands of newly active women listeners to state their views of radio output. The BBC experience of broadcasting to women was based in programmes which 'talked down' to the audience, an approach unsuited to the wartime discourse of 'togetherness' and equal opportunities for sacrifice. A gradual shift in content and address took place, but only as a result of a willingness to learn from another more successful area of women's media – print magazines.

The women's weekly magazines of the 1930s had been less patronising than the voice of the BBC in their offers of advice and exemplars of social attitudes and behaviour to the rising white-collar shop and office workers of the period. Under the conditions of war, the print magazines were marginally better able to adapt and to build on an existing successful mode of address. One reason for this may have been their patchwork format of serialised fiction, articles on household subjects, 'beauty and fashion' as well as interviews and features on 'well known personalities'.

The *Radio Times*, published by the BBC, contained programme schedules and articles showing clear journalistic links with women's magazines in its use of certain feature writers. The November 1939 special wartime women's issue of the *Radio Times* includes articles which could fit easily into any women's magazine of the time. Alison Settle, women's magazine journalist, writes about the conflicts of class and culture which centred on evacuation experiences in the optimistically entitled 'The greatest revolution of our time'. A prominent feature of this *Radio Times* is the rhetorical tone, appealing to women as homemakers and already indicating a concern for post-war domestic stability. Irene Veal, for example, a regular *Radio Times* writer, suggests that:

> Behind the men in the fighting forces Home Defence Services and Armaments Factories, as well as the workshops and commercial enterprises that must provide money and goods for the nation's needs, the women of the Home Keeping Front must stand firm ... In their hands lie the roots of civilisation. For it is from these homes that men draw courage and inspiration to serve and work. It is in these homes as well as the schools that the children must be taught and trained so that they shall be fitted for the important work which lies before them. Each one in every way must play its part in the work of reconstruction that will follow this war. Its success lies fundamentally in the hands of the women, since they run the homes.[3]

In this early period before compulsory mobilisation of the female population, domesticity and childcare are emphasised as fundamental 'backup' roles in the war effort, even with an increasing number of women becoming 'mobile'. The 'home' in 'home front' was a core concept linked to family and nation and essentially portable, literally embodied in all women wherever they were drafted.

The discourse of femininity and the importance of maintaining 'beautycare' standards was an obvious theme in women's magazines. It was less obvious as a theme for broadcasting but nevertheless featured in *Radio Times* articles and later in programmes – for example, 'Beauty in Battledress', a regular item in *Women at War*. The emphasis was often on 'make do and mend', 'recycling' resources and adapting to the prevailing conditions of austerity. Whether the experts also took their own advice was unclear and the hints were sometimes bizarre and impractical. Tips from Irene Veal in the *Radio Times* included domestic and fashion advice:

> Have you ever thought of cutting bread and dripping as thinly as bread and butter and sprinkling the delicate slices with pepper and salt? … See to it that your clothes defy the blackout. Buy as few as you can reasonably need, if you feel that way; but choose with care. A woman's appearance is always important.[4]

Ludicrous though the underlying assumption of this statement seems, it may indicate the difficulty of discussing 'fashion and beauty' at times of official shortage and national restraint. Antonia Lant's book on women in wartime British cinema suggests that the austere conditions of the war were incompatible with the more excessive image of Hollywood glamour previously dominant in the discourse of femininity in cinema.[5] In the context of radio, however, an emphasis on 'natural' beauty was linked to an invocation of national imagery and patriotism which were already part of the 'Britishness' of BBC output. The 'naturalness' of the 'English rose' (an icon readily utilised in the 1990s representation of Princess Diana) was in the 1940s deeply marked in the upper-class southern-counties rural idyll so predominant in previous radio output. But the wartime presentation of this image posed problems since *Women at War* listeners were critical of the 'dull, patronising approach' and perceived elitism of the 'beautycare' professionals. The 'Beauty in Battledress' slot eventually became 'Forces Forum' with round-table discussions and a greater use of 'voices of the forces' as opposed to 'the dictum of the expert'. Planned items for the slot proposed by Archie Campbell, the co-producer, included 'My idea of an ideal dancing partner', 'Books to read', 'Christmas in the forces', 'Hobbies', 'Service slang'. But Campbell still felt a basic uncertainty about the programme, indicated in the comment 'the new formula is likely to be more popular than the old, although we have not found the right presiding genius'.[6]

The programme's weaknesses became more apparent when early in 1942 the government issued new regulations to widen the range of women liable for compulsory mobilisation into the services or work in industry. Sweeping proposals for a co-ordinated radio response to this came from Janet Quigley, the producer mainly responsible within the BBC Talks Department for programmes for women.

Quigley is critical of government departments and their public relations officers for using only press and film and for failing to see the value of broadcasting in the war effort on the home front, but she also argues for a more explicit and vigorous intervention by the BBC in the construction of government propaganda campaigns. The BBC Director of Talks grudgingly gave his support to Quigley's proposals since 'she has got in on the ground floor with this particular campaign'. But he is dubious about whether broad-casting 'can assist the callup of women to run efficiently and happily' to any extent.[7]

In this interchange between a woman producer and her boss at the BBC the pressures of wartime force a normally cosy middle-class consensus into a debate on fundamental issues concerning women in society – in particu-lar working women, and especially working women doing manual, indus-trial jobs. The argument was certainly not about equal rights but rather that the 'nation's interests' in times of war required a temporarily different address to women as workers and not simply in their role in the family. Of course this arose from a pragmatism of which Quigley seemed much more aware than her bosses at the BBC. She writes convincingly of the need to 'present industry to the workers in a way that will fire their imagination and enthusiasm … to make factory workers feel that they are appreciated and that their share in the war effort is fully recognised'.[8] She considers that *Women at War* can do more than any other programme to achieve that *if* it is allowed to appeal to *all* women workers and not just those in the armed forces. Even as early as October 1941 Quigley wanted to widen the focus of the programme, writing to her co-producer: 'I do not think we can afford to ignore any longer the letters that are coming in from nurses and landgirls protesting at the fact that they are not included in the women at war to whom this programme is addressed'.[9]

Appeals to the Director of Talks from both Quigley and Campbell proved useless. He insisted that the programme should continue with its lim-ited focus but seemed to accept part of the argument, asking Quigley to pro-vide guidelines for producers to help in the campaign to mobilise women. Her subsequent report entitled 'Women and the call-up' poses a key question intended to set a new agenda for the BBC in mobilising women for the war effort: 'Why are women not pulling their weight, particularly in industry?'[10] In attempting to answer this question Janet Quigley makes assumptions which seem to be rooted in traditional attitudes of class and privilege, as she assesses the 'girls already in industry but not pulling their weight':

> We are up against very low average mentality and extreme narrowness of out-look. These women are said to be interested in nothing but getting, with the least possible effort, more money to spend on clothes, make-up, going to the pictures etc. untouched by appeals to patriotism or other abstract sentiments, no realisation of what the war is about; no pride in job for its own sake, no sense of job as a vital part of great national effort; all this resulting in general apathy and discontent.[11]

Quigley goes on to suggest reasons for this outlook which logically connect with her earlier plea to use radio to 'ennoble' women workers in industry:

'there is also in this audience the feeling that industrial workers are looked down upon in comparison to women in the uniformed services ... and that much heavier sacrifices are demanded from some sections of the people than from others'.[12] Living conditions, problems with transport and shopping hours, childcare, are briefly cited as possible reasons for discontent, but Quigley stops short of a wider social or political explanation for these disparities.

However, Janet Quigley was keen to see radio used as a catalyst to change women's views of themselves and what they might achieve. This was in the service of war propaganda and ultimately in the interests of maintaining the dominant order. But the contradictions in the situation meant that a different role for working women was being proposed for radio programmes in 1942. Of course many women in war work were middle-class. But Quigley's objective was clearly to do with the mobilisation of working-class women to the war effort and what radio could do in that. For example, as well as featuring more women industrial workers in radio programmes she also wanted a new series for working women which would be broadcast in the evening, after work, and a Sunday morning programme with less on domesticity and more on 'public questions'.

Janet Quigley spoke from the privileged perspective of the middle-class women of her era and reveals attitudes which sit comfortably among the moral judgements made by Tory ministers in Britain about single mothers in the 1990s. However, she still had to combat the men of her class in powerful positions, attempting to convince them of the importance of radio in the lives of the majority of women. It took persistent argument and extensive memos from Quigley and another producer, Bill MacLurg, to get *Women at War* extended to encompass all women.

The Assistant Controller of Programmes, Norman Marshall, was vehemently opposed to this initially, saying that to widen the programme would lead to 'scrappiness and lack of real character' and that 'women are already catered for in programmes such as *Calling all Women, Wise Housekeeping, The Kitchen Front, Exercises for Women, Health Magazine* and talks on subjects such as the making of new clothes from old etc'.[13] Apart from Marshall's adherence to traditional notions of women's interests, there is also a hint that, to him, women in the uniformed services constituted an elite corps, superior to women war workers in industry. He found in discussions with servicewomen that they 'were obsessed, whether rightly or wrongly, by the fact that they are doing a man's job' and he recommends that the programme should have 'dignity and guts, without being pompous or heavy. It needs to be gay and light, but not frivolous ... not too feminine or too sentimental, but at the same time it must not be hearty'. Marshall also found amongst women 'of all ranks', a 'completely unanimous demand for a woman compere' who, unlike the male compere, 'would not attempt to make feeble and facetious jokes'.[14]

Another highly critical memo indicated listeners' criticisms of the upper-class accents of some participants, taken for granted only two years previously, but which in a wartime context grated: 'the three girls were too county to be representative of the women's services, or to be popular with mass audiences'.[15] The search for 'acceptable' women's voices had always been a problematic issue for the BBC. The Talks Department in 1942 wanted regular broadcasters with voices giving a hint of Scottish, Irish or Welsh origins, not upper-class or southern English, but also 'not West Ham or Wigan'. The wartime need to find voices more representative of the majority of women was important to that wider notion of national unity discussed by, for example, Angus Calder in *The Myth of the Blitz*.[16]

However, to bracket factory and agricultural workers together in a programme with uniformed servicewomen may have been too much of a political and cultural leap for BBC executives at the time – until the pressures of war left no choice in the matter. The reshaped version of *Women at War*, launched in April 1942, made a clear turn to a wider audience of women working in industry. Bill MacLurg was the producer and he co-edited the programme with Janet Quigley. A *Radio Times* article introduced the new series in a style which combined the intimate, direct address of women's magazines with images of social realism typical of wartime rhetoric. MacLurg justified the restricted focus of the earlier series:

> It's going to cause trouble said the critics … it's going to annoy a lot of women who are doing other war jobs [but] there was a job to be done in putting on this special programme for women with His Majesty's Forces. Now … the job of putting on a programme for all women in organised war work is more important. In the new edition of the programme you will hear something of the work women are doing. There will be visits to factories, canteens, hostels, and rest centres. We shall take the microphone to railway stations and organising offices and out to the country where women are ploughing, sowing, and looking after the forests.[17]

He concludes on a note of high rhetoric: 'It is your programme, *Women at War*, so come and take it with both hands'. Yes, but invitations were still a prerequisite and the programme was carefully organised around particular wartime needs of the authorities – which sometimes coincided with the needs of the listeners.

The new *Women at War* series contained regular slots such as 'Introductions' in which a munitions worker was 'introduced at the microphone to someone who uses them'. The programme for 18 May 1942, for example, was structured, with musical interludes, around the theme of nursing and included a talk by a hospital matron and two teams of nurses competing in a quiz entitled 'Nurses' Playtime' and chaired by Bill MacLurg.[18] A reading of the script reveals that the entertainment aspects of the programme are highlighted with a generally humorous tone and musical interludes. However an underlying seriousness is marked out by the narrator in his announcement that to commemorate Florence Nightingale's birthday, £10,000 had been collected by nurses to buy two night fighter aircraft, with Sheffield nurses collecting most. Both a regional and international flavour is introduced in the programme with a discussion about the backgrounds and experiences of the nurses – from Eire, Belfast, South Africa, the United States.

Bill MacLurg had promised in the *Radio Times*, 'We shall bring you stories of the women of other countries and of what they are doing – stories to convince you of the worth of your work and of the greatness of its purpose'. Whether the programme achieved this objective is difficult to assess. The struggle to establish the validity of a radio programme which set out to present women working in industry as heroines, even in terms of war propaganda, is a special episode in media history and full of contradictions. The myth of national unity was undoubtedly reinforced by programmes like *Women at War* which, thanks to Quigley and MacLurg, finally addressed a notionally unified body of women working across class divisions towards a common goal in the war effort. The social and political reality, of course, was, and is, somewhat different from this.

To her credit, Janet Quigley continued to argue within the BBC for more serious programmes directed towards a wider female audience. As producer of the series *Mostly for Women*, broadcast in 1942 at noon on Sundays and targeted at all working women, she made the case for more discussions of 'public questions' on the basis that, 'Considerable evidence has come in both by letter and verbally ... to suggest that discussions on public questions affecting women would be more welcome than anything else'.[19] The proposed topics included such political questions as wartime nurseries, equal compensation for war injuries, and women for Westminster. The Director of Talks approved all three topics but wanted government ministries represented in the first two topics and an emphasis in the third on a 'realist' approach and 'the less pleasant sides of work involved in parliamentary elections and being an MP'.[20]

As one of the few women working at the production level in the BBC Quigley would have been under pressure to subsume her criticisms into an ethic of professionalism, particularly where difficult issues were concerned such as gender and class. In the particular circumstances of wartime her perceptions of what should be done were sharper and more responsive to the situation than the perceptions of those in charge at the BBC. In the tradition of Hilda Matheson, Head of Talks Department at the end of the 1920s,

Quigley was ready to argue that the institutions themselves should recognise how they could benefit from a more effective use of radio in the lives of the majority of women. This argument did not require any basic change in class position but, in the historical context, it did require persistence and courage in confronting those in authority at the BBC. Janet Quigley continued to work in and defend women's programmes into the post-war period, becoming editor of *Woman's Hour* in 1950, when in the face of a threat to reduce the programme length to forty-five minutes she launched a vigorous defence of the hour for *Woman's Hour*!

## Notes

This article is partly based on research carried out for an M.Phil. awarded by the University of Kent. I wish to thank the staff at the BBC Written Archives Centre in Caversham for their help and advice in finding the relevant files.

1 Memo from Janet Quigley to BBC Director of Talks, 12 February 1942.
2 The first programme for women was broadcast in April 1923 by a Captain Lewis and was entitled 'A talk to women'.
3 *Radio Times*, 17 November 1939.
4 *Ibid.*
5 A. Lant, *Blackout* (Princeton, Princeton University Press, 1991).
6 Memo from Archie Campbell to Assistant Controller of Programmes, 10 December 1941.
7 Memo from Director of Talks to Assistant Director of Talks, 13 February 1942.
8 Memo from Janet Quigley to Director of Talks, 19 February 1942.
9 Memo from Janet Quigley to Archie Campbell, 21 October 1941.
10 Memo from Janet Quigley to Director of Talks, undated.
11 *Ibid.*
12 *Ibid.*
13 Memo from Norman Marshall to Assistant Controller of Programmes, 12 February 1942.
14 Memo from Norman Marshall to Assistant Controller of Programmes, 10 February 1942.
15 Memo entitled '*Women at War*', unsigned, 2 February 1942.
16 A. Calder, *The Myth of the Blitz* (London, Jonathan Cape, 1991).
17 *Radio Times*, issue dated 17 April 1942.
18 *Women at War* script, 18 May 1942.
19 Memo from Janet Quigley to Director of Talks, 11 May 1942.
20 Memo from Director of Talks to Janet Quigley, 12 May 1942.

# 7

## Putting the black woman in the frame: Una Marson and the West Indian challenge to British national identity

DELIA JARRETT-MACAULEY

The black woman has almost lost her place in British history. It is hardly ever remembered that she played an active part within the Second World War, in the services, in munitions factories, in the media and in a multitude of other areas of life. This erasure is the result of a historiography unconcerned about racism and sexism, unwilling to grasp the significance of the link between imperial centre and margin and inexperienced at exploring multiple identities. This essay discusses the impact of 'race' and gender policies and practices on black colonial women from the West Indies and considers, in particular, the role of the BBC as an institution which reflected British government attitudes towards black service people.

Throughout the twentieth century there have been black women living in Britain. During the 1930s, in ports such as Liverpool, Cardiff, Bristol and London there were sizeable black communities which faced discrimination even from their unions, disproportionately high levels of unemployment, poor housing conditions and chronic lack of opportunity. In the nineteenth century sailors based in Liverpool had come from Somalia and other African trading centres. Later they were joined by soldiers from the colonies who fought in the First World War. Yet scarcely had the war ended, when in 1919 African people were attacked in all the major cities and the government responded by deporting some ninety-five West Africans that year. War and peace have always been markers for change in race relations.[1]

Prior to the Second World War black men in Britain continued to work as seamen, dockers and labourers while the women ran boarding houses, took factory jobs or, where possible, worked as domestics. Alongside these working-class communities were a handful of middle-class black professionals – doctors and lawyers – students turned into settlers. All these men and women, and those who came later, were restricted by the colour bar which substantially limited their lives, both economically and socially.[2]

Differences between classes had little impact on the representation of black people within the media. Men of all classes were portrayed as social troublemakers and criminalised. The middle-class professionals sometimes wrote letters to the press objecting to the 'colour bar' in Britain and to race discrimination policies within their countries of origin; they set up their own journals, wrote their own plays, and held concerts of 'Negro' music.

The sociologist Kenneth Little found, when researching his *Negroes in Britain* (1947), that the black woman was viewed negatively by the press: for example the *Daily Express* series on cities ran with a Cardiff report entitled: 'Half-caste girl: she presents the city with one of its big problems'.[3] One way for such women to eschew this hostile representation was through the performing arts, singing and dancing on stage and screen for a guinea a day in films such as Paul Robeson's *Sanders of the River*. A passable way of making oneself visible was to appear alongside African-American singers such as Marion Anderson and Adelaide Hall who were famous on both sides of the Atlantic.

The BBC, which was to become a key outlet for advancing better race relations during the war, paid little attention to these black artistic talents during the 1930s. There were, however, exceptions. Elizabeth Welch first took part in a radio programme *Soft Lights and Sweet Music* in 1934 in which she was singing with a band.

> We used to have to worry a lot about what clothes we wore because, in those days, there was no wardrobe department. We wore our best clothes even when we were doing radio things at the Big House in Portland Place … The BBC was called 'Auntie' because it had a reputation for being prim and prissy. The ladies, for example, never had plunges in their dresses – the BBC were very strict about that.[4]

### 'Race' and war service

In *Out of the Cage*, Gail Braybon and Penny Summerfield demonstrate how the advent of the war put conventional views about roles for British women under strain.[5] Black women, both those who were already living in Britain and colonial subjects, were caught in a similar mire. Colonial subjects had played a significant role in the economic development of Britain and were educated to view England as their country. However, attempts to bring them into view alongside white British women or their white peers from the dominions went against the long-held colour bar which placed black people at the bottom of the social pile.

During the first year of the war colonial subjects were not seen as necessary to the effort, but from the end of 1940 the idea of forming a West India combat force was being mooted.[6] (This was dropped in early 1942.) A role for West Indian women in a non-combatant force was under consideration from the closing months of 1941 and while the recruitment of white West Indians did not present the War Office with any dilemmas, the recruitment of black women was to become a major battleground in its own right.

Every memo, letter and telegram that passed from the War Office to the Colonial Office or between Washington and London bore testimony to the strange hypocrisy that was at work. After all only Hitler could be considered guilty of segregation, oppression and ruthlessness. The BBC put out a series of broadcasts in which service personnel would send messages home. In one of these aircraftsmen from Jamaica closed with a wartime version of the Jamaican song, 'Slide Mongoose', that went:

> Hitler come with him bluff and shoutin',
> Say Brown Boys don't worth corn meal dumplin',
> But we-all gwine show him somepin',
> Slide Hitler!'[7]

But while Hitler was being told off in public for undervaluing black men, the British government was privately doing its best to keep black women out of the forces as Ben Bousquet and Colin Douglas have shown in their valuable book *West Indian Women At War*.[8] This depressing story tells of a determined group of educated Caribbean women attempting to play a meaningful role in the war through joining a British-based service, while the officials of the country they wish to serve are equally determined to keep them away. In the end, the pressures of war, the perseverance of the West Indian women themselves and the demands of the Colonial Office won the day. In autumn of 1943 thirty West Indian women, new recruits of the British Auxiliary Territorial Services (ATS), arrived in England. But throughout the whole saga, the War Office was bent on protecting the British colour bar and American Jim Crowism.[9] There were several instances in which the combined effects of sexism and racism led to fudged decisions and dissimulation. One example will have to serve here as an illustration.

Towards the end of 1942 the RAF mission in Washington reported to London that sixteen black women from the Bahamas had applied to join the Women's Auxiliary Air Force (WAAF). The Air Ministry, not wishing to set a precedent by accepting black Caribbean members, was in a dilemma. Further, the island's governor, His Royal Highness the Duke of Windsor, insisted that the applications be processed speedily. To protect the status quo, it was decided to find suitable local employment for these candidates.

Within days, it was discovered that these black candidates were in fact 'white women of excellent type'. Panic ceased. Arrangements were immediately made for them to travel to England via the United States and everyone breathed a sigh of relief. But this incident had alerted the Air Ministry to possible difficulties with its own colour bar and it told Washington:

> Applications from coloured women in colonies for WAAF have been received from time to time. In view of certain difficulties attendant upon employment of coloured air women, it has been our policy not to accept offer of their services but to encourage them to join local auxiliary forces ... [and] it is immaterial that Bahamas volunteers are white. Their acceptance for service in the UK must lay us open to acceptance of coloured women with requisite qualifications.[10]

The WAAF remained closed to colonial black women. One black British woman, Lilian Bader, whose story is also told by Bousquet and Douglas, was recruited however. The only service to accept colonial women was the ATS.

British weather and modes of life had been two of the grounds for refusing recruitment. But there was also an ungrounded fear of being seen to lower standards by accepting black women. When the decision was reached to allow recruitment, it was reluctantly agreed that only a quota of thirty highly qualified women would be allowed in. As the *Picture Post* reported, 'most of them had excellent jobs ... They're all educated beyond the School Certificate Standard and some of them were school mistresses before they joined up.'[11]

Nevertheless, the privately held War Office view of these women remained hostile:

> I don't at all like your West Indian ATS ideas. However, my people say that they can manage up to 30 in this country without any discomfort ... I don't like it and I think it is possible that the 30 will go back to their own place very sour and just as most of the Indians at Oxford and Cambridge used to do and probably do.[12]

The West Indian women who joined the ATS in 1943 were fighting Britain as a colonial power which, during the 1930s, had abandoned its Caribbean territories to poverty, inadequate health and educational facilities, and disenfranchisement. There had been little socio-economic improvement since the end of slavery a century before. The middle classes were pressing for fairer and better opportunities in public life, especially the Civil Service, political representation to match taxation, and improvements in social facilities. In short, most black West Indians had had enough of being treated as second-class citizens in their own countries. Caribbean people had rebelled in a series of labour uprisings and tension about race discrimination had reached a new pitch. At no point did the British authorities wish to inflame this tension, but neither was there much enthusiasm for granting black West Indians equal status with their other British counterparts.

### 'Race' and media representation

War meant that 'Auntie's' family had to be extended with foreign language services, the establishment of a separate European service and the trebling of overseas output during 1940–41. The basis of the BBC's overseas broadcasting was the Empire service but its achievements in terms of covering West Indian issues or engaging West Indian personnel during the 1930s was an inadequate forerunner to the semblance of racial unity and equality which the war required. The Director of Empire Services, R. A. Randall, put together a team of 'men from the Dominions and Colonies' and invited them over to Britain as his colleagues. 'It has been his doing that the Empire Service of the BBC is very largely run by *men* from the Dominions, namely Canada, Australia, New Zealand and South Africa', but it was different for Black countries in Africa and the West Indies.[13] He did not have black staff; relations were not easy.

The BBC, working as a propaganda machine, advanced a liberal race relations stance and from 1943 there were on the Home Service distinct attempts to suggest the ideal of unity among peoples of all races across the Empire. For example, for the Home Service on Sunday 16 May 1943 'Empire youth talks things over' brought together a group of people under twenty-five from 'different parts of the Empire' including West Africa, Jamaica, South Australia and India to discuss features characteristic of 'their homes which they think might be shared by young people over here and about things here which they would like to see transplanted overseas'.[14] Empire Day, a week later, was celebrated by a multi-racial group of people from the dominions and the colonies sharing in music 'the rich variety of the Empire … [and] the unity of purpose which has brought them together'. In addition, there were, predictably, stories from Harlem and the Caribbean (16 June 1943) and a few more black artists than had appeared before the war.[15] Naturally, Britain wanted to diffuse any notion of being a racist country which was as unsympathetic to black people as Hitler's Germany was to the Jews. The Home Service liberally suggested that all was well on the race relations front.

It was not just at home that the BBC needed to speak with an authoritative voice during the war. By April 1941 the BBC had decided to extend its services to the West Indies and to institute three programmes a week

in addition to *News Daily*, *News Commentaries* and *Radio Newsreel* which include political commentaries, eye-witness accounts of events in the news, talks by men of the fighting services and some sound pictures, recorded on the spot, of wartime life in Britain. As far as is possible West Indians and people of West Indian interest over here will be brought to the microphone in talks, special West Indian News, interviews and variety.[16]

The BBC's need for suitable West Indian personnel was filled by a clever, articulate and imaginative Jamaican journalist and freelance broadcaster who had been living in London for almost twelve years; her name was Una Marson. Una was in her mid-thirties when she joined the Empire Department as Programmes Assistant on the West Indian service. Well versed in West Indian politics, social activism, cultural forms and literature, she was able to combine in-depth knowledge of both West Indian tastes and English life. She had never worked as a full-time employee within an English company, but she was au fait with English culture, English racism and English manners.[17] In the BBC's own journal *London Calling*, the arrival of this new black employee was signalled as the welcome inclusion of 'one of us':

> Since the outbreak of the war she has been a freelance broadcaster, as well as lecturing to schools and at the Imperial Institute. She has had the experience of having her house fired by one of Hitler's incendiary bombs, and her spare time is taken up as an air-raid shelter marshal in Hampstead.[18]

During the 1930s Una Marson had been one of the leaders of London's black community, speaking at conferences, schools and churches on race and gender issues, campaigning for better treatment for black students, nurses and other workers. Her literary and cultural achievements in Jamaica had made her into a household name in the West Indies and by the beginning of the war she was gaining a considerable reputation among Colonial Office contacts in London also. But her role was not entirely that of liaison between West Indian interests and the British establishment. She was one of the few black, middle-class women resident in London who was able to befriend, support and on occasion house her fellow West Indians. As such Una played an important, maternal role within the West Indian community of RAF men who would drop into her home or office at any time to chat, to borrow some money, share news of home and provide a touchstone in a foreign land.[19]

The bare titles of the regular West Indian programmes which Una Marson was producing give little indication of the attempts which she and her colleagues were probably making to reshape West Indian thinking, suggesting that better times lay ahead for colonial peoples and that they were included in questions of British identity. The staple diet of 'Calling the West Indies' was a space for West Indian servicemen and women to send messages home to family and friends, but also broadcast were lectures such as 'Trade unionism in the Colonies' (20 August 1942); a talk by Mrs Arthur Creech Jones on wartime nurseries (23 August 1942); discussions on West Indian problems by students (27 August 1942); and a forum on politics, 'Red on the map', involving politicians and activists such as Creech Jones and Donald Cameron, a former governor of Nigeria. The talks and other programmes were developed with such effect that they would have important implications for the future of the West Indian people. English experts speaking on science and agriculture, education and women's issues geared the West Indian audience towards the post-war period.

For West Indian listeners this expanded programme would have appeared dramatic. For whereas pre-war broadcasting had been limited to occasional coverage of important events such as the test match commentary of summer of 1939, now the broadcasts drew colonial people into a more consciously British way of life and envisioned a future for them based on well tried English models like trade unionism. Una Marson's programmes also enabled them to see themselves as successful artists within the metropolitan centre – a morale booster for West Indian audiences.

## Conclusion

Una Marson's work at the BBC amounted to an attempt to reframe 'race' and to a lesser extent 'gender' by drawing black experiences and concerns into the studio. She herself, along with the colonial women who joined the ATS, were protesting against the continuation of their marginalisation within the British Empire. Their protest contained an essential ambiguity, however, for the black woman's attack on the colonial power's ideology could not be waged outside the domain of that colonial power, but in fact was enabled by the war and their desire to contribute to the war effort. Their contributions should have shattered the tired and negative images of black women in Britain. Sadly they didn't. The British media went on with depressing fixity, to image the black woman as 'sapphire', 'whore' and 'mammy' or to ignore her totally. The collective experience of black women in the war demands a change in the analysis of cinema and other forms of representation; above all it requires an analysis large enough and subtle enough to bring together the complexities of their involvement and perceptions. Only by taking account of the extent to which 'race', gender, class and nationality continue to govern our social relations and shape the study of culture can we hope to imagine a better frame for their works.

## Notes

1  For background on the history of black people in Britain see: P. Fryer, *Staying Power: The History of Black People in Britain* (London, Pluto Press, 1984) and R. Ramdin, *The Making of the Black Working Class in Britain* (London, Gower, 1987)

2  D. Jarrett-Macauley, 'Interviews with Black British Women' (unpublished).

3  K. Little, *Negroes in Britain* (London, Kegan Paul, 1947).

4  Jim Pines, *Black and White in Colour* (London, British Film Institute, 1992), p. 22.

5  G. Braybon and P. Summerfield, *Out of the Cage* (London, Pandora Press, 1987); see the introduction, pp. 1–7.

6  For a wider discussion of this see Ben Bousquet and Colin Douglas, *West Indian Women at War* (London, Lawrence and Wishart, 1991) pp. 83ff.

7  Quoted by Ivor Brown, *The Listener*, 3 April 1941.

8  Bousquet and Douglas, *West Indian Women at War.*.

9  Jim Crow was the US policy and practice of segregating black people which ended only with the Civil Rights Movement of the 1960s.

10  Air Ministry to RAFDEL Washington, 31 December 1942, CO/968/81. Quoted by Bousquet and Douglas, *West Indian Women at War*, p. 93.

11  *Picture Post*, 4 December 1943.

12  James Grigg to Oliver Stanley, Colonial Secretary (source unknown), quoted in Bousquet and Douglas, *West Indian Women at War*, p. 103.

13  *London Calling*, No. 110, 16–22 November 1941, p. 20 'The man who directs the BBC Empire Services', emphasis mine.

14  'Empire youth talks things over', *Radio Times*, 14 May 1943.

15  For background reading on some of these artists see John Cowley, 'West Indian gramophone recordings in Britain, 1927–1950', in *Under the Imperial Carpet* (Crawley, 1986), pp. 245–58.

16  'Extended service for the West Indies', *London Calling*, No. 81, 20–26 April 1941, p. 13.

17  D. Jarrett-Macauley, 'Una Marson (1905–1965): a literary biography', PhD, University of Kent, 1994.

18  'Una Marson joins the BBC staff', *London Calling*, No. 80, 13–19 April 1941, p. 13.

19  So it was with her younger Caribbean 'sister' more than ten years later when Claudia Jones, the Trinidadian communist, opened her newspaper office for the *West Indian Gazette* in Brixton, south London; that too was a meeting place for the local community. See B. Johnson, *I Think of My Mother: The Life of Claudia Jones* (London, Karia Press, 1986).

# 8

## Women's magazines: times of war and management of the self in *Woman's Own*

JANICE WINSHIP

During the war years women's magazines were directly recruited into the war effort with a close liaison being established between magazine editors and the war ministries. Yet references to wartime meetings by Mary Grieve, editor of *Woman* magazine from 1940 to 1962, hardly indicate a doormat press. One liaison officer at the Ministry of Information found himself 'warily confronting a score of frustrated editors, mostly women, all bristling with questions and disinclined to take evasive answers'.[1] The description of magazines' dual role in wartime as 'handmaiden of government, *and* hand-holders of the female population' is nearer the mark, raising the issue of how that potentially conflictual dual role was managed.[2]

According to Grieve 'the women's magazines entered the war as the Cinderellas of the British publishing industry'.[3] But their prestige grew as their effectiveness in speaking to, and on behalf of, women was established: 'A tremendous unsatisfied demand built up. Copies were passed around three or four households with a readership of half a dozen per copy. Finally, the tattered remains were bundled off to a Service camp or hospital'.[4]

Looking back at wartime magazines, the unrelenting evidence of war is striking: direct references to war permeated virtually every page, and as print rationing hit, women's magazines became thin shadows of their former selves.[5] With their pages unable to provide any simple escape from the experiences of war, there is a question as to their appeal for readers.

Here I explore two aspects which open up these issues. First I examine the two halves of *Woman's Own*: the largely practical feature pages, and fiction.[6] In the former, efficiency, planning, 'make do and mend' and 'smiling through' prevail as modes of living the present. Above all emotions are to be kept firmly under wraps. In the latter, women's emotions partly escape the controlling straitjacket exhorted by public discourse. Second, I examine the ways that the difficult present is also managed by selective memories of a past used to shape a much-anticipated future. The hope for this future is that it is to be planned, by women no less than by men.

### Efficiency on the home front: pre-war precursors

The conditions of the Second World War – in which the battle engaged in by civilians, especially women, and their 'commitment and cohesion on the home front'[7] was deemed by the state to be as important as the loyalty of the troops and the battles they were engaging in overseas – enabled the virtues of domestic efficiency to flourish and its regime to be thought appropriate for women across the class spectrum. As David Morgan and Mary Evans put it, 'Wartime propaganda extended the language of the work place to the management of home'.[8] But it is debatable whether its virtues would have flourished quite so vigorously if the principle of domestic efficiency had not already taken root in the interwar period.

Explanations of the take-up of domestic efficiency tend to emphasise its retrogressive attributes, suggesting that after the feminist advances of the First World War it becomes mobilised within an ideology of, to recall the title of Deirdre Beddoe's book, *Back to Home and Duty*.[9] Following Alison Light's lead, however, I would like to suggest a review of the interwar years:

> as marking for many women their entry into modernity, a modernity which was felt and lived in the most interior and private of places. If we assume the inter-war years were in many ways a period of reaction, we have also to make sense of it as a time when older forms of relationship and intimate behaviour were being recast and when even the most traditional of attitudes took new form. If the English middle classes found themselves in retreat after 1919, and the idea of private life received a new enhancement, nevertheless it was not the same old private life – the sphere of domestic relations, and all which it encompassed, had also changed. And even if a new commercial culture of 'home-making' was conservative in assuming this to be a female sphere, it nevertheless put woman and the home, and a whole panoply of connected issues, at the centre of national life.[10]

Light uses the phrase 'conservative modernity' to capture the changes which 'simultaneously look backwards and forwards'.[11] The scientific management of housework represents one component of such modernising but conservative trends. It was introduced in the context of a 'servant problem' and the move by some of the middle classes to smaller and cheaper suburban housing.[12] In these new homes which, by the mid-1920s, were wired up for electricity and had the convenience of Ascot (gas) water heaters, women increasingly performed domestic tasks which their nineteenth-century counterparts would merely have supervised. If adopting Taylorist time and motion studies for the home was misplaced as a practice,[13] as a rhetoric and fantasy it powerfully elevated the housewife and distanced her from the manual labour of servants. In this way, by making her part of a progressive move hailing the future in technology,[14] her 'descent' into manual labour was legitimised.

Notwithstanding sharp class differences,[15] working-class women were also touched by modernity if by the latter, admittedly a fluid and problematic term,[16] we are referring to a break away from various traditional ties and the adoption of new modes of living associated with urban, consumer and media culture. For those in employment, particularly in the south-east and the Midlands, standards of living rose and, with the aid of contraception, family size diminished.[17] Increasingly, young unmarried women could find alternative employment to domestic service in the new light industries making wirelesses and electrical goods. They were also the consumers in an expanding ready-made clothes market and an important audience for cinema.[18] Like their middle-class counterparts, many young and aspirant working-class households also moved out to suburbia where the absence of family and community ties enforced a self-reliance (as well as loneliness) for wives.[19] They were a ready market for the new women's magazines, which led the way in extolling the virtues of a domestic management aided by technology and consumer goods.[20] As one of these titles, *Woman's Own*, was launched in 1932: "'The new big-value weekly for the *up-to-date* wife and wife-to-be'" aimed primarily at 'women in charge of small homes'.[21] A survey in 1939 revealed that in contrast to the readership of *Woman* magazine, whose readers were spread fairly evenly across social groups C and B, those of *Woman's Own* were solidly of social group C.[22] *Woman's Own* thus appealed to the expanding, and newly constituted, lower middle class.

### Wartime entreaties

For all women the conditions of war marked a deeper step into modernity, by enabling a partial break from the assumption that they were *only* housewives and mothers, and by facilitating various moves out of the family and community. Wartime also extended the ethos of domestic efficiency across all social classes, invigorating it with a new rationale. In winning the war (and later in winning the peace) domestic efficiency and success on the home front was the necessary complement to military planning and prowess on the battle fronts. The ethos of domestic efficiency also made possible the acceptance of some socialisation of domestic responsibilities. Only with support services, like day nurseries, could women push their efficiency further by engaging in the paid work the country also needed them to do. In women's magazines, a veritable orgy of planning advice for the home front ensued. But another significant strand to women's overall efficiency was their management of the material self: the disciplining of body and emotions.[23] I want to turn now to the pages of *Woman's Own* to explore these aspects in more detail.

A cover from 1942, 'I am doing everything I can', captures the address to women during wartime. Smiling as she bundles up newspapers for recycling on the domestic front, she is also represented as a (smiling) cog in a machine as she engages in factory work. Two of the elements constituting 'efficiency' are in play: the saving of resources, and an increase in (manufacturing) productivity. The first marks a difference from the pre-war discourse of 'labour saving' in which time and effort saved were foregrounded. Wartime efficiency frequently meant *more* time and effort expended. An advertisement 'Issued by the Board of Trade' declares '8 coupons saved' and shows a small boy proudly wearing a 'snug Battle Blouse': 'Look what Mummy's done with my old overcoat'.

The importance of taking the material self in hand is stressed in Ursula Bloom's weekly slot interestingly called 'In defence of beauty'. Not a trivial matter, it is women's duty to look after their looks as part of their overall war effort. Proficiently fashioning the attractive face and body becomes the public masquerade that all is well with the nation. In the succinct copy of a Yardley advertisement we read: 'No surrender ... Our faces must never reflect personal troubles. We must achieve masculine efficiency without hardness ... Put your best face forward'.[24]

The column 'What women are doing and saying' is a tribute to women 'putting their best face forward' on all possible fronts. The thumbnail reports convey an impression of busyness and occasionally celebrate the woman who has pushed herself to the limit: ' "I didn't mind because I felt I was making the future safe for my children." Mrs. Mary Knowles, Manchester, mother of two, who took munitions job, cycled 3 miles at 4.30 a.m., 11.30 p.m., in all weathers' (9 January 1942). Another report more directly invokes women as (part of a) machine:

> 'Every time my leg goes up and down I feel I'm giving Hitler a kick in the pants.'
> – Mrs Clara Evans, Hall Green, Birmingham, who works 100-ton press which makes containers for tank shells in munitions factory. Leg goes up and down over 3,500 times a day; says 'I'm working even faster now the Japs are in.' (30 January 1942)

In the same issue in 'It's Rosita Forbes's weekly letter' the lead-in declares, 'YOU are a weapon against Germany' with Forbes gently admonishing: 'Don't, for one second, let the "Don't care – there's nothing in it for me" feeling get hold of you. It's a disease ... Say to yourself, "That is a ridiculously selfish feeling'" (30 January 1942). The onus was on women to push feelings aside. Like 'Four British mothers – who have taken with typical British courage and reserve the hardest blow of all [losing a son]'. The feature concludes that all such mothers 'can do what these four women are doing to-day – carrying on, *smiling in their courage*, proud in their memories' (9 October 1942, my emphasis).

It is difficult to convey the relentlessness of the exhortations to 'efficiency' in just a few extracts. Looking only at that aspect it is also difficult to see why women would continue to read a literature which so constantly 'got at' them.[25] However, many features do acknowledge the difficulties of women's lives even whilst urging them to contribute yet more. There *are* signs of the costs to women, particularly in advertisements: 'Take 10 drops when you feel exhausted. In 15 minutes Phosferine begins to replenish your strength. Countless thousands are carrying on in this period of undue stress and strain by the regular and timely use of Phosferine' (20 April 1940).

Strikingly anomalous, not least in its humour, Mrs Fusspottle's 'Letters from the home front' pulls the rug from beneath the 'process of public glossification in war'.[26] This is 'Mrs Fusspottle on war factories':

> I told you last week didn't I how I discussed the Call Up with my brother-in-law Chalmers Whittlenap and he said I wouldn't do for the WRENS ATS or WAAFS only a War Factory or Secret Service Well I told him that wouldn't hurt me because War Factories were so wonderful these days you live in a Hostel sometimes called a Hovel by mistake ...
>
> Of course the work is just child's play the machines are so wonderful now they really work themselves the wireless plays all the time because it helps what they call Physchology [sic] and Output you dance in the gangways and keep laughing at little jokes to show your Moral [sic] ha-ha-ha then just now and then you say *Oh la la* and turn a little screw or bolt and up goes Output 50 per cent and Mr. Bevin sends a telegram *Well done thou good and faithful servants.* (30 January 1942)

Only (worthless) feminine prattle, Mrs Fusspottle's ramblings also challenge the wartime ethos of efficiency and 'smiling through'. The lack of punctuation is arguably an analogy for the wishful upturning of rule-bound Britain. Complementing this 'subversive' discourse, the currency of fiction is the emotional life that wartime dictates strive so hard to discipline.

### Emotional narratives

As *Woman's Own* became more utilitarian, fiction was foregrounded, with cover promotion and its pages pushed largely to the front. Compared to the practical side of magazines a 'more sympathetic tear-letting is encouraged'.[27] The name for those cultural genres whose main effect is the 'stirring up of the emotions' is, of course, 'melodrama'.[28] But melodrama's trade is over-dramatisation and heightened emotion, and what Ien Ang refers to as the 'tragic structure of feeling' and 'melodramatic imagination'. When life itself was (potentially) melodramatic, fictional escape – at least that which was largely enjoyed in the context of home – could not itself be melodramatic.[29]

The stories in *Woman's Own* are emotionally restrained – shades of Mrs Miniver[30] crossed with Laura Jesson/Celia Johnston of the 1945 British classic *Brief Encounter*. The latter character, as Light points out, is 'remarkable for what she doesn't do and for what she does not say: the film is her imaginary confession to her husband as he sits opposite her on the sofa, all unsuspecting, plying the *Times* crossword, but it is all the more eloquent for being ultimately unspoken'.[31] *Woman's Own* fiction offers a modest working through of what Light graphically refers to as 'throttled emotion'.[32] It allows a play with emotions – fear, anguish, unhappiness, tiredness and boredom, love – which, made problematic by war, it would have been unwise to rehearse and experience too strongly in other contexts, and which perhaps *could* not be fully felt, if 'normal' life were to proceed.

At the outset of war many stories deal with wives' distress over husbands' signing up for active service. As the war proceeds stories tackle loss, and the temptations and loneliness of separation. By 1945 stories in which women are low in spirits and deeply tired become more common. Female protagonists may be in the forces or engaged in war work but emphasis in the fiction is on private life and on women as girlfriends, wives and mothers.

'Clipped wings' by Vera Wynn Griffiths is typical of stories early in the war but also more generally illustrative. The story revolves around Irene's anguished discovery that husband Gilbert wishes to join up, and her own painful realisation that since she has prevented him – having clipped his flying wings after the First World War and in this war too put her own desires before his – she must now persuade him of her change of heart.

The story's conventional narrative structure – the equilibrium of fifteen years of marriage disrupted and then worked through to the new equilibrium of Gil able to do his masculine bit in the war – follows Irene's emotional state. Her calm is unsettled, her feelings unleashed, only to be contained at the end. Irene's pain is a wholly private experience shared neither with her husband, in front of whom she adopts a mask of composure, nor with her daughter. Irene is alone; except her feelings *are* shared with the reader. Though to Gil she indicates, 'it would be nice to see you in uniform again', the reader is party to her more honest self-reflection: 'She heard the echo of her own words. Silly, inane words, but they didn't matter. All she wanted now was to finish off this situation quickly; before she burst into tears and clung to him, pleading frantically: "I didn't mean it. Don't listen to me. Don't go, Gil, don't go.'" Irene's composure is rewarded by Gil's decla-ration of love: 'He was more hers now in this moment of renunciation than he had ever been'. In the secure knowledge then that 'THE END' brings emotional control *and* happiness there is the possibility that the reader, with Irene, might temporarily and partially let loose *her* feelings. In this way women's war self is managed.

### Memories and dreams of the future

Another strategy for the management of women's war self involves dreams of the future. Jane Waller and Michael Vaughan-Rees indicate that 'maga-zines discouraged people from looking backwards'.[33] Sometimes the editor-ial voice and fiction do express concern about such dangers, especially around memories of the past blocking the path to the future. But the mate-rial I've looked at points to more complex relations between present, past and future. Nostalgic memories can be a means of coping with the difficult present, as in this Patience Strong verse from her weekly 'Corner':[34]

> The guest room is deserted now for no-one comes to stay – all dear friends, by duty called, are scattered far away ... But sometimes when my heart is heavy with the thoughts of war – I tip-toe up the creaking stairs and peep in at the door. Through the little lattice window comes the moon's white glow. I stand and listen, hearing voices from the long ago. Ghosts are there; the place is haunted. Faces I can see. And the air is fragrant with the breath of memory. The sheets are laid in lavender. The chintz is fresh and gay – All is ready for the coming of that happy day – when once again within these walls a friend will come to rest – and beneath my roof there'll be a dear and welcome guest. (*Woman's Own*, 12 November 1943)

But this remembrance of things past is also a means for imagining life after the war ('the coming of that happy day'). Memories, and the sketching of a future, focus on the domestic – a room, possibly a cottage room: 'The sheets are laid in lavender. The chintz is fresh and gay.' A series of (rare during wartime) full page advertisements for Brasso and Reckitt's Blue echo similar sentiments: 'Scene: the dining room at Aunt Helen's. Time: Summer in peace time' (see Figure 7).

Herbert Shaw's romantic story 'City for two' (28 January 1944) con-trasts the grey, noisy, industrialised, inland city of wartime with the quiet, coastal town of peacetime memories. Vivienne makes gun parts: 'Even in the bright factory Vivienne was oppressed by the drabness and hard clamour of the big town nearby ... You didn't mind a scrap, either. You were doing your bit, and you took care to do your very best. Day after day. But you had to have something from the old days to which you could cling, and Vivienne

[ 133 ]

thanked her lucky stars for her memories of Burldon.' A painting of Burldon in an antique shop (a romanticised illustration offers 'bygone – probably Victorian – days') puts Vivienne in touch with Michael. At the end of the story and in anticipation of the end of the war, Michael expresses his hopes of becoming manager of Burldon's hotel: 'I shouldn't be surprised if you and I were among the prominent inhabitants of Burldon very soon – how would you like that?'

Where aspects of the past are seen as 'bad', the key dimension enabling a shift from 'bad' traditional pre-war days to 'good' modernity after the war is *planning*. Having roots in the interwar period, planning is fed and nourished during war, in the hope not only of producing victory but of reaping a rich, peacetime harvest. Almost from the outset of war planning for peace is widely discussed, but increasingly so from 1942.[35] Towns, social welfare, education, family size, women's and men's roles, jobs for women, kitchens and homes are all debated.

Enjoining women to be active players in post-war planning is a continuation of their embrace by the ethos of wartime efficiency at which they have shown themselves so adept. It is a declaration that their entry into modernity is not (or should not be) just 'for the duration'. Nevertheless, discussion indicates that the role is still a new one, and not one with which writers (middle-class women) think 'other' women will necessarily feel comfortable. Nan Gordon in 'Where are you going?' carefully balances 'old' (care of family) and 'new' (contribution to the bigger world):

> With an eye on the future we plan. In the past we have been too inclined to let things slide, and our horizons have been too near. We must realize that the world needs us – and learn to look outwards. Perhaps we have been too self-satisfied. Too inclined to burrow into our own homes and bolt and bar the door, then grouse about the happenings outside that displease us. We should go outside and take a peek ... Our families and homes take up a lot of our time, but there should be some over for the rest of the world. (30 January 1942).

There is no sense that in 'sow[ing] the seeds for a world at peace by making our homes calm refuges for our husbands and children' women were perhaps not best prepared to 'make our minds more elastic' (30 January 1942).

### 'Back to real life'[36]

Given women's magazines' close association with the war effort and their consumption largely in the domestic sphere, escape into their pages could only be partial compared to the kind of escape possible in relation to the feature film within the darkened auditorium of a cinema.[37] It would seem that women's magazines both keyed women into the war effort and allowed them

SCENE: *The dining-room at Aunt Helen's.*

TIME: *Summer in peace time. Sunday morning.*

7   Brasso and Reckitt's Blue advertisement, *Woman's Own*,
    25 November 1943, p. 10

limited space to indulge the dispiritedness which inevitably ensued. The rigorous and continual management of the self, articulated by magazines in order that women manage the war, was not a strategy that could be pursued indefinitely. Yet in some respects, as austerity continued – the battle of peace simply replacing the battle of war – women were 'got at' until the early 1950s.[38] It is not surprising that, when consumption became a possibility, women (and their magazines) enthusiastically embraced its potential. Not just because they had been deprived of commodities but because consumption represented an expressiveness, a letting go, an excess, a fulfilment of dreams, that had for so long been denied them. The skills related to wartime efficiency were now transferred to this new terrain.[39] The narrowing of women's focus from 'home front' to 'home' can also be seen as the lifting of this burden of altruistic self-management. It would be inappropriate, however, to suggest that the post-war promises of women's involvement in 'the outside world' and their entry into modernity were thus curtailed. The 'conservative modernity' Light refers to, in its emphasis on women and home and 'its minimalist management of emotional and social life which would rather leave things as they are than suffer the pain of disturbance',[40] and which had been thoroughly mobilised during war, continued.[41] But arguably it began to be transformed by a newer ethos of modernity engendered by a more full-blown consumption.

### Notes

1 Mary Grieve, *Millions Made My Story* (London, Victor Gollancz, 1964), p. 126.
2 Marjorie Ferguson, *Forever Feminine: Women's Magazines and the Cult of Femininity* (London, Heinemann, 1983), p. 19, my emphasis.
3 Grieve, *Millions Made My Story*, p. 123.
4 *Ibid.*, p. 134. Notwithstanding print rationing, circulations blossomed during the war.
Magazine circulations 1938–46

|  | Woman | Woman's Own | Woman's Weekly | Woman and Home* |
|---|---|---|---|---|
| 1938 | 750,000 | 357,000 | 498,000 | 301,000 |
| 1946 Jan–June |  | 670,000 | 727,500 | 405,000 |
| 1946 July–Dec | 1,079,900 |  | 785,200 | 461,000 |

*Woman and Home* was a monthly but with a circulation comparable to that of the big weeklies.
Source: Cynthia White, *Women's Magazines 1693–1968* (London, Michael Joseph, 1970), p. 324.
5 Print rationing was introduced in 1940. Further controls restricting the space devoted to advertising were brought in during 1942; see James Curran and Jean Seaton (eds), *Power Without Responsibility: The Press and Broadcasting in Britain*,

4th edn (London, Routledge, 1991).

6 The choice of *Woman's Own* was pragmatic: wartime copies of this title rather than others were to be had in Sussex University library. However, I was reassured that this was also a sound choice when I read that other commentators believed that *Woman's Own*, led by Constance Holt, 'had the strongest editorial team' during wartime (Jane Waller and Michael Vaughan-Rees, *Women in Wartime: The Role of Women's Magazines 1939–1945*, London, Macdonald Optima, 1987, p. 7). The mix of entertainment and service elements was by no means the prerogative of *Woman's Own*. Even a magazine like *Good Housekeeping*, which it might be thought would have offered only the practical side, also carried fiction, which it boldly advertised on its cover (Brian Braithwaite, Noelle Walsh and Glyn Davies (eds), *The Home Front: The Best of Good Housekeeping 1939–1945* (London, Ebury, 1987).

7 David Morgan and Mary Evans, *The Battle for Britain: Citizenship and Ideology in the Second World War* (London and New York, Routledge, 1993), p. 39.

8 *Ibid.*, p. 83.

9 Deirdre Beddoe, *Back to Home and Duty: Women Between the Wars 1918–1939* (London, Pandora, 1989); see also Dena Attar, *Wasting Girls' Time: The History and Politics of Home Economics* (London, Virago, 1990); Barbara Ehrenreich and Deidre English, *For Her Own Good: 150 Years of the Experts' Advice to Women* (London, Pluto, 1979).

10 Alison Light, *Forever England; Femininity, Literature and Conservatism Between the Wars* (London and New York, Routledge, 1991), p. 10.

11 *Ibid.*, p. 10.

12 John Burnett, *A Social History of Housing 1815–1985* (London, Methuen, 1986).

13 Taylorist principles as applied to factories and later offices broke tasks down to create a division of labour along mental and manual labour lines. Whilst supposedly creating more efficient production it also gave more control to a managerial level at the expense of workers. The latter no longer had a sense of the whole labour process, only the bit to which they were allocated (Harry Braverman, *Labor and Monopoly Capital: The Degradation of Work in the Twentieth Century*, New York, Monthly Review Press, 1974). Applying this to the home made little sense in two ways: first, the scale of tasks and output were not sufficient for any rationalisation of labour to make any significant 'productivity' gains; second, the housewife had to be both manager *and* worker (Suzette Worden, 'Powerful women: electricity in the home 1919–40', in Judy Attfield and Pat Kirkham (eds), *A View from the Interior: Feminism, Women and Design*, London, Women's Press, 1989). It is interesting though that women appear to have internalised that double role. Ann Oakley's research on housewives in the 1970s showed a conflict and difficulty for women: having set themselves standards they were then their own judges (*Housewife*, London, Allen Lane, 1974).

14 Caroline Davidson, *A Woman's Work is Never Done: A History of Housework in the British Isles 1650–1950* (London, Chatto and Windus, 1982); Adrian Forty, *Objects of Desire* (London, Thames and Hudson, 1986); Worden, 'Powerful women'.

15 Beddoe, *Back to Home and Duty*; Jane Lewis, *Women in England 1870–1950: Sexual Divisions and Social Change* (Brighton, Wheatsheaf, 1984) and (ed.) *Labour and Love: Women's Experiences of Home and Family 1850–1940* (Oxford, Blackwell, 1986); Marjorie Spring Rice, *Working Class Wives* (London, Virago, 1981).

16 Joli Jenson, *Redeeming Modernity: Contradictions in Media Criticism* (Newbury Park, Sage, 1990).

17 Mark Abrams, *The Condition of the British People 1911–1945* (London, Victor Gol-

lancz, 1946); Lucy Bland, 'Purity, motherhood, pleasure or threat? Definitions of female sexuality 1900–1970s', in Sue Cartledge and Joanna Ryan (eds), *Sex and Love: New Thoughts on Old Contradictions* (London, Women's Press, 1983); Diana Gittens, *Fair Sex: Family Size and Structure 1900–39* (London, Hutchinson, 1982).

18  Jeffrey Richards, *Age of the Dream Palace: Cinema and Society in Britain 1930–39* (London, Routledge and Kegan Paul, 1984).

19  Alan Jackson, *Semi-detached London* (London, Allen and Unwin, 1973).

20  Largely 'domestic' titles launched during the interwar period included: *Good House-keeping* (1922), *Woman and Home* (1926), *My Home* and *Modern Home* (1928), *Woman* (1937), and the titles aimed at a higher-class readership, *Woman's Journal* (1927) and *Harper's Bazaar* (1929). There were also two new service magazines aimed at a more working-class readership: *Woman's Friend* (1924) and *Woman's Companion* (1927) (Cynthia White, *Women's Magazines 1693–1968*, London, Michael Joseph, 1970, pp. 95–6).

21  White, *Women's Magazines*, p. 96, my emphasis.

22  Cited in Joy Leman, ' "The advice of a real friend": codes of intimacy and oppression in women's magazines 1937–1955', *Women's Studies International Quarterly*, Vol. 3 (1980), pp. 63–78.

23  This emotional management is also in accord with Light's characterisation of 'conservative modernity' as implying an almost masculine playing down of the emotions by women.

24  Reprinted in Braithwaite *et al.*, *The Home Front*, p. 63. It is worth quoting all of this advertisement which shows a woman's face wearing a service-type cap: 'War gives us a chance to show our mettle. We wanted equal rights with men; they took us at our word. We are proud to work for victory beside them. And work is not our only task. We must triumph over routine; keep the spirit of light-heartedness. Our faces must never reflect personal troubles. We must achieve masculine efficiency without hardness. Above all, we must guard against surrender to personal carelessness. Never must we consider careful grooming a quisling gesture. With leisure and beauty-aids so rare, looking our best is specially creditable. Let us face the future bravely and honour the subtle bond between good looks and good morale. Put your best face forward. YARDLEY.'

25  See article headed 'Do you feel "GOT AT"?' in *Woman's Own*, 9 January 1942.

26  Tom Harrison, *Living Through the Blitz* (London, William Collins, 1976), p. 324.

27  Braithwaite *et al.*, *The Home Front*, p. 9.

28  Ien Ang, *Watching Dallas: Soap Opera and the Melodramatic Imagination* (London and New York, Methuen, 1985), p. 61.

29  Stuart Hall ('The "social eye" of *Picture Post*', Working Papers in Cultural Studies 2, Centre for Contemporary Cultural Studies, University of Birmingham, 1972) notes a similar absence of melodramatic photos and copy in the mass weekly publication *Picture Post*. The success of Gainsborough Studio costume melodramas from 1943 to 1947 is interesting. But note that these were set in the past not the present, and they were also distanced by being about 'the upper reaches of the landed classes' (Sue Harper, 'Historical pleasures: Gainsborough costume melodrama', in Christine Gledhill (ed.), *Home is Where the Heart is: Studies in Melodrama and the Woman's Film*, London, British Film Institute, 1987).

30  Jan Struther's *Time* column describing the fictional life of Mrs Miniver (October 1937–December 1939) and the film of that name (1942) are discussed by Light (*Forever England*). Jan Struther's journalism and her character in Mrs Miniver are at the heart of Light's thesis concerning 'conservative modernity'.

31  Light, *Forever England*, p. 208.

32  *Ibid.*, p. 212.

33  Waller and Vaughan-Reese, *Women in Wartime*, p. 120.

34  Patience Strong was the pseudonym of Winifred May. Light suggests that her verses expounded 'sentiments similar to Mrs Miniver's. Though there was more religiosity and sentimentality in Patience Strong's offerings' (*Forever England*, p. 145). Wartime print restrictions meant that extracts like that cited here were not set out as verse.

35  When the Americans enter the war at the end of 1941 peace can perhaps more easily be envisaged. Beveridge's milestone report revising social security was published in December 1942.

36  This is the title of a piece by Norah C. James, *Woman's Own*, 5 January 1945.

37  Jackie Stacey, *Star Gazing: Hollywood Cinema and Female Spectatorship* (London and New York, Routledge, 1994). Stacey's study of the place of cinema and of female stars in women's lives is based on material from questionnaires gathered in the 1980s. I am merely speculating about the satisfactions magazines might have provided on the basis of their texts alone. On two counts I am doubtful about what exactly a study asking women to remember their wartime magazines would produce. First Joke Hermes's ethnographic research on readers of contemporary women's magazines (*Reading Women's Magazines: An Analysis of Everyday Media Use*, Cambridge, Polity, 1995) points to women remembering remarkably little of the content of what they have read because the activity of reading magazines is not actually that important in their lives. Hermes criticises other researchers for what she refers to as the 'fallacy of meaningfulness' which they have attributed to women's magazines. Even if we concede that wartime magazines were more memorable and the activity of their reading more significant, there is perhaps a problem about that memory. I am struck by Tom Harrison's observations (*Living Through the Blitz*) about people's wartime memories as opposed to their thoughts and feelings at the time. Their memories of the Blitz uphold the myth of Britain at its best – everyone working efficiently together, deeds of heroism and so on – and yet at the time, these very same people gave accounts of local and national mismanagement, and of people's often low morale. I would suspect that in the case of women's magazines, because of their close association with the war effort orchestrated by government and its numerous ministries, and the way that role has subsequently been perpetuated in popular memory, if anything is remembered it will be 'make do and mend' and exhortations to 'efficiency'.

38  Janice Winship, 'Nation before family: *Woman* the National Home Weekly 1945–53', in *Formations of Nation and People* (London, Routledge and Kegan Paul, 1984).

39  Janice Winship, 'Woman becomes an "individual": femininity and consumption in women's magazines 1954–69', Occasional Paper 65 (Centre for Contemporary Cultural Studies, University of Birmingham, 1981).

40  Light, *Forever England*, p. 212.

41  We can perhaps see in Betty Friedan's 'The problem that has no name' the far reaches of this management and its costs (*The Feminine Mystique*, New York, Dell Publishing, 1963).

# 9

## The Family Firm restored: newsreel coverage of the British monarchy 1936–45

ROSALIND BRUNT

Immediately after the abdication of Edward VIII on 10 December 1936, the British newsreel organisation Pathé News had to decide on the presentation of their next cinema bulletin. How were they to set about promoting the new King, formerly Albert Duke of York, as George VI? Pathé plumped for full ceremonial regalia. They filmed the whole speech of the Garter King of Arms proclaiming the accession of 'the High and Mighty Albert to the Imperial Crown' and followed up with a montage of ritual occasions entitled 'Our King and Queen: Pathé Gazette's pictures of episodes in the life of their Majesties'. The sequence consisted entirely of a series of 'journeys which have helped forge ever more strong links with Empire' and showed the then Duke and Duchess (but repeatedly called 'their Majesties' in the commentary) being saluted and waved at in Africa, Australia and New Zealand. The bulletin concluded, 'Such, in brief, is the story of the King we have just seen proclaimed, and his Queen. We *know* that they will uphold the glorious tradition of King George V and Queen Mary. God bless them both!'

There is desperation in Pathé's assertive 'knowing'. That autumn's abdication crisis had caused a major constitutional wobble that rendered the future of the British monarchy quite precarious – especially when their European cousins were being reduced to exile, collaboration with fascism, or silence. So Pathé's bulletin required considerable 'ideological labour'[1] to naturalise and legitimate a dynasty suddenly in crisis and fighting for its very survival. Hence the elimination of all reference to the former King Edward whose style and charm as Prince of Wales had captured the popular imagination. The bulletin assumes a direct line of succession from George V to George VI and attempts to transfer onto his little known, unprepared second son some of the popularity of the old King which had reached its height in the Jubilee Year of 1935 and earned him the widespread soubriquet 'Father of the Nation'. Describing George V's funeral in January 1936, Pathé News had called it 'the Empire taking leave of its beloved Father'. Now with the accession bulletin and its emphasis on regal continuity, Pathé implicitly responds to widespread anxieties about the new King's stamina, health and personality. But its images of imperial deference and royal heritage are unconvincing; they try too hard to counteract current concerns about the new King's fitness to reign. However, as we know, the British monarchy not only survived the abdication crisis, it managed to relaunch itself as both a popular and revered institution. So how did its success relate to the circulation of images and what other symbols were invoked than those originally chosen by Pathé? In this article, I want to look at some examples of newsreel presentation of royalty during the three years following the abdication up to 1939 and how the images established then were consolidated in wartime. I will consider how newsreels, along with radio broadcasts, documentary and photography, contributed to a rehabilitation of monarchy in Britain and to a particular identification of monarchy with 'the people'. I'll also be noting how television and the press repeatedly recycle royal wartime imagery in contemporary celebrations of both Britishness and the monarchy.

When Edward VIII announced in his abdication broadcast that he could not be King without 'the help and support of the woman I love' (Wallis Simpson), he commended his brother to the nation pointing out that 'he has one matchless blessing ... not bestowed on me – a happy home life with his children'. In this phrase he recognised both his own 'lack' and the significance of what was to become the key factor in a new 'restoration' of monarchy: the representation of royalty as a family group. The importance of family had been quite overlooked by Pathé's early bulletins but the lack was soon compensated. In common with other image-makers, Pathé had realised by 1937 that what was required was a combination of both imperial and familial images. In this year it had two royal scoops. The Coronation of George VI in May was the first occasion the actual service was filmed: 'With the most solemn and sacred pictures ever taken by a newsreel, we show you, inside the Abbey, the supreme moment.' The Coronation commentary reverts to the grandiloquence of the accession bulletin, repeating its theme of dynastic legitimacy: 'Once again, the Sovereign comes to the throne, fitted by character and upbringing to carry on a great tradition ... in the magnificent pattern of his great father. On him the Crown is safe. Long may it rest there!' The second occasion, the annual Derby Day horse race in June, again allows Pathé to crow about their unique facilities. The bulletin relies on perpetuating the Coronation aura, but at the same time stresses the informal intimacy of family through the new use of close-up:

This year [the Derby] is especially honoured in being the first great sporting event attended by their Majesties the King and Queen, and the Royal Family, since the Coronation. [*Shots of royal procession to the grandstand; then location shots accompanied by 'natural' wildtrack of racegoers' voices.*] Facing the grandstand, Pathé is once again using the world's largest newsreel lens [*Large mounted camera and operator in shot.*] to get these *amazing* close-ups of the Royal Family! [*Queen Elizabeth chats excitedly to a male companion with a cine camera; smiling, turns to engage King and mother-in-law, Queen Mary, in conversation.*] And watch the royal thrill of a superb finish! [*Friend, Queen, King with field glasses.*]

These close-ups are still of a rather fuzzy quality, but their liveliness is striking after the more formal composition of the longshots adopted at the Coronation and at most public royal events. They also indicate how, just as Queen Elizabeth[2] is the focus of the frame at the Coronation Derby, so she is central to the familial image of royalty. In her role both as wife of a king and mother of a possible future monarch, Elizabeth embodies all that Mrs Simpson, as the woman 'behind' the abdication, patently could not offer as a consort.

Biographical anecdote suggests a personal rivalry between these two women, amounting to enmity on Elizabeth's part. But more to the point, regardless of any actual evidence, there was clearly an ideological opposition at stake in their two versions of competing femininities. At the emblematic level, Wallis Simpson, model-thin, chic and 'childless', a twice-divorced American, was obviously out-royalled by a pretty plumpish chiffony person with Scottish ancestry whose daughters, Elizabeth and Margaret Rose, aged ten and six at the accession, were already familiar from press photographs, as the little golden-haired princesses. This was the fairytale femininity which replaced the figure of a threatening femme fatale who, in the public perception, if not according to her own account,[3] had forced a monarch to make the wrong choice between love and duty. Queen Elizabeth became the country's consolation as its former prince charming was 'banished' to the Continent. When Mrs Simpson finally married the former King at a French chateau in June 1937 and the pair became Duke and Duchess of Windsor, a kind of visual banishment ensued. Although the wedding is well-documented in film and photograph, it was given no contemporary currency by mainstream British newsreels. This was presumably because it provided too uneasy a comparison with the visual panoply of the Coronation, which had occurred barely three weeks before. Similarly, the filmed record of the Windsors' unofficial visit to Nazi Germany that summer, where they had cordial meetings with Himmler, Goering and Hitler, was probably deemed both too politically sensitive and damaging to the new monarch to be shown by the newsreels in Coronation Year. It appears that the only 'safe' footage of the Windsors shown on the newsreels from the time of the abdication up to the end of the war features their ceremonial arrival at Nassau in August 1940 to take up a five-year governorship of the Bahamas. This event and subsequent filmed images of the Duke in colonial regalia taking the salute and the Duchess in Red Cross uniform helping the war effort demonstrated to the British public that the Windsors, suitably humbled, had been well-contained as a threat to the monarchy and demonstrated to the government that they could no longer function as potential fascist collaborators.

The fate of the Windsors, inhabiting a world of tarnished glamour and shady realpolitik, thus never contaminated the public roles of the new King and Queen. In the brief span of their reign before the war they emerged from the abdication crisis to assume personas that were overwhelmingly safe and nice, whilst still bearing the weight of royal and imperial heritage.

After listening to the broadcast of the Coronation in May 1937, the socialist and feminist writer Beatrice Webb recorded in her diary the return to 'the dominating ideology of a divinely appointed King, of a chosen people, to rule by the sword, over the rest of mankind'. Yet she also noted that the entire historical panoply that combined medieval pageant, Old Testament, Alice in Wonderland and imperial glorification, focused around 'two little robots in the glass coach'. Two years later Webb extended the 'robot' comparison to make a more general comment about the current impact of photography and newsreels. Discussing the first visit by a reigning British monarch to the United States in the summer of 1939, she notes in her diary:

> How amazingly personal the world has become: the mob idolizing particular individuals instead of claiming, as they did in the nineteenth century, the right of groups to govern themselves ... And this idolization of persons on account of their assumed and exceptional goodness and infallible wisdom is not confined to the so-called totalitarian states. The British people, with their genius for compromise, have lit on the device for a robot King and his wife – who have no power but are treated with extreme deference and arouse in the mob worshipful emotion. The efficiency of the device has been shown by the enormous success of the British King and Queen not only in Great Britain but in Canada and the USA. They are ideal robots: the King kindly, sensible, without pretension and with considerable open-mindedness, and the Queen good-looking and gracious and beautifully attired, who blows kisses to admiring Yankees in New York but looks the perfect dignified aristocrat in London.[4]

Webb's account is useful in identifying particular characteristics adopted by the royal couple and indicating how rapidly and extensively they had come to appeal to both national and international publics. But her extended 'robot' metaphor overemphasises the degree of passivity involved on the part of both 'the mob' and royalty themselves. Indeed, Webb's elision of the concept of ideology with that of propaganda to imply something of a deliberate conspiracy is rather undermined by her own references to the very plasticity of the two royal personas.

I would suggest that a manipulative model, inferring that the public, royalty or both are somehow dupes of the visual image-makers, cannot adequately explain how successful representation must 'work' to engage experience, memory and fantasy. To interpret royalty as robot figures does dramatically illustrate how much they come to 'bear' the load of British cultural history; but it downplays the extent to which they may also actively collaborate in its remaking. For instance, in looking through the available newsreel material of the period, I've noticed how there is nearly always a brief point where the Queen, in the midst of carrying out her official duties as if the cameras aren't there, looks directly at the lens and thereby breaks the convention of 'acting naturally' in order to achieve the best camera compositions. As with the present-day debate around images of the Princess of Wales, it leads nowhere to pose the question in the moralistic terms of 'who is manipulating whom?' I think it's more productive to take as a given of modern monarchy that they are bound to be in various ways participants in their own mythologising, and then consider what repertoires of imagery are actually drawn upon, and with what possible 'ideological effect'.

From this perspective, Elizabeth has probably been the most successful member of royalty to collaborate with the image-makers since she first entered public life as the Duchess of York on her marriage in 1923. Her first journalistic epithet was 'The Smiling Duchess' and the early portraits by John Singer Sargent and the Rubens-inspired Philip de Laszlo, reproduced as postcards for mass consumption, established Elizabeth as a worthy object of courtly homage. After the Coronation, the unthreatening image of sweet old-fashioned glamour was further enhanced by what became her 'trademark' Norman Hartnell dresses, starting with the crinolines he designed that caused a sensation when Elizabeth accompanied the King to Paris in July 1938. The following July, her status as chivalric icon received its ultimate confirmation in a series of photographs taken by Cecil Beaton. In these, Elizabeth is posed against pillars and balconies as an early Victorian heroine with parasol, creating what Beaton called 'lovely pictures that should be very romantic – of the Fairy Queen in her ponderous Palace'.[5]

Two months before the declaration of war with Germany seems at first an unlikely moment to be creating Ruritanian idylls in photographs. On the other hand, 'lovely pictures' of the Queen may well have fitted a desperate 'if only' slot in the public imagination: 'if only' a nervy present could do a magical dissolve into a permanent summer's afternoon in fairyland. One explanation of this phenomenon is offered by that 'other' socialist and feminist writer, Virginia Woolf. Writing about royalty on the eve of the war, she was struck by the way in which, especially at crisis points in British history, all manner of collective fantasies can be projected onto the royal family.

Woolf's starting point is a series of reflections about the apparently insatiable public need 'to see the Dukes and Kings' and a set of photographs of a royal visit to the zoo. Struck by the incongruity of 'the Princess who was feeding the panda' appearing in the picture papers 'at times which it is sufficient to call "like these"', she poses the question: what can the audience's fascination possibly consist of? As a fascinated observer herself she notes that 'the matter is complex', but answers by suggesting that:

> perhaps the most profound satisfaction that Royalty provides is that it gives us a Paradise to inhabit, and one that is much more domestic than that provided by the Church of England …
>
> Moreover, real people live in Buckingham Palace, but always smiling, perfectly dressed … it is a consolation to know that such beings exist. If they live, then we too live in them vicariously.[6]

Following Woolf's notion of the 'domestic paradise', royalty can appear to function both as a real and an ideal family. They may act to focus a perceived national need, to, as it were, escape into normality in the face of impending disruption. Moreover, the rehabilitation of monarchy as a charmed and charming family circle with Queen Elizabeth at its heart – the very 'pink of grace and charm', in Woolf's words – allows for an easy and 'naturally' assumed identification between subjects and Crown. Because 'everybody' has some experience of family, it is possible to discern 'family likenesses', projecting our own experience of bits of family life onto members of the royal family and combining it with the common stock of cultural values.

Thus in Woolf's account, royal mythology does not operate quite the way Beatrice Webb sees it, as a kind of imposition or con-trick from above. Rather, there is always some degree of 'fit' with what we, their subjects, know and want. So the princesses at the zoo can be at once quite ordinary, just 'little girls feeding the sea lions' in the magazines, but they also function as the idealised daughters we might all wish to have, as we bring to bear on those pictures 'many ghosts and glories' and a 'good deal of gilding of the imagination'.[7]

A newsreel sequence from September 1938 well illustrates Woolf's point. While the King is detained in London at the height of the Munich Crisis over appeasement, his two daughters accompany the Queen to Clydebank where she's launching the Cunard liner named after her. The Pathé cameras pull out to establish massive cheering crowds stretching far below the three distinctive regal figures. Then, in the current documentary style, they pick out individual families to show in close-up. Hopeful and respectful working-class faces gaze upwards listening to the Queen's message from the King: 'He bids the people of this country be of good cheer in spite of the dark clouds hanging over them'. At her side, well-behaved but attractively animated, the princesses stand out in matching Bo-peep hats and sailor collar coats. Although over four years apart in age, the two sisters were always pictured like twins at all public events until 1944 when Princess Elizabeth reached eighteen. It's as if, just through their identically dressed visual presence, not a hint of sibling rivalry could ever infect these fairytale daughters. For this was a family keenly aware of the need to maintain 'front'. The King took a constant interest in matching the family's clothes to the occasion and it was he who coined the epithets 'Us Four' and 'The Family Firm'. These became shorthand for insider use to underline the royal requirements for a united group effort.

In the period up to the war, then, the figure of the family in domestic paradise had, in various guises, effectively neutralised the damage caused to the monarchy by the abdication. But it had also in that short time managed to establish a repertoire of themes that could be drawn on for explicit morale-boosting purposes in the subsequent war effort. In fact the last pre-war newsreel film of the family serves to prefigure much wartime imagery. The sequence, shot in August 1939, shows Us Four together, all informally dressed: King in open collar and kilt, Queen and daughters in country style dress surrounded by young men in shorts. Broadly smiling, they are attempting to fit the right gestures to the comic song, 'Under the spreading chestnut tree'. The Pathé commentator remarks: 'The Queen and Princess Margaret, watching the King out of one eye and the singing director out of the other, win our sympathy by getting some of the actions wrong!' The whole group laughs.

The setting for this bulletin is Abergeldie Castle, Scotland where the last Duke of York's camp is being held. Started in 1921 out of the Duke's involvement in the Industrial Welfare Society which aimed to promote better employer–worker relations, the camp brought together equal numbers of public school boys and industrial apprentices for a week of games, practical skill-sharing and visits from prominent people. How the camp features in this newsreel implies the kind of link between the royal Family Firm and a unified nation that is to be a central theme of subsequent wartime coverage. It involves an approach that makes class differences visible but at the same time dissolves them into triviality. On the assumption that families are what bring people together and classes are what divide them, the newsreels are to demonstrate throughout the war that royals and their subjects can unite as one big national family. The national family transcends class division because it is composed essentially of individual families, of which the royal family is only the most exemplary.

In his treatise on revolutionary socialism, *The Lion and the Unicorn*, published in February 1941,[8] the English essayist George Orwell offers an illuminating contemporary analysis of national identity and how it inter-plays with class. In common with many of the Left intelligentsia at the time, Orwell sees the war as already providing the preconditions for a 'realisable policy' of socialism. But he prefaces his political programme with a detailed ideological examination of some of the 'peculiarities' of Britishness. His argument is that although Britain is actually a number of nations and although the material inequalities of class are greater than in any other European country, nevertheless,

> the vast majority of the people *feel* themselves to be a single nation and are con-scious of resembling one another more than they resemble foreigners. Patrio-tism is usually stronger than class-hatred ... England [sic] is the most class-ridden country under the sun. It is a land of snobbery and privilege ruled largely by the old and silly. But in any calculation about it one has to take into account its emotional unity, the tendency of nearly all its inhabitants to feel alike and act together in moments of supreme crisis.

This account of how a national consensus operates to deny the realities of class division and separate nations is encapsulated in the central organising metaphor of 'family'. According to Orwell, consensus in Britain reproduces itself not by any official philosophy of statehood, but through a dense inter-texture of unspoken, spontaneously assumed and deeply ingrained beliefs: Britain 'is a family ... It has its private language and its common memories, and at the approach of an enemy it closes its ranks. A family with the wrong members in control.' Nowhere in the essay does Orwell specifically mention royalty but he does refer to the importance of 'symbolic figures' in main-taining the myth of family. These people represent 'the strange mixture of reality and illusion, democracy and privilege, humbug and decency, the subtle network of compromises by which [Britain] keeps itself in its familiar shape'.

Coming finally to wartime images of royalty, I want to gloss Orwell's reflections on the family metaphor and take the Family Firm as 'symbolic figures' that act as embodiments of national consensus. There are three main types of newsreel sequence: first, coverage of a public event (morale-boosting royal visit, inspection or ceremony); secondly, speeches made for media audiences, either direct to camera or radio broadcasts illustrated with stills and cinematic montage; and thirdly, informal occasions illustrating family and palace life.

From the first category come the images most familiar to British audi-ences through post-war compilations for press and television: the King in uniform and Queen in smart hat and coat inspecting the bomb damage to their official residence, Buckingham Palace; or stepping through debris to meet bombed-out families, particularly those of the East End of London at the height of the Blitz in Autumn 1940. The symbolism of this footage is heavily reinforced when the material is recycled. In recent compilations, the images' appeal to a national family that transcends class barriers to pull together for the war effort is further underlined by reference to two 'legendary' remarks made by the Queen during the Blitz. One in reply to the suggestion that, given the fears of imminent invasion, the children should be sent to Canada: 'The Princesses cannot go without me. I cannot go without the King. The King will never go'. And secondly, 'I'm glad we've been bombed. It makes me feel I can look the East End in the face'.[9] These remarks, probably from letters or diaries, and only published in the 1950s, highlight the significance of the royal family as 'just like us', the representatives of 'ordinary people'. For if families in both palaces and slums could be bombed indiscriminately, then the 'emotional unity' Orwell describes could overcome the material divisions of privilege in the national consensus to win the war.

The overlay of the Queen's remarks onto original wartime coverage of public events also emphasises how much the focus of the newsreels was both maternal and matriarchal. Throughout the war, the Queen made radio broadcasts and newsreel speeches from her palace sitting-room. These were addressed primarily to women and invoked her own role as wife and mother in the context of the national home front. The aim of this second type of message was to sympathise with women's current privations whilst encouraging them to value their achievements.

Speaking to women by radio and screen across her palace desk in 1940, the Queen stresses a national identity of interests: 'Many of you will have had to see your family life broken up: your husband going to his allotted task, your children evacuated to places of greater safety … The King and I know what it means to be parted from our children and we can sympathise.' Later on in the war, she widens her address, exhorting women to see themselves as full and equal participants in the war and challenging any attempt to downplay their contribution. In a Pathé newsreel from 1943 the Queen starts by disclaiming any special occasion or specific message, and goes on to say:

> But there is something deep in my heart I know ought to be told you and probably I am the best person to do it. So often when I have talked to women engaged in every kind of job, sometimes a physically dangerous one, so often when I have admired their pluck, have I heard them say, 'Oh well, it's not much, I'm just doing my best to win the war.' And have you not met that enemy too? [*The Queen then lists women's war achievements, accompanied by a montage of women's labour in heavy industry and amidst bombed-out people. She thanks people for their prayers and prays in turn:*] for victory for our people in this country and our great family throughout the Empire.

When this speech was included recently in a video compilation to celebrate Elizabeth's ninetieth birthday, the commentary remarked that Hitler had described her as 'the most dangerous woman in Europe' because of her ability to focus national loyalty around herself and the King.[10] A second birthday video, also using wartime newsreel extracts, commented that Charles de Gaulle, leader of the wartime Free French Army, had referred to the Queen as the only person in Britain he could trust.[11] In this way, wartime newsreel imagery acquires the symbolic accretions of matriarchy, presenting the story of a woman who held the national family together at its most testing time: hence the title of the first video: *Elizabeth: The Heart of a Nation.*

But this is a matriarchal order that is understated, unassuming – and thereby all the more effective as wartime propaganda. The third type of newsreel coverage, the informal occasion, is again widely quoted in recent compilations. Familiar images include the Queen's twice-weekly sewing circle, bringing together aristocrats and palace servants in an early 'make do and mend' exhortation from 1940; and the family visiting Princess Elizabeth during her truck maintenance course in the Auxiliary Territorial Service, the women's unit of the British army, in April 1945.[12] These show Us Four prepared to 'muck in' and do their ordinary bit, nothing special. But they form a striking contrast to the hectoring declamatory style associated with Hitler – no family man, he. Thus the most evocative informal images, shown throughout the war, feature quiet domestic or rural settings. These served as propaganda cameos: the family simply 'being' a family; sitting round the fire, reading, knitting, listening to the wireless; or out walking at Windsor, playing with the corgis, getting into the family car. The classic idyll involves the family inspecting the harvest at their Sandringham estate (ploughed up for wartime production). Recalling the pre-war paradise, the Queen, accompanied by a retainer, drives an old-fashioned pony and trap past ancient English woodland, followed by the smiling King and two princesses on more democratic bicycles.

This sunlit cameo from near the end of the war[13] typifies the link between Britishness and monarchy constructed in all three types of wartime newsreel. It highlights the continuity of an old order, the very apex of the class system, maintained despite the massive upheaval of war, whilst also pointing to the post-war class settlement to be established with the new Labour government. And both the images of class hierarchy and class settlement are mediated through the restored royal family and the symbolism of delightful and enduring family values.

'The camera has an immense power in its eye, if it would only turn that eye in rather a different direction.' Concluding her 1939 essay on royalty, Virginia Woolf tentatively imagines the camera being used to help the British adopt a more rational enlightened viewpoint, transcending their fascination with royalty: 'It might wean us by degrees from the Princess to the panda, and shunt us past religion to pay homage to Science, as some think a more venerable royal house than the House of Windsor'.[14]

But for all the wartime discussion of the need for a new socialist order, republicanism was mostly absent from the agenda. The newsreels appealed to the conservative loyalties of British subjects and remained transfixed by the glamour of an ordinary-yet-extraordinary family. In this way they mainly eschewed the 'different direction' Woolf points to: the democratic possibilities that open up when the camera begins to picture for its audience, 'the drudgery, about which there is no glamour, of being ourselves'.

## Notes

1 Stuart Hall's term is explained in his seminal essay, 'Culture, the media and the "ideological effect"', in J. Curran *et al.* (eds) *Mass Communication and Society* (London, Edward Arnold, 1977).

2 As the Consort of George VI, Elizabeth took the title of Queen until her husband's death in 1952. At that time, she became known as Queen Elizabeth, the Queen Mother, and her daughter, Princess Elizabeth, became Queen Elizabeth II.

3 See Frances Donaldson, *Edward VIII* (London, Weidenfeld and Nicolson, 1974) and the Duchess of Windsor's own (ghosted) account in *The Heart has its Reasons* (London, Michael Joseph, 1956). These indicate that Wallis Simpson was more concerned about her own reputation than marriage to the King. Fearing to become 'the most hated woman in Britain', she struggled, with the support of several courtiers, to make the King give her up and go on to his Coronation.

4 *The Diary of Beatrice Webb*, Vol. 4 1924–43, ed. N. and J. MacKenzie (London, Virago, 1985), pp. 389, 435.

5 Quoted in 'The Queen Mother and her painters', Sir Roy Strong, *Sunday Times Magazine*, 29 July 1990.

6 Virginia Woolf's essay, 'Royalty', is reprinted in *Collected Essays*, Vol. 4 (London, Hogarth Press, 1967), p. 212. A note says only that it was written in 1939 but does not date the essay more precisely or give any publication details. From the content, it appears to have been written before July, certainly before the outbreak of war.

7 Woolf, 'Royalty', p. 212.

8 George Orwell, *The Lion and the Unicorn: Socialism and the English Genius* (London, Secker and Warburg, 1941). This was the first volume in the radical series, '*The Searchlight Books*', edited by T. R. Fyvel and Orwell himself. Throughout the treatise, Orwell renders 'Englishness' problematic but also tends to elide 'English' with 'British' in his writing.

9 I don't think these remarks were public knowledge during the war. I've had considerable difficulty tracing their source. Most post-war royal biographies simply quote them as already well-known without any reference! John Wheeler-Bennett's authorised biography, *King George VI*, commissioned in 1952 and first published by Macmillan in 1958, gives as source for the second statement, Betty Spencer Shew, *Queen Elizabeth, the Queen Mother*, 1955 (p. 76) – a book I've been unable to trace. But for me, the 'point' of these quotations is rather their widespread symbolic resonance in post-war commentaries than questions of authenticity.

10 *Elizabeth: The Heart of a Nation* (Parkfield Publishing video, 1990) – again, no source is given for this, or the following remark.

11 *The Queen Mother: A Life of Our Times* (Independent Television News video, 1990).

12 See Roland Flamini's biography, *Sovereign Elizabeth II* (London, Corgi, 1992) for an assessment of this ATS episode, which relates to Orwell's notions of what 'symbolic figures' represent. Flamini points out that, although it appeared in newsreels and press photography that Elizabeth was just an ordinary subaltern, she maintained special privileges throughout, avoided most of the drudgery of army life and completed only three weeks' training. Her role, similar to that of Hollywood movie stars' wartime service, was entirely morale-boosting.

13 I've been unable to ascertain the exact date of this Sandringham sequence because I have only seen it – many times – in contemporary compilations. But judging by the age of the princesses, it belongs to the latter stages of the war.

14 Woolf, 'Royalty', p. 215.

# 10

## Fashioning the feminine: dress, appearance and femininity in wartime Britain

### PAT KIRKHAM

Keep beneath your Dungaree
dainty femininity!
Wearing while you do your bit
Wolsey undies fairy-knit
Emerging from your Chrysalis
a Wolsey jersey frock is bliss! (Wartime advertisement, Wolsey)

Fashion has never died in this War (*Vogue* 1944)

50 years from now, how shall we look to the women of that day? Perhaps they will laugh at us ... for something called glamour, for slim females with shoulder length manes who became the feminine prototypes of an era (*Vogue* 1944)

This article considers three areas of women's culture traditionally associated with the construction and expression of femininity – dress, body shape and making oneself attractive – which were affected by shortages and government regulations during the Second World War. It challenges claims that there was no such thing as fashion during the war and examines the extent to which female dress was 'masculinised' and, by implication, '*de*-feminised'. Most accounts of women's wartime dress overemphasise the extent to which it was different from what went before, depicting it as uniform, utilitarian and 'masculinised', the latter sometimes crudely attributed to war economies and women taking over male jobs.[1] However, the adoption of elements of male dress by women was neither new nor necessarily linked to wartime; indeed since the 1850s, it has taken place more frequently outside wartime than within and the most commonly quoted examples of the masculinisation of female dress *during* the Second World War – the wearing of trousers, tailored suits and wide shoulders – were present *before* the war. Both civilian dress and female uniforms were based on the fashionable, 'rational', up-to-date dress of the late 1930s which is not regarded as either unfeminine or de-feminised. A modern 'mobile' femininity – a femininity without fussiness, of the sort discussed by Annette Kuhn elsewhere in this anthology in relation to Deanna Durbin and embodied in the star persona of Katherine Hepburn – was strongly in evidence by the late 1930s and featured in much wartime dress, illustrating that there was much more to women's dress in the war years than a simple 'masculinisation'. Although there was some reorganisation and destabilisation of male codes in women's dress during the war, the resultant dress was not considered unfeminine by the standards of the day.

Any discussion of women's dress during the years 1939 to 1945 has to be considered against the widespread wearing of military uniform by men which not only emphasised their masculinity but also created a space for women to adopt more 'masculine' styles without seriously threatening either men or their own 'femininity'.[2] The latter was redefined and re-adjusted but by no means refused or rejected. Women were not seen and did not see themselves as *taking over from men* but rather as *taking on* jobs vacated *by men* or acting as helpers or ancillaries. The status quo was temporarily disrupted but not essentially challenged. Women did not throw away major aspects of their collective culture and individual identities just because there was a war on – indeed, it could be argued that it made them cling to what they knew more tenaciously than before. At the same time as certain aspects of dress became more rational and 'masculine', considerable care was taken to beautify and feminise female appearance and the processes were not necessarily contradictory. Rather than seeing 'masculinisation' and 'feminisation' of dress during the war as necessarily opposing tendencies, related to entry into or retreat from new areas of the labour market, it is more useful to consider a complex continuum wherein elements of the feminine and the masculine each played shifting parts in often delicately balanced dress codes.

'Masculine' dress styles can *accentuate* the femaleness of the wearer and during the war, as at other times, 'masculine' elements were offset by more explicit signifiers of femininity; from waists rendered small to make-up and jewellery, from scarves tied in the hair to the display of ankle and lower leg. No matter how small the signifiers, they inflected the representation of the 'masculine' elements and confirmed gender difference (and generally heterosexuality). This was not a period of androgyny in dress, nor was it one in which women suddenly or simply adopted male dress, or suddenly and differently 'masculinised' their appearance as they took on certain male roles.

[ 153 ]

## Beauty as duty

Fashion and femininity were far from invisible during the Second World War but they were sometimes found in different places and spaces and referred to differently. As such, they are not always readily recognisable to historians using Paris fashions and/or Hollywood glamour as yardsticks. My focus on how fashion, femininity and glamour remained part of women's culture during the war is in no way meant to minimise the many hardships suffered. Indeed, that so many women gave 'beauty' the priority they did during a period of national crisis, indicates the importance attached to it. Despite national austerity the government encouraged women to beautify themselves to maintain morale – not only the morale of the home front but also that of the men in the armed forces.

The government established a committee comprised of the editors of women's magazines and others deemed to represent the interests of women in order to ensure that official 'lines' on matters related to women were put over as powerfully as possible.[3] One result was that 'beauty as duty' became a recurrent theme in features and advertisements in women's magazines and in others such as *Illustrated* and *Picture Post* (which, in 1941, appointed a woman's editor with a brief to cover fashion, beauty and comfort). Femininity was foregrounded during this concerted effort to forge a common outlook and national identity amongst women. What had previously been a private matter became the mainstay of the home front. Morally worthy overtones inflected discussions of how to make a fashionable hat out of odd scraps of material or choose appropriate shades of nail polish for the parade ground or the dance floor. The ideal woman became the one who, in the words of the Yardley advertisement *No Surrender*, honoured 'the subtle bond between good looks and good morale'.[4]

## Body shape

My concerns include body shape, alongside dress, make-up and hairstyles, not least because it was through body shape that I first made sense of clues which had been staring at me from the pages of women's wartime magazines. As a multitude of images and descriptions of body shapes fused into a comprehensive body of evidence, I became intrigued by the neat waists and 'natural' rounded breast shapes of wartime women. I fell to wondering why, if the New Look of 1947 'brought back' the 'naturally' curvaceous figure, I was seeing so much of it in the early 1940s. It seems an obvious enough point but it was an important moment of recognition for me – one which made me ponder on the 'visibility' of evidence. Here is an aspect of women's culture that has been 'hidden from history', but it has not been uniformly hidden. Indeed, body shape and the role of corsets and undergarments in achieving it are staples of orthodox fashion history. Largely because dress is so often discussed without reference to body shape (a topic even more marginalised than clothes within design history) and because the New Look is almost exclusively presented as a return to femininity (with the notable exception of Elizabeth Wilson who writes of the stiffness, sharpness and spikiness of it as 'weirdly masculine'[5]) it has somehow been assumed that the wartime female body was not 'feminine'. But, if the shaping of the waist and an emphasis on the bust are seen as important elements in the process of the construction of the feminine in the late 1940s, and if the eroticism of wearing restrictive garments such as corsets can be highlighted in relation to the New Look, such criteria should at least be considered in relation to wartime body shapes, undergarments and dress.[6]

There was no 'masculinisation' of women's body shape during the Second World War. One of the main features of the 'New Look' fashion, associated with a post-war re-assertion of femininity, namely the small waist, was also a feature of the fashionable wartime body shape. Although it was not so exaggerated as in 1947, the smallness of the waist was given *added emphasis* by the fashionable broader shoulder. Indeed, it could be argued that in order to retain a proportionately similar relationship between 'small' waist and shoulders, the New Look waist needed to be even smaller than the wartime one once the shoulders had been slimmed and softened. Similarly, although the emphasis on the bust was not so great as after 1947, 'natural' full and rounded busts were fashionable during the war and many clothes 'flattered' or drew attention to them. There was certainly no flattening of the bust, as in certain other periods when women's fashions have been 'masculinised'.

Although the skills of 'putting on a front' in terms of appearance were those acquired by most girls as part of learning to be a woman, keeping up appearances was more greatly entrenched in British middle-class culture than it was in that of the working class. Furthermore, beauty as duty discourses conveyed something of the stiff upper lip associated with the British upper classes. The wearing of corsets, however, which was common before the war, suggests more the stiff upright back associated with middle and upper-class modes of comportment as well as with the military. The upright back acted as a metaphor for moral rectitude and fortitude, a theme explored by Jeanne Allen in relation to the Hollywood 'home front' film *Mrs Miniver* (US, 1942).[7]

Some young women started to go without corsets, wearing bras and suspender belts, but the majority of older women continued to regard the corset as essential to their constructions of femininity.[8] Manufacturers and wearers alike claimed that corsets helped women maintain 'feminine' shapes as well as endure longer periods of work and, despite acute shortages of materials, particularly rubber and steel, the government directed valuable resources into the making of corsets. They also offered psychological protection to the wearer against the enemy, giving a degree of 'body armour' more generally associated with the military male.[9] The War Office commissioned corset, designed by the Berlei foundation garment company and issued to women serving in the armed forces, was 'a garment designed to safe-guard women's femininity for the duration'.[10]

## Grooming

'Good grooming', which featured strongly in wartime discourses of appearance, had connotations of the well turned out fashion model as well as of the military (and horses). It was central to 1930s notions of femininity, its precise codes endlessly relayed through women's magazines and advertisements, many of which offered the well-groomed mannequins of Paris and/or female stars of Hollywood as role models. Although one should not underestimate just how 'smart' were many young wage-earning working-class women in the years before and during the war, middle and upper-class women had always had more time and money for grooming. The widespread emphasis on smartness, neatness and cleanliness during the war, therefore, can be viewed as part of a much longer and complex process of the 'improvement' of working-class appearances and the encouragement of more middle-class sartorial sensibilities. Grooming, like 'correct' deportment, accorded well with the new military and quasi-military life of the 'mobile' woman and, together with military codes of self-presentation, was used to contain and discipline the 'untidy' working-class elements in the armed forces.

## Utility, uniformity and individuality

There was much greater choice of attractive clothing within wartime female civilian dress than the term utility implies; it was hated in the dress trade because it was felt to misrepresent their products. Its equation with standardisation and drabness has led to a simplistic picture of wartime dress and, by implication, issues of female identity and femininities. Modish pre-war clothes – including the tailored suit, complete with longer jacket (25 inches) and knee length skirt (16 inches off the ground), slacks, rope-soled sandals and the turban – dictated the terms of wartime dress as much as war economies. Had economy or rationality been the only criteria, shorter jackets, softer shoulders and shorter and straighter skirts would have prevailed.

[ 156 ]

As it was, the economies of scale achieved were within broadly acceptable versions of fashionable dress.

From June 1941 a coupon system was introduced for rationing clothes and in order to ensure that the clothes were fashionable as well as durable, leading designers such as Molyneux (recently returned from Paris) and Hardy Amies were involved in the scheme which aimed at quality affordable clothes for all.[11] Styles were published and prototypes produced. Manufacturers were allocated utility cloth to produce their clothing, 85 per cent of which had to be devoted to the utility scheme. In 1942 a series of Making of Clothes (Restrictions) Orders established regulations relating to the number of pockets, buttonholes and pleats in a skirt, as well as the width of sleeves, hems, seams and collars, but many manufacturers seem to have circumvented them in one way or another. Major 'seasonal' changes of style diminished but we should not forget the changing fashions in colours, patterns, hem lines, accessories, hairstyles and head gear from year to year. As *Vogue* put it in an article titled 'Fashion moves': 'there is plenty going on – all nicely calculated to make new clothes pleasing without putting old ones out of countenance ... War conditions have made developments slow – but sure!'[12] There were pastels for the spring and summer of 1942, greater mix and matching of colours in spring 1943 (featured first in *Vogue* as the 'New Look' and by the more popular magazines later in the year), and 1944 favoured bold vivid contrasts. Manufacturers were allowed to make up to 15 per cent of clothing outside the utility scheme but one of the most remarkable features of wartime dress is the extent to which utility and non-utility clothing resembled each other. It was not that one was fashionable and the other was not: fashionable dress was provided within the utility scheme itself.

In attempting to re-evaluate questions of uniformity, choice and preference in relation to wartime dress and femininity, several points need to be considered. Firstly, within fashion itself the pressures to conform to a particular 'look' tend to make clothing uniform. The variety of choice and the desire to express individuality within the parameters of the fashionable partly mask the similarities between fashion garments but certain features have to be common or else the clothes would not be recognisably fashionable. Secondly, the large-scale production of similar garments during the war needs to be contextualised against the increasingly popular ready-to-wear fashions of the 1930s which were based on standardised ranges and batch or mass production. Even a middle-class purchaser of an expensive Jaeger or Harella garment ran the risk of seeing others like it, though not so great as those who bought the cheaper ranges from the big department stores or through mail order catalogues and Provident clubs.[13] Although during the war choice diminished, great efforts were made to add 'individual touches' to garments and the energy and creativity involved in improvisation marked not only 'femininity' but also a determination to remain fashionable. The 'make do and mend' campaign incorporated more tips and aids to fashionable dressing than its dour name conveys and the popularity of agencies for remodelling clothes also indicates that fashion did not remain static.

Colourful, intricate and often witty small prints enlivened the fabrics used for frocks and blouses and fashionable details were used to ring the changes: beautifully scalloped overlocked collars, white cotton or lace collars, neck ruffles, pin-tucked bodices, artistically positioned buttons, moulded glass buttons, half-belts adding interest at the back, waist and stomach panels in contrasting colours, inventive use of patterns, quilting, piping, gathered work, clever folds, double peplums, bows, back buttoning, rouleau button loops, open work (cut and overstitched), folded and twisted lapels, to name but a few examples from a handful of dresses in Leicester's costume museum alone. The colours were far from drab and the dresses cited above came in a variety of colours including grey and purple, tartan, dark red, maroon, purple, multi-coloured (floral), black and white (stripes), red and white (stripes), yellow (with white spots and black circles), red (with white trims), and purple, green, red, yellow and white mixed together in an exotic print, while the materials include cotton, wool, moyagashel, and synthetic materials including artificial and watered silks. Professional dressmakers had to conform to changing governmental regulations but if a woman was sufficiently skilled and could obtain the fabric, she could make what she wanted at home; many women worked miracles from old curtaining, bedspreads, disused clothes or fabrics sent home by men serving abroad.

### Uniformed dress

One visible sign of a common national female identity was the woman in uniform. The wearing of military uniform by women (500,000 by the end of the war)[14] represented a far greater degree of the 'masculinisation' of female dress than did civilian garments such as utility suits. Nevertheless, it remained female dress. What took place was not the adoption of male uniforms by women so much as a transposition of elements of the male suited uniform to women's suits to form a female suited uniform. Military uniforms (rather like school uniforms) were such that there was never any question of gender confusion in terms of the appearance of male and female personnel; just as the women's auxiliary services were clearly differentiated from the male services, so too were the uniforms. The dialogue about power relations within and between genders that women's wearing of suits produced shifted during the war, especially when some women went into military uniform, but the main issues about women wearing elements of 'male' dress had been well aired before 1939.

The effects of women wearing clothes that visually referenced those of the male military were rather like those which result from women cross-dressing more generally. Indeed, the effect was often to *foreground* rather than blur or deny gender difference. Uniforms that retained an emphasis on the waist, did not negate the bust, and revealed the legs from the knee downwards, while revealing curls or rolled hair beneath hats, highlighted femininity. To note that female uniformed dress lay within the parameters of fashionable femininity is not to deny that the uniforms offered practical utilitarian clothing or that they related to male uniforms. Here was a version of rational dress, campaigned for by dress reformers and modernists since the turn of the century, which in its *apparent* emphasis on utility and form following function rather than fashion, signalled the wearer as thoroughly modern – the latter adding to its cachet. Nevertheless there was considerable 'subversion' of women's uniformed dress to make it more fashionable and attractive and this was not always done by 'feminising' it; the case of using government supplied sanitary towels to add extra padding to the jacket shoulders of women's uniforms is my favourite example of the further 'masculinisation' of an already 'masculinised' shoulder in order to render it more fashionable.[15] As one WAAF said 'we might have been in uniform but we were still women, still interested in fashion and still wanted to be attractive'.[16] The 'masculine' feature was emphasised to make it better conform to female fashions and fashionable femininities; in other words, some signifiers of the 'masculine' acted as central features of certain types of fashionable femininity.

Some uniforms were thought more attractive than others and many women based their choice of service and/or occupation on the apparel.[17] WRNS (Women's Royal Navy Service) and WAAF (Women's Auxiliary Air Force) uniforms were generally more popular than that of the ATS (Auxiliary Territorial Service) but that gained status after Princess Elizabeth's association with it. Civilian conventions of gendered dressing were observed; women wore a skirt, stockings and make-up as well as a jacket which was cut differently to the male one, and hairstyles were markedly different from those of male soldiers. Women's uniforms, like those of nurses, did not include trousers. Exceptions were made for certain types of work including lorry or ambulance driving, flying, mechanical and other dirty jobs. Trousers were included in the uniform of the ATS, the female director of which had some say in the design of the 'smart, workmanlike uniform', but the trousers were for specific jobs only and women were not allowed to wear them off-duty.[18] Like recalcitrant personnel, trousers were restricted to base. WRNS working clothes included bell-bottomed trousers and jerseys but these too were restricted to base. Women in the WAAF who worked part of the time in the open were issued with a blue serge 'battledress' top and trousers. Some thought the combination of the 'softer' battledress top and uniform skirt the most 'feminine' and flattering combination and, despite the fact that it was banned, risked wearing that particular 'mix and match' to dances.[19]

It was because they represented 'maleness' more than any other item of the male uniform that trousers were the only part of it deemed inappropriate for female dress uniform.[20] Military hats, shirts and ties were accommodated more easily because they were more established within women's pre-war dress practices. Shirts and ties were part of the neat school uniforms for girls on which female military uniforms were partly based and service hats could be seen as masculinised versions of an object which when worn by women signified smartness and respectability, even chic. The various branches of the women's forces had two hats: one for duty wear and a more becoming one for off-duty days, again suggesting the more extreme references to male dress were confined to barracks.

Civilian women ambulance drivers, air raid wardens and dispatch riders were also allowed to wear trousers but some chose to wear skirts with stout shoes or wellingtons, even if their work took them to bomb-damaged sites.[21] Photographs show that some of the women working from a Chelsea garage in 1940 who donned boiler suits signalled their femininity and individuality by tying their hair up in fashionable styles with scarves and turbans, wearing a patterned scarf at the neck or, in one case, extremely smart two-tone 'co-respondent' shoes.[22] The occupation which more than any other signified femininity – nursing – was considered too sacrosanct for any changes to be made to the uniform. Redolent with references to Florence Nightingale and wartime nursing, its symbolic functions outweighed others. Nurses were expected to attend to the most gruesome injuries at scenes of great devastation and climb over heaps of dirty rubble in white aprons, stockings that laddered easily and skirts that, though slightly longer than the fashionable knee length, were far less practical than trousers.[23]

An additional uniformity for women was achieved by skirt hems being a uniform distance from the ground (16 inches), no matter what the height of the wearer. In 1939 16 inches from the ground was the fashionable length but by 1943 it was 17 inches[24] and it was fairly common practice for women in the services to surreptitiously roll up their skirts at the waist to achieve a more fashionable hem length. There was even greater incentive to roll up the skirt and assert one's individuality when on leave and the illustration from *Punch* 1942[25] (see Figure 2, p. 25) of a woman on leave indicates the letting down of hair, a tighter waist, broader shoulder and a shorter flared skirt to be preferred indicators of fashionable femininity. What is fascinating about the parody of the neat on-duty woman is that the cartoonist radically altered the uniform: the shoulders are softened, the waist thickened and the shape of the skirt changed (from the regulation slight flare to straight) in order to enhance the 'transformation'. In January 1943, *Woman* implored service women on leave not to 'hitch up the skirt ... by turning it over at the peter-sham waistband. It makes the skirt look far too short for the uniform and makes it full and baggy over the hips.'[26] Many women aimed at a little of the 'on leave' look when on duty. They risked punishment by doing it, by alter-ing their uniforms so as to obtain a better fit or by having their hair 'too long and wearing too much make-up' in their attempts to assert their more glam-orous versions of femininity over those imposed by their senior officers.

## Cosmetics

By the outbreak of war, make-up had become so central to fashionable fem-ininities that the government was unable to cease production of cosmetics. Supplies of raw ingredients fell dramatically but demand remained high for both legal and illegal cosmetics. In an effort to maintain morale certain high-grade face powders were reserved for key women workers in the muni-tions industry[27] and the labyrinthine governmental regulations were cir-cumvented, most notably when cosmetics were manufactured and distributed as medical items.[28] Nella Last described her delight at finding a range of cosmetics on sale on the streets of Blackpool in 1942, and a year later she looked like a miser at her 'little cherished hoard of perfumes, lip-sticks and powder'.[29] Fifty years later, women still recall the excitement when supplies of well known brands such as Coty came into the shops.[30] Many women who regarded it as immoral to obtain other items illegally had few scruples when it came to cosmetics or stockings, for which they paid quite high prices; 'we didn't think of it as black market, it was more like, well, we had worked and saved for it, so why not?'[31] The general sanctioning of the illegal purchasing of such items central to women's identities and feminini-ties suggests that they were somehow re-classified in people's minds as necessities or at least as necessary luxuries.

## Stockings

Another crucial signifier of femininity was stockings. Legs signified femi-ninity and not since the 1920s had fashion revealed so much of them. This was the leg of the active woman and carried connotations of modernity and movement. Yet it was also a sexualised leg; the most sought-after stockings were fully-fashioned seamed ones with some women paying up to 15/- a pair on the illegal market[32] and part of the popularity of the American GIs was that they came bearing silk stockings and nylons (the most up-to-date female legwear, invented by Dupont chemists at about the time Europe went to war). Flesh-coloured lisle stockings were available but they were thick, sensible and generally considered un-sexy. Manufacturers desperately tried to come up with a more popular alternative stocking. In 1941, for example, magazines proclaimed vividly coloured lace wool stockings 'all the thing' and new ranges of mesh, crepe and rayon stockings appeared.[33] Ankle socks were a cheaper alternative.[34] Some younger women wore them with panache, making a fashion accessory out of a necessity, but generally they were regarded as a poor second best to sheer stockings and were far less popular than is often supposed.

Another alternative to stockings was to go bare-legged but that was considered as somewhat less than respectable, especially by middle-class women, besides proving cold in winter. As with ankle socks, it was the younger and/or working-class women who tended to go bare-legged, particularly those who could tan their legs in the summer sun. Many spent their money on one of a variety of leg paints available and hoped, usually in vain, that they would not streak. Some used gravy browning which attracted flies in the summer heat while others found their 'tan' rubbed off on clothes and bedclothes. To complete the disguise, 'seams' were drawn up the backs of legs with eye-brow pencil.[35]

### Shoes

Contrary to popular understanding, there were few flat shoes for women during the Second World War. There were plenty of shoes suitable for the 'mobile' woman but they usually came with a wedge or platform, re-shaping the calf and ankle into what was considered a more attractive shape by being higher at the heel than the toe. 'High-heeled' shoes as such, were generally not overly high and were usually, but by no means exclusively, reserved for evening wear and special occasions. Worn with seamed sheer stockings, they added instant glamour to many an outfit. There was a far greater difference between utility and non-utility shoes than was the case with clothes. Utility shoes came in black, brown and navy only – although it has to be said that these were popular colours for shoes, especially with less well-off people who could not afford several (or even two) pairs – whereas those made outside the scheme came in a panoply of colours and were used like scarves and other accessories to enliven plain outfits. One woman remembers the shoes she bought in wartime London as more interesting than at any subsequent period.[36] Reasonably well-off, she bought crocodile skin lace-ups and five pairs of suede shoes – in emerald green, royal blue, black, deep purple (with small Louis heels) and navy blue. The latter pair came with leather flaps and tied with an assortment of different coloured laces (an easy and cheap way of ringing the changes) or a tiny handkerchief or scarf. Joyce, Brevitt and Dolcis advertisements for the war years all show shoes in a variety of brilliant shades.

### Hats, headscarves and hair

Social regulations related to female dress became somewhat less formal during the war and even the customary wearing of hats in church was

8   Cover of *Woman*, 14 November 1942

relaxed. Hats were never rationed and I am constantly surprised when studying contemporary photographs at just how many women continued to wear them – when queuing for food, for the cinema or going away to join the armed forces. At the same time, the headscarf established itself as one of the most popular fashions in headwear of the war. Inexpensive and yet stylish, it epitomised the dialectic between high fashion and popular use in wartime female dress.

Hair was a major coder of gender difference and a range of attractive hairstyles were used by women to mark their femininity and maintain morale. Long hair meant that instant glamour could be achieved by letting down shoulder-length tresses which had been rolled up for everyday work and home duties. Despite a shift to jobs and responsibilities formerly undertaken by men, there was no move to copy male hairstyles. It is true that the Liberty Cut, the V-ingle and the Regimental Curl were more rational, 'modern' and shorter styles than the more popular longer glamorous ones, but they were a far cry from the Eton crop of the 1920s and far from masculine.[37] In the forces long hair had to be rolled up to the regulation two inches above the collar and many women were disciplined, or ran the risk of it, because they wore their hair longer than allowed.[38] As the war went on, longer hair became even more popular after Veronica Lake appeared with flowing locks in *I Wanted Wings* (US 1943).[39]

### Underwear and nightwear

Scarcity enhanced rather than reduced the significance of strongly female-coded objects such as alluring 'feminine' underwear, which was hoarded for high days and holidays. So precious were her three pairs of silk stockings and satin and crepe de Chine underwear, that the eminently practical and sensible Nella Last stored them, rather than more obviously useful or valuable objects, in a 'safe' reinforced corner under her stairs during periods of bombing.[40] Many women had been brought up to consider underclothing as important as outer clothing, and found it difficult to shed these old markers of respectability and wear shabby underwear in order to have nicer outerwear. Product advertisements stressed the necessity of pretty underwear to feeling good, feeling 'feminine' and keeping up morale. Even in the coldest winters many women, particularly younger ones, resolutely refused to wear 'sensible' warm underwear because they did not find it sufficiently 'feminine'. For many working and service women, no matter how unflattering or utilitarian the outer garment, 'true femininity' was maintained in the layer that lay closest to the 'real person', to the body. It was not just that woolly vests and service issue knickers were 'passion killers' in their lack of direct erotic appeal but that the *absence* of a particular kind of delicate underclothing (associated with both a delicate femininity and a sexual allure) suggested an absence of femininity. Lingerie (the word itself implying so much more than underwear), which included nightgowns and negligees, was in particular demand for trousseaus and many brides had to choose between new outer garments and sensual lingerie for their honeymoons as they juggled to make the coupons go round.

'Feminine' underwear in delicate fabrics with lace and/or embroidery became increasingly scarce and expensive as the war wore on. At the top end of the market, the most exquisite silk lingerie was available throughout the war in exclusive small shops, particularly those in the West End of London.[41] The majority of women supplemented their pre-war garments with ones bought early in the war but the shortage of materials such as elastic meant that many well-loved undergarments 'died'. Items were either replaced by home-made (or dressmaker-made) items using the ubiquitous parachute silk, rayon or one of the other new and cheaper silky artificial fabrics, delicate curtaining or fabric taken from old dance dresses or by items from a range of six basic styles offered in a variety of colours and fabrics under the utility scheme from 1941.[42] Although fancy lace and other trimmings were officially banned, extant garments reveal that the regulations were flouted. An extremely well-made utility petticoat (with adjustable straps) and matching french knickers in pale blue artificial silk, for example, has lace insets,[43] and home-made lingerie was often lovingly embroidered and trimmed with lace or tiny buttons removed from worn-out garments.

In the 8 March 1941 issue of *Picture Post*, the cover of which showed a woman trying on a new spring hat with the help of a modish milliner's assistant, Anne Scott Jones argued that as opportunities for dressing up in public diminished, they were partly transferred to the private sphere, particularly the bedroom where women could satisfy their passion for 'dressing up after dark' – or dressing down in the case of some of the more scanty items. In one of her first pronouncements on women's issues, this newly appointed women's editor of a very respectable magazine featured nightwear, half of which was diaphanous and modelled in pin-up style poses, in an article which acknowledged women's desires to 'dress up' in sexually alluring clothes (see Figure 9). She also featured more practical yet fashionable and, in their own ways, 'feminine' nightclothes (some of which were more appropriate for an evening in bed with a good book rather than a good lover), revealing a sensitivity to the often abrupt switches of 'costume' in the wartime masquerade – in this case between the 'practical' working woman who, married or otherwise, slept on her own when lovers were away at war and the sexually active woman. At a time when it was virtually impossible to address female sexuality directly in a public forum, the article used these two different types of nightwear as well as illustrations and double entendre to reference not only dual and multiple femininities but also sexuality and dressing up for sex. The practical cosy 'envelope' suit and the one with the pixie hood referenced adolescent and pre- if not a-sexual femininities and look as if they were designed for the adolescent (and older) Deanna Durbin fans discussed elsewhere in this anthology. Neither was easy to get out of, in contrast to the more brazenly named 'Next to Nothing' garments about which Scott Jones pulled few punches, stating 'there's nothing cute about these nightgowns', and describing them as 'essentially languorous ... very sheer, very elegant ... thin, filmy ... low-cut ... the "undress" type of night-gown'. Any article or advertisement which offered a range of images was, of course, likely to be plundered by women in a variety of ways not necessarily intended by fashion writers or product manufacturers. This fashion feature offered, more openly than most, clothes to assist individual readers in the construction of more than one type of femininity; it offered, like Madonna today, more than one way of dressing up.

### Glamour and special occasion dress

It has been argued that Hollywood-style glamour was out for the duration of austerity[44] but the desire to be glamorous did not abruptly end with the beginning of war, particularly in the case of younger women. Glamour did not disappear from women's vocabulary and, within the changing defini-tions of appropriate femininity, there were sanctioned spaces for glamour in real life as well as in women's magazines, some of which, at times, fore-grounded what approximated to movie glamour – even if it took on more makeshift qualities as the war progressed. The official stress on beauty as duty fed rather than restrained women's more glamorous inclinations and fantasies even while they were restricted by material shortages and pressures not to indulge in overly ostentatious display.

Glamour took on different material forms on occasions such as wed-dings, honeymoons, 'big dances' or when a lover or husband returned on leave. It was on these special occasions that a variety of femininities gave way to more glamorous, sometimes overtly sexy ones which were sanctioned and celebrated – particularly in the case of honeymoons and men home on leave – when beauty as duty and sexual duty were subtly inter-linked. But women's wartime magazines recognised the varied roles women were expected to play and what that implied in terms of appropriate presenta-tions of self. Articles regularly addressed a multi-faceted woman; the service woman, for example, was assumed to want at least three different basic pre-sentations of self (on duty, off duty and on leave), as was the factory worker (work, home and leisure).

A garment which signified luxury and added instant glamour to any

**9**    Practicality and glamour, *Picture Post*, 8 March 1941

outfit in the 1940s was the fur coat. Rather than dismissing such items as extravagant and superfluous, the Board of Trade encouraged their purchase because of savings made on fabrics which could then be used elsewhere, particularly for military uniforms.[45] There was a steady trade in furs, new and second hand; women with 'new' money and little else to spend it on often conspicuously displayed what others thought of as brash by purchasing fur coats.[46] Fur coats were planned for the utility range and were available towards the end of the war. Popular with the newly demobbed – one woman spent all of her £28 demob pay plus clothing coupons on a Beaver Lamb coat – they saw many women through the next few years of austerity.[47] They were also one of the items most frequently borrowed for that extra special occasion, usually a dance or a winter wedding.

Dances were a central feature of wartime social life, and for the more special of these the women's magazines agreed that an extra touch of glamour was needed. It was for these that the special dress should be bought, begged or borrowed, if not made or made-over at home. Dances were arenas for the display of the most eye-catching jewellery, new hairstyle, hair adornments, corsages on the bodice, sequinned snoods, velvet capes (made from old curtains if you had them), and your best high heels. According to 'Look

10  Cover of *Home Notes*, 18 December 1943

your best for him', published in *Home Notes* in December 1943, the glamour necessary to get your man at the big Christmas dance involved 'exaggerating your makeup ideas quite a lot – using more lipstick, accenting your eyes with just that faintest touch of mascara, using a heavy "film type" powder foundation to give your skin that matt velvet look. The great thing to remember, if you want to look attractive and interesting on the dance floor, is to *dramatise yourself. Forget about being a "nice girl" for a while.*[48]

11    Beryl Lewis and Michael Brooshooft, 18 May 1943

That such an overt emphasis on glamour came from one of the cosier, more family- than fashion-orientated of the cheaper women's magazines reinforces the suggestions (also raised by the *Picture Post* article on nightwear) that we need to re-assess the extent to which more overt forms of glamour were considered unpatriotic in wartime Britain. Furthermore, we need to recognise that context was crucial in signifying whether or not an article of clothing or adornment was regarded as being on the right side of glamorous or denoted the 'easy' woman. Seamed stockings, heavy make-up, exotic hats and diaphanous nightwear all potentially put respectable women at risk of censorious remarks if their attire were read 'wrongly'. The orchid hat of the famous wartime VD poster is regularly and correctly cited as having 'sensual connotations', connotations which are spelled out in the accompanying text about 'The easy girl-friend' who spreads VD.[49] However, very similar hats, with exotic flowers and veiling, adorned the heads of virginal fictional heroines in women's magazines and novels and also of real life women, virginal or otherwise, particularly at weddings.[50]

For those women not able to marry in the 'traditional' long white dress and veil, the choice was usually a suit with hats, sheer stockings, high heels and bouquets adding glamour. Yet for many women to have a 'white wedding' was especially important and it is remarkable just how many women managed to walk down the aisle in a 'traditional' wedding dress during this period of national austerity. It symbolised a past of peace and security; normality in the midst of disruption. The refusal of women to let 'Hitler' interfere with their dream of a white wedding reflected some of the deeper defiances, resolution and resistance that kept them going the rest of the time.[51] Some women were fortunate enough to buy material before war broke out, others borrowed dresses. Two Leicestershire women, one of whom was married on the last day of peace and the other shortly after war was declared, both lent out their wedding dresses throughout the war.[52] Beryl Lewis, who lived in Hampshire, managed to find some non-couponed pale cream cotton curtain lace which was made into a dress worn over an underslip made from a piece of satin given to her as a wedding present (see Figure 11). Someone else gave her some veiling. It was white, the dress cream and so the veiling was sent to Pullers of Perth for dyeing. Not terribly well-off, this lower-middle-class daughter of a foreman engineer had good 'clothes sense' and knew what she wanted for her 'dream day'.[53]

## Conclusion

I have attempted to suggest some new ways of considering issues of femininity, dress and female appearance and glamour during the Second World War. Despite all the hardships, what they looked like remained a central concern for millions of British women throughout the war. Far from being ignored, fashion and femininity remained firmly on the female agenda. The adoption of late 1930s fashionable styles which incorporated 'masculine' elements into stylish women's clothes did not necessarily mean either a de-feminisation or a 'masculinisation' but rather a continuing feminising of the self through attention to one's looks and dress. Aspects of the masculine as played out in women's fashionable dress heightened its chic and did not necessarily lead to confusion as to the gender of the wearer. I hope to have shown that 'femininity' was not an absolute. Femininity needs to be considered as a plural term; there were many wartime femininities, some of which were produced, in part at least, through 'masculine' forms. The interplay between 'masculine' and 'feminine' was largely within the terms of reference of fashionable femininities. The wearing of trousers and/or wide shoulders during the war did not necessarily or simply signify the assumption of male power, or even the desire for it, just as the wearing of the longer full-skirted New Look in 1947, complete with softer shoulders and wasp waist, did not necessarily or simply mean that individual women suddenly abandoned the entire social and ideological frameworks within which they had previously operated. As one working-class woman put it:

> I might have desperately wanted – and got – a dress like I saw on the pictures or like Princess Margaret's New Look ones but that didn't mean that I stopped thinking the royal family a bunch of parasites or that we – the working class that is – deserved attractive clothes and glamorous dresses a million more times than them, any more than it meant I had stopped thinking that women were the salt of the earth – every bit as good as men – and should have decent jobs and equal pay.[54]

Rather than viewing the war years as a dull backwater in terms of female self-expression, femininity and fashion, it seems appropriate fifty years on to acknowledge the extent to which those issues remained part of the lives of ordinary women during the years 1939 to 1945.

### Notes

1 See Jane Ashelford, 'Utility fashion', in *CC41 Utility Furniture and Fashion 1941–1951*, catalogue, Geffrye Museum (London, ILEA, 1974), p. 33. The better accounts of women's wartime dress are Lou Taylor and Elizabeth Wilson, *Through the Looking Glass* (London, BBC Books, 1989), esp. chapter 4; Elizabeth Wilson, *Adorned in Dreams: Fashion and Modernity* (London, Virago Press, 1985), pp. 80–2, 219; Elizabeth Ewing, *History of Twentieth Century Fashion* (London, Batsford, 1986), esp. chapter 7; Joan Heath, ' "Fashion by government order": fact or fiction?', unpublished undergraduate thesis (History of Art and Design and Complementary Studies), North Staffordshire Polytechnic (now Staffordshire University), 1988, p. 29, and Peter McNeil, '"Put your best face forward": the impact of the Second World

War on British dress', *Journal of Design History*, Vol. 6 No. 4 (1994), pp. 283–99. Heath and Maggie Wood, *'We Wore What We'd Got': Women's Clothes in World War II* (Warwickshire Books, Warwickshire County Council, 1989) (an oral history compilation) redress the balance and challenge what has become an orthodoxy in dress history. It is particularly important when dealing with issues of dress and appearance not to let personal and contemporary (1990s) tastes cut across contemporary (*c.* 1939–45) views of what was and was not attractive. One problem with aesthetic judgements in relation to the years 1939–45 is that a great deal of what fell well within the parameters of fashionable femininity and afforded women the complex pleasures derived from owning and wearing clothes has been dismissed as unattractive, unfashionable and old-fashioned from the late 1940s until fairly recently. Despite and because of the 'post-modern' raidings of history by dress designers, the re-use and re-working of styles and images from the years *c.* 1939–45 in recent fashion 'revivals', together with other factors such as the wearing of stout, clumpy 'male' footwear by young women, have probably done as much as feminist scholarship to open minds and eyes to the attractiveness of such dress and the complex negotiations of the 'masculine' and the 'feminine' in relation to fashion and femininity.

2  Lisa Tickner, 'Women and trousers: unisex clothing and sex role changes in the twentieth century', in *Leisure in the twentieth century* (Design History Conference Papers, The Design Council, 1976), p. 62.

3  Jo Spence, 'What did you do in the war mummy? Class and gender in images of women', in *Photography/Politics One* (London, Photography Workshop, 1977), p. 33. For a discussion of 'beauty as duty' see Pat Kirkham, 'Beauty and duty: keeping up the (home) front', in Pat Kirkham and David Thoms (eds), *War Culture: Social Change and Changing Experience in World War Two Britain* (London, Lawrence and Wishart, 1995).

4  July 1942. Cited in Jane Waller and Michael Vaughan-Rees, *Women in Wartime: The Role of Women's Magazines 1939–1945* (London, Macdonald and Co. (Publishers) Ltd, 1987), p. 102.

5  Elizabeth Wilson, *Adorned in Dreams: Fashion and Modernity* (London, Virago Press, 1985), pp. 44–6.

6  My concerns went far beyond a regret that this evidence had been ignored. Because women's bodies were involved it seemed almost sacrilegious to ignore evidence related to what had been flesh, bones and blood. I found myself wondering why we feminist historians had been able to find living sensual bodies beneath the clothes of the late 1940s but had not looked beneath those of five years earlier. It was as if the 'real' bodies of wartime women were nothing more than the dummies on which their clothes now hang in museums and second-hand shops. In the rush to ask properly important questions about working in munitions factories, evacuation, making do and mending, living through the Blitz and changing sexual practices, we forgot the culturally shaped physical bodies of our subjects. For me, once 'seen' these women's bodies refused to become invisible again.

7  Allen's paper on this topic is available from the Education Department, The British Film Institute. Although I do not accept Allen's contention that 'the stiff upper back' was gendered as feminine (partly because of the strong military associations and partly because women used the corset to achieve the same degree of bodily control and moral rectitude as men, thereby suggesting that it was the *corset* and not the stiff upper back which was gendered), it played a part in representing 'true womanhood' as a fortress that could never be conquered.

8  *Woman's Magazine*, November 1940, cited in Caroline Lang, *Keep Smiling Through: Women in the Second World War* (Cambridge, Cambridge University Press, 1989), p. 100.

9  See Klaus Theweleit, *Male Fantasies*, 2 vols (Minneapolis, 1987 and 1989 respectively), especially Vol. 1.

10  *Picture Post*, 2 March 1940, p. 26.

11  See note 1 for works outlining the utility scheme.

12  *Vogue*, December 1943, quoted in Heath, '"Fashion by government order"', p. 28.

13  Taylor and Wilson, *Through the Looking Glass*, pp. 95–102; Ewing, *History of Twentieth Century Fashion*, pp. 119–38.

14  Eric Hopkins, *The Rise and Decline of the English Working Classes 1918–1990: A Social History* (London, Weidenfeld and Nicolson, 1991), p. 60.

15  Gladys Pate, Interview, December 1993.

16  *Ibid.*

17  Lang, *Keep Smiling Through*, pp. 34–6; Waller and Vaughan-Rees, *Women in Wartime*, pp. 58–62; Wood and Wood, *'We Wore What We'd Got'*, pp. 40–3; and interviews with Elsie Lyall, Beryl Brooshoft and Gladys Pate (who decided to join the WAAF after seeing the film *The First of the Few* (1942)).

18  Lang, *Keep Smiling Through*, p. 34; *Woman*, 29 May 1943 (Lifebuoy Toilet Soap advertisement); and Anne Coleing (Interview with Linda Coleing, to whom I am grateful for the information about her mother and the ATS uniform).

19  Joan Beech, *One Waaf's War* (Tunbridge Wells, D. J. Costello, 1989), pp. 45, 133.

20  Tickner, 'Women and trousers', p. 56.

21  Arthur Marwick, *The Home Front: The British and the Second World War* (London, Thames and Hudson, 1976), plate 69.

22  Ewing, *History of Twentieth Century Fashion*, p. 140, plate 143.

23  *Ibid.*, plate 144.

24  *Vogue*, September 1939 and *Woman*, 2 January 1943, respectively.

25  'John and Joan', *Punch*, 2 September 1942.

26  *Woman*, 2 January 1943.

27  Ashelford, 'Utility fashion', p. 33.

28  E. L. Hargreaves and M. M. Gowing, *The History of the Second World War: Civil Industry and Trade* (London, HMSO, 1952), p. 533. See also Angus Calder, *The People's War: Britain 1939–45* (London, Panther, 1971), pp. 436–7.

29  Richard Broad and Suzie Fleming (eds), *Nella Last's War: A Mother's Diary 1939–45* (London, Sphere Books Ltd, 1981), pp. 200–66.

30  Beryl Brooshooft (nee Lewis), Interview, June 1994.

31  Cited in Heath, '"Fashion by government order"', p. 23.

32  *Ibid.*, p. 23.

33  *Ibid.*, pp. 11–12.

34  In 1942 they cost 2/- per pair as opposed to 3/6d for stockings (legal prices). See Celia Fremlin, *War Factory: Mass-Observation* (London, The Cresset Library, 1987), pp. 93–4.

35  Wood and Wood, *'We Wore What We'd Got'*, p. 13. The countless variations on this theme constitute some of my favourite stories of women's wartime 'beauty' practices. Since a child I have been fascinated by the sheer inventiveness and creativity of this period; some of my earliest memories are of my mother and her friends endlessly recalling the lengths to which they had gone to be smart and glamorous (their words) during the war, including my mother using old billiards chalk as eyeshadow – an act considered somewhat daring even at the time of re-telling in the 1950s (at

least in our Northumbrian pit village).

36 Heath, "'Fashion by government order"', p. 35.

37 Waller and Vaughan-Rees, *Women in Wartime*, pp. 82–3; *Picture Post*, 22 June 1940 (for Kemt Hair Lustre Restorer advertisement).

38 Beech, *One Waaf's War*, p. 133; Wood and Wood, *'We Wore What We'd Got'*, p. 42; Christine Jope-Slade, 'Cold Cream Hour', *Woman and Beauty*, July 1942, p. 52.

39 Wood and Wood, *'We Wore What We'd Got'*, p. 44.

40 Broad and Fleming (eds), *Nella's Last War*, p. 128.

41 Heath, "'Fashion by government order"', p. 21.

42 Calder, *The People's War*, p. 23.

43 Heath, "'Fashion by government order"', p. 21. Heath is good on the dialectic between 'make do and mend' and 'fashion'.

44 See Antonia Lant's essay in this anthology and her *Blackout: Reinventing Women for Wartime British Cinema* (Princeton, Princeton University Press, 1991), p. 60. Calder, by contrast, argued that it was patriotic to be chic (*The People's War*, p. 435).

45 Elizabeth Ewing, *Fur in Dress* (London, Batsford, 1981), p. 131. Cited in McNeil, "'Put your best face forward"', note 68.

46 Elsie Lyall, Interview, December 1993; Broad and Fleming (eds), *Nella Last's War*, p. 93.

47 Wood and Wood, *'We Wore What We'd Got'*, p. 70.

48 *Home Notes*, 18 December 1943 (my emphasis).

49 Illustrated in McNeil, "'Put your best face forward"', p. 291. The poster was designed by Reginald Mount in 1943–44. See also Antonia Lant in this anthology.

50 Raynes Minns, *Bombers and Mash: The Domestic Front 1939–45* (London, Virago, 1980), p. 177, top illustration.

51 Elsie Lyall and Beryl Brooshooft, Interviews, December 1993 and June 1994 respectively.

52 Pat Kirkham, *Wedding Belles*, exhibition catalogue (Leicester Polytechnic, 1988).

53 Brooshooft, 1994. The dress, which she has to this day (and it still fits), was not only fashionably softened under the bust but came with two sets of sleeves – the long ones for the wedding and very formal occasions, the short 'puff' sleeves for dances. It was not only women who wanted to look glamorous on their wedding day. A former service man (Mr Fenn) told me of the efforts gone to in his unit to ensure that he had a dashing dress uniform to get married in – not all of which he was entitled to wear. Interview, December 1993.

54 Interview, February 1976, with Gladys Dodd, my mother, to whom this article is dedicated with love and gratitude.

# Part three

Nationalising femininity:
the case of British cinema

12    At the boundaries of class in *Millions Like Us*

# 11

## Cinema culture and femininity in the 1930s

ANNETTE KUHN

Gracie Fields's gritty but upbeat first feature film *Sally in Our Alley* (1931) is set in the slums of London's East End. In it the Fields character – Sally of the title – rescues a motherless young woman, Florrie (Florence Desmond), from a brutal and violent father. But Florrie, unaccustomed to decent treatment, repays her benefactress with dishonesty and deceit. 'There's a devil inside me', explains Florrie: when people show kindness towards her, she says, 'it makes me want to smash things'. Florrie nevertheless contrives to find some escape from her joyless existence in the fantasy world of cinema. She spends what little money she comes by (not always honestly) on film magazines and going to the pictures. She hones her skills of deception by imitating the acting styles of her favourite stars. Her pathetic dreams are exposed most poignantly in a scene in which, sitting at Sally's dressing table in grubby and ragged petticoat, she tries to copy Greta Garbo's make-up techniques from a picture feature in a magazine. But Florrie's eventual redemption through Sally's generosity and goodness involves an exorcism of her obsession with cinema, and an acceptance of the limitations – and the less glamorous if more communitarian pleasures – of 'real' life.

A similar motif surfaces in a later Gracie Fields vehicle, *Sing As We Go* (1934). When the mill where she works closes down and she is thrown out of a job, Grace Platt (Fields) travels to Blackpool and gets work in a boarding house. She shares an attic room with the skivvy, Gladys, whose last act before settling down to sleep at night is to moon over portraits of her favourite film stars. 'Come on, hurry up. Put that light out, and take Clark Gable with you', chides Gracie, indulgently.

In both *Sally in Our Alley* and *Sing As We Go* a preoccupation with films and film stars is represented as a silly, even as a damaging (but nonetheless happily a passing) obsession. In both films, too, the foolishness of the starstruck girls is set against the no-nonsense big-sisterliness of our Gracie. It is as if in the characters she plays Gracie Fields the film star absolves herself from involvement in the peculiar fascinations cinema held for its – and her – fans, while the pitiable and slightly ridiculous figures of Florrie and Gladys stand as embodiments of the typical contemporary film fan. That the impulses which drew audiences into cinemas can be subject to such mockery within popular cinema itself suggests that an ambivalent, if not a negative, attitude towards the pleasures of this popular medium was not confined to the guardians of 'high' culture in 1930s Britain.

Cinema has never enjoyed greater popularity than in the 1930s, when Britain had the highest annual per capita cinema attendance in the world, and film-going held centre stage among favourite leisure activities, playing an integral part in the everyday lives of millions. The editors of *Mass-Observation at the Movies* suggest that 'while a large proportion of the population at large went to the cinema occasionally, the enthusiasts were young, working class, urban, and more often female than male'.[1] The starstruck servant girls of the popular imagination translate as the young, urban, working-class females of the social historians' account. However characterised, though, these young women are all undergoing the passage from girlhood to womanhood: they are growing up, in process of being formed. Like Florrie, with her film magazine propped by the mirror, they are experimenting with identities, with ways of being women. Alongside their dreams, they must negotiate family ties and obligations, school or work, friendships, and the anxieties and pleasures of consumerism and courtship. For these young film-goers of the 1930s, adolescence is constrained and shaped in specific ways by circumstances of social class, gender relations, and economics. The enthusiasms of the typical 1930s film fan may be understood as a moment – shortlived, undoubtedly – of aspiration and possibility, a small space of imagining and yearning, to be tolerated, and finally to be dismissed, as merely a passing phase.

At some level, we know who the keenest cinema-goers of the 1930s were, and even perhaps something of their tastes and preferences. We can speculate, too, about what was at stake for them, affectively, in their enthusiasms. But even so, there is a very real sense in which we know them not at all. Their moment as fans lies within living memory; yet as women, their voices remain unheard in historical record: such accounts of popular cinema culture in 1930s Britain as exist are rarely told from the standpoint of the 'ordinary' cinema-goer. As cultural icons, Florrie and Gladys may be noticeable enough; but as cultural producers, they remain invisible. In such circumstances, perhaps the best the historian can do is to ask the right questions.

What did the typical British film fan of the 1930s bring to her cinema-going? What did she take from it? How did it fit in with other areas of her daily life – with school, work, leisure, friendship, courtship? In what ways was she formed by all this, not simply in the activity of 'going to the pictures', but through all of the various cultural competences and social discourses surrounding, and at whatever remove hinging upon, that activity? And how, finally, might such apparently mundane activities connect with the broader, the contradictory, the fluctuating social conditions of 1930s Britain: economic depression and the birth of consumer culture at home, mounting world crisis and ultimately outbreak of war in Europe?[2] Such questions are a great deal easier to pose than to answer; although to pose them is in itself to challenge not only the silencing of 'ordinary' women's voices in standard historical accounts, but also the virtual absence of the social audience (as against the implied spectator) from studies of film reception, historical and contemporary.

I propose here to begin to tackle some of these issues by taking a brief look at discourses around femininity at work within, and produced by, the cinema culture of 1930s Britain, and by tracking changes in these over the course of the decade. To take cinema culture as a starting point implies a concern with the *reception* of films; and indeed my premiss is that, in the moment of reception, an array of social conditions and cultural competences is brought together with the identifications proposed in the organisation of meanings and pleasures within film texts. At all these levels, femininity figures as a site of negotiation, sometimes even of contradiction and struggle. How, then, was the typical young female cinema-goer of these years positioned in relation to the various conditions, competences and discourses mobilised in the activity of cinema-going?

In the virtual absence of direct evidence from cinema-goers themselves, in any attempt to answer this question we must attend to other voices: those of film exhibitors and critics, say, and of columnists and advertisers in popular cinema magazines and women's magazines. From these sources it is possible to sketch a profile of the typical 1930s cinema-goer's preferences – in films, in film genres, and especially in stars; and also to get some sense of how these changed over the course of the decade, of normative models of femininity in cultural circulation, and of the cultural competences which framed and interlinked discourses around femininity and cinema.

The discussion opens with an examination of films, genres and stars which appealed distinctively to British cinema-goers of the 1930s, and of the cultural significance of their preferences. This is followed by a consideration of some intertextual constructions of femininity and cinema culture in the period; and finally by a case study of one of the most popular figures of 1930s cinema: a star with special appeal to young women, whose films, star image, and cult of fandom condense key contemporary discourses around both cinema culture and femininity.

## Cinema-goers' tastes and preferences

Critics and historians of cinema agree that Hollywood's command of the world's cinema screens was well under way by the mid-1920s; and that – potential language difficulties notwithstanding – this domination was more or less secured by the early 1930s when the 'talking picture' was established.[3] It is certainly true that the majority of films released in Britain during the 1930s were Hollywood productions. But what is less commonly acknowledged is that British-made films enjoyed more exposure and possibly greater popularity than their comparatively small numbers would suggest. It has been calculated that in the mid-1930s British films exhibited in British cinemas exceeded the legally imposed quota by between 70 per cent and 120 per cent, and on average had longer runs in cinemas than foreign productions.[4] While bare statistics tell us nothing about either the films themselves (how much of the figure is accounted for by the despised 'quota quickies', for example?), or about their reception (how enthusiastically were they received? would audiences have wanted to see more British films had they been available?), it does appear that Hollywood was not quite so pervasively dominant in 1930s British cinema culture as is often supposed.

Nevertheless, since Hollywood still provided the majority of films screened in Britain, British cinema *culture* was far from co-extensive with British cinema. And indeed, Hollywood's influence is very apparent in British fans' tastes throughout the 1930s. But if British film-goers took Hollywood to their hearts, the Hollywood they embraced was distinctively their own, and certainly not the 1930s Hollywood which has been canonised in film history.[5] Among British cinema-goers, the most consistently popular type of film was without doubt the musical comedy. The early 1930s in particular saw a cycle of well-received 'Viennese musicals', most of them from Hollywood. Among these are Ernst Lubitsch's *The Love Parade* (1929, UK general release 1930), voted Best Film of 1930 by readers of *Film Weekly*; and Victor Saville's *Sunshine Susie* (1931, UK general release 1932), a depression-era Cinderella tale of an indomitably cheerful office girl (Renate Muller) who wins her boss's (Jack Hulbert) affections. Winner in the 1931 *Film Weekly* readers' poll for Best British Film, *Sunshine Susie* was also a huge box-office success, running for as long as a year in some cinemas: its unremittingly optimistic tone is perfectly caught in the film's catchy theme song, 'Today I Feel So Happy'.

The musical maintained its appeal throughout the decade, with British-made musical comedy films functioning largely as showcases for the talents of musical stage entertainers. Prominent among these is Gracie Fields, already well-established in music hall when she went into films in the early 1930s. During the early and middle years of the decade, Fields was incontrovertibly Britain's favourite home-grown film star (Table 1), and even against competition from Hollywood proved a major British box-office draw (Table 2).[6] When Fields surrendered top ranking in 1938, it was to another music hall performer, George Formby; while another very popular star of British-made films, Jessie Matthews, had also established herself on the musical stage (though in revue rather than in music hall) before making her first film.

The distinctive national quality of British cinema-goers' tastes emerges particularly strongly in their preferences among Hollywood films and stars. Although this is true across the board (for example, among Hollywood stars favoured particularly by British audiences are the 'quality' actors Ronald Colman and Norma Shearer), here again a predilection for the musical sets British film-goers' preferences apart. Thus although Shirley Temple was top box-office on both sides of the Atlantic for several consecutive years, a number of other Hollywood musical stars scored degrees of success in Britain that they did not enjoy in their own country: Astaire and Rogers, Jeanette MacDonald, and Deanna Durbin, for example (Table 2).

But perhaps the most striking finding to emerge from this study of the tastes of the cinema-going audience of the 1930s relates to paradigms of femininity embodied in the personae of Britain's favourite female stars, all of whom conspicuously lack attributes of overt, adult, sexuality. While the more glamorous Hollywood stars of the 1930s found little favour (according to the Bernstein surveys, the raunchy Mae West was positively detested), performers who were, or appeared to be, pre-pubescent, rated very highly with British audiences. If the Hollywood stars Shirley Temple and Deanna Durbin are the most prominent instances of this tendency, there are plenty of others. The British juvenile player Nova Pilbeam enjoyed a large following among some sections of the audience, as did Elisabeth Bergner, an actress adult in years but gamine in image. Both Pilbeam and Bergner received awards voted by cinema-goers: Pilbeam from readers of both *Picturegoer* and *Film Weekly* for her role in *Tudor Rose* (1936); and Bergner likewise for *Escape Me Never* (1935).

The persona of song-and-dance star Jessie Matthews was markedly 'little-girlish', too, and in this context it is worthy of note that she was never partnered for her dancing in films by any man deemed worthy of her talents. And if Gracie Fields can hardly be regarded as juvenile either in years or in image, her screen persona – the sensible big-sisterly figure who always loses the man to someone more glamorous – is arguably as asexual as Shirley Temple's. Or possibly more so: Graham Greene got into trouble for suggesting that the child star's infancy was actually a disguise for a 'more secret and more adult' appeal.[7] But in the 1930s, such perverse readings remained firmly repressed: British cinema-goers evidently preferred femininity to be youthful, innocent, asexual.

While these general trends in cinema-goers' tastes run throughout the 1930s, a number of changes are observable towards the end of the decade. Although the musical continued to maintain its appeal, for example, a new generation of musical stars emerged. In 1938, the year in which George Formby ousted Gracie Fields from her long-held position as top money-making star of British-made films, the Canadian-born Hollywood singer/actress Deanna Durbin shot virtually overnight into the position of Britain's overall favourite star. Another juvenile musical performer, Mickey Rooney, also entered the British ratings in the late 1930s and, along with Durbin, displaced Shirley Temple from her top ranking (see Tables 1 and 2). But these transitions are by no means confined to cinema culture: they coincide exactly with significant shifts in discourses around femininity.

Table 1  Box-office rankings: stars of British-made films

| 1936 | 1937 | 1938 | 1939 |
| --- | --- | --- | --- |
| Gracie Fields | Gracie Fields | George Formby | George Formby |
| Jessie Matthews | George Formby | Gracie Fields | Gracie Fields |
| Jack Hulbert | Jessie Matthews | Will Hay | Robert Donat |

Source: *International Motion Picture Almanac*, 1937–41

Table 2  British box office: all-star rankings

| 1936 | 1937 | 1938 | 1939 |
| --- | --- | --- | --- |
| Shirley Temple | Shirley Temple | Shirley Temple | Deanna Durbin |
| Astaire/Rogers | Clark Gable | Jeanette MacDonald | Mickey Rooney |
| Gracie Fields | Gracie Fields | Spencer Tracy | Shirley Temple |

Source: *International Motion Picture Almanac*, 1937–41

Table 3  United States box-office rankings

| 1932 | 1934 | 1935 | 1936 |
| --- | --- | --- | --- |
| Marie Dressler | Will Rogers | Shirley Temple | Shirley Temple |
| Janet Gaynor | Janet Gaynor | Will Rogers | Clark Gable |
| Joan Crawford | Clark Gable | Clark Gable | Astaire/Rogers |

## Cinema culture and femininity: some intertexts

The enthusiasms of the fictional film fans Florrie and Gladys in *Sally in Our Alley* and *Sing As We Go* are referenced through intertexts figuring in the films' fictional spaces: Florrie has her film magazines, Gladys her portrait of Clark Gable. These references within films to film fandom speak to certain cultural competences on the part of the audience. They assume prior knowledge about cinema, films and stars, and about the place of these in the culture of the everyday; about stars currently in the ascendant; and about the character of film fan culture itself. They also point to a cinema culture thriving off the screen and outside the doors of the picture palace: in books and magazines about films and stars; in organisations such as fan clubs; in newspapers and other media consumed by film-goers but not concerned centrally with cinema; and finally in the routines, habits, and talk surrounding the very ordinary activity of 'going to the pictures'. How is the cinema-goer addressed and positioned in these intertexts? How does this intertextual address connect with the address of the films themselves? And, more specifically, to what degree and in what ways is the cinema-goer constructed in terms of gender?

The 1930s saw a boom in popular film-related print media, notably in magazines directed at cinema-goers. A large number of such periodicals, some of them more enduring than others, were published during the decade. The most widely read of these – *Film Pictorial, Picturegoer, Film Weekly*, and *Picture Show* – appeared weekly throughout the 1930s and until the outbreak of the Second World War, when *Film Weekly* was absorbed by *Picturegoer*, and *Film Pictorial* by *Picture Show*. In the mid-1930s, the four magazines had a combined weekly circulation of more than 300,000 copies, indicating an actual readership in excess of one million – approaching one in ten regular cinema-goers.[8]

In addition to the 'big four', a number of more ephemeral titles appeared from time to time, most of them during the early 1930s. Among these was *Girls' Cinema* (1920–32), which after a change of title to *Film Star Weekly* (1932–35) merged with *Picture Show*. After the mid-1930s, the

Table 3 cont.

| 1937 | 1938 | 1939 |
|------|------|------|
| Shirley Temple | Shirley Temple | Mickey Rooney |
| Clark Gable | Clark Gable | Tyrone Power |
| Robert Taylor | Sonja Henie | Spencer Tracy |

Source: *International Motion Picture Almanac*, 1933–41

scene is dominated by the big four weeklies, differences between which vary over the years. One key indicator of a film magazine's self-image appears to be the amount and the nature of its fashion and beauty coverage, which varies considerably between the magazines – and even within any one title – over the course of the decade. This perhaps suggests a degree of uncertainty of address: to what extent is it assumed that the bulk of the readership is female?

The title of *Girls' Cinema* bespeaks no such uncertainty: the comic-style pulp format, advertisements, and regular editorial features all suggest a readership of young working-class women. Indeed, in a number of respects *Girls' Cinema* resembles the weekly women's magazines of the 1930s – also relatively downmarket – more than other film magazines. It has an agony column; features romantic short stories and serials which are not always based upon films; and sports cover pictures showing boy–girl movie clinches. *Girls' Cinema*'s successor, *Film Star Weekly*, moves somewhat further towards the contemporary women's magazine format, perhaps addressing a somewhat older readership: in 1934, the cover 'clinch' is replaced by pictures of individual stars modelling knitwear, the patterns for which appear inside the issue.

*Picture Show*, which absorbed *Film Star Weekly* in 1935, is itself rather downmarket by comparison with other film magazines and, while not always adopting a lighthearted tone, over the years does feature a considerable amount of material addressed to a female readership. *Film Pictorial*, with higher production values than *Picture Show*, nonetheless also appears to address itself to a more downmarket and feminine readership than either *Picturegoer* or *Film Weekly*. In *Film Pictorial*, there is a marked emphasis on personalities and, certainly until the mid-1930s, a greater bias towards Hollywood than is apparent in the other film magazines. *Film Pictorial*'s film reviewer also shows a consistently favourable attitude towards pictures likely to appeal to female audiences; and from 1937 a regular agony column, with Jessie Matthews as agony aunt ('tell all your problems, your worries, or ask any questions you like, and Jessie Matthews will answer'), highlights some of the preoccupations of adolescent girls: parent–child conflicts, courtship problems, and the like.

*Picturegoer*'s and *Film Weekly*'s aspirations to 'quality' are perhaps evident in their somewhat ambivalent attitude towards features with a feminine slant. Writers, regular and occasional, for *Film Weekly* include the upmarket Ethel Mannin, Paul Rotha, Oswell Blakeston and Lotte Reiniger. The magazine's 'serious' tone is apparent also in its regular campaigns on behalf of the cinema-goer (for a reduction in the delay between West End and general releases of films, for example), and, especially during the early 1930s, its low quotient of fashion and beauty features. *Picturegoer*, however, whose aspiration to quality is allied with a much larger circulation, appears to be trying to cater to all cinema-going tastes: this is apparent in its fluctuating commitment to feature material designed to appeal to female cinemagoers. Nonetheless, in all the magazines many column inches are devoted to advertisements for products aimed at female consumers: make-up, skin products, soap, hair treatments, and suchlike.

Variations in tone and address notwithstanding, a degree of duplication in content between film magazines and women's magazines is discernible, suggesting an overlap between the constituencies of each. And a feminine cinema-goer/reader is quite frankly constructed in a type of popular periodical which appears to be peculiar to the 1930s, a hybrid of women's magazine and film magazine. *Film Fashionland*, with a broad emphasis on lifestyle, consumption and leisure, was published monthly between March 1934 and April 1935. It includes features on stars' homes, cooking and beauty tips from the stars, and stars' horoscopes. A dress pattern is given away with each issue, while readers unskilled in dressmaking may send away for readymade 'film fashions' based on outfits worn by the stars. *Women's Filmfair*, which appeared monthly between 1935 and 1941, offers similar material, but over its lifetime moves towards a more straightforward women's magazine formula.

The popular women's press of the 1930s offers some impression of the normative modes of femininity in circulation throughout the decade, but until the late 1930s and the birth of the mass circulation woman's magazine as it is understood today, there is a dearth of models of femininity for younger women. The weekly woman's magazine scene had been dominated by such titles as *Woman's Weekly*,[9] in which femininity is constructed in terms of a comfortable, but far from affluent, domesticity. The implied reader is married, and her main concerns are her husband and children in general, their health in particular. Advertisements in *Woman's Weekly* in the early 1930s suggest preoccupation to the point of obsession with such threats to family integrity as tiredness, poor hygiene, dandruff, 'nerves', and above all, constipation. If the unmarried woman is addressed at all here, it is assumed that she is in domestic service, or perhaps in office work: it is taken for granted that married women do not have jobs outside the home. The only references, explicit or otherwise, to cinema appear occasionally in advertisements, usually for products endorsed by film stars, and in small ads for film magazines and similar publications. The picture here, then, is of a domestic femininity which is incompatible with an enthusiasm for cinema. Specifically adolescent femininities are addressed not in magazines such as *Woman's Weekly* but in film periodicals like *Girls' Cinema*.

In 1937, however, a marked shift in constructions of femininity becomes apparent. The summer of that year saw the launch of the weekly magazine *Woman*, which was to change the face of the woman's popular periodical press. Produced with the aid of new print technology which permitted rapid production of large runs of full-colour magazines, *Woman* addressed itself to a readership younger ('in tune with the changed ideas of the woman of TODAY') than that of the established women's magazines, and soon achieved a circulation of unprecedented proportions.[10] It also foregrounded the contradictions of femininity in an almost explicit manner. The writer of a feature in the first issue, for example, opines that paid employment can be a preparation for marriage, but that once married, a woman must certainly not submerge herself in domesticity.[11]

Unlike the more traditionally inclined *Woman's Weekly*, *Woman* advanced a heterosexual, rather than a domestic, ideal in which marriage is regarded as companionate, and in which family building is not necessarily a *sine qua non*. Nor was it taken for granted that marriage in itself excludes paid employment. At the same time, variant models of femininity are constructed: in one issue, a regular column on jobs and careers offers advice on working abroad, cheek-by-jowl with an article on the virtues of the stay-at-home mother.[12] By the end of 1939, by which time the magazine is throwing its weight fully behind the war effort, these new models of femininity are well established in *Woman*; so that in this context the wartime exhortation that 'women must work' is by no means out of key with what has gone before.

Unlike the implied reader of *Woman's Weekly*, moreover, *Woman's* modern woman is unequivocally a cinema-goer. Aside from the familiar advertisements for products endorsed by the stars (Jessie Matthews and Gracie Fields recommending Potter and Moore's face powder; Madeline Carroll, Carole Lombard, and numerous other stars featuring in advertisements for Max Factor cosmetics, and so on), the reader's enthusiasm for cinema is solicited both explicitly and implicitly: explicitly, from late 1937 until the outbreak of war, in a regular column on films by Freda Bruce Lockhart, who also wrote for *Film Weekly*, and in occasional features on films and stars; implicitly in an assumption of cultural competence in matters cinematic. A column on ice skating includes, without comment, a photograph of the Hollywood skating actress Sonja Henie; a knitting pattern for a hat and scarf is headlined, in an allusion to Deanna Durbin's film hit, 'Two smart bits of fluff!'[13]

### A case study: Deanna Durbin

If the late 1930s saw transformations in cinema culture and discourses of femininity, 1937 emerges as the key moment of transition. In the year in which *Woman* magazine launched the 'woman of TODAY', a musical comedy featuring an unknown teenage soprano scored a surprise hit. *Three Smart Girls* (1936) co-stars Deanna Durbin, Nan Grey and Barbara Read as sisters who conspire to remove their father from the clutches of a gold digger and effect a reconciliation between their estranged parents. On its British release in May 1937, *Picturegoer*'s reviewer Lionel Collier ranked *Three Smart Girls* 'outstanding', calling it 'one of the year's most entertaining pictures'; and in his annual survey of the year's films, *Film Pictorial* columnist John Milford hailed Deanna Durbin as the success of 1937.[14] On this occasion at least, the critics were completely in tune with the mood of the cinema-goer: in 1938, readers of *Film Pictorial* voted Durbin the year's most popular star, and by the following year she had moved to top ranking at the box-office.

Unusually, there exists considerable direct evidence from contemporary cinema-goers concerning the appeal of this young star. The *Picturegoer* reader who wrote to the magazine to praise Durbin ('In these days when the world is topsy-turvy with so much to make humanity weep, it is good to ... render utmost gratitude for a talented, youthful star's contribution to every film-goer's happiness')[15] catches the mood, the spirit and the content of the admiration, the adulation even, inspired by Deanna Durbin, and suggests that her popularity was as deep as it was wide. There was clearly something about the Durbin image which seized the imaginations and stirred the hearts of millions of young British cinema-goers.

A study of film stars and of audiences' responses to them offers a useful route to understanding those affective aspects of film reception which are the key to any proper understanding of cinema culture. Film stars being at once real (they are living human beings) and unreal (their presence on screen is in effect an absence) constitute ideal figures of fantasy, objects of desire, identification and projection. In the film industry, particularly in the 'age of the dream palace', film stars stood for ideals of glamour and success of a sort which could scarcely figure in the day-to-day lives of most cinema-goers. They also held out models for the era's nascent consumerism, and models of success based on an individualistic ethos.[16] To this extent, there is a considerable element of aspiration in many forms of fan worship. Such aspiration may then translate itself into consciously held beliefs and attitudes and outwardly expressed behaviours.

This seems to be true of what is clearly a widespread cult of fandom surrounding Deanna Durbin in the late 1930s and early 1940s. In 1945, in a pioneering in-depth study of cinema-goers' 'experiences and self-interpretations', the sociologist J. P. Mayer visited cinemas to talk to audiences and distribute questionnaires. Through the pages of *Picturegoer*, he invited readers to write essays and letters expressing their feelings about the films and about how cinema had affected their behaviour. Despite the fact that in 1945 her heyday as a star had already passed, Deanna Durbin is mentioned spontaneously, and always with great enthusiasm and warmth, in many of the replies Mayer received. These responses suggest that Durbin inhabited the inner lives of her male fans as a much idealised fantasy object; while for her female fans she offered a model for behaviour and self-image in their own daily lives:

> I fell in love with Deanna Durbin and my love has grown for her every day. It is not just calf love or a passing infatuation but it's the real thing. (male, age 28)

> Deanna Durbin ... not only inspires both young and old with the melody of her voice, but also has the power to stimulate and sustain me ... When Deanna sings she seems to sing to me alone. (male, age 39)

> I wanted to be as much like her as possible, both in my manners and clothes ... If I found myself in any annoying or aggravating situation ... I found myself wondering what Deanna would do, and modified my own reactions accordingly. She had far more influence on me than any amount of lectures or rows from parents would have had. (female, age 22)

> It was Deanna whom I have to thank for initiating me into my first attempt at curling my hair ... Of course, my mother had to be consulted, but she agreed with me that if it was all right for Deanna, then it should be all right for me. (female, age 22)

> I used to tell my 'boy-friend of the moment' to note the way Robert Stack held Deanna in his arms and kissed her [in *First Love*]. (female, age 19)

> I wore boleros, when I was fourteen or so, because Deanna Durbin did, and boleros were obviously youthful and becoming to girls of that age. (female, age 19)

> I model the majority of my wardrobe on the clothes Miss Durbin wears. I pride myself they suit me, and therefore I feel confident in myself (for surely you know how much nice clothes go towards a woman's poise and mannerisms!). (female, age 19)[17]

These testimonies indicate that for her fans Deanna Durbin in various ways represented 'higher things'. For the women at least, this sense of elevation and inspiration translates itself into modes of self-expression and behaviour in their day-to-day lives, into their images of themselves as young women, and into their experiments with clothes, cosmetics, and courtship behaviour.

It is often noted that a keystone of star appeal lies in the capacity of a star image to appear at once extraordinary and ordinary. A gap between star and fan is opened up, and in it flourishes desire ('I *want to be* like her'); while at the same time there is a sense of familiarity, attainability ('I *can be* like her').

The Durbin star image mobilises this play of ordinary and extraordinary to construct, *inter alia*, a model of youthful femininity which sits well with the newly aspirational and slightly daring modern woman who enters cultural currency in late 1930s Britain. At the same time, the image lies within the reach of the 'ordinary' adolescent girl, rendering it both acceptable and attainable ('if it was all right for Deanna, then it should be all right for me'). This offers a mix of safety and risk which might have obvious appeal to an adolescent at a time when girls in their teens were still regarded as children, and when there existed few models to help them negotiate the transition from girlhood to womanhood.

**13** Publicity photo for Deanna Durbin: 'The sensational fourteen-year-old star discovery with the fully developed voice and magnificent acting ability is shortly to be seen in this country in the new Universal picture, *The Three Smart Girls*, to be presented by General Distributors Ltd.'

From the start of her film career, articles about Deanna Durbin in the popular press stressed both her extraordinary musical gifts and her very ordinary qualities as a schoolgirl. A month or two before the release of *Three Smart Girls*, for example, *Picturegoer* alerted its readers to the forthcoming debut of 'a young girl with a fully matured voice of opera quality', who nonetheless must carry on attending to her lessons and taking care of her pet spaniel. As Deanna rose to fame, emphasis was laid increasingly upon her normality and naturalness: she is just 'an ordinary nice American girl' who happens to love music and can't help singing. And she is being sensibly brought up by a caring and watchful mother for whom Deanna is 'that rare, refreshing combination of youth, sophistication and talent that every mother hopes her daughter will be'.[18] As the Durbin cult filtered into the cultural competences of young British women, references to 'smart girls' became ubiquitous.

In her screen characters as much as in her star image, Deanna Durbin figures as the ideal local role model for the adolescent girl negotiating familial constraints and nascent femininity. The basic Durbin film character is a matchmaker, an effervescent teenager who innocently – but not without encountering trouble on the way – meddles in the affairs of adults. In the end, she always wins through to a happy ending, an uplifting song and a beaming smile.[19] The screen persona of a young woman whose youthful enthusiasm and energy fuels her determination to solve the problems of the adults around her endeared Durbin to her young fans – and rendered her acceptable to their parents into the bargain.

The fuss about Durbin's first screen kiss (in *First Love*, 1939), is most revealing in this context. Anticipated in the British popular film press for nearly two years, and already held out as a tease in at least two of her films (the titles of *That Certain Age*, 1938, and *Three Smart Girls Grow Up*, 1939, reveal much about the nature of the Durbin image and the discourses around adolescence and femininity it embodied), the long-awaited clinch was characteristically esteemed by British critics to be in the best of taste, eschewing 'the polluting influence of Hollywood's diseased mind', and 'handled with the most immaculate respect for standards of good taste and common sense'.[20] It is perhaps a sign of the times that, unlike Shirley Temple and Gracie Fields, Deanna Durbin did make a move towards adult sexual womanhood, even if its circumstances were very strictly controlled.

The star persona of Deanna Durbin and the cult of fandom which surrounded her in the years immediately before and after the outbreak of the Second World War condense key discourses around cinema culture and femininity in circulation during that period. Durbin stands at once for the consistent popularity of musical comedy films and stars with British cinema-goers, for the distinctiveness of British audiences' preferences among Hollywood stars and films, for an idiosyncratically British predilection for juvenile stars, and for the 'good taste' and 'quality' demanded by many sections of the British film-going public. At the same time, her rise to fame forms part of the broader shift in British film-goers' tastes apparent after 1937. As an adolescent girl, Durbin also stands for a typical British cinema-goer of the period; while her unusual musical talent gestures towards a world distant from that in which the average working-class and lower-middle-class British girl lived her daily life. Leaving behind the pathetic Florries and the silly Gladyses of the earlier years of the decade, Durbin stands above all for the new femininities which entered cultural circulation in the late 1930s and fed into wartime models of British womanhood. The figure of Deanna Durbin, then, stands for a cluster of cultural transformations which – contrary to received wisdom – antedate, rather than follow on from, the outbreak of the Second World War.

## Notes

My thanks to Christine Gledhill and to Jean Barr for comments on earlier drafts of this essay, research for which was made possible by a grant from the Carnegie Trust for the Universities of Scotland.

1 Jeffrey Richards and Dorothy Sheridan (eds), *Mass-Observation at the Movies* (London, Routledge and Kegan Paul, 1987), p. 41. For further discussion of cinema-going in Britain in the 1930s, see Jeffrey Richards, *The Age of the Dream Palace: Cinema and Society in Britain, 1930–1939* (London, Routledge and Kegan Paul, 1984). Contemporary evidence suggests that cinema-going was in fact more than 'occasional' for the majority of the population – two-thirds of which went to the cinema once a week or more: see Simon Rowson, *The Social and Political Aspects of Films* (London, British Kinematograph Society, 1939).

2 See C. L. Mowat, *Britain Between the Wars, 1918–1940* (London, Methuen, 1955). For a contemporary account which gives a good idea of the 'feel' of the times, and of how conditions varied in different parts of England, see J. B. Priestley, *English Journey* (London, Heinemann, 1934).

3 Kristin Thompson, *Exporting Entertainment: America in the World Film Market, 1907–34* (London, British Film Institute, 1985); Margaret Dickinson and Sarah Street, *Cinema and State: the Film Industry and Government, 1927–34* (London, British Film Institute, 1985).

4 Simon Rowson, 'A statistical survey of the cinema industry in Great Britain in 1934', *Journal of the Royal Statistical Society*, Vol. 99 No. 1 (1936), pp. 67–129; Tony Aldgate, 'Comedy, class and containment: the British domestic cinema of the 1930s', in James Curran and Vincent Porter (eds), *British Cinema History* (London, Weidenfeld and Nicolson, 1983), pp. 257–71.

5 For a full discussion of research methods and source materials deployed in assessing the tastes of 1930s cinema-goers, and of the methodological questions that arise in such a project, see Annette Kuhn, 'Researching popular film fan culture in 1930s Britain', in J. Gripsrud and K. Skretting (eds), *History of Moving Images: Reports*

*from a Norwegian Project* (Oslo, Research Council of Norway, 1994). Although a distinctively national set of tastes and preferences is observable, there are significant regional variations within this overall profile: see, for example, 'Census tells what film stars Britain prefers', *Daily Express*, 14 November 1933, p. 8; 'Conflicting tastes of British film-goers', *World Film News*, February 1937, pp. 6–7.

6 For an account of Gracie Fields's films and an assessment of her appeal, see Jeffrey Richards, 'Gracie Fields: the Lancashire Britannia', *Focus on Film*, No. 33 (1979), pp. 27–35; No. 34 (1979), pp. 23–38.

7 In his review of *Wee Willie Winkie* in *Night and Day*, 28 October 1937, p. 31.

8 W. N. Coglan, *The Readership of Newspapers and Periodicals in Great Britain, 1936* (London, Incorporated Society of British Advertisers, [1936]); Nick Hiley, 'British cinema fan magazines in 1936', unpublished manuscript (1991). The latter calculation is based on a figure of 20 million, assuming an average of two admissions per capita per week.

9 In 1936, *Woman's Weekly* was Britain's highest circulation weekly woman's magazine; Coglan (*The Readership of Newspapers*) cites a figure of 238,071.

10 On the launch of *Woman*, see Cynthia L. White, *Women's Magazines, 1693–1968* (London, Michael Joseph, 1970). White cites an average weekly circulation of 750,000 for the years 1938–45.

11 *Woman*, 5 June 1937; see also Ellen Wilkinson, 'Women must work', *Woman*, 12 June 1937. For a general discussion of women's magazines and their positioning of readers in relation to cinema in the US context, see Susan Ohmer, 'Female spectatorship and women's magazines: Hollywood, *Good Housekeeping*, and World War II', *The Velvet Light Trap*, No. 25 (1990), pp. 53–68.

12 *Woman*, 17 July 1937.

13 *Woman*, 23 October 1937; 27 May 1939.

14 *Picturegoer*, 22 May 1937; *Film Pictorial*, 1 January 1938.

15 *Picturegoer*, 28 January 1939.

16 For discussions of the phenomenon of stardom, see Richard Dyer, *Stars* (London, British Film Institute, 1979); Christine Gledhill (ed.), *Stardom: Industry of Desire* (London, British Film Institute, 1991), especially the essay by Jackie Stacey, 'Feminine fascinations: forms of identification in star–audience relations', pp. 141–63. On British stars of the 1930s, see Richards, *The Age of the Dream Palace*.

17 The first, and the last two, quotations are from J. P. Mayer, *Sociology of Film: Studies and Documents* (London, Faber and Faber, 1946), pp. 182, 237 and 188; the rest are from his *British Cinemas and Their Audiences: Sociological Studies* (London, Dobson, 1948), pp. 60, 90, 83, and 42.

18 'Fair, famous and fourteen', *Picturegoer*, 6 March 1937; 'Schoolgirl star', *Film Weekly*, 29 May 1937; 'Bringing up a breadwinner', *Picturegoer*, 4 February 1939.

19 William K. Everson, 'The career of Deanna Durbin', *Films in Review*, Vol. 27 No. 9 (1976), pp. 513–29.

20 'Deanna's first kiss', *Picturegoer*, 30 December 1939.

# 12

## The years of total war: propaganda and entertainment

### SUE HARPER

Great care is required in discriminating between the policies of various official bodies, and in distinguishing between the means whereby they attempted to orchestrate film production. At the same time, we should be wary of inferring too mechanical a congruence between institutional desires and film texts. To be sure, official discourses do partially construct social frames of reference, and these can have measurable effects. But it is rarely profitable to underestimate the adroitness displayed by particular groups when they wish to evade official propaganda. It is possible that subordinate working-class and female audiences selected and preferred those films which permitted them to stand at a distance from official realities.

The wartime Ministry of Information (MoI) was in a very powerful position vis-à-vis the film industry. The existing legislation imposing quotas on film exhibitors and distributors was augmented by the increased involvement in feature film production by the MoI. Initially, it tried to influence production by close liaison with co-operative film producers such as Michael Balcon, and it directly subsidised such films as Powell and Pressburger's *The 49th Parallel* (1941). Following the 1940 report of the Select Committee on National Expenditure, which discouraged direct subsidies for film-making, the MoI developed a different strategy. It opted for a carrot-and-stick approach. On the one hand, it could exert influence on film producers by controlling supplies of film stock, and by releasing stars and key technicians from military service. On the other hand, it effectively subsidised compliant producers by giving them administrative and practical support. The MoI also established an 'Ideas Committee' which organised informal discussions between its own personnel and hand-picked directors and scriptwriters co-opted from the Screenwriters' Association. The Ideas *male attitudes in film*

Committee discussed topics which were aligned to government propaganda policy; and as far as is known, all the committee members were male.

How did the MoI nuance its film policies on the gender issue? In spite of its reputation for Leftism, early Ministry pronouncements were notable for their conservatism on propaganda matters. Ministry personnel were attracted by the findings of the International Propaganda and Broadcasting Enquiry; this argued that propaganda bodies should 'in a stratified society, persuade the dominant group', and should use imagery from the past which would 'form valuable propaganda for stability'.[1] At the outset, therefore, the Ministry was not inclined to instruct the Films Division to give subordinate groups like women any privileged address in their feature films policy. Moreover, the Ministry stubbornly refused to avail itself of other types of propaganda expertise. The British Psychological Association was roundly rebuffed, although it provided the Ministry with a register of willing, largely Freudian-trained workers.[2] Professor F. Bartlett, the author of the influential *Political Propaganda*, offered help; and his work usefully took account of class-specific discourses, symbolism, subliminal messages, the sporadic nature of emotion, and sexual difference.[3] But the MoI rebuffed him savagely.[4] Instead, it favoured the ideas of Dr Edward Glover, largely because they thought he dismissed 'the more morbid aspects of the science of psychoanalysis'.[5] Glover's views on propaganda were markedly mechanistic, and were premised on models of social symmetry and emotional predictability. He did not, of course, forswear psychoanalysis as the MoI mistakenly thought. He suggested that the important emotions were anxiety, depression, rage and indifference, and he insisted that subjectivity and gender were less worthy of attention than empirical or economic constraints. By favouring Glover's more mechanistic ideas, and by recommending them to the Films and other Divisions as officially-blessed policy, the Ministry effectively banished subjectivity and gender from its repertoire. This, of course, considerably impoverished its resources.

Consequently, the Films Division formulated a number of directives on feature film which were seemingly bland; but their uninflected quality masked some elitism and misogyny, and notions of 'Englishness' and 'the Common Man' were simplistically conceived. Early in 1940, the Policy Committee had argued that, as a matter of priority, they should promulgate films glorifying 'histories of national heroes', since 'it might be possible to do a great film on the institution of liberty and its repercussions in the world'.[6] These suggestions, of course, were invented without reference to the instincts of commercial producers or the tastes of their customers; Ministry personnel expressed increasing contempt for the industry, and saw its protestations of patriotism as 'little more than the timely use of an unusual opportunity of getting something for nothing'.[7]

Until mid-1941, the Films Division gave some priority to history as a tool in the propaganda war. But it was opposed to sensational or spectacular histories of the type that had been popular in the 1930s, such as *The Scarlet Pimpernel* (1934). The MoI viewed history as an instructive parallel. For example, Arthur Elton inserted the following into a proposed scenario: 'owing to the explorers of the sixteenth and seventeenth centuries, the standard of life began to rise. People were demanding more and more commodities and ornaments ... but we are not blinded by temporary fashions as are the Germans'.[8] History should be used to sell the idea of Britain's heritage, particularly to the Americans.[9] The lesson to be learned was that 'in human history Britain has the special contribution of fair play'.[10]

After mid-1941, MoI film policy altered drastically; film-makers were encouraged to concentrate on purely contemporary issues and problems. *Kinematograph Weekly* noted in 1942 that the MoI now only wanted films 'which were not nostalgic about the old ways and old days ... but realistic films of everyday life'.[11] It feared that 'light, frothy subjects [would] be in the minority' if the Ministry had its way, and that the changing recreational needs of the mass audience would not be met.[12] As the war progressed, the MoI put a veto on historical films because their type of fantasy was thought to encourage jingoism: 'we may be the benefactors of the human race, but to rub it in can easily cause irritation'.[13] This change in orientation towards realism and the contemporary was probably due to two factors: firstly, there was an intensification of interest in the American market, and secondly, Brendan Bracken was in post as Head of the MoI from June 1941. Bracken was an ebullient and energetic minister, but his pronouncements in MoI files do not display liberalism on propaganda issues, and they show no concern with female audiences or the issue of subjectivity.

I suggested at the outset that the Films Division of the MoI had considerable power, and, although it did not produce its own feature films as such, it could significantly skew production. The MoI was composed of middle-class and male personnel in all but its lower echelons, and its files contain overwhelming evidence that while the idea of socialism was tolerated, feminism was anathema. The Ministry was thus constitutionally disabled from addressing gender as an issue in its propaganda policy. Many policy documents and private memoranda displayed a puritanical contempt for mass taste, and an irritation for those parts of the audience which persisted in a preference for fantasy and escapism. Certainly, many of the documentaries produced by or for the Crown Film Unit were addressed to females, usually by a male voice-over who instructed them about the correct compilation of a pie, for example. The short 'message' films such as *Miss Grant Goes to the Door* (1940), and documentary films on domestic or security matters, did engage with gender difference.[14] But feature film policy did not; and as I shall show, the full-length feature films encouraged by the MoI constructed women as either vapid or dangerous.

Further clarification of MoI thinking on film may be gained from an analysis of its rivalry with the Foreign Office. The FO had a long history of involvement in the film industry since the 1930s, when it had intervened in a number of cases to defend British films shown abroad. It had also covertly made overtures to favoured directors such as Korda. In all its 1930s dealings with film, the Foreign Office showed a broad, catholic and permissive tendency. This continued into the war period, and provided a strong contrast with the shrill moralism of the MoI.

Bad relations between the two bodies began in September 1939, when Lord Lothian, Britain's ambassador to Washington, castigated MoI efforts to influence American audiences. Lothian disliked the MoI's 'condensation and presentation of the story of England into narrow limits'.[15] He later emphasised the potency of British history for propaganda purposes, 'because Britain, owing to ancestral tombs, Magna Carta, the Bill of Rights, Shakespeare and Milton and so on, is able to exercise a profound influence over feelings'.[16] Lord Vansittart, the Permanent Head of the FO, replied to Lothian's first memo that he, too, thought the MoI was incapable of making films that could reach millions by 'getting at the feelings'. What was needed was a 'big film' which would deploy history and a high emotional tenor, and he recommended that Korda was ideal for the job, which would best be made in Hollywood by personnel who would 'be delighted to make films which would work our way'.[17] *Lady Hamilton* (1941) was this 'big film'. As I shall show, its covert Foreign Office backing cast it in quite a different propaganda mould from MoI films. And *Lady Hamilton* foregrounded female sexuality and visual pleasure.

However, the Ministry of Information defeated the Foreign Office on larger matters of film policy. It was jealous of the FO's international work on film; and although the FO itself could not be formally routed, its cultural agency, the British Council, might be. Accordingly the MoI began to chip away at the Council's film remit, which naturally displayed its parentage. By the end of the war, the MoI had hogtied both FO and British Council by a series of impossibly restrictive directives on their film-making policy and practice. The battle was fought out on the grounds of history and national culture. To the FO and its acolytes, history was the site of pleasure; to the MoI, it had come to be the site of oppression. Some of the memos produced during this debate are invaluable for our purposes. The MoI insisted that the best films for propaganda purposes were 'simple, direct, and man to man'.[18] Quite. MoI representatives on the Political Warfare Executive wanted films to lay 'particular emphasis on our positive achievements and wartime advances – not the past'.[19] Throughout the debate, the Ministry developed a coercive policy towards the mass audience and its pleasures. Jack Holmes, the MoI documentarist, bewailed audiences' fondness for Gainsborough historical melodramas, and argued that producers should be encouraged to deal with contemporary life: 'I don't know that history as such interests cinema audiences much, unless it is a bastard kind of dress-up story of some picturesque characters, with all the historical effects suitably distorted and with plenty of love-life thrown in for seasoning. Most people can easily be made interested in contemporary life'.[20]

We can conclude that, because of institutions' relative strengths and weaknesses, official film policy in the Second World War was irredeemably biased against spectacle; there was no consistent address to female audiences. *Lady Hamilton* was the only film to be made, as it were, under more liberal Foreign Office auspices. The other body (this time quasi-official) to attempt to influence film production was the British Board of Film Censors. The Scenario Reports for the war period display a predictable preference for projects favoured by the government; the script of *Thunder Rock* (1942) was praised because it corrected those 'who had suffered poverty, persecution etc., and had not stood up to their troubles, but had run away from them'.[21] The Board took a dim view of the sexual content of *The Wicked Lady* (1945), insisting on a deletion of a Bible verse, the lightening of a love scene, the removal of the words 'cheap though she looks', and the toning-down of the hanging scene.[22] But their strictures were ignored by the producers. Clearly, the BBFC's puritanism was of an ineffectual type, and it had insufficient clout to dissuade determined producers from challenging it. Its standards were out of joint with the times, and the odd rearguard action it did mount came to grief.

But what of the producers during the wartime period? Some of them clearly felt able to flout the censor; were they also unconvinced by the nostrums of the MoI? Walter Mycroft, a producer of low- and middle-brow orientation, was enraged by the Ministry's elitist attitudes, and he berated 'intellectuals who have attached themselves like limpets in decorative clusters to film production'. Rather, Mycroft thought, the instincts of the popular audience were more trustworthy: 'outwardly untutored people react instantly against anything phony, anything pretentious'.[23] John Baxter, too, insisted that the Ministry was mistaken in its insistence on contemporary realism.[24] He argued that even the Old Mother Riley films were potentially more useful as propaganda than officially-sanctioned ones, since only in escapist entertainment could 'problems be faced and opinions ventilated'.

Other producers and directors expressed resistance to MoI attitudes. Gabriel Pascal argued that wartime conditions intensified audience needs for non-realist films.[25] Del Giudice thought that historical and spectacular films were 'of the greatest artistic and cultural propaganda value'.[26] Bernard

Miles argued that the homogeneity desired by the MoI could not lead to a popular national cinema, which should rather display 'visual mastery'.[27] Even Rank was chary of MoI behests, and he emphasised the necessity of 'entertainment of integrity that will bring happiness'.[28] And at the end of the war, Maurice Ostrer noted that 'costume melodramas pack the box-office. I suggest that this is an escape from the drabness of the present-day world of clothes coupons and austerity'.[29]

This indicates that most producers were suspicious of the MoI's crusading attempts to reform film. The papers of the British Film Producers' Association provide valuable evidence too. The Minutes of the Executive Council display some tensions between Michael Balcon, a doughty supporter of MoI propaganda policy, and the other producers.[30] They also show the extent to which producers were prepared to band together to lobby the Ministry and to operate restrictive practices. For example, in 1941 the government wished, not unreasonably, that 400 film technicians be released from the industry for active service, and be replaced by fully trained female workers who would of course be paid less. The Association's ire was roused, and it vetoed the suggestion. It was only interested in women as consumers, and in the type of visual pleasure they were prepared to pay for.

As the war progressed, the BFPA appeared to be stricken with mass deafness where Ministry demands were concerned. The producers loudly ignored Jack Beddington's suggestion that a film be made about the historical changes in women's social roles.[31] The President was instructed to include in his annual address for 1942 a stringent critique of the Ministry, and an alternative suggestion that the public 'was asking for films which took their minds off the tragedy now taking place'.[32] The Association responded very negatively to an MoI memo which warned that 'special support would be given to films dealing in a realistic way with everyday life'.[33]

We can conclude that during the war many producers objected to government meddling in the free market, particularly when it was coloured by interventionist notions of state power and the desire to reform popular culture. The producers had developed a sophisticated sense of the changes in audience taste and composition, and they wished this to operate alongside their own definition of propaganda. To be sure, they wished to provide pleasure for the female audience, because that would have an automatic effect upon profits. But producers (and directors) rarely developed an explicitly gender-specific response. Gainsborough was the only exception, advising cinema managers about 'curiosity, that great feminine characteristic. Trade on this!'[34] And Leslie Arliss, the director of *The Man in Grey* (1943) and *The Wicked Lady*, welcomed the appellation of 'a women's director': 'I am not afraid of sentiment, and am working to overcome this shyness and to put unashamed feelings on the screen, rather than to depend on speed of action'.[35] But the unusually frank gender orientation of Gainsborough gave rise to unparalleled hostility from 'quality' critics.

We are now in a position to make sense of the different patterns of gender representation in feature film in the war period. Some career advantages would certainly accrue to those who produced images of women which were roughly commensurate with government propaganda policy. Others were simply motivated by profit, or by the urge to make their voice heard in the prevailing babble of cultural forms. Otherwise, it was in no one's direct *interest* in the film industry to represent women in one way or another, since women were of course excluded from any major part in the production process. But neither are the discernible trends in the way women appear in commercial film the result of some sublime accident. Rather, they have to do with the studio system, which at that time was perfectly competent for the cultural job in hand. The producers, who co-ordinated all film labour and generally took overall intellectual responsibility, were responsible for delivering films to the major investors, and the producers' cultural competence and sexual politics informed the films.

Let us now analyse a range of films, and categorise their sexual politics and propaganda orientation, considering firstly films with a degree of official support. The MoI was involved in many commercial features across a range of genres, and production companies responded in different ways. I have already suggested that, early in the war, the MoI actually funded some projects. Powell and Pressburger's *The 49th Parallel* was a case in point. Powell relates in his autobiography how he was encouraged in the early stages of the project by Kenneth Clark and Duff Cooper, heads of the Films Division and the MoI respectively, to the tune of £60,000.[36] The film, patriotic though its intentions are, is conceived in the thriller and 'chase' genre, and plays against a backdrop of rugged scenery. What are the film's sexual politics? All the communities visited by the Nazi interlopers are hierarchical; the Eskimo village is portrayed as traditionalist along Western lines, for example. The backwoods retreat of the anthropologist Scott (Leslie Howard) is exclusively masculine; there are men who do the rough work, and Howard, 'the Boss', who studies Indian culture and the European avant-garde. Females are an irrelevance to both forms of labour. Of even greater interest is the German Hutterite community. This is clearly chosen so as to function as a positive point of reference, and the gender roles of this miniature Utopia are rigidly stereotyped. The women are biddable and permanently headscarved; they are chiefly represented by Anna (Glynis Johns), who is generally content in traditional tasks. We should note that, as Powell and Pressburger's partnership developed, women played quite a different symbolic role in films they made outside the aegis of the MoI. The emphasis on the ideal female type as asexual and malleable in *The 49th Parallel* should probably be attributed to MoI 'authorship', rather than to Powell and Pressburger's.

Other production companies responded to Ministry initiatives in different ways. Two Cities, under the tutelage of del Giudice, was dedicated to the production of 'quality' films which would reform audience desires for low-status bromides. In 1945 he remarked that 'the masses are unfortunately more inclined to enjoy a *Wicked Lady* than one of our pieces of art which have brought such a credit to the British film industry ... my contention is that if we make a film comparable to Cartier's jewels we ought to sell it only in specialised shops like Cartier's'.[37] But his ideas were well in evidence in Two Cities' practice before then, and there was a clear consonance between the company's cultural and sexual politics, which are visible in its quasi-official as well as purely commercial products. Antonia Lant has valuably shown the effects of Ministry views on Two Cities' *The Gentle Sex* (1943). She demonstrates how this film, made partially as a recruitment aid for the ATS, was unable to provide a consistent mode of address to its female audience, and instead produced mixed allusions for the male and national community; the film condescended, but at the same time could not combine old and new images of femininity in a meaningful way.[38]

Two Cities produced *The Demi-Paradise* later in 1943. *The Way Ahead* was released in 1944 and *The Way to the Stars* in 1945. There is a clear similarity in the films' conservatism on sexual matters. Laurence Olivier noted in his autobiography that there was considerable government backing for *The Demi-Paradise*.[39] Certainly, the director Anthony Asquith was on the MoI Ideas Committee with the producer, Anatole de Grunwald, and both were experienced in propaganda work. The main purpose of the film was to express, in a coded manner, the official position on the Anglo-Russian alliance; but it also held a position on sexual alliances as well. Anne the heroine falls in love with the Russian engineer Ivan, and takes the initiative in confessing her feelings. But all she gets for her pains are well-kissed knuckles from mumbling Ivan, and he deploys her passion as a mere source of inspiration for further industrial designs. So the film repositions Anne into village society, where she plays precisely the same role as the older, desexualised ladies such as Margaret Rutherford; Anne's real task is to broaden the class 'spread' of women who provide encouragement and support. The second pageant scene clarifies the role allotted to females, when a local woman, in classical attire and teetering on a column, symbolises liberty. Neutral, heroic and uncomfortable, she is an icon whose personal feelings are expendable.

*The Way to the Stars*, made by the same team and with even stronger MoI support, displays the same sexual politics. The female protagonists, plucky and lively though they are, are born to suffer and sacrifice. Their behaviour under stress is rigorously modelled upon a middle-class ethic of impassivity. This ethic, although it has been 'argued up' into a national characteristic by male historians and critics, is based on weakness rather than strength; there is nothing inherently praiseworthy about emotional inexpressivity. But *The Way to the Stars* mounts a forcible argument in favour of such repression, and the performance of the actresses is probably a testament to their compliance in the face of forceful direction. Rosamond John, in particular, makes it seem 'natural' not to weep on hearing of the death of one's beloved. The film's aims are twofold: to sing an elegy for the lost young men of the RAF, and to encourage stronger emotional links between Britain and the USA. The female characters are comprehensively absorbed into both schemes.

The propaganda aims of Two Cities' *The Way Ahead* were just as firmly welded to MoI directives. Vincent Porter and Chaim Litewski have convincingly demonstrated that, due to a mixture of official tardiness and hamfistedness, the film missed the propaganda boat, and was released too late to be really effective.[40] But here too the function allotted to females had a family resemblance to the other Two Cities films mentioned above. In *The Way Ahead*, women exist in order to be left behind; they provide a secure backcloth for the real action, which is military. The nation's morality and culture is entrusted into female hands, so long as those hands are engaged in ratified activities.

Other production companies worked closely with the MoI. I have already suggested that Michael Balcon, Head of Ealing Studios, was the producer most in sympathy with government aims. Two of his productions are of particular interest for us. *The Next of Kin* (1942) was originally commissioned by the War Office as a training film, and as the project took shape, its aim became more consonant with the 'Careless Talk Costs Lives' campaign being mounted by the MoI. It is clear that the enemy within, as constructed by *The Next of Kin*, is the sexually active female. The original sin of indiscretion is committed by a dancer who is first seen on stage dwarfed by a gigantic grotesque silhouette of a woman. She is both Pandora and Circe, and leaves her illicit messages of national betrayal written in lipstick on a mirror. Thus female duplicity and vanity are ineluctably linked to a sense of national risk.

Ealing's *Went the Day Well?* (1942) was, as Antony Aldgate has demonstrated, a quasi-official film which 'carried the MoI stamp of approval ... and neatly encapsulated much of what the MoI stood for by 1942'.[41] It was a successful enterprise insofar as its arrangement of class values was coherent and its visual style was consistent throughout; there is evidence that it did reasonably well at the box-office. *Went the Day Well?* is interesting from our perspective because of the exclusion of sexually active females from the canon of heroism. To be sure, the lady of the manor, the vicar's daughter, and the postmistress all display initiative and the propensity for self-sacrifice, but they are all women 'of a certain age' whose maturity clearly makes them both undesirable and reliable. The correlative of this is that the sexuality of younger women renders them dangerous and thus outside a ratified cultural system.

American companies could sometimes be persuaded to part with money for MoI-approved projects. *The Young Mr Pitt* (1942) was one such, which Twentieth Century Fox produced as a prestigious and popular biopic. However, this was a view of history which rigorously excluded females. *Thunder Rock* was another, which was financed by MGM, but made by the liberal and highbrow Boulting Brothers. They recalled that 'at the behest of Duff Cooper, [we] were released to make *Thunder Rock*. Though in retrospect it was philosophically naive, as a film it was way ahead of its time. *Thunder Rock* matched the need and mood of everybody'.[42] *Everybody?* Dorothy Sheridan and Jeffrey Richards have demonstrated that it was mainly the intelligentsia who responded positively to the film.[43] Certainly the narrative techniques which the film deployed – the set built at an angle of 12 degrees and called 'Boulting's Folly' – are redolent of the avant-garde. And another significant part of the mass audience, women, were probably discomforted by the film. To be sure, one of the discrete biographies in the film deals with the vicissitudes of an early feminist, played by Barbara Mullen. But she suffers obloquy and imprisonment for her devotion to the writings of Mary Wollstonecraft, and finally in despair she plans to become a subordinate Mormon wife in Salt Lake City. What is significant about this feminist history is the way it compares to the other cautionary tales in the film. It is more detailed and more pessimistic in tone; the whole narrative is proportioned so as to underplay the possibility of a positive outcome for those espousing radical sexual views. *Thunder Rock's* aim was to inspirit those intellectuals who felt that they were in a cul-de-sac of history, but en route it offered its female viewers the sense that they were irrevocably caught in a backwater of biological determinism.

All the films mentioned above had propaganda aims specifically to do with the conduct of the war, and were aimed at general audiences. *Millions Like Us* (1943), which was made at Gainsborough, is particularly important for us, since it was an exception on both counts. It was specifically commissioned by the government to address a female problem: the low recruitment and morale of women in factory work. Frank Launder, who was Honorary Secretary of the Screenwriters' Association and a member of the Ideas Committee, liaised with the MoI when it wished to contract the Association as a voluntary intellectual workforce; its first project, which Launder and Sidney Gilliat masterminded, was *Millions Like Us*. The film was produced by a team which had an honourable history of popular feature film work: Ted Black as producer on the studio floor, Jack Cox on camera, Louis Levy as musical director and John Bryan as art director. But *Millions Like Us* was not able to combine its various visual languages in a homogeneous way. It was shot in actual factories and used serving soldiers as extras, but there was a confused sense of cinematic space, and the combination of documentary and fictional modes was inconsistently managed. The film tended, moreover, to elide the discourses of patriarchy, class and culture. Traditional working-class life was shown under the thumb of the repressive father; the new, post-war life envisaged was similarly structured around the dour will of the new patriarch, played by Eric Portman. More importantly, the preferred model of ideal female behaviour was of a sweet vacuousness. The heroine Celia (played by Patricia Roc) was diffident and agreeable, and her body language, with its consistently lowered gaze and closed posture, expressed a demure primness; only such a female could, by implication, inspire the war effort. *Millions Like Us* suggested, with some rigour, that female happiness could only be assured within the normalising rituals of society. The film was originally intended to alleviate female anxieties about industrial labour; in the event, it repositioned those anxieties in the context of emotional and familial experience, where they could be resolved in a familiar way.

There is little evidence about whether *Millions Like Us* achieved its propaganda aims. Those female Mass Observation respondents who did mention the film were all middle-class, rather than being from the target group. Nonetheless they all thought that the film was 'true to life' in the way it dealt with working-class culture.[44] J. P. Mayer's 1948 book on film response was published too late to demonstrate any direct propaganda effect, but it did contain suggestions that female viewers were only interested in the love story and the star values.[45] This evidence is too flimsy to allow of any firm conclusion, but it is difficult to imagine that the chaste female stereotype played by Patricia Roc struck really significant chords in the audience, especially when we recall the radical liberalisation in sexual mores in the wartime period. What is certain is that the image of desirable femininity she portrayed was thoroughly consonant with MoI intentions.

We can conclude that there was a very clear 'family resemblance' in the representation of gender relations within films promulgated or encouraged by the MoI. Across a range of studios and genres, Ministry attitudes to women were perceptible in the speech, actions, body language and emotions of the actresses paid to play their roles; official views were also more indirectly evident in the narrative structure and visual style of the films. Throughout, women were rigorously reminded of the supposed advantages accruing to patriarchal structures, and the ills likely to befall those who challenged them. What should be stressed is how much is *missing* from the 'rat-ified women' in MoI films. They do not laugh; they do not move with any sensual grace; they do not enjoy their own bodies or anyone else's. They are respectable, and never reckless in love. Half of their identity has been sliced away, in the interests of the state.

However, I suggested at the outset that there was another official body engaged in the film business, and that it had more liberal sexual politics. I showed that the Foreign Office did not share the puritanism of the MoI and that, under the leadership of Lord Lothian and Sir Robert Vansittart, it pro-moted *Lady Hamilton* as a more appropriate propaganda vehicle. The story of Lord Nelson and national crisis had obvious contemporary parallels. Alexander Korda, whose films had been in high favour with the Foreign Office in the 1930s, directed and produced the film in Hollywood. It attracted the attentions of the America First Committee, since it was thought to exert undue influence on neutral Americans, and the Senate Committee investigating the film was informed that Nelson 'is ostensibly talking about Napoleon and the events of that particular period, but he is actually addressing it to the times'.[46] Korda was about to be subpoenaed to defend the film, but the entry of America into the war demolished the isola-tionist case. In spite of (or perhaps because of) the publicity surrounding the film, it was a resounding box-office success on both sides of the Atlantic, as Kenneth Short has indicated.[47]

Korda had remarked that 'propaganda ... can be bitter medicine. It needs sugar coating – and Lady Hamilton is a very thick coating of sugar indeed'.[48] The propaganda message was cloaked in a disguise of sexual plea-sure, and moreover one which was constructed in such a way as to appeal specifically to women. There were endless wrangles between Korda and the Hays Office over the degree of moral condemnation they required in the script; but in the completed film, Grundyisms are subordinated to the dom-inant visual language of the *mise en scène*. The pleasures of sight and touch are emphasised, and its erotic aspects are foregrounded; Korda insisted that the sets should all evoke 'a bedroom'. The techniques used stimulate the eye to maximum creativity. The line of vision is frequently broken up to produce a serpentining, 'picturesque' perspective appropriate for the period por-trayed, and the decor is richly evocative. One volatile scene has a smoulder-ing Vesuvius in the background; the foreground shows, at right, a painting of Emma which gazes left towards the real Emma, who also looks left towards a naked female statue, in turn gazing left at a shadowy, half-hidden male figure. Such attention to detail makes maximum use of cultural codes, such that the braided hair, postural behaviour, and tight collar of Lady Nelson connote an unacceptable sexual frigidity.

Indeed, *Lady Hamilton* celebrates female desire, and examines its arousal by male vulnerability. The film presents the female audience with the possibility of a freer mode of libidinal life. Emma, as played by Vivien Leigh, forcefully implies that the more variously a woman is loved, the greater her significance; she is not besmirched by sexual exchange. The film also expresses some cynicism about the 'ownership' arrangements in ratified monogamy, which have similarities to ideas expressed in *The Wicked Lady*. Both films clearly address the changes in wartime sexual mores.

But what is really significant for our purposes is that the erotic charge of *Lady Hamilton* is augmented by an argument about class, and one which is very different from that contained within MoI propaganda features. In *Lady Hamilton*, it is Emma who can negotiate her way through any class dialect, and who can teach Nelson to inhabit the opera and the public house with equal ease. In the balcony scene on Nelson's return, the only reciprocal gaze is between Emma and the crowd; she *enables* Nelson's identification with popular naval tradition, which is most marked in the set-piece rendering of popular songs such as *Hearts of Oak*.

*Lady Hamilton*, then, suggests that the only viable leadership is a quasi-aristocratic one which works by excluding the middle class and forging links with the working class. But the 'glue' holding this transaction together is, as it had been in Korda's 1930s films, female desire. Accordingly the film was sold by aiming exclusively at the female audience; suggested tie-ups were with local beauty shops, for example. This female orientation may have accounted for the film's unpopularity with 'quality' critics: the *Observer* suggested that 'these are not the days when we have much patience for looking at history through the eyes of a trollop'.[49] The mass audience disagreed, however. I suggest that *Lady Hamilton* was successful because of Korda's polished combination of the aristocracy/proletarian topos with the theme of female sexual pleasure. It is of the greatest possible significance that this arrangement of class and gender issues obtained under the aegis of the Foreign Office. It could never have occurred under the leadership of the MoI, in whose propaganda films, as we have seen, women were rigidly clamped into a middle-class ethic of respectability, routine, and impassivity.

But what about the representation of women in films made outside any specific government remit? To be sure, no studio could afford to ignore the political situation in wartime, and every entertainment film displayed an awareness of it, either explicitly or implicitly. Is it possible to categorise 'unofficial' images of women? There is clear evidence of different studio styles in gender representation: women appeared as neutral and accommodating in Ealing films, flamboyant and aggressive in Gainsborough films, regally polysemic in The Archers films, and so on. A really thorough analysis along these lines would take account of smaller outfits such as Butcher's and British-National. Such work is feasible because it deploys the explanatory model of producer-authorship; it relies upon the notion that the producer is the determinant in the last instance. A film will always have some relationship to the cultural competence of its producer, and its gender and class attitudes can usually be seen as part of a larger studio position.

But it is unsatisfactory to remain at that descriptive level. We should now attempt to establish what conditions were conducive to the production of *non-traditional* images of women. By this I mean women who appeared autonomous and wilful, women who were resourceful and demanding, women who took as well as gave. Such figures appear frequently in Second World War films, and in those which have a coherently female mode of address. What patterns, and what class alliances, obtain in these films?

For example, let us consider the symbolic uses to which aristocratic style is put in a range of films. I have already demonstrated that, in the work of Alexander Korda, the alliance between the working class and the aristocracy is a means of evading bourgeois narrowness and puritanism. But Korda was, cannily, deploying a very fertile topos in British cultural life, and one whose roots go back to the early nineteenth century. Since the Regency, aristocratic style has been used as a way of accruing confidence and status by any group experiencing anxiety, and the exiled aristocrat has been a potent symbol of marginality and energy. The work of Byron, the Chartist poets, Wilde and even Yeats should be interpreted in this way. What is remarkable is that this trajectory clearly extends to Second World War film culture. It is no accident that a whole range of 'wilful women' (a group acutely on the boundaries of hegemony) appear in films in a firm alliance with aristocratic style.

Consider, for example, Herbert Wilcox's *Yellow Canary* (1943) and his *I Live in Grosvenor Square* (1945). In both, the heroine (played by Anna Neagle) actively engages her own destiny; in both, she is allied to the aristocracy, and has absorbed its style, thus ensuring her own survival. In *Yellow Canary*, as an aristocratic socialite, she has the confidence to assume the disguise of a quisling, and manages to expose traitors through her own initiative. In *I Live in Grosvenor Square*, Neagle plays a duke's daughter who refuses to do the expected thing; wilfully, she plights her troth to a sergeant from the aptly-named Flagstaff, Arizona. In both films, the bouncy female protagonist is empowered, by her aristocratic connections, to make surprising alliances which derail the predictable train of events. It is worth contrasting these with Wilcox's *Piccadilly Incident* (1946). This deals with a 'Wren', supposed drowned, who returns from a desert island to find her husband remarried. She has no aristocratic or gentry position of her own, and (it is no coincidence) she has a propensity for self-sacrifice and conformity absent from the other two heroines.

Or consider the case of Gainsborough. I have written at length about this studio elsewhere.[50] I argued that the studio, organised in a classically 'Taylorist' manner, produced a number of films which provided intense pleasure for the females in their target audience. Within the film texts there were contradictions between the different languages of script, decor and costume. But it is important to discriminate *between* Gainsborough melo-dramas, and to note that those films containing the most 'wilful' women are also those with the strongest use of the aristocratic motif. In *Fanny By Gaslight* (1944), *The Man in Grey*, or *The Wicked Lady*, the aristocracy is deployed as a symbol of a dark, unspeakable sexuality which provides inspi-ration, fascination or sustenance for the heroines. Each of them goes on to make links with the residuum: with public house society in *Fanny*, with the stage in *The Man in Grey*, with the highwayman in *The Wicked Lady*. The heroines are empowered to make these connections by the outrageous energy and confidence they have gained from the symbolic exchange with aristocratic culture. Significantly enough, when Gainsborough heroines are placed in an unremittingly bourgeois setting, they are far more biddable and conventional; consider *They Were Sisters* (1945), for example.

A final example of aristocratic substitution can be found in the films of Powell and Pressburger. *The Life and Death of Colonel Blimp* (1943), *A Can-terbury Tale* (1944) and *I Know Where I'm Going* (1945) should be read as a sustained meditation on the fertility of the gentry topos, in which females are both its inspiration and its apotheosis. *Blimp* is an elegiac paean to a van-ished, gentrified officer class which could once have unified Europe. The three females attached to this group (all played by one actress, in an auda-cious evocation of *Das Ewig-Weibliche*) challenge traditional roles: Edith by engaging in political action and marrying a foreigner, Barbara by marrying out of her generation, and 'Johnny' by her generally aggressive behaviour. Gentry style also enables self-realisation for the heroine of *A Canterbury Tale*. By her acquaintance with the Squire/'Glue Man', the land-girl Alison (Sheila Sim) comes into real contact with history. He is a conduit through which a sense of the past can flow; and through him she gains real blessings. And finally, the clearest example is *I Know Where I'm Going*, in which wilful Joan Webster (Wendy Hiller) decides to marry sensibly for money. But she falls in love with Torquil, the virile, charismatic owner of the isle for which her fiancé can only pay rent. His mystical, aristocratic attraction encourages her to transcend the limitations of common sense. In an important scene, in which the two are divided by careful composition within the frame, Joan asks Catriona Potts (of the wild hair and Irish wolfhounds) why she does not sell her patrimony. Catriona, of the same class as Torquil, replies in a classic formulation of aristocratic style, that 'money isn't everything'. Powell signif-icantly remembered that this took twenty-two takes because 'there's only one way to say it, and that's the right way'.[51] Precisely; the Herculean efforts required to find 'the right way' are akin to a stammerer struggling to articulate a crucial word. It is difficult because it is important.

We can conclude that, across a range of studio contexts, the aristocratic or gentry topos was a key *enabling device* for the production of iconoclastic images of women. Such images, dangerous as they were, could not enter 'naked' into the world of art: they required protective clothing. But the aristocratic motif was not the only enabling device for images of wayward females. And here some care is required. Female waywardness can take many forms; it is not always manifested by sexual banditry. It can simply be a wilfulness about getting one's own way. And here again we notice that this theme in British film culture of the period is thoroughly informed by a pattern of class allegiance.

Consider the Old Mother Riley films made by British National, or Butcher's Gert and Daisy cycle. Both appeared regularly in *Kinematograph Weekly*'s bestseller listings, and they had absolutely minimal status. Both contain female (or imitation female) protagonists who, freed by age from time-consuming wantonness, get down to other types of serious fun and mayhem. Two things are noteworthy: that they totally disregard the standards of dignity and good taste, and that their vigour derives from a solid alliance with working-class modes of behaviour and entertainment. Arthur Lucan, in films like *Old Mother Riley in Society* (1940), comes from a long line of music-hall drag artistes whose role has always been to provide a terrified homage to female energy. His body language also clearly owes much to more traditional performers such as Gus Elam. Gert and Daisy too, in such films as *Gert and Daisy's Weekend* (1941), display a kind of portly nonchalance in the face of polite society; their accents and physical behaviour are unremittingly working-class. In short, they hugely enjoy outraging middle-class shibboleths.

We can conclude that a tactical (albeit symbolic) alliance with proletarian modes of behaviour provided another 'enabling device' whereby wilful females could appear in films. But there were other devices, which *circumvented* middle-class dominance on a symbolic level. One recurring in different production contexts is that of the musical creativity of female artists. Films dealing with this theme all derive from an essentially bohemian notion: that the creative force should be allowed free play regardless of the gender or class of its possessor, and that its repression is fatal. This explains the wilful energy which inhabits the female protagonists of *Love Story* (1945) and *The Seventh Veil* (1945), for example. Their artistic virtuosity gives them the confidence to seek love in the unlikeliest places. Gainsborough's *I'll Be Your Sweetheart* (1945), too, is a relevant case. It deals with copyright wars at the turn of the century. This is a subject which does not, at first glance, seem rife with allure. Yet it did well at the box-office, and this is doubtless because of the nuancing of the performance of the music-hall star, played by Margaret Lockwood. Full of vitality and confidence in her artistry, she performs a range of songs in which she plays an aggressive role. In the old music-hall song 'You Are The Honeysuckle, I Am the Bee', gender roles are reversed and she even pollinates the flower. But the most interesting example is a key scene from *Madonna of the Seven Moons* (1944). The heroine (Phyllis Calvert) is, unbeknown to herself, split between her frigid bourgeois side and her wild gypsy self. This split surfaces for the first time while she is playing the piano. Initially, with her whole body held in a rigid tension, she plays a tinkling classical piece. Then the tune changes to a sweeping romantic one, and the impassioned self emerges, full of confidence, desire and expressivity. The whole narrative takes off from that moment.

So the motif of musical artistry is another means whereby 'wayward' women could be permitted an appearance in commercial feature film. This phenomenon consistently disfavoured a representation of the bourgeoisie as the dominant class. My last, and in some ways most problematical, example of a 'wayward' film also falls into this category. *Great Day* (1945) was produced by the British arm of RKO, ostensibly as a tribute to the Women's Institute. It was directed by Lance Comfort, who had made the successful Gothic *Hatter's Castle* (1941) and who went on after the war to make a number of films specifically on female topics.[52] *Great Day* deals with the combined labours of a group of women from all classes, when Mrs Roosevelt visits their Women's Institute; it also tells the story of wilful land-girl Margaret, who spurns her rich farmer fiancé in favour of a penniless soldier.

Quite simply, *Great Day* is a masterpiece, which combines radical sexual politics with a ravishing visual style; the latter owes much to the superb camerawork of Erwin Hillier. It is the only film of the period I have seen which successfully maintains a coherent mode of address to the female audience, while at the same time insisting on the pleasures of female energy and sisterhood. The film did not do well at the box-office, probably because of an unbelievably ham-fisted publicity campaign by the production company.[53] The condescending tone of critics did not help either, although the low status of 'women's films' often produced this response.[54]

*Great Day* makes a strong argument, on both the script and visual level, for the vigour, inventiveness and communality of women. They can turn their hands to anything, whereas the males in the film, in three set-piece scenes, are presented as more emotionally vulnerable and dependent. Of greater interest is the way class relations are handled. Bourgeois restraint is explicitly mocked in the women's speech and actions, and anything that looks like an attempt at social control by the middle class is roundly rebuffed. The final shot is a leftwards pan after the arrival of Mrs Roosevelt. The women are seen, as it were, from her point of view, and the camera sweeps across them as they prepare to display the products of their labour. It shows them, young and old, British and Irish, barmaid and lady of the manor, to the heart-wrenching strains of *Jerusalem*. The camera finally rests on Flora Robson's face, whose plainness is transfigured in an extraordinary manner. *Great Day* is clearly powerful because it combines an argument about female autonomy with one about the inefficacy of a middle-class explanation of the world.

In conclusion, wartime feature film has much to teach us about the representation of socially subordinate groups, particularly women. I have demonstrated that, due to a certain stubbornness, narrowness and puritanism, personnel at the Ministry of Information were unable to develop a propaganda theory that permitted a coherent mode of address to female audiences. Feature films endorsed by the Ministry imposed a rhetoric of bourgeois restraint on the female protagonists. The 'ratified women' displayed respectability, rather than any propensity for pleasure; they were constructed on screen in such a way as to imply that the national interest which they represented was rigorously middle-class. By contrast, the Foreign Office held more liberal views than the Ministry, and *Lady Hamilton* was an example of a quasi-official film which was able to deploy the aristocratic topos as an efficient propaganda tool.

But it is to non-official feature films that we must turn for more unpredictable conclusions about gender representation. I suggested that, for wilful, wanton, or iconoclastic women to appear in film, certain clusters of meaning were a prerequisite. The social power of the middle class had to be circumnavigated, on a symbolic level. The most hidden and threatening group of all – women who wanted to own their own lives – could not appear naked in films, as it were. One 'enabling device' was to deploy the metaphor of artistic creativity; another, more crucial stratagem was to don the disguise of aristocratic interest, or of traditional working-class culture. Only thus was it possible to cloak the terrifying spectacle of women getting their own way.

### Notes

1 Public Record Office (PRO) INF 1/724, 1 June 1939, recommendations 28, 29, 31.
2 PRO INF 1/318. The whole file is relevant.
3 F. Bartlett, *Political Propaganda* (Cambridge, Cambridge University Press, 1940), pp. 56, 63, 83, 155–6.
4 PRO INF 1/318. See exchange of letters between the Parliamentary Secretary and the Director-General, November 1940. Lord Hood, Churchill's Private Secretary, favoured Bartlett, but he was overruled; see *ibid.*, Hood to Fairburn, 9 April 1940.
5 *Ibid.*, unsigned handwritten MoI memo dated 1 May 1940.
6 PRO INF 1/867, Policy Committee document, undated, but from internal evidence January 1940.

7　PRO INF 1/196, undated MoI memo, which must from internal evidence be early 1940. See also INF 1/615, Fenton to Hodson, 5 March 1940, which contains acrimonious remarks about the trade.

8　PRO INF 1/615, Arthur Elton to Oliver Bell, 13 March 1940.

9　PRO INF 1/196, MoI memo, 18 April 1941. See also Policy Statement in *ibid.*

10　PRO INF 1/251, MoI memo, 27 May 1941.

11　*Kinematograph Weekly*, 30 July 1942.

12　*Ibid.*, 6 January 1943.

13　PRO INF 1/867, Feature Films Policy, March 1943.

14　See Mass-Observation File Report No. 458, *MoI Shorts*. There is an admirable account of some of these shorts by Antony Aldgate in A. Aldgate and J. Richards, *Britain Can Take It* (Oxford, Blackwell, 1986). For a full survey of official films, F. Thorpe and N. Pronay, *British Official Films in the Second World War* (Oxford, Clio Press, 1980), is invaluable. From this we see the extraordinary range of independent production companies who worked for the MoI. Analysis of those shorts on 'female' topics which are available in the National Film Archive indicates that, although conforming to a coherent propaganda framework, there are slight differences in the nuancing of gender issues. These are doubtless due to the different production contexts.

15　PRO FO 371/22839, Lord Lothian to FO, 28 September 1939.

16　PRO FO 371/24227, memo from Lord Lothian to FO, 11 February 1940.

17　PRO FO 371/22839, memo from Vansittart, 21 October 1939.

18　PRO BW 4/21, MoI memo, July 1942.

19　PRO FO 371/34386, Political Warfare Executive, 24 May 1943.

20　PRO BW 4/40, Holmes to Bundy, 18 August 1944.

21　BBFC Scenario Notes (in BFI library), 4 July 1941.

22　*Ibid.*, 29 December 1943.

23　*Kinematograph Weekly*, 14 January 1939.

24　*Ibid.*, 14 January 1943.

25　*Ibid.*, 11 January 1940.

26　F. del Giudice to J. Arthur Rank, 8 August 1943, in Bernard Miles Papers, BFI library.

27　J. Arthur Rank from Bernard Miles, 13 March 1944, in Bernard Miles Papers.

28　*Kinematograph Weekly*, 16 August 1945.

29　*Ibid.*, 20 December 1945.

30　British Film Producers' Association Executive Council Minutes, 6 March 1940, 5 June 1941, 2 October 1941.

31　*Ibid.*, 7 May 1942. See also 19 March 1942, where they scotch Beddington's suggestion that a film be made about Mary Kingsley and her life on the Gold Coast.

32　*Ibid.*, 25 June 1942.

33　*Ibid.*, 13 July 1942.

34　Publicity material for *Madonna of the Seven Moons*, in British Film Institute library.

35　*Picturegoer*, 3 April 1943.

36　Michael Powell, *A Life in Movies* (London, Heinemann, 1986), pp. 345–8.

37　Del Giudice to Bernard Miles, 12 November 1947, in Bernard Miles Papers.

38　Antonia Lant, *Blackout: Reinventing Women for Wartime British Cinema* (Princeton, Princeton University Press, 1991).

39　L. Olivier, *Confessions of an Actor* (London, Weidenfeld, 1982).

40　Vincent Porter and Chaim Litewski, 'The way ahead; the case of a propaganda film', *Sight and Sound* (Spring 1981).

41　See A. Aldgate, in Aldgate and Richards, *Britain Can Take It*.

42 Bernard Lewis, *Always and Everywhere*, unpublished manuscript in BFI library, p. 171. For other evidence on official support for the film, see PRO LAB 26/35 and PRO BW 4/18. Antony Aldgate has given a thorough account of the film in *Britain Can Take It*.

43 J. Richards and D. Sheridan, *Mass-Observation at the Movies* (London, Routledge, 1987), p. 221.

44 *Ibid.*, pp. 263, 277, 278.

45 J. P. Mayer, *British Cinemas and Their Audiences* (London, Dobson, 1948), pp. 169, 177.

46 *US Senate, 77th Congress*, 1st Session, S. res. 152, 9–26 Sept. 1941, US Govt. Printing Office 1942, p. 117.

47 K. R. M. Short, '*That Hamilton Woman* (1941): propaganda, feminism and the production code', *Historical Journal of Film, Radio and Television*, Vol. 11 No. 1 (1991).

48 Olivier, *Confessions of an Actor*, p. 91.

49 *The Observer*, 3 August 1941.

50 'Historical pleasures: Gainsborough costume melodrama 1942–47', in C. Gledhill (ed.), *Home Is Where The Heart Is* (London, British Film Institute, 1987).

51 Powell, *A Life in the Movies*, p. 491.

52 He made *Bedelia* (1945), *Daughter of Darkness* (1948), and *Portrait of Clare* (1950). A complete filmography is in *Filme Cultura*, Vol. 4 No. 18 (January/February 1971).

53 The publicity material in the BFI library suggests that the film be sold along realist lines: 'So True-To-Life It Could Happen to Anyone!', 'A Love Story That Could Happen In Your Home Town'. The romance aspect of the tale predominates, and the fact that it is about the work of the WI is not mentioned at all.

54 The tone of all critics was either hostile or lukewarm: see *The Spectator*, 20 April 1945; *The Lady*, 19 April 1945; *Daily Telegraph*, 16 April 1945; *The Standard*, 14 April 1945; *The Observer*, 15 April 1945.

# 13

## 'An abundance of understatement': documentary, melodrama and romance

### CHRISTINE GLEDHILL

The 1940s constitute a period not only of self-conscious production of films for a national cinema, but of considerable dissension about the kind of cinema which could serve the conflicting needs of government policy, propaganda, national morale, and the box-office. It is within the context of these debates that this essay approaches the question of the representation of women and femininity in wartime British cinema. I want to focus in particular on the role of documentary realism, melodrama, and romance in renegotiating the place of woman and female desire. For while wartime cinema continued to produce the full range of pre-war genres, simply inserting wartime plot devices or ignoring the war altogether, two new categories emerged from British studios as conflicting answers to national needs: the documentary-realist 'home front film' and costume melodrama, both of which are significant for the representation of women.[1]

### Home front realism v. costume melodrama

Realism and melodrama are conventionally seen as mutually exclusive opposites and indeed this was true of the liberal intelligentsia of the Ministry of Information's (MoI) Films Division and the critics of the day.[2] However, the terms realism and melodrama have a complex and contradictory history at all levels of film culture, meaning one thing to the film industry, another to intellectuals, yet another to the swelling audiences of the 1940s, and again another to contemporary cultural and feminist theorists. For many during the war, realism became central to British cinematic identity, opposing Hollywood as a marker both of national experience and of 'high' cultural value.[3] However, film theory's later critique of realism as complicit with bourgeois ideology led to a correspondingly positive evaluation of Hollywood's genre conventions and expressionist *mise en scène* as a potential means of formal rupture and ideological subversion.[4] Feminists have found particularly interesting the family melodramas of the 1950s, which with their female protagonists, familial crises, excessive desires, heightened and circular plotting, and baroque *mise en scène* seemed to raise more than could be contained within the ideological straitjacket of classic realism. Thus melodrama was constructed as a transgressive, anti-realist mode, mirroring in reverse the commonsense opposition of melodrama and realism.[5] While British cinema has frequently been berated for failing to produce the sophistication of European Art cinema, its attempts to produce a popular cinema are equally denigrated for their failure to achieve the stylistic virtuosity of Hollywood's genre system. Instead the British contribution to Art cinema has long been associated with documentary and social realism, while its popular cinema, locked in 'old-fashioned' melodrama or a 'dependency' on theatre and the variety stage, was thought too uncinematic to consider. British cinema, it seemed, lacked the opportunity for aesthetic and ideological transgression so prized in Hollywood genre films and in the family melodrama in particular.[6]

This exacerbated the perception by feminists of a gender bias in British realism in its association with male-dominated public discourse, characterised in the cinema by the high cultural values of documentary objectivity, class-bound characterisation, emotional restraint and underplaying. André Bazin quotes Hitchcock's mordant observation that 'In Hollywood films are made for women, and it's in line with their sentimental tastes that one constructs scenarios. In England films are made for men, and that's why they never make any money.'[7] The recent recovery of the Gainsborough melodramas, then, has represented for feminist criticism a break in the defences of a masculinised culture.[8] The home front film is closely associated with the paternalism of Michael Balcon's MoI-favoured Ealing Studios and of the British documentary movement, both of which marginalised women,[9] while the box-office winning Gainsborough melodramas, with their demanding and transgressive heroines, are seen as the property of their female audiences and the largely female authored novels from which they were adapted. This reversal has led to their valorisation at the expense of the home front films: realism is identified with repression; melodrama with transgression. But I want to resist this critical reverse canon and to suggest that, despite the efforts of the intelligentsia to maintain a distinction, the relationship between the home front films and Gainsborough melodramas is closer than might at first appear. I shall argue that documentary is not immune to the investment of melodramatic meaning, nor is the costume melodrama remote from social reference. Equally documentary is not just a matter of patriarchal repression, nor does melodrama speak only to transgressive female desire. Class as a central factor in British society is crucial to the evolving relationship between melodrama and realism and I want to suggest that cinematic constructions of femininity are caught up in the negotiation of aesthetic and class codes.

The cultural traditions out of which these wartime films come and the discourses through which they circulate are complex and contradictory, as a cursory glance at the terms used by industry and audiences suggest. For example, the thumbnail sketches offered by 'The Cinema Booking Guide' in *Today's Cinema* for 20 October 1943 do not use 'melodrama' to suggest a feminine category. Rather the term, deriving from the 'blood and thunder' strand of nineteenth-century melodrama, includes espionage, western, detective, and wartime adventure melodrama.[10] Feminine interest is associated not with melodrama but with comedy, including romantic, marital and domestic comedy. While there is considerable evidence to support Gainsborough's contention that by mid-war audiences were weary of war films, the response of those *Picturegoer* fans who took pleasure in writing to the sociological researcher J. P. Mayer about their film preferences is remarkable for the catholic lists which both men and women provide, frequently including both home front films and Gainsborough melodramas.[11] Moreover the respondents who declare they are heartily sick of war films often make conscious or unconscious exceptions for the home front or documentary reconstructions which belong to the 'Golden Age' tradition. Most interesting are the criteria used to support these choices, whether realist home front or costume melodrama: a good story, good acting, sincerity, truth. This suggests, in popular experience, not the opposition of melodrama and realism, but their symbiosis.

## Melodrama and realism in British culture: a historical digression

If the terms repression and transgression and their aesthetic complements, realism and melodrama, are to offer any purchase in the analysis of British wartime cinema their meaning cannot be taken as self-evident, but must be located historically and culturally. In nineteenth-century culture melodrama and realism are neither opposed aesthetics nor gender defined. Melodramas were taken as a valid way of representing life and judged for their truthfulness and realism of presentation. Moreover they appealed to male and female, working- and middle-class audiences alike. In Peter Brooks's influential formulation melodrama emerges to fill the need of a secular capitalist order based on the individual for a source of social cohesion and moral legitimation.[12] A dramaturgy of polar oppositions, heightened performance and spectacular staging bears witness to the work of moral forces in everyday, ordinary lives – a project that depends on the authentication of the codes of realism. Melodrama, Brooks argues, in terms to which I will return, combines document and vision.

A major source of melodramatic polarisation in the nineteenth century was that of class. Increasingly, it was felt, revolution could only be staved off by a social democratic project, which began to emerge in the work of the philanthropists, and more pertinent to my concerns, in the rise of the social documentarists. Arguing that the foundations of the British documentary movement – so important to British wartime film production – should be located within this earlier journalistic movement, Robert Colls and Philip Dodd draw a striking parallel between the terms of Grierson's project and that of George Sims in *How the Poor Live* (1883). Where Sims writes of the need to travel 'into a dark continent that is within easy walking distance of the General Post Office', Grierson declares his intention to 'travel danger-ously into the jungles of Middlesborough and the Clyde'.[13] What Colls and Dodd don't mention is that George Sims was equally known as a theatrical melodramatist and poet (author of 'Christmas Day in the Workhouse'). In this respect he draws on a tradition of journalistic investigation which com-bines in equal measure document and vision, charting the stark polarisa-tions between the rich and the poor, upper and working class, the respectable and a subculture of poverty and crime that appeared to the Vic-torians as melodramatic oppositions in order to shock and stir the con-sciences of the middle classes.[14] However, in his anthology *Into Unknown England*, Peter Keating shows how the documentarists gradually shifted from the sensationalism of personal exploration to the scientific methods of sociology.[15] Their link with Grierson lies in their shared response to the polarisations produced by industrialisation and capitalism, whereby they seek to avert the social melodrama of revolution by promoting a process of democratisation aimed at rational understanding, social harmony and uni-versal citizenship through social observation.[16]

This exploration of one class by another, shared by nineteenth-century documentarists, the 1930s documentary movement and arguably by Mass Observation, is variously described as 'surveillance' (Griselda Pollock), voyeuristic class domination (Robert Colls and Philip Dodd), or the de-personalisation of the public sphere (Andrew Higson).[17] However, the process of locating and mapping social boundaries brings difference into visibility even as it attempts to contain it. For a boundary not only divides, it is also a meeting place. Revelation of life on the other side of the divide produces sensation, surveillance is a form of fascination: such responses suggest attraction as well as fear. Thus the forces that must be controlled threaten not only from without but also from within. If fascination threat-ens to dissolve class boundaries, middle-class hegemony requires they be internalised. Accordingly the shift from personal exploration to sociological documentation is paralleled in the transformation of melodrama by the Well-Made Play, and later the New Drama, which seek to restrain melo-drama's polarities and intensities in line with a middle-class verisimilitude. As G. H. Lewes writes, 'There are scoundrels in high life – but they are per-fectly well-bred'.[18] The new realism identifies and so repositions subjects in their proper class locations, while suppressing gestural, visual and emo-tional expressiveness in favour of the subdued tones, decorous phrases, and restrained behaviour of hegemonic middle-class public discourse.

## Femininity and class

These cultural and aesthetic transformations have profound consequences for the representation of women. 'Virtue' is now a matter of self-suppression rather than the defiant innocence of nineteenth-century melodrama's hero-ine. Control will become the mark of the modern woman displayed in effi-cient household management and care of her family's psychic health, but at the same time her role shifts to the sidelines of a masculine drama.[19] William Archer complains of Wilde's *A Woman of No Importance*: 'The young man's crude sense of the need for some immediate and heroic action is ... entirely right; but how much better ... would the scene be if the mother met his Quixoticism with sad, half-smiling dignity and wisdom, instead of with pas-sionate outcries of unreasoning horror'.[20] Thus the melodramatic becomes identified with excessive female emotion or working-class lawlessness. The control of social spaces and their threat of class conflict is linked to the con-trol of interior spaces and those desires, emotions and psychic undercur-rents which threaten to cross social divisions, whether emerging through the working-class and female protagonists of popular genres, or within the psy-chic economy of middle-class self-regulation.

## Realism, melodrama and British cinema

British cinema's inheritance of this visionary structure of separate but inter-related psychical and geographic spaces is eloquently described by Charles Barr in his seminal reassessment of British cinema: 'It is as though a social world were distinguished from an imaginative world ... the social world elicits the "aloof", objective look ... the imaginative world is viewed from a different position and its rules are those of subjectivity and stylisation'.[21] The observational mode of documentary and the understated mode of perfor-mance and characterisation of English dramaturgy holds social boundaries in place against the fluidity of subjectivity and melodramatic desire which threatens to cross them. However, restraint functions as an aesthetic

[ 217 ]

dynamic because there is something to restrain. 'The two modes or sides may coexist, or the one may be seen as reacting against and challenging the other's dominance ... But above all they interact and interpenetrate, all the time and in a variety of ways.'[22] This suggests that although melodrama and realism may have become disjoined in British culture, they remain in tense relationship. A remarkable series of echoes occur between nineteenth-century theatrical critics ('Mr Harvey made a great impression ... by his composure, by the sobriety of his words and the suppression of his emotions'), the film critics of the 1940s ('Rosamund John's characterisation is sure, restrained but intense') and the audience preferences elicited by J. P. Mayer (for example the wonderfully oxymoronic praise of *The Way Ahead* for its 'abundance of understatement').[23] This suggests a national aesthetic which is for at least certain sections of the population deeply ingrained. The dominance of acting over stardom in Mayer's respondents' film preferences suggests further the cultural value of control: restraint, repression of feeling become a moving display of virtue, a source of imaginative power, in direct correlation with what is held back.

### Wartime cinema and the home front film

It is in this historical and cultural context that I want to look at the home front film as an MoI-sponsored attempt to mobilise the populace. Considered as propaganda, these films seem surprisingly unmelodramatic, eschewing the polar oppositions which divide allies from enemies. In particular they lack the dominating centre of melodrama – the villain. This may in part be to do with a conscious concern to avoid the hate campaigns that brought the initially successfully pioneered propaganda techniques of the First World War into disrepute as lies. Moreover, Nicholas Pronay suggests, a culturally ingrained suspicion of demagoguery rejected techniques associated with the emotional extremes of Nazi propaganda which threatened to make 'us' like 'them'.[24] An American review of *Night Train to Munich* (1940) comments, 'Like the best of British melodramas ... the incredible adventure ... has been made credible by underscoring its terrors quite casually, even humorously'.[25]

Against the popular perception of propaganda as 'lies', official thinking in the Second World War developed the notion of 'propaganda with truth'.[26] However, this depended for its populist appeal on a greater recognition of social conditions and internal differences than was permitted in the censorship-ridden 1930s. While the documentary movement had developed techniques for penetrating different social spaces and suggesting links between different sectors of the population through montage editing and the inter-cutting of sound and image, it encountered considerable difficulty in finding an appropriate address for the total mobilisation required for the war effort. Whereas the observational mode maintains a division between observer and observed, Second World War propaganda entailed crossing these divisions in an address to the working class and women, an address that could be neither of one class or gender to another, nor simply to the private desires of the individual. As Andrew Higson has shown, a conjunction with fiction promised a means of intersecting with individual subjectivities in public contexts, as documentaries expanded into feature films and documentary personnel joined commercial feature producing studios.[27] But the dynamic of this intersection, I would suggest, lies in the changed function of the boundary, now called into play less to demarcate than to join. In this context, the recentring of female protagonists (remarkably absent from the portrait of Britain provided by the 1930s documentaries) provides a key to the problems and management of the move towards the edges of social division required by total mobilisation. But while figures such as Celia Johnson and Phyllis Calvert may provide the stability of the maternal, others entail the fluidity of the romantic, for example Margaret Lockwood, Anne Crawford. Female protagonists may stabilise the boundaries, but also threaten to slip over them.

### 'Woman' and women: relocating the maternal figure in the home front film

As well as the villain, the home front films lack another traditional figure from war propaganda: the waiting woman or woman as victim, the symbolic threatened woman who elides nation with the image of wife, mother, dutiful daughter or sister. As Antonia Lant and Alison Oram suggest elsewhere in this book, female conscription underlines the distinction between women as socially and historically constituted subjects and 'woman' as a melodramatic signifier in patriotic, nationalist discourse. In dealing with the home front, these films had to negotiate between the role of woman as stabiliser of patriarchal society and her new historical mobility. For mobilisation refers not just to the movements of bodies but also to movements of desire. The construction of the home front required the redirection of the personal into the public sphere. If women are drawn out of the home, an image of 'woman' must be refound which reties female desire to nation and redirects male endeavour to the defence of a national rather than private home.

This is not, however, a one way process, since the populist address pulls nation out of a centrist and hierarchical configuration towards a more local and egalitarian image of community. Both the mobile woman and woman as maternal icon participate in this construction. The changed function of marriage is instructive. As Gillian Swanson and I have argued elsewhere,

[ 219 ]

weddings are celebrated not as private family gatherings, but rather as signs of communal bonding and the reconciliation of social differences.[28] So, for example, in *The Bells Go Down* (1943) Nan and Bob's wedding postponed at the beginning of the film is eventually celebrated by a gathering not of family relations but of the local AFS as a sign of their integration into a communal firefighting force. Similarly Celia and Fred's marriage in *Millions Like Us* (1943) is celebrated in the factory hostel lounge, linking factory women, including the heretofore unintegrated upper-class Jennifer, and the locally based airforce. That marriage is a communal rather than private act is underscored by the recognition of separation and loss whereby the death of lovers (*The Gentle Sex*, 1943), of husbands (*Millions Like Us*) or sons (*The Bells Go Down*) produces the icon of the maternal woman capable of securing the communal home. In this respect these films tap into the emotional core of melodrama: home as the switching point between, to borrow from Laura Mulvey, inside and outside; or, in Geoffrey Nowell-Smith's terms, negotiating the need of individuals to feel at home in the world.[29]

If melodrama invests the social with personal desire, documentary provides a rhetoric for nationalising the idea of home, releasing a stream of acculturated images which in the context of war become deeply invested with communal and patriotic meaning and emotion: St Paul's Cathedral, the crossing searchlights of the ack-ack batteries, barrage balloons, dance floors, community singsongs. In their repetition from film to film such images cease to be incidental markers of local detail but function as documents of a shared experience, recalling Peter Brooks's characterisation of melodrama as the conjunction of document and vision.[30] Analysis of melodrama has concentrated on 'vision' but the *Oxford English Dictionary*, in tracing the evolution of the term document from teaching or warning (medieval) to evidence or proof (nineteenth-century) to a cultural artifact, 'something written, or inscribed ... as a manuscript, title-deed, coin' (twentieth-century), suggests the symbolic and emotional potential of documentary film.[31] The production of the document as evidence or proof parallels melodramatic rhetoric which seeks proof in its concrete verbal or visual signs of that for which no empirical evidence exists. As Antonia Lant notes, the ordinary/extraordinary paradoxes of daily living on the home front provided the conditions for turning documents of national life and landscape into signs: St Paul's silhouetted against the Blitz, the London bus in wrecked streets, the ghostly barrage balloons. Arguably the techniques of documentary itself invite communal recognition: the montage of workers and machines, or the slow track across collective faces in factory, canteen or railway station, even the avuncular tones of the male voice-over. It is no accident that photographs rather than the event itself represent both the communal weddings described above, offering documentary proof of community that outlasts an individual union, which may be lost through separation or death.

The ending of *Millions Like Us* provides a rich example of the way these processes interact. In the communal ritual of the canteen singsong, the choreographed documentary camera movement from the music-hall singer to the back of the canteen, which cuts together documentary footage and fiction, invites us not simply to join a public gaze, but to become a part of what we gaze at. Central to this process is the cipher-like image of Celia, who at the first sound of the planes overhead, and in a gesture typical of the melodramatic heroine, turns her eyes heavenwards. More significant, however, is the role of the socialist Gwen who catches her look and pulls it back so that not only does Celia join in the community singing, she almost looks at us. In this look at us, knitted into a montage of Britain at war – factory and airforce – and reached at the end of an all-embracing documentary tracking shot which splices actuality footage with the fictional, vision and document are combined. The closure of the film in community singing speaks in a self-reflexive way to the social role of cinema in wartime as itself a communal home. Indeed community singing was frequently a part of the cinema-going experience.[32]

There is considerable debate as to whether such strategies represent a repressive displacement of the private by the public, and the containment of female mobility by the production of woman as maternal icon. Andrew Higson, for example, while acknowledging the positive sense of community at the close of *Millions Like Us*, suggests that both audience and Celia are 'punished' by Fred's death in a mission over Germany.[33] However, 'punishment' does not seem to me to match the bitter-sweet euphoria of the film's ending. Fred's loss is less repression of private desire than the construction of a new form of desire – for the communal bond, evoked in the hostel dormitories and on the factory floor and fed as much by documentary as by the film's attenuated melodrama. Moreover, if Celia as maternal icon, a melodramatised sign, speaks to the community as a whole, the film's constitution of this moment in the all-female group, embracing mobile women differentiated by class and region, suggests a rather different euphoria that might emerge out of the pathos for the female audience: the extended mutual gaze between Celia and Gwen promises to displace the heroine's confinement within the private nuclear family through the bonding of women.[34] Put in this context, Celia's newly confident look at the female audience documents the strength discovered by many women in their movement into directed or voluntary service outside the confines of the home and which for some produced a corresponding feeling of flatness with the end of the war.[35] This constitutes, perhaps, what Ann Kaplan calls a transvaluative moment: the belief that the values of the domestic can be extended to a wider social sphere and society turned into a home for women.[36] The public sphere is infiltrated by emotion, feminised: while men are not excluded, 'social motherhood' is extended to women themselves.[37]

### Romance at the boundaries

In countering the notion of a leftward shift in wartime cinema, Jeffrey Richards links the box-office successes represented by Ealing's early wartime efforts, *Ships With Wings* (1941) and *Convoy* (1940), and the more insistently class-bound Coward/Lean home front films, *In Which We Serve* (1942) and *This Happy Breed* (1944), with Gainsborough's melodramas in what he sees as a popular 'celebration of the class system', indicative of an essential British conservatism.[38] However, as I have suggested, that unity depends on the representation of difference: arguably, rather than celebrating class hierarchy, class difference is evoked to celebrate contact. The encounter at the boundary produces a thrill of recognition, the fantasy of mutual respect, and of co-operation across the barriers in a shared enterprise. This fantasy is played out in film after film, between officers and men, between factory owners and employees, between authority figures and new recruits (see *Western Approaches*, 1944; *Convoy*, 1940; *The Demi-Paradise*, 1943; *The Lamp Still Burns*, 1943). Arguably Celia's look to the skies at the end of *Million Like Us* marks less the division of the air and the land by gender noted by Antonia Lant than their wished-for conjuncture.[39] The narrative problem for these films is how to manage these encounters at the edges of social difference, particularly when sex becomes an issue. The boundary can represent contact, but equally a potential crossing-point of desire, and produces moments tense with social fascination and expectation. Romance feeds on difference and (im)possibility, eroticising social hierarchy: for example the play of romance between the upper-middle-class Jennifer and working-class factory foreman Charlie in *Millions Like Us*;[40] the female architect and factory boss in *The Lamp Still Burns*; or the Russian engineer and the English rose in *The Demi-Paradise*.

### Gainsborough and transgression

If the conjunction of documentary and fiction in the home front film sought energy from the approach to boundaries of social division, the question remains as to how far the transgressive narratives of the home front film's alter ego, Gainsborough costume melodramas, represent a flight from contemporary realities or, rather, a different way of addressing the needs of the present. The mobile woman who replaced the waiting woman as dominant type of the Second World War implied not simply the entry of women into national service but an address to that most troubling source of desire – female desire. *The Man in Grey* (1943), for example, appears to counter the home front film in two main ways. First, it returns to the female figure a type of glamour made problematic to the national culture because associated not only with Hollywood but also with those class elements – the working classes or decadent aristocracy – that British culture's class-bound realism seeks to contain. Secondly, in the figure of Margaret Lockwood, the film embraces not simply the *desirable* woman but the *desiring* woman. However, the appeal of Lockwood's desires may well be less to do with sexual transgression and more perhaps with female revolt at the demands of the time, at 'being got at' as Janice Winship describes it in this volume. It is less sexual passion that Hester asserts than material need, linked to a refusal of the symbolic role of woman in national identity. She refuses to sink her individuality within the collective. She is a home breaker not a home stabiliser and she refuses to smile through her troubles. She is both angry and makes excessive material demands. It is haute cuisine, unconditional heating, a mansion that she wants: 'I never knew ... that fires could burn so recklessly all day for people who sometimes never come in'.

But even while Gainsborough melodramas make a space for the release of unsocialised, personal demands of female desire, and indulge in the social freedoms exercised by those at the extreme boundaries of British society – the aristocrats and the déclassé – their plots organise a complex network of social positions through which the protagonists make a series of transitions to arrive at a point where the boundaries no longer exclude but integrate. The class and gender shifts of the protagonists in *The Man in Grey* and *The Wicked Lady* (1945) are as much a geographic remapping of social relations as occurs in any home front film. For example, as Janet Thumim notes below, the shifting class positions of Lady Rohan and Rokeby in *The Man in Grey* converge in its opening and closing 'bookends' which are enacted in the present and encompass the liquidation of Clarissa's inheritance, of Rokeby's troubled Jamaican estates – which, consciously or not, echoes, perhaps, the political unrest in the West Indies during the 1930s described by Delia Jarrett-Macauley above – and the integration of the film's acceptable protagonists into national service in respectively the WRNS and RAF. The flight to the past, then, is neither irrelevant escapism nor obliterated from the present: Clarissa appears on the steps of the auction rooms in a WRNS outfit that echoes the riding habit she wore in her brief moment of fulfilled romance with Rokeby. The class privilege and patriarchal dominance disturbed by the social upheavals of the 1940s have been fiercely contested: the empty shell marriage, the brief romantic idyll, the pain of parting and betrayed friendships recognisable as contemporary experiences are staged with full melodramatic intensity rather than stoically endured. The return to the war-torn present is paradoxically a return to a new ordering of social and gender relations which in comparison with the violent passions set in an imaginary past offers a fresh sense of self-assurance and possibility.

### *The Lamp Still Burns* and the productivity of documentary, melodrama and romance

I want to conclude by looking at a film that is neither quite home front movie nor costume melodrama, but which drawing in equal measure on the rhetorics of documentary, melodrama and romance, demonstrates how these modes construct wartime negotiations around femininity. *The Lamp Still Burns*, a project begun by the hugely popular yet critically prestigious Leslie Howard, was taken over on his death by a veteran of British popular cinema, Maurice Elvey. In his hands it became a nursing drama that reconstructs the Florence Nightingale myth for wartime Britain, thereby exploring the challenge of changing roles of women to the gender ideology that constructs woman as a maternal icon.

The film, which adapts Monica Dickens's novel *One Pair of Hands*, charts the conversion of a successful female architect to nursing. Thus a career woman, Hilary Clarke (Rosamund John), moves from competing in a male world to a socially sanctioned traditional female vocation. This shift in Hilary Clarke's life story is paralleled by a romantic trajectory signalled in the film's sexually charged opening encounter between the architect and factory owner, Larry Rains (Stewart Granger), for whose engineering works she is to design an accident room. Rosamund John's professional but 'proper' middle-class femininity confronts the seductive insolence of the Granger star persona. Countering his concern for production quotas, Hilary insists he give up the square footage demanded by the Factory Act from which she authoritatively quotes. Romance is thus constructed not at the boundaries of class but of gender, which Hilary Clarke in her knowledgeable professionalism threatens. Melodrama produces the series of fateful coincidences that make dramatic changes in and intertwine the lives of this couple, eventually bringing Nurse Clarke to the bedside of Larry Rains as the image of the woman he has 'always been looking for'. But arguably these are not quite the simple devices of ideological containment they might at first seem. For the career switch and the romance are played out within a home front context evoked through documentary strategies which both appeal to audience recognition of contemporary realities and intervene in contemporary debates about the nature of women's work and their future role in society.

It is instructive to compare Hilary's conversion to nursing with Celia's mobilisation in *Millions Like Us*, for unlike Celia, Hilary is already established outside the home. The national demand is for a shift from an individualistic career to public service, but the change comes about as a matter of personal conversion rather than government conscription. However, the orchestration of this conversion as a dramatic switch of personal desire and changing identity further suggests that what is involved in both cases is not a repression of desire but the emergence of a new one. Melodrama provides the pretext for Hilary's conversion, significantly substituting the injury of her office boy in a car accident for the occasion used by the novel – identification with the star of a Hollywood nursing film. Hilary accompanies Jimmy to Queen Eleanor's Hospital where she is shocked to find that despite her professionalism she can be of little help. Later in Sir Marshall's Harley Street surgery, for which she is designing a new waiting room, Hilary's gaze is caught by a quasi-surreal painting of a nurse before the same hospital which hangs over his fireplace, as if a mirrored answer to her felt inadequacy. In a moment of epiphany, and to the bemusement of the surgeon, she declares her intent to be a nurse. A dissolve takes her back to the hospital and, while the camera tracks past the waiting patients, her voice-over takes on a documentary intonation, as she explains her perception of a different order of female competence and assurance – their 'air of calm efficiency, of unhurried speed'. This documentary moment is thus infused with personal desire, as the camera track merges Hilary's gaze and the return look of the patients, marking her emotional response to a social demand. In a sequence of sharp shot-reverse-shots in which the surgeon in the style of 1930s documentary voice-over retails the military regime of hospital life: 'It's like training to be a commando, there's no room for someone who can't take it … when you're in the uniform, everyone expects everything of you … Like any soldier you must be ready for any sacrifice. Do you want that life?' Hilary replies 'I want that letter of introduction', identifying her desire with vocational service on the home front.

Superficially, the romance trajectory is blocked because hospital hours and the dedication expected of a nurse rule marriage out. As if to underline the problem, two other characters face similar dilemmas, playing out traditional solutions to the career versus marriage plot: Pamela Siddell, Rains's former girlfriend, realising he is in love with Hilary, nobly frees him, declaring that she has her violin and is 'just another career woman'. In the next sequence the staff nurse who befriends Hilary in her early days, makes the decision to leave nursing and marry, confessing her lack of 'moral courage' to face the financial implications of old age alone. However, in the context of the upheavals in social organisation and personal identity involved in the home front, Hilary's romantic encounter confronts less the career–marriage conflict than male investment in the icon of woman. In a moment of extraordinary masculine beauty and, for Granger, exceptionally sincere playing, the amnesiac Rains regains consciousness in Queen Eleanor's Hospital to recognise in Hilary the picture he has been carrying at the back of his mind: 'You're not a nurse. I'm glad you've come at last. I've been looking for you; always looking for you.' In the following moment Sir Marshall arrives at the bedside and, noticing Hilary, engages in an exchange that is repeated several times through the film: 'It's you', 'Yes, it's me'. This play with personal pronouns addresses directly the problematic placement of 'woman' in the male imaginary and the female attempt to own the male 'you' as 'me'. The romantic melodrama played out around Stewart Granger's Rains dramatises the gap between male projection and a woman's self-defining identity: Hilary finally blocks his increasing pressure with the declaration, 'I want to be a nurse'.

Melodrama provides a denouement which orchestrates the film's intersecting strands of romance and home front documentary. After infringing a number of hospital rules, including drinking beer with a junior doctor and passing a note from Rains to Pamela's private ward in an attempt to reunite the couple, Hilary is threatened with dismissal. A hearing at the hospital board functions like a public trial in which Hilary addresses both her fictional judges and the audience of the film in a speech which begins with acceptance of the hospital discipline necessary to keeping her job and shifts into an impassioned plea for reform. The validity of her arguments is partially recognised, overpowering the nineteenth-century Nightingale tradition of female sacrificial service, as well as rehearsing the negotiations that prepare a shift from charity to a professionalised National Health Service. Hilary is reinstated. The coda enacts a further encounter with Rains, waiting outside the boardroom: if she is dismissed she will marry him, if not she will stick to her profession. Rains declares his intent to fight for reforms: 'one day you're going to have a job *and* a home'. But as in the closing home front coda of *The Man in Grey*, the film hesitates to confirm a romantic couple in the face of an uncertain future. The wish expressed here seems to express as much men's need for reassurance that women will still want a home as to assert women's rights to marriage and career.

## Conclusion

My purpose in this essay is to stress the concepts of negotiation and contest in analysing representations of women in the 1940s. Documentary, romance and melodrama all produce 'woman' and negotiate her relation to the changing historical roles of women in different ways. *The Lamp Still Burns* is interesting because its narrative seems propelled towards a realisation of the Gainsborough-style nursing fantasy indulged by Celia in the employment office of *Millions Like Us*, and which recurs in films such as *The Life and Death of Colonel Blimp* (1943) and *Perfect Strangers* (1945). However, romance is deflected by the new sense of female social purpose and energy which emerges when the home front documentary gaze and voice is given over to a female protagonist. At the other extreme awaits the Florence Nightingale bio-pic with its endorsement of female self-sacrifice, but this trajectory is turned by both the eroticism of romance and the frisson of egalitarian contact at the boundaries of gender on the home front. As modes of imagination, documentary, melodrama and romance guarantee nothing in themselves. For all her splendidly aggressive personal demand, Margaret Lockwood's Hester is brutally exterminated at the close of *The Man in Grey*. It is the return to the documented present and the professional self-sufficiency of the now déclassé Clarissa in her WRNS uniform that makes Hester's demands relevant to a modernising femininity. In other words it is in the intersections of these modes and in the clash of ideological and emotional investments which they carry that we can trace the work of social, cultural, and subjective change and the negotiations between atavistic and forward-looking male and female desires.

## Notes

This essay is a revised version of a paper given at the British Film Institute Conference, 'Melodrama: picture, stage, screen', in 1992. Subsequent versions were given at University College, Dublin, Staffordshire University and the University of Lancaster. I am grateful to colleagues and friends for their helpful feedback and especially to my co-editor, Gillian Swanson.

1 For the home front movie see A. Lant in this volume and A. Lant, *Blackout: Reinventing Women for Wartime British Cinema* (Princeton, Princeton University Press, 1991). For Gainsborough melodrama see Sue Harper in this volume, and in S. Aspinall and R. Murphy (eds), *Gainsborough Melodrama: BFI Dossier 18* (London, British Film Institute, 1983); C. Gledhill (ed.), *Home Is Where the Heart Is: Studies in Melodrama and the Woman's Film* (London, British Film Institute, 1987); and S. Harper, *Picturing the Past* (London, British Film Institute, 1994).

2 See Sue Harper on the Ministry of Information in this volume.

3 See Antonia Lant's essay in this volume.

4 For the realist/anti-realist debate see amongst others: C. MacCabe, 'Realism and the cinema: notes on some Brechtian theses', *Screen*, Vol. 15 No. 2 (1974); C. Williams, *Realism and the Cinema: A Reader* (London, Routledge & Kegan Paul, 1980); Terry Lovell, *Pictures of Reality: Aesthetics, Politics and Pleasure* (London, British Film Institute, 1980).

5 See Gledhill, 'Mapping the field', in *Home Is Where the Heart Is*, pp. 5–13 and L. Mulvey, 'It will be a magnificent obsession: the melodrama's role in the development of contemporary film theory', in J. Bratton, J. Cook and C. Gledhill (eds), *Melodrama: Stage, Picture, Screen* (London, British Film Institute, 1984).

6 For a summary of denigratory comments on British cinema see C. Barr, 'Introduction: amnesia and schizophrenia', in *All Our Yesterdays* (London, British Film Institute, 1986).

7  Quoted in P. Houston, 'The figure in the carpet', *Sight and Sound* (Autumn 1963), p. 160.

8  See articles by S. Aspinall, P. Cook, S. Harper in Aspinall and Murphy (eds), *Gainsborough Melodrama*; Harper in Gledhill, *Home Is Where the Heart Is*; and M. Landy, *British Cinema Genres: Cinema and Society, 1930–1960* (Princeton, New Jersey, 1991).

9  See M. Dickinson and S. Street, *Cinema and State* (London, British Film Institute, 1985), note 14, p. 258 on Muriel Box's rejection as a woman director by Arthur Elton of the documentary movement and later by Michael Balcon.

10  Stephen Neale discusses this in relation to Hollywood in 'Melotalk: on the meaning and use of the term melodrama in the American trade press', *The Velvet Light Trap*, Vol. 32 (Autumn 1993).

11  See J. P. Mayer, *Sociology of Film* (London, Dobson, 1946) and *British Cinemas and Their Audiences* (London, Dobson, 1948). Examples of catholic film preferences collected in the latter study include the following lists: * *The Demi-Paradise*, *English Without Tears* (1944), *2000 Women* (1944), * *This Happy Breed* and *Love Story* (1945) – from a seventeen-year-old woman; * *The Way to the Stars* (1945), * *Waterloo Road* (1944), *Goodbye Mr Chips* (1939), * *This Happy Breed*, *Fanny By Gaslight* (1944) and *They Were Sisters* (1945) – from a twenty-year-old woman; * *Waterloo Road*, *They Were Sisters*, *Love Story*, *Madonna of the Seven Moons* (1944), * *A Canterbury Tale* (1944), * *Great Day* (1945), *The Man in Grey* and *A Place of One's Own* (1945) – from a twenty-five-year-old man. A twenty-two-year-old man, who distinguishes his interest in performance from his girlfriend's interest in 'the dope and dirt of the stars' private life', nevertheless lists alongside * *The Way to the Stars*, *The Man in Grey*, *King's Row* (1942), and *They Were Sisters*. Films that might be considered as belonging to the cycle of home front films are marked *.

12  P. Brooks, *The Melodramatic Imagination* (New Haven, Yale University Press, 1976).

13  R. Colls and P. Dodd, 'Representing the nation – British documentary film, 1930–45', *Screen*, Vol. 26 No. 1 (Jan–Feb 1985), pp. 22–3.

14  For example, Henry Mayhew's *London Labour and the London Poor* (1851) and the joint Blanchard Jerrold/Gustave Dore anthology, *A London Pilgrimage* (1872).

15  P. Keating (ed.), *Into Unknown England* (London, Fontana, 1976).

16  See I. Aitken, *Film and Reform* (London, Routledge, 1990).

17  See Keating, *Into Unknown England*, p. 13; G. Pollock, 'Vicarious excitements: London: a pilgrimage by Gustave Dore and Blanchard Jerrold, 1872', *New Formations*, Vol. 4 (Spring 1988); Colls and Dodd, 'Representing the nation'; A. Higson, 'Britain's outstanding contribution to the film', in Barr (ed.), *All Our Yesterdays*, p. 83.

18  G. H. Lewes reviewing *A Day of Reckoning*, anthologised in G. Rowell (ed.), *Victorian Dramatic Criticism* (London, Methuen, 1971), p. 206.

19  For notions of household management and maternal care as they developed in the 1930s and 1940s see Gillian Swanson and Janice Winship in this volume.

20  See Rowell (ed.), *Victorian Dramatic Criticism*, p. 230. I make this argument at greater length in 'Between melodrama and realism: Anthony Asquith's *Underground* and King Vidor's *The Crowd*', in J. Gaines (ed.), *Classical Hollywood Narrative: The Paradigm Wars* (Durham, North Carolina, Duke University Press, 1992).

21  C. Barr, 'Introduction: amnesia and schizophrenia', p. 24.

22  *Ibid.*

23  J. T. Grein reviewing *The Only Way*, an adaptation of *A Tale of Two Cities*, in Rowell (ed.), *Victorian Dramatic Criticism*, p. 230; *Monthly Film Bulletin*, No. 10 (1943), p.

119; Mayer, *British Cinema Audiences*, p. 194.

24  N. Pronay, 'Introduction' to F. Thorpe and N. Pronay (eds.), *British Official Films in the Second World War* (Oxford, Clio Press, 1980), p. 5.

25  *New York Times*, 30 December 1940.

26  See Pronay, 'Introduction', p. 7 and Harold Nicholson, 'Propaganda', in *BBC Year Book 1941*, pp. 27–32.

27  Higson, 'Britain's outstanding contribution to the film', pp. 81–8.

28  C. Gledhill and G. Swanson, 'Gender and sexuality in Second World War films – a feminist approach', in G. Hurd (ed.), *National Fictions: British World War Two in British Film and Television* (London, British Film Institute, 1984).

29  L. Mulvey, 'Melodrama inside and outside the home', in her *Visual and Other Pleasures* (Houndmills, Macmillan, 1989); Geoffrey Nowell-Smith, 'Minnelli and melodrama', in Gledhill (ed.), *Home Is Where the Heart Is*.

30  'The melodramatic imagination needs both document and vision'. Brooks, *The Melodramatic Imagination*, p. 9.

31  *The Shorter Oxford English Dictionary* (Oxford, Clarendon Press, 1968). Philip Rosen has similar recourse to the *OED* for an interesting argument about documentary film which he takes in a somewhat different but related direction in 'Document and documentary: on the persistence of historical concepts', in M. Renov (ed.), *Theorizing Documentary* (New York and London, Routledge, 1993).

32  See 'Show business in wartime', *Kine Weekly*, 1 January 1942; Guy Morgan, *Red Roses Every Night: An Account of London Cinemas Under Fire* (London, Quality Press, 1948); and Janet Thumim who discusses this film and its audience in this volume.

33  A. Higson, 'Five films', in Hurd (ed.), *National Fictions*, p. 26.

34  For a feminist argument on the mutual gaze between female characters see Jackie Byars, 'Gazes, voices, power: expanding psychoanalysis for feminist film and television theory', in D. Pribram (ed.), *Female Spectators: Looking At Film and Television* (London, Verso, 1988).

35  See R. Broad and S. Fleming (eds), *Nella Last's War: A Mother's Diary, 1939–45* (London, Sphere Books, 1983); Dorothy Sheridan (ed.), *Wartime Women: An Anthology of Women's Wartime Writing for Mass-Observation, 1937–45* (London, Mandarin, 1991).

36  A. Kaplan, 'Mothering, feminism and representation: the maternal in melodrama and the woman's film 1910–1940', in Gledhill (ed.), *Home Is Where the Heart Is*.

37  Sheila Rowbottom at a recent talk on 'Social Motherhood' quoted from S. Koven and Sonya Michel (eds), *Mothers of a New World: Maternalist Politics and the Origins of the Welfare State* (London, Routledge, 1993).

38  J. Richards, 'Wartime British cinema audiences and the class system: the case of *Ships With Wings (1941)*', *Historical Journal of Film, Radio and Television*, Vol. 7 No. 2 (1987). In my view this account makes a somewhat misleading separation of *In Which We Serve* and *This Happy Breed* from the category of the home front film and raises the problem of using box-office figures to imply a homogeneous audience taste. In particular it evades the issue of the role of the intelligentsia in framing cultural attitudes and practices through education, journalism, opinion formation and so on.

39  Lant, *Blackout*, pp. 51–2.

40  Geoff Brown notes as recurring plot motif in Launder and Gilliat films the 'couple, flung together by the bizarre circumstances and temperamentally at war' in *Launder and Gilliat* (London, British Film Institute, 1977), p. 11.

# 14

## Disguises and betrayals: negotiating nationality and femininity in three wartime films

CHRISTINE GERAGHTY

This essay explores the way in which women are represented in three films whose main focus is the question of national character. The three films, *The Silver Fleet* (1943), *Went the Day Well?* (1942) and *Yellow Canary* (1943), all deal with problems of allegiance which arise in the context of narratives of occupation and betrayal. The three films are different in genre and tone: *The Silver Fleet*, made for The Archers by Vernon Sewell and Gordon Wellesley, tells a story of resistance in Nazi-occupied Holland in the heroic but whimsical style of Powell and Pressburger; *Went the Day Well?*, made at Ealing Studios by Cavalcanti, imagines the fantasy of the German invasion of an English village with ruthless realism; *Yellow Canary*, a star vehicle for Anna Neagle directed by Herbert Wilcox, tells the story of Sally Maitland whose cover as a pro-German English aristocrat enables her to act as a uniquely effective undercover agent for the British forces. All three films try to secure an English national identity by testing it against alternative allegiances.[1] In the process they also have to address questions of sexual difference and the way in which women's identity can be established within that of the nation.

The narrative structure of these films is crucial to the audience's ability to read actions appropriately and hence to identify the traitor correctly in these narratives of betrayal. Questions of collaboration are bound up with questions of national identity because traitors or quislings are effective only insofar as they cannot be recognised as having crossed sides. The traitor figure must conform to national characteristics even though the feelings of loyalty and patriotism which animate those characteristics and give them meaning have been diverted to an alien cause. A secret agent or resistance worker reverses the process, adopting the marks of the enemy and thus disguising identification with a just cause. Both figures are sites of semiotic confusion whose true meaning cannot be read from outward signs. In their different ways, the three films under discussion here try to ensure that the audience has appropriate knowledge to avoid confusion and judge properly the key characters who move on the boundaries of nationality.

In *The Silver Fleet* and *Went the Day Well?* this is done through a flash-back structure which puts the events of the narrative into the past and reas-sures us that they have been resolved before the films begin. In *The Silver Fleet*, the story is told through the diary of Jaap Van Leyden (Ralph Richard-son) which his wife Helene (Googie Withers) reads after his death and so finds out the true nature of her husband's heroism. *Went the Day Well?* opens with a direct address to camera by Sims (Mervyn Johns) who greets the audience as visitors to the village and points out the grave of the dead Germans before the story reverts to 1941 and the 'invasion' begins. In addi-tion, ambiguity is eliminated by the way in which the audience is given nar-rative access to the private moments of the transgressive figure. In *The Silver Fleet* Van Leyden is accused of being a collaborator by the workers in his shipyards, by the local people and ultimately by his wife because he works for the German invaders, receives gifts from them and entertains them at his house. The audience, however, does not doubt him because we have access to his real motivation through following the action with him. In *Went the Day Well?*, Oliver Wilsford (Leslie Banks) appears to be the perfect English gentleman, organising the home guard, friendly with the vicar's daughter and dining at the manor house. The audience, however, is privy to his con-versations with the invading German officers and is thus aware of Wilsford's treachery almost from the beginning. In the cases of the male characters in these stories, therefore, the narratives adopt an ironic mode and the double game of the collaborator is acted out with the audience's full knowledge of what is false and true.

*Yellow Canary* operates rather differently. Its narrative appears to look forward rather than back to events which have already happened. It follows Sally Maitland's (Anna Neagle) rejection by English society, her voyage to Canada, her meeting with Jan, the Polish captain who turns out to be a German secret agent; it culminates in the revelation that Sally is actually a British secret agent who heroically thwarts the attempt by the Nazi spy ring to blow up Halifax harbour. In fact, though, *Yellow Canary* operates less like a thriller and more like a mystery story, centring on the real nature of Sally's national identification. Her mask never slips and the audience has no access to private thoughts which might reassure us. It is only at the end when she is revealed as an effective agent that her previous actions can be explained. Thus, her first act in the film – signalling to German bombers over London – is narratively understood as treachery until the end when it is revealed that she has sent misleading information to the pilot and saved the royal family.

The resolution of the film then is not so much the saving of Halifax but the revelation of Sally as truly part of the national effort; in the final scene, she is joyfully welcomed back into her family and the nation.

Across the three films, therefore, there seems to be a contrast along gender lines. Male identity, as English or alien, is secured through the narrative so that the undercover work in which the male characters engage does not threaten it. Female undercover work, however, is used to express ambivalences about femininity and doubts about the secure identification of the female agent with the nation. It should be noted, however, that the ambiguity surrounding the character of Sally and the narrative in which she is placed could be resolved by the star image of Anna Neagle which would have reassured the audience as it tried to follow the twists and turns of Sally's manoeuvrings. Anna Neagle, as her fans would have known, was a well established star whose roles in the 1930s had included the British queen in *Victoria the Great* (1937) and *Sixty Glorious Years* (1938), both directed, like *Yellow Canary*, by her husband Herbert Wilcox. With this kind of stable star image firmly rooted in a pre-war depiction of England, *Yellow Canary* could afford to run the risk of a heroine whose nationality appeared unstable.

Central to the establishment of national identity in British war films is the concept of what is being fought for. Once this is established, different groups – men, women, young and old, aristocrats and 'ordinary people' – can be encouraged to identify with the cause. *The Silver Fleet* establishes this concept early in the film when a young woman schoolteacher (Kathleen Byron) tells her pupils about Piet Hein who defeated the Spaniards, 'a little man … but when our country is in danger it doesn't count how big we are. What counts is to love our country and be brave.' Van Leyden overhears the passionate speech and takes it to heart, adopting the name of the Dutch national hero, Piet Hein, as his pseudonym in his resistance activities. In *Went the Day Well?*, the cause is less overtly expressed but no less present. The villagers take up arms to defend their way of life – the English way of life – which is expressed in the film through the landscape, the grazing fields dappled with shadows, the country park around the manor house, the timbered cottages surrounding the medieval church. At stake too are the rhythms of village life – the gossip, the gardening, the weddings, the poaching – activities which provide the basis for the villagers' resistance. *Yellow Canary* begins with an air raid observer quoting Shakespeare ('This isle is full of noises') but is finally less concerned with a communal definition of what is being fought for than with Sally's reasons for involvement. For that we have to wait to the end when Sally finally tells her family 'One thing you don't know … Something that even justified deceiving all of you. I actually heard Von Ribbentrop tell the Führer that the British were decadent and wouldn't fight. Do you think I was going to stand that?'

In all three films, the occupation/collaboration motif is used to set an English identity against that of other nationalities. In *The Silver Fleet*, this is complicated by the fact that the story, since it deals with Dutch resistance, has no English characters. This problem is solved by emphasising the similarities between the Dutch and the English. The Dutch are presented as a small sea-faring nation and Van Leyden builds ships and submarines – war work which would have been familiar to British audiences; the resistance fighters meet in a grocer's shop, providing analogies for 'a nation of shop-keepers' for whom rationing and food were also constant preoccupations; Piet Hein, whose name Van Leyden uses, is a folklore figure who, like Sir Francis Drake, teased the Spaniards. In this context, Ralph Richardson's Van Leyden is an English hero – modest, ingenious, cool and inventive – sacrificing himself to sink the submarine he has built so that it will not fall into German hands. The Germans, in contrast, are not only brutal and destructive but also loud, vain and greedy: the Gestapo organiser slurps over a plate of soup while issuing brutal orders; the Nazi Protector of Holland is fooled by Van Leyden's flattery and his vanity allows him to be lured on to the submarine which is to be sunk.

In *Went the Day Well?*, the Germans are given less detailed attention. They are ciphers, necessary for the 'what if?' of the narrative but lacking the range of characteristics of their counterparts in *The Silver Fleet*. What is clear is their ruthless behaviour towards the villagers, threatening the children and gunning down the home guard as they cycle down the sunny country lane. Such behaviour is standard in representations of the Nazis in British war films but less standard is the way in which the initial amateurishness of the villagers' response gradually becomes more efficient and effective. The normal notion of the British muddling through is here replaced by resistance, planning and even, in the final defence of the manor house, pleasure in killing. In case this is misread as adoption by the English of German ruthlessness, the villagers' behaviour is balanced and excused by comparisons with another nation, the French, who allowed themselves to be overrun. As Nora pointedly comments, 'I haven't much sympathy for the French, they let us down so abominably'.

*Yellow Canary* displays considerable confusion about different national identities, but significantly what emerges is a solid, commonsense stability around male Anglo-Saxon behaviour and values contrasted with the unstable and emotional response from male and female European characters. On the Anglo-Saxon side, Sally is surrounded and supported by reliable men. The British secret service and the Canadian Mounted Police are presented as pragmatic, dogged and unassuming. Respect for the Canadians is particularly underlined; they are doing 'a grand job' comments a British intelligence officer. The position of the other allies in the film, the Poles, is by contrast

[ 233 ]

marred by the revelation that Jan, the tragic Polish captain, and his exiled mother, Madame Orloc, are Nazi saboteurs. The emotion which Jan brings to his descriptions of the bombing of Warsaw and the passion with which his mother toasts the European past are transformed by the revelation of their true identity. With equal emotion and equal passion, they fight for a Nazi future. Passion and commitment are thus linked to instability and excess in stark contrast to the phlegmatism of the British approach.

National identity is thus clearly marked out in each film and it is against that background that the identity of the traitor figure is created. In *The Silver Fleet*, Van Leyden is presented as modest, restrained and pragmatic. His love for his son and his wife is expressed with a passion that belies his conventional appearance but he is prepared to sacrifice domestic happiness for his nation. *The Silver Fleet*, like *Went the Day Well?*, addresses the question of occupation, asking 'How should we behave if the Nazis ran the country?' *The Silver Fleet* suggests that resistance is in the heart, not in outward behaviour. Van Leyden's compatriots misconstrue his behaviour – his socialising with the enemy, his refusal to join in subversive activity – because they do not know his true motivation. National identity cannot be understood through outward signs but through inner feelings which are known to the individual concerned. It is possible to conform *and* resist so judgements cannot be made about a person's actions without knowledge of their secret loyalties. Nationalism is thus not a public posture but a private negotiation within a given context.

*Went the Day Well?* also bases its occupation scenario on the difficulty of reading identity through outward signs of conformity and gives it a specifically class dimension. Here, the traitor figure Oliver conforms to the mores of the English upper middle class. He is accepted by the villagers on these terms and is so plausible that he is elected to represent them in the 'negotiations' with the Germans. Although the audience is alerted very early on to his true intentions, Oliver retains the trust of the villagers almost until the end. This automatic acceptance of the gentry's credentials is reinforced by the fact that no motivation is given for Oliver's treachery. His behaviour thus seems to be part of his character, as automatic as the commitment of other characters to fighting the invaders. Unlike *The Silver Fleet*, therefore, which suggests that one can fight the Germans under the cover of conformity, *Went the Day Well?* makes the more uncomfortable proposition that conforming to middle-class manners is no guarantee of national identity.

*Yellow Canary* offers a more reassuring account of classes united through nationalism in the war effort. Sally Maitland's upper-class background is initially part of the problem she presents. References to pre-war trips to Germany for meetings with Hitler create a character which would have had resonances with audiences looking back to the behaviour of certain members of the English upper classes in the 1930s. Sally's upright blondeness and her manner of innate superiority create a traitor figure who is convincing precisely because of doubts about the position of her class. Once again, though, like the other films under discussion, *Yellow Canary* suggests the deceptiveness of outside appearances in judging national identity, the misleading nature of signs of identification. Sally is finally revealed as an English heroine, the mismatch between outward appearance and inner commitment resolved by her adoption of the WRNS uniform.

The national identity of the traitor figure is also bound up with questions of gender. A secure sexual/romantic relationship is a sign of a secure national identity. In *The Silver Fleet* Van Leyden's deep love for his wife is expressed in his need for her to find out the truth about his actions after his death. The renewal of her love is important to his securing an identity as a hero. Similarly, in *Yellow Canary*, Sally returns to her family after her successful mission to reveal her true nature *and* her new husband, a secret agent who had known her identity all along. Thus, Sally's position in the family and the nation is secured. In contrast, in *Went the Day Well?*, the first sign of Oliver's potential for betraying his country is his ambiguous behaviour towards Norah in the opening scenes of the film. His willingness to use her evident feelings for him prefigures his lack of loyalty to the village and the nation; when she kills him, it is because he has betrayed his national identity but the emotional force of the action is linked to a sense of more personal betrayal.

Sexual identity and security is thus linked in all three films to national commitment, but the films also explore the specific roles which women can undertake within a broad national identity. In *The Silver Fleet*, Helene Van Leyden is narratively an outsider who knows less than the audience. She tries to understand her husband through the outward signs of his compliance with the Germans and loses touch with his inner allegiances. On the night before the sabotaged submarine test, Helene finally loses faith as Van Leyden ingratiates himself with the Nazis. On what will be the last night of his life, Helene locks the bedroom door to her husband. The camera frames him on the staircase; below is the German soldier left to 'protect' the household, above is the locked door of the bedroom. Like the Germans, Helene is excluded from true knowledge of her husband's heart, her faith has failed in the final test and she can do no more than read her husband's loving words after his death.

In *Went the Day Well?*, on the other hand, the women play an active part in the defence of the village. In typical Ealing fashion, the characters cover a wide range of ages and positions and as the villagers begin to develop a group identity and plan their counterattack, women of various ages and different classes contribute to the effort. The lady of the manor and the working-class postmistress, for instance, both show resourcefulness in trying to seek help and courage in fighting for the village. The two land-girls – one working-class, the other the more refined Peggy whose wedding is interrupted by the invasion – both take up arms to kill the invaders and the former gleefully relishes a hit. And it is Nora, the vicar's daughter, who finally discovers Oliver's true allegiances and kills him to prevent him from assisting the Germans further.

In *Yellow Canary*, a woman takes the central part in the action of the film. What is striking here is how doubts about Sally's national identity are tied up with her assertion of femininity. Her femininity is indeed part of her disguise; it marks her out as different from the other women in their uniforms, as one who can avoid clothing restrictions and the adoption of uniform. She dresses glamorously, flinging her fur coat across her shoulders in defiance, and uses lipstick to write a message on her mirror. She controls men and uses them, initially for minor purposes to get a table in a restaurant, later for the major activity of espionage, luring Jan into falling in love with her in order to fulfil her mission. Her style and glamour are the outward signs of her ambiguity, of our inability to understand her behaviour. At the end, when the truth is revealed, her femininity is banished. Secured by marriage and safely dressed in uniform, she becomes once again the well-scrubbed English rose.

Sexual and national identity are linked in all three films but they are mapped out in different ways and potentially offer quite different pleasures for women in the audience. *The Silver Fleet* puts its leading woman character on the sidelines, in the traditionally feminine position of trying to understand her husband's actions. It may be, however, that Helene's position as an outsider, reading the diary after the event, accurately acknowledged the feelings of exclusion and frustration experienced by women whose husbands, lovers, sons were away and whose only contact was by letter. Helene's position outside the narrative, trying to understand male action through hints and observations, may have had resonances with women who had experienced the same sense of distance. *Went the Day Well?*, on the other hand, shows women as central to the action of a group. It offers the pleasures of identification with realistic women characters whose lives are suddenly transformed by action. Women help to plan the resistance and their actions are amongst the most violent and striking: Mrs Collins throwing pepper in the eyes of the German soldier to distract him before she kills him and Nora confessing she has never used a gun before and promptly shooting her deceitful lover. Identification is also a possibility for women viewers of *Yellow Canary*. The risk-taking, ambiguous, glamorous Sally is a figure whose femininity both challenges and reassures. She offers an outlet for an expression of rebellion by women who might feel regimented and de-feminised by war but she also suggests that women's difference should not be read as treachery but as a different way of negotiating national identity.

In analysing the way in which these different narratives work with issues of nationality and femininity, I am suggesting that an examination of the textual complexity with which they are handled is important for understanding the range of pleasures they offer. The independent assertiveness of Sally in *Yellow Canary* is balanced by her return to the fold, predictable through Anna Neagle's presence; the ordinariness of the women in *Went the Day Well?* reinforces their extraordinary actions; and Googie Withers lends a poignant and erotic resonance to the familiar waiting role in *The Silver Fleet*. There has been a tendency in feminist criticism of British wartime films to value the excesses of fantasy and melodrama as the only way in which women's desires can be expressed. Sue Harper, for instance, stresses the way in which Gainsborough costume melodramas provide expression for female pleasure which, she claims, the more realist approach of other studios, particularly Ealing, does not.[2] This seems to underestimate the complex way in which films of this period acknowledged and reworked women's wartime experiences. Flamboyant heroines like Sally Maitland allowed for an expression of ambivalence about the reconciliation of femininity and national identity. But it is also important to recognise the way in which a particularly feminine discourse of waiting, grieving and loss finds a voice in the more restrained character of Helene Van Leyden, and that *Went the Day Well?*'s vigorous representation of older women, throwing pepper and bombs, has a force precisely because it occurs within a realist context. To impose too rigid a model on the films of this period is also to impose too rigid a view of the range of experiences the films were addressing for and with their female audiences.

### Notes

1  There is not space to discuss fully the way English identity is often assumed to stand for Britain in films of the Second World War. The three films discussed here follow the common practice of asserting a largely English identity as the basis for British national feeling.

2  See, for instance, S. Harper, 'Historical pleasures: Gainsborough costume melodramas', in C. Gledhill (ed.), *Home Is Where the Heart Is: Studies in Melodrama and the Woman's Film* (London, British Film Institute, 1987).

# 15

## The female audience: mobile women and married ladies

JANET THUMIM

### 'Audience' as a site of struggle

The state's hegemonic relation to its female subjects in wartime is fraught with contradictions: nowhere are these clearer than in the space between the fictional women on the cinema screen and the real historical subjects sitting in darkened auditoria up and down the country. For a balancing act is required here which entails a recognition, in the interests of wartime production, of the heterogeneity of female experience, at the same time as ensuring that women's necessarily subordinate position in patriarchy is not unduly jeopardised. Wartime propaganda ostensibly addressed to women spoke also to men: for the patriotic endeavours of the men serving in the armed forces were secured by reference to their paternal and filial duties to women – by putting themselves at risk they were protecting wives, mothers and daughters waiting in their homes. Despite the fact that, in the urban centres at least, 'the home' was at least as dangerous as 'the front', the rhetoric of patriotism required this trope which was, arguably, put into question by the more specific demand that women themselves should put their homes second to the interests of the nation – for the duration.

The autonomous female citizen, ready to go anywhere, do anything, in the interests of her beleaguered country, was a creature constructed by state propaganda in the interests of the war effort, but the very same state required too that its female subjects maintain their proper domestic destiny, although this was sadly disrupted by the temporary exigencies of war. And though propaganda skilfully deployed the forms of documentary to assert an interpretation of the mobile woman in the here and now which would serve the state's interests, the filmic devices of melodrama were also essential in securing audiences' attention to the decorative and dependent 'married lady'. The picture that emerges of the female cinema audience in wartime Britain thus entails a complex and fascinating interweaving of different interests, those of the state's wartime propaganda, of the film industry and of the audiences themselves. In exploring these often conflicting interests I have called on a range of different sources, many of which inform other essays in this collection. The Mass Observation archives yielded useful material about the habits and opinions of various sectors of the population on the home front. Many of their reports were commissioned by the state in order to gauge popular feeling about initiatives departing from pre-war conventions. Though Mass Observation reports occasionally considered the question of popular cinema and audience tastes, it is the film industry's trade magazines, serving the interests of distributors and exhibitors by recording which titles secured the best response at the wartime box-office, which give the most reliable sense of which films were most enjoyed by audiences. And, not least, many of the films themselves are still available.

But a simultaneous perusal of these disparate sources confirms the difficulty of ascertaining how this historical audience used the film images, raising questions about the extent to which popular cinema *was* instrumental in securing the dissemination of state propaganda and about how far our own readings of the films, informed as they must be by hindsight and scholarly preoccupations of one kind and another, can be expected to deliver a sense of this audience. In short, we have to consider a range of vested interests in a struggle for the meanings of the wartime cinema audience. What I want to explore in this chapter is the gap between filmic representations of and address to its audience, that is to say the film's explicit and implicit representations of its intended audience, and the category 'cinema audience' as a part of demographic data about Britain at war. Many of the home front films – which were by no means the most popular amongst contemporary audiences though they have fascinated later generations – did indeed seek to represent the audience to itself, deploying a complex mélange of realist and melodramatic modes in order to do so. In considering wartime women's understandings of such films – and of others with which they would appear to have engaged rather more fully – I call on the idea of the reader's negotiation of the film text, referencing the nuanced readings which must be the consequence of the individual's private use of the film text in producing her pleasure, engagement, and satisfaction. Thus the concept of the *use-value* of the film is one which has different meanings for the audience member, the cinema manager, and the state, as the film is evaluated according to the different criteria of individual pleasure, audience popularity, or effectivity as propaganda.

In pursuit of a fuller understanding of the female audience in wartime I have considered the question from different angles: I have considered the audience as it was represented *in* the films, observations made at the time *about* the cinema audience, and the relative popularity of various films as indicated by the *choices* audiences made at the box-office. Finally, I note the 'return' of the domestic as a preoccupation of the post-war cinema and audience in reviews of the 1950 film *Odette*. By comparing wartime representations of women with those popular with post-war audiences we can perhaps come to a fuller understanding of the complex relations in play between wartime images and their consumption. I hope to show that in this play, the hegemonic operations of the patriarchal state are especially, and unusually, visible.

### The audience in the film: *Millions Like Us* (1943)

Had a surprise today, Dad.
Got to go for my interview tomorrow at the labour exchange.
It's my call-up, Dad.
I'm a mobile woman.
They can put me anywhere, into anything.
I've no obligations.

As Celia (Patricia Roc) announces her call-up in *Millions Like Us*, a family discussion ensues in which the advantages of work in a munitions factory near her home are urged over her preferred option of conscription into one of the forces. The project of the film, to solicit the readiness of the female workforce to go willingly wherever they were needed, is announced in Celia's tearful remonstrance as her father attempts to keep her at home – 'Besides, I'm mobile'. The connotations of this term may be lost on us today, but to the cinema audiences of 1943 it signalled the latest intervention of the wartime state into the domestic life of British families. Not only were (some) women accepted into the various branches of the forces, the WRNS, the WAF, the ATS, but they were *conscripted* into these or, as this film demonstrates, into the equally crucial task of munitions production. Much of the film's narrative organisation is directed at the perceived opposition for the young women concerned – both those on the screen and, the film assumes, those in the audience – between the glamour of the forces and the tedium, already familiar to many, of local factory work. As Celia's fantasy in the labour exchange next day while she awaits her interview suggests, the glamour of the forces resided chiefly in the thrilling promise of romance, in an exciting and alluring contrast to the arguably less exotic pleasures of female camaraderie in the hostel, the air raid shelter and the production line. For Celia's family, however, the reverse is the case: her access to legions of unknown young men is a prospect fraught with dangers, while work in a factory, especially one near home, would entail minimal disruption to the established routines of domestic life. The work of the film, then, is to distance the supposed glamour of the forces while simultaneously emphasising the romantic possibilities of industrial conscription, and to substitute the peer group for the family group as the locus of individual identity and security. Celia's father may protest, 'I didn't know they were calling you up as quick as that, can't you say you are looking after the house?' Her sister-in-law, struggling to feed and clothe two children on an army wage supplemented by her own earnings, might depend on Celia's support, 'Can't you tell them you've got an old father to look after, and two children? They don't take you if you've got encumbrances, you know'. But neither of them has the right to compete with the need of the state for Celia's services[1] and, as Celia and millions like her were invited to acknowledge, taking their place in the adult world meant identifying their own needs with those of the state.

The conscription of women up to the age of forty-five from 1942[2] entailed what for most British subjects was an unprecedented departure from the prevailing ideas of appropriate female behaviour, and for some, no doubt, the first direct conflict between the requirements of the state and those of the family. It was hard to reconcile the prospect of hordes of autonomous young women with the twin ideals of filial respect and matrimonial duty which, in 1942, determined the social position of women. Mass Observation reported in May 1942 on attitudes to the conscription of women:

> nearly everybody found something to complain about in this matter. Rationing, previous conscription (including fire-watching and the Home Guard), restrictions and regulations, security measures and uniformities, have been accepted by the great majority of people. Conscription of women has aroused a type of response new in our experience – and we have studied the impact of every big new legislative measure since 1936.[3]

It was necessary to 'sell' the idea of the Mobile Woman not just to the women themselves but also to their fathers, brothers, husbands and mothers.[4] If Celia is obliged to make a 'sacrifice' in the interests of national survival, so too is her father, henceforward to be deprived of her care and obliged to fend domestically for himself. He too must be persuaded. The narrative carefully negotiates its address to parents who must be reassured about the well-being of their suddenly-independent daughters, with that to the young women themselves whose new found and paradoxical 'freedom' is at issue. It proceeds to demonstrate the positive benefits such an enforced departure from the confines of the parental home might have. In the case of the fictional Celia these are new friends, new places, new work and even a short-lived marriage with a very young airforce gunner, Fred Blake (Gordon Jackson), tragically curtailed by his death in action over Germany. At the end of the film Celia, by now no longer a tearful daughter but a full-blown tragic heroine, joins in the lunchtime factory singing as another wave of planes takes off in the valiant national struggle to which all other considerations must be subordinated until its successful conclusion. In this scene the film's moves between the documentary realism of the lunchtime ENSA concert in the factory canteen, an image familiar from many sources, and the heart-rending melodrama of Celia's pale but beautiful face and raised eyes exemplify the way in which the interdependence of these modes works in home front films to secure audiences' allegiance to the collective project.[5]

But an understanding of the national need for munitions was not in itself, it seems, a sufficient incentive for a life on the factory floor far from home. As the same Mass Observation report wryly noted: 'It may be good propaganda to say that conscripted factory girls are burning with zeal to have their smack at Hitler; but it is certainly not good policy to be taken in by your own propaganda and to spend time and effort appealing to emotions which aren't there, simply because one thinks they *ought* to be there'.[6] One of the tasks the producer-director team, Launder and Gilliat, set themselves in this film, which began its existence as a commissioned Ministry of Information propaganda short, was to persuade young female conscripts that munitions work was just as vital, and could offer just as much access to young male conscripts, as membership of the various women's branches of the forces – the WRNS, the WAF, the ATS. Running counter to the requirements of an appeal to the young women themselves (the conscription regulations specified women without dependants between the ages of eighteen and forty-five which in practice generally meant the younger of the specified age range) was the need to reassure men, largely those in the forces, that 'their' conscripted women would be adequately protected and cared for. Mass Observation reported in February 1942, for example, on the negative opinion of the ATS currently prevailing in the army: 'In view of the millions of men now in the army, each one of whom may be presumed to have influence over at least one woman, this anti-ATS complex among soldiers is an extremely important factor and obstruction to be overcome by ATS recruiting propaganda'.[7] These paternalist assumptions, no doubt well-founded, are ubiquitous amongst the volunteer observers. The importance of cinema as a means of disseminating propaganda to the people was not lost on Mass Observation:

> Women are doing a terrific job of work in this war ... they are if anything more patriotic and more unselfish than men. At the same time their patriotism is less directed, less based on a coherent appreciation of what is going on. They have not nearly enough information put across in ways that will hold their attention

... Women always read less than men, are less interested in newspapers, radio news and other forms of national propaganda. But they are particularly susceptible to films, illustrated posters, and other pictorial material.[8]

The question, however, of exactly how the contemporary female audience members may have understood, or used, the filmic constructions which aimed to stimulate their participation in the war effort, and what habits of viewing may have been engendered in the process, is not one that exercised Mass Observation. The attention of Mass Observation was in fact turning, during 1943, to *post-war* social aspirations. Early in 1942 the urgency of the need to mobilise all available resources, including female labour, overrode all other considerations. As the war progressed, however, the validation of female autonomy which was a consequence of the propagandist emphasis on women's democratic equality – their rights as well as their responsibilities – began to exceed its original propagandist requirements.

Though the most popular box-office hits of the mid-war years 1942 and 1943 were not, on the face of it at least, directly concerned with such details as conscription, many did deal in fictional terms with events and emotions close to the surface of wartime lives. How far did such films articulate the aspirations and problems of female experience, under the spotlight of propaganda attention? Here the concept of use-value and the idea of negotiation together acknowledge the co-existence, in the readerly construction of meaning, of imperatives which are not necessarily contradictory but may simply be different: the personal agenda informing the individual reader's activity may not have been imagined by the film-makers. We might speculate about the response of a young woman viewing Celia's argument with her father in *Millions Like Us*. Prior to this scene the text has already offered Celia as the central protagonist, encouraging spectatorial identification in various ways including a voyeuristic access to her fantasy imaginings of various conventionally romantic encounters in her possible future as a 'Wren', a member of the WAAF, and so on. This is the stuff of romance: the familiar narrative devices banishing realism and basking in a succession of semi-erotic fulfilments, one well-tried form of the pleasures of fiction. Yet at the same time the business of the film is to point out that this is, precisely, a fantasy, to put it on one side as it were, in the interests of a more prosaic and immediate concern which is essentially a demonstration of the more accessible and dependable social attractions of munitions work. The fantasy engagement ring slipped onto Celia-the-WAAF-nurse's finger by a grateful (and handsome) RAF officer is, in the end, no match for the real gold band symbolising her marriage to Gunner Fred Blake. The film's gold band is of course just as fictional a construct as its diamond ring, yet the diegetic opposition of the two and the narrative focus on Celia's 'real' experience in preference to her fantasy imaginings invites the spectator to read them differently, to read them as though the first (the diamond ring) *was* fictional whereas the second (the gold band) *is* real. Once again, melodrama and realism are skilfully deployed together. The filmic proposition about the two rings assumes that spectators – particularly the young women so clearly solicited as primary targets of the film's address – will be persuaded by recourse to their own experience of wartime Britain. Here the extra-cinematic knowledge and experience of audiences are, almost, included in the fiction through the device of the male narrator which asserts the relation between 'millions like us' and 'millions like you':

> *Voice-over:*
> Remember those gay carefree days before the war when eggs still came out of shells and the government only took some of your money, when you and millions like you swarmed to the seaside ... You could taste the salt in the air and the hops in the beer and still slip up on a piece of orange peel.
> *Written note on screen:*
> The orange is a spherical pulpish fruit of reddish yellow colour.

In other words the intended audience is figured in the film in the group of young women with whom Celia eventually finds herself. Here is another kind of pleasure. Although the second pleasure (the gold band) is in a sense predicated on a rejection of the first (the diamond ring), it is in practice possible for the audience to enjoy both at the same time. From the picture offered, through Mass Observation and other reports, it would seem likely that the young women whose possible real and fantasy experiences are the subject of the fiction were also likely to have recognised the substantial distance between Patricia Roc's life as a fictional munitions worker, and the tedium and isolation which must certainly have constituted at least part of the young conscript's experience in the service of the war effort.

### The audience observed

One of the more straightforward pleasures to be had from attending the cinema during wartime was the simple matter of being somewhere warm and dry for a few hours: of being one of a crowd taking time off from the gruelling realities of daily life. For many of the predominantly youthful audience too, it was a matter of being somewhere relatively (if paradoxically) private. Amongst the surviving ephemera of the period the picture of cinema-going that emerges is rather different from that derived from a study of the films alone. For the group of young female welders in Yorkshire, for example, whose letters to their former instructor during the year following their training are preserved in the Mass Observation archives, 'going to the pictures' is mentioned as a pursuit equivalent to 'going to the pub' or, in summer, 'going out to the country'. Though the letters contain much entertaining description of drinking, eating and dress, not to mention graphic details of new boyfriends, courtship exploits, and the intrigues of the factory canteen and shop floor, not a single film title is mentioned nor, perhaps more surprisingly, a single film star.[9]

In an historical conjecture such as this, therefore, it is important to remember that what comes before any consideration of what the audience did, what was understood from the available films, what pleasures may have been constituted, is the question of how they came to be in the cinema. How was the audience persuaded to *be* an audience? Amongst the tasks undertaken by the (largely middle-class) Mass Observers were periodic studies of various social groups, pursuits or venues. A January 1941 record of street life in various parts of London yielded some peripheral but nonetheless interesting notes on the frequency of groups looking at the displays outside cinemas without going in – as though the display was in itself a focal point.[10] Inside the cinemas, Mass Observers noted the greater proportion of 'youth' than was to be found in the streets, and noted also that same-sex pairs or groups were more usual than male–female couples, that there were almost no family groups and that there were more single boys than girls. This suggests that prior to its importance as a courtship venue for young people during wartime, the cinema was a meeting place. The audience, we might conclude, was just as interested in itself as it was in the films to be shown, a point not lost on Launder and Gilliat who as we have seen explicitly represented the audience to itself in *Millions Like Us*. It is also worth noting that cinema-goers habitually purchased entrance to a 'show' comprising several parts rather than to a specific title, and that their choice of venue was determined as much by the degree of comfort it offered as by its programming. Cinemas, not films, incited audience loyalties.[11]

The ideological work which, with hindsight, we may ascribe to particular films or to the institution in general was conducted against this background. Hence, perhaps, the perennial importance of clearly established generic frameworks in soliciting audiences and, in the cinema of the Second World War period, the frequently emphatic presence of such narrative supports as diegetic music, stylised and spectacular costumes and *mise en scène* characteristic not of all, but certainly of an appreciable proportion of the films achieving large scale box-office success. Despite the fact that the audience was in the cinema, the film still had to work hard to claim and maintain its attention. We might conceive of filmic 'address' not just as the textual analysts' term for particular details of narrative organisation, but in the rather more practical and immediate sense of an unmistakable yell to the audience to pay attention to the narrative. Nevertheless, whether or not the audience did pay any attention to the film on the screen, in mid-1943 the cinema was 'an important form of recreation for one-third of the adult civilian population, who go once a week or more often'.[12]

One-third of the adult civilian population is a lot of people. In addition there was the large number of cinema-going children whose habitual presence augured well for the post-war cinema, as well as the forces audience, many of whom would have been on leave in the urban centres at any particular time, not to mention the army camp cinemas which attracted sizeable audiences, including civilians. Because of the size of the audience and because of the importance of utilising as effectively as possible all available means of communication between the government and the people, the cinema audience was the subject of special enquiries by the Ministry of Information in June and July 1943 – that point in the war, we should note, when the prospect of an Allied victory began to be clear, if not imminent – and in March and October 1946, soon after the cessation of hostilities. The timing of the first survey suggests that, perhaps not altogether consciously, the question of the shape of post-war Britain was beginning to exercise Ministry officials. The Beveridge Report, the blueprint for the post-war establishment of the 'Welfare State', had been published in December of the previous year. It is also the point, according to Angus Calder's useful study of the home front, when domestic politics began once more to preoccupy the citizens of Britain, evidenced in the attention generated by the spate of by-elections early in 1944.[13]

For all these reasons the 1943 MoI audience study paid particular attention to the composition of the audience on the one hand, and on the other hand to the declared cinema-going habits of particular population groups. Indeed this is the limit of the survey: the question of *how* the audience, or individual members of it, experienced the cinema in general or specific films in particular is beyond its scope. Not a single film title, nor a single actor, is mentioned in the survey. Nevertheless it does offer an invaluable resource to cinema historians, enabling us to note the important differentiations of the cinema audience which, en masse, was responsible for the box-office successes of some films and stars rather than others.

The picture of the mass cinema audience in mid-1940s Britain which emerges in this survey is one which accounts, to some extent, for the noticeably class-based scorn of film critics in the 1940s for the tastes of this audience.[14] According to the survey about two-thirds of the adult population attended 'sometimes', of which over half were regular attenders (once a week or more). Amongst this large group the less well-off, the less well-educated, urban dwellers, the young – particularly the fourteen to seventeen age group – and women are disproportionately represented, there being considerably more of these groups in the cinema audience than in the national demographic breakdown. This fairly crude differentiation is slightly refined by the observation that amongst occupation groups, factory, clerical and distributive workers attended with the greatest frequency and that while women accounted for a slightly larger proportion than men, housewives were less frequent cinema-goers. The conclusion, which recalls in its language the function of the survey, notes that: 'In general it may be said that the larger groups of the population are relatively better represented in the cinema audience than they are in the publics reached by other visual publicity media such as newspapers and books'.[15] During the war, then, the 'female audience', though occasionally including women of all ages and from all walks of life, implies a grouping of adolescent or young adult women, probably with low-paid and minimally skilled jobs in factories, offices and shops, living and working in the urban centres. They worked hard, too, as other sources testify. The routine evident between the lines of the young women welders' letters was a punishing one, and another Mass Observation report specifically investigating the activities of girls between school leaving age (then fourteen) and the registration age of eighteen noted of the urban group that 'of those with jobs, over four-fifths work over 8 hours a day, and of those at school seven-tenths work these hours. Coupled with the very considerable amount of housework, which few of them escape, it really does seem that the majority genuinely have very little time to spare.'[16] The other feature of the mid-1940s population that begins to emerge, both inside and outside the cinema, is of a nation far less united than subsequent, post-war accounts of Britain under siege would have us believe. Not only were party politics apparent once more, but there is also some evidence of a perennial mistrust of government edicts as well as of a greater awareness of gender inequities than is usually associated with the images purveyed during the war and those constructed later, in re-tellings of the period. Some of these sentiments surfaced in the responses to a survey investigating the proposed call-up of 'older' women (over forty-five), a proposition which was, in the event, abandoned.

> There are a lot of men wandering around and pleasing themselves what they do. Any man who isn't accepted for the army is allowed to choose for himself what he'll do and where he'll be. Women aren't allowed to do that. (woman, age 40)[17]

> Oh, I'm not worrying about it too much because I don't think they'll ever put it through. Not with the end of the war in sight. It may be a long way off, but it's in *sight*. And people who would be willing to give just that extra shove to the wheel, if things were desperate, aren't willing now. *Nobody* believes things are desperate. No, I don't think they'll ever get this call up through. Everybody's against it. I don't know anybody that isn't. All this talk about peace and planning and reconstruction, and then they suddenly behave as if we had our backs

[ 247 ]

to the wall. Just like all that yelling about the birth-rate when there's more babies than ever before. (woman, age 45)[18]

These statements give the impression of a degree of dissent, of a distinct *lack* of consensus. If this has any foundation – and there is plenty of evidence to support the proposition that audiences were both alert and hostile to overt propaganda – it would follow that the idealised imagery to be found in popular cinematic hits of the day, both of the nation and of the feminine, would certainly have been taken with a pinch, if not a large handful, of salt by contemporary female audience members. The questions of use-value, of nuanced readings and of the negotiations involved in the readers' acceptance or refusal of textual propositions are all crucial here in considering what audiences did with the films they chose to watch.

## Audience choice: *Mrs Miniver* (1942) and *The Man in Grey* (1943)

Despite these caveats about the composition of the audience and its undoubted distance from the object of its attention, the films, the question of which of the many films on offer *were* most successful remains central to my enquiry: which films *did* the wartime audience find most pleasurable, valuable or useful? A correlation of the main annual assessments of box-office success in the trade papers *Kinematograph Weekly* and *Motion Picture Herald* with the annual poll of readers' opinions conducted by the fan magazine *Picturegoer*, yields a list of popular titles and/or stars' names which provide a sufficiently accurate picture of contemporary popularity for this discussion of the female audience and its activity.[19] In addition to these sources Mass Observation issued a directive in November 1943 to its regular respondents which, among other questions, asked about cinema-going and in particular about respondents' recent favourite films. The largely middle-class respondents included many who were not cinema-goers or who went so rarely that they were hard put to it to recall any titles from the war years at all, let alone the current year, confirming the MoI 1943 audience survey observation that British cinema audiences were predominantly composed of people from the lower socio-economic groups. But among those Mass Observers who did name up to six films which they had enjoyed, many mentioned the titles which also dominated the correlation outlined above.[20] According to this correlation, then, the most popular films at the British box-office in 1942[21] were, in this order:

*Mrs Miniver*
*The First of the Few* (1942 )
*Sergeant York* (1941)
*Captains of the Clouds* (1942)

*Holiday Inn* (1942)
*How Green Was My Valley* (1941)

and in 1943 they were:

*The Man in Grey*
*The Life and Death of Colonel Blimp* (1943)
*Random Harvest* (1942)
*In Which We Serve* (1942)
*Casablanca* (1942)
*The Black Swan* (1942)

A closer look at the themes of these films shows that they fall into two distinct categories. The majority deal directly with war experiences, though not exclusively those of the current war, while wartime concerns are markedly absent, at least overtly so, from the rest. It is also true to say that the terms 'realism' and 'fantasy' are not at all useful in summarising the differences evident here. Not only do many of the films draw freely on both sets of conventions, as we have seen in the case of *Millions Like Us*, but they also deploy them hermeneutically – here again, we might note, it's a question for both film historians and contemporary audiences alike, of negotiating plural frames of reference.

I want to look a bit more closely at the 'top hit' of each year, *Mrs Miniver* in 1942 and *The Man in Grey* in 1943. Not only was each title markedly the most popular in its release year, but also both films, according to trade paper and critical summaries, were thought to have a particular appeal for a female audience. Perhaps this accounts for their contemporary box-office acclaim which, with hindsight, might seem surprising given the more durable reputation of some of the other titles. Both films place the experiences of female protagonists at the centre of their narratives, and both, interestingly, deal with the relations *between* female characters as well as with their plot-specific experiences. There are, clearly, many differences between these two films. The American *Mrs Miniver* offers an unashamedly romantic and idealised 'Hollywood' version of a British wartime experience, first published in fictional form as a serialised diary.[22] It is a study of a rural English village, its ancient customs, practices and class structures rudely interrupted by the drama of war. The British *The Man in Grey* is a period melodrama dripping with excess in its study of the callousness of dynasty and the hopelessness of penury in Regency England. The film opens and closes with a relatively realist portrayal of contemporary blacked out, blitzed London, imbricating the past and present through the device of the pairs of lovers, one Regency (and doomed), one present-day (and full of hope), both played by Phyllis Calvert and Stewart Granger.

Despite their differences, however, and despite the conceptual distance between Hollywood's version of the home counties middle classes and Gainsborough's fantasy of the Regency aristocracy, their central female protagonists have many features in common. In *Mrs Miniver* there are three women: Mrs Miniver herself (Greer Garson), her daughter-in-law Carol (Teresa Wright), and Carol's grandmother, the irascible Lady Beldon (Dame May Whitty). *The Man in Grey* has two central female characters: Clarissa (Phyllis Calvert) and Hester (Margaret Lockwood). In both films these characters meet, or, in the cases of Mrs Miniver and Lady Beldon, have to endure the consequences of, violent and tragic deaths. In both films too, class divisions are shown to be responsible for the inappropriate discord which threatens social cohesion, and the narrative resolutions also entail the resolution of class divisions. The aristocratic Lady Beldon is initially resistant both to the marriage between her family and the thoroughly middle-class Minivers, and to the prospect of the station porter's success in the village's annual prize rose contest, a trophy she herself was accustomed to winning. The rose, in this Hollywood confection, is imbued with all the perennial qualities of Englishness which will survive the national crisis (a British film might have been more alert to the potentially divisive nationalist overtones), although, as the narrative suggests, outworn structures such as those of class will have to be jettisoned in the interests of survival. At the beginning of the film the two old bell-ringers consider whether the onset of war will put the annual flower show in question:

> 1st old man:    If war comes, it's good-bye roses.
> 2nd old man:    Don't be silly, you might as well say good-bye England.
>                 There'll always be roses.

Needless to say, the flower show is held, though it is dramatically curtailed by the aerial attack from which Mrs Miniver and Carol are fleeing when the latter is killed by a stray bullet. And, also needless to say, Lady Beldon overcomes her scruples and awards the prize to the station porter Mr Ballard for his rose, named for Mrs Miniver. This proletarian, not to say peasant compliment to a middle-class heroine provides a nicely ambiguous solution to the question of class, in which the dominance of the bourgeoisie in exchange for that of the aristocracy is offered *as if* it were equivalent to an egalitarian classlessness.

In *The Man in Grey* the damaging strictures of class division are located in the distant past of the Regency period. Their absence in the egalitarian (though still noticeably middle-class) present is signalled in the new and promising liaison between Clarissa, the last of the Rohan line, and the descendant of Rokeby, the Regency Clarissa's lover, which frames the narrative by means of the device of the auction rooms in blacked out London.

'Isn't it a lovely day?' Clarissa asks, echoing exactly her ancestor's words to the Regency Rokeby as, at the end of the film, they leave the sale and run for a passing bus, in a realist version of the wartime here and now. The present-day frame for *The Man in Grey*'s narrative of passion, suffering, desire and death asserts that there is no place in the present for outmoded class constraints and their superfluous and destructive intervention in human relations. Hence the experiences of suffering and death which dominate the narratives of both films are endowed with meanings which attempt to validate, if not always to justify, them. In these two films, as in many other popular successes of the mid-war period, it is the women whose suffering, stoicism, courage and restraint is recognised and celebrated by demonstrating its vital function in maintaining the meta-structures of family and nation – though not, as we have seen, of class – and so of ensuring the postwar future.

There were other pleasures to be had from an evening at the pictures – the spectacle of dress, style, interiors and so forth being one which drew frequent comments – this pleasure residing precisely in its *difference* from day-to-day wartime. Gainsborough discovered this with *The Man in Grey* and produced a series of costume dramas during the 1940s, of which the *The Wicked Lady* (1945) was the most successful. Though such films were routinely vilified by the critics of the day, they were enjoyed by large audiences and therefore found favour with exhibitors. The relatively simple pleasures of spectacles of dress, luxury and of other times and places, were imbricated in the more complex satisfaction to be had from the cathartic release of emotion which could be the consequence of a therapeutic engagement with narratives of emotion and fantasy, indicating diverse 'use-values' for the individual reader. Every audience in 1942–43 was more likely than not to have included those who had recently suffered bereavement, displacement, or other traumatic fracturing of their daily routines. Such experiences surely encouraged a heightened susceptibility to the workings of melodrama in general and to these stories of war and suffering in particular. Another part of the package is the development of habits of viewing, the gradual and no doubt unconscious use of cinematic imagery as a source of information about the moral values attached to various forms of behaviour, or to the consequences of one or another kind of decision. Hence we can speculate that by the end of the war there was a mass audience accustomed to receiving ideological propositions in a fictional context. Particular ideological suggestions were additionally privileged by means of their imbrication with the satisfaction produced in the audience by the narrative closure, though, as I have suggested, this was always likely to have been inflected by the readers' own nuancing of fictional constructs. Despite such nuancing, however, the cinema was consciously employed by the state as a propaganda device in films such as *Millions Like Us*, and doubtless in this case the audience too was conscious of the propagandist intention and methods.

But there's an important difference between the rousing factory lunchtime chorus of 'There was I, waiting at the church' with its documentary *mise en scène* in which the bereaved (and melodramatic) Celia joins through her tears as the RAF flies overhead on another mission at the close of *Millions Like Us*, and the priest in his pulpit preaching the 'peoples' war' in *Mrs Miniver's* finale as the survivors of the air raid, in which Carol was killed, mourn their dead. Though the ideological project of each scene is the same – the united and class-free British demonstrating their invincible solidarity – the former proposes itself as co-extensive with the 'real' experiential world of its audience whereas in *Mrs Miniver* the significatory excesses of the closing scene are in danger of producing a *reductio ad absurdum* in which state, Church, and patriarchy are conflated. Its symbolic reductions risk, in the process, the audience's refusal of its propositions.

At issue here is the question of how contemporary women might have used such images to negotiate their own paths through patriarchal social structures. To what extent did the patriotic insistence on the concept of the nation enable the female audience to distinguish between the state, which proposed itself as an ungendered entity, and oppressive social structures which they were invited to understand as a legacy of the past, no longer appropriate to the 'modern' world? In *The Man in Grey* the class-free and gender-egalitarian wartime present is celebrated; in *Millions Like Us* Celia's tragedy is endowed with national significance. But at what points, we could ask, was there an evident conflict of interests between the (arguably) legitimate demands of the (ungendered) wartime state, and the (arguably) illegitimate demands of a repressive patriarchy? Where, in these filmic propositions, does patriarchy reveal itself?

### Conscripts go home: *Odette* (1950)

It is striking to note that in the small groups of top box-office hits between 1940 and 1950, the clearest opportunities for readings subversive of patriarchy tend to cluster in the immediate post-war period rather than at the height of the wartime crisis. Films such as *The Wicked Lady*, *Brief Encounter* (1945), or *Piccadilly Incident* (1946) detailed the extreme emotional traumas of their heroines and also demanded substantial sacrifice of them, locating these traumatic experiences firmly in the individual psyche – the *collective* significance of the heroine's moral choice being consequently diminished. In the more speculative climate stimulated by consideration of the post-war world it becomes possible for the audience to read the required sacrifice as unreasonable, if not entirely unnecessary.[23]

In the post-war society of reconstruction conflicting interests could surface. Though the popular cinema of the later 1940s, both in the UK and in the United States, is notable for its thematic concentration on female experience, it is the punishment of the transgressive female, or the repositioning of the mistaken woman, that forms the basis of most such narratives. *Mildred Pierce* (1945), *It Always Rains on Sunday* (1947), and *Gilda* (1946), for example, all demonstrate that women *cannot* be permitted to act autonomously but must be secured within the heterosexual couple, the prelude to the nuclear familial unit, for their own protection. Thus post-war cinema offered rich terrain for nuanced readings often directly opposed to those urged in the narrative closures, an opportunity seized with pleasure by many audience members.[24]

What is so interesting about the later 1940s is the extent to which this routine negotiation threatens to identify the arbitrary nature of social and sexual hierarchies. The fairly savage attack on the concept of the autonomous woman typical of immediately post-war films is in marked contrast to the box-office hits of 1950 and 1951 which celebrated the 'rebirth' of the domestic, dependent woman fulfilled by her dependence, sated with her domesticity. Though such titles as *All About Eve* (1950), *Born Yesterday* (1950), *Annie Get Your Gun* (1950) and *Odette* still centre on a female protagonist, their narratives are devoted to a demonstration of the difficulties she experiences in her autonomous activities, and their narrative resolutions, their 'happy endings', have her firmly and happily re-placed in the arms of a husband, a proper married lady at peace in her domestic context.

*Odette* is of particular interest in connection with this discussion of the female cinema audience since it chronicles, in a fictional reconstruction, the real-life exploits of a war heroine and her undercover experience working for British Intelligence with the French Resistance and, later, incarcerated in a German prisoner-of-war camp. Can Odette be understood as a paradigm for the conscripted women of the war period? Wrenched from her pre-war life as an 'ordinary' mother of three and plunged into unlooked-for braveries, hardships and heroism, she not only survives with her morale intact but also sacrifices herself for her colleague, lover and post-war husband Peter Churchill (Trevor Howard). At her rescue she happily abandons her military career and her wartime self, returning – so the film suggests – to an untroubled domesticity. Both the cost of victory and its reward are summarised in the haggard, shuffling and unkempt figure of Odette in the film's final scene which takes place in the War Office where her 'adventures' had first begun. When she turns to see Peter at the door, however, the film cuts in to a close-up of her tear-stained face as she begins to smile: now their romance – tentatively suggested in Annecy just before their capture – can blossom in the spring sunshine of London visible through the open window behind them.

The veracity of the film's account was emphasised in reviewers' references to her participation in the production. 'Herbert Wilcox ... had Odette by his side throughout the picture and turned to her for guidance in this respect throughout the filming of her own story.'[25] 'The real Odette, Mrs Peter Churchill, advised on every phase of the production and the film emerges as dramatic entertainment rather than a documentary.'[26] Odette's involvement was also underlined by her attendance with Peter Churchill (they had married in 1947) at the film's royal premiere on 6 June 1950. Whether or not the truth of Odette Sansom's life was different from this account is beside the point: it is this version, personified by that icon of British womanhood, Anna Neagle, which earned the approval of the post-war audience. In the flurry of publication which accompanied the release of the film emphasis was placed on Anna Neagle's 'bravery' in playing a part 'without glamour'[27] as well as on Odette's own bravery chronicled in the film. In the conflation of two kinds of bravery a connection is suggested between Neagle's 'work' and Odette's, and, by extension, with the wartime work of the film's female audiences. But just as Odette's exploits were offered as exemplary of the sacrifices many 'ordinary' women had been required to make, so her post-war aspirations were also suggested to be universal ones. A feature in the magazine *Woman* emphasised her wartime experiences as disruptive of more appropriate aspirations:

> We found the house at the end of a steep, narrow road ... the same impulse, or 'hunch' which launched me on my wartime adventures in France and Germany seemed to be at work again, compelling me to linger in this quiet place ... I should explain that one of my chief occupations during periods of solitary confinement had been to furnish and refurnish all the houses I had known or lived in.[28]

Odette's wartime task is completed, but the work in which many female subjects engaged during wartime was not, was never completed – particularly that of the many left to raise families without the support of a male partner or even of a male wage. The idea of women's work, in these 'reconstructive' films of the early 1950s, is *in itself* suggested to be temporary, to be unnecessary to the 'norm' of peacetime society. Odette's emphatic and understandable relief at the prospect of post-war domestic anonymity was linked with comments on Neagle's own domesticity and her pronouncements on 'the feminine'. A *Picture show* reporter found her 'busy in a gingham apron' and went on to note that 'Anna loves her home life just as much as she loves making films';[29] while a more 'in depth' two-page feature in *Picturegoer* noted:

[ 254 ]

Anna is a man's woman. All her life she has enjoyed the society of men, man's talk, man's games ... Women, she holds, have their own place and their own function in life which is, according to some modern standards, restrictive. Women should go about the business of being women a bit more, thinks Anna. They should study the graces of the home and of deportment.[30]

The same theme informs William Whitebait's *New Statesman* review of the film and, in particular, his response to Odette's 'look': 'Her photograph, back among her children after the war, shows a young smiling mother who might have been no farther than picnicking at Henley'.[31]

Celia's wartime mobility in *Millions Like Us*, which asserted both the duties and the rights of women's democratic autonomy, is transformed, in the figure of Odette, into an extreme and even 'unnatural' act of bravery for which there is no longer any necessity. In between Odette and Celia is the transitional figure of Barbara in *The Wicked Lady* whose equally 'unnatural' behaviour is condemned precisely because it is in her *own* interests which, in this post-war fiction, are carefully shown to be opposed to the effective and harmonious maintenance of the social order. Hence the historical experience of the female subject is denied in the post-war period; her mid-wartime centre-stage position refused. With hindsight the extraordinary precariousness of the constructs of 'the feminine' offered to wartime audiences becomes clear: less than ten years from the mid-war *Millions Like Us* the mobile woman gives place to the married lady, busy in her gingham apron, happy in her kitchen.

## Notes

1  See Penny Summerfield's essay in this volume for a full discussion of wartime legislation, recommendations, and practices of 'call-up' for various categories of women.

2  *Ibid.*

3  Mass Observation 1 May 1942 File Report No. 1238, p. 17.

4  See Summerfield in this volume.

5  See Christine Gledhill's much fuller discussion of this point, in this volume.

6  Mass Observation 1 May 1942 File Report 1238, p. 5.

7  Mass Observation 2 February 1942 File Report No. 1083, p. 9.

8  Mass Observation 1 May 1942 File Report No. 1238, p. 33.

9  Mass Observation Box 3 File F; see also D. Sheridan (ed.), *Wartime Women* (London, Mandarin, 1991), pp. 176–180.

10  Mass Observation Box 2 File F.

11  Mass Observation October 1946 File Report No. 2429, p. 2; March 1947 File Report No. 2464, p. 15.

12  MoI Wartime Social Survey June/July 1943 *The Cinema Audience*, p. 3.

13  See A. Calder, *The People's War* (London, Granada, 1971), pp. 636–40.

14  J. Ellis, 'Art, culture, quality: terms for a cinema in the forties and seventies', *Screen*, Vol. 19 No. 3 (1978).

15 MoI Wartime Social Survey, June/July 1943, *The Cinema Audience*, p. 2.

16 Mass Observation 12 January 1943 File Report No. 1567, p. 4.

17 Mass Observation August 1943 File Report No. 1980, p. 6.

18 *Ibid.*

19 See J. Thumim, *Celluloid Sisters: Women and Popular Cinema* (London, Macmillan, 1992); J. Thumim, 'The "popular", cash and culture in the post-war British cinema industry', *Screen*, Vol. 32 No. 3 (1991); and J. Thumim, 'Film and female identity: questions of method in investigating representations of women in popular cinema', in C. McCabe and D. Petrie (eds), *New Scholarship from BFI Research* (London, British Film Institute, 1996), pp. 157–86, for fuller discussions of my correlative method.

20 The total number of titles appearing in any of the correlated listings was thirty-nine in 1942 and fifty-one in 1943. The total number of films on release would have been substantially larger: these titles appear because they were considered noteworthy in at least one of the categories correlated.

21 Annette Kuhn, in this volume, makes an important distinction between British cinema culture and British cinema in the 1930s: 'since Hollywood still provided the majority of films screened in Britain, British cinema *culture* was far from co-extensive with British cinema', which is also true of the 1940s and 1950s.

22 Jan Struthers, *Mrs Miniver* (London, Virago, 1989).

23 J. Thumim, *Celluloid Sisters*, pp. 57–63.

24 *Ibid.*, pp. 167–8, 178.

25 *Picturegoer*, 1 July 1950, p. 5.

26 *Motion Picture Herald*, 6 January 1951.

27 *Picturegoer*, 1 July 1950, p. 5.

28 'Odette Churchill, G.C. looks forward to happiness', *Woman*, 12 August 1950, p. 13.

29 'Round the British Studios', *Picture show*, 25 August 1951.

30 'Twenty glorious years' in *Picturegoer*, 10 June 1950, pp. 7–8.

31 *New Statesman*, 17 June 1950.

# 16

## Stepping out or out of step? Austerity, affluence and femininity in two post-war films

MELINDA MASH

The negotiation of possible femininities in post-war Britain took place in a climate of tension: that between the experience and expectations of the post-war years and the stimulus of wartime identities and desires. Expressed in a variety of contexts (government reports, surveys, psychological and psycho-analytic studies and theories, popular newspapers, women's magazines) and naming a range of 'problems' (women and work, women and the family, motherhood, domesticity), the various discourses surrounding women attempted to contain the contradictions and tensions that abounded in a period of uncertainty and reconstruction.

The movement between an immediate post-war 'age of austerity' and the 'affluent society' of the mid-1950s was inscribed onto both the bodies of real women and their cinematic representations. Throughout this period, 'austerity' and 'affluence' had a complex existence and operated across different spheres: economic, social, and ideological. Hence they encompass material conditions, 'imagined relations' invoked to hold together a fractured and rapidly changing nation, and specifically gendered discourses addressed to women. The material conditions of 'austerity' and 'affluence' (the shift from a culture of shortage, rationing and sacrifice to an apparent abundance and the rise of expansive consumption) were underlined by a popular rhetoric that also foregrounded particular assumptions about femininity and womanliness. Women were stitched into this rhetoric in ways that advanced notions of appropriate feminine behaviour and particular patterns of consumption. In this sense 'austerity' and 'affluence' can also be understood in relation to post-war attempts to reconstruct and resituate dominant notions of femininity and female sexuality.

It is my intention to demonstrate that popular cinema in the late 1940s and early 1950s was determined by and contributed to this restructuring process. Moreover, I would suggest that the representation of women in British films narrowed down possibilities for audiences, resulting in a national cinema that offered only limited strategies for the exploration of desires and ambitions other than those in accordance with dominant attitudes.[1] Indeed, I would argue that the femininities represented were contained within a rigid hierarchy and were deeply rooted in the construction of class identities. Thus, British films of this period were bounded by the rhetoric of 'austerity' and 'affluence'. Certain class-specific notions of femininity and sexuality were key elements in British films and these played upon ideas of women as unreliable, subject both to the lures of glamour and to the 'pernicious' influence of 'Americanisation' with its attendant threat to preferred notions of Britishness.

To this effect, I shall discuss two films: *Dance Hall* (1950) and *Turn the Key Softly* (1953). These films position, present and characterise women in quite specific ways through the prescription of 'proper' modes of feminine behaviour and patterns of consumption. Furthermore, they clearly demonstrate the centrality of femininity to concepts of 'austerity' and 'affluence'.

### 'Let's dance, I haven't danced for ages'

*Dance Hall*, released in 1950, clearly evokes the 'age of austerity' and women's position within it. As with *Millions Like Us* (1943), *Dance Hall* at times uses a quasi-documentary style to align itself with a mobilised female workforce. However, whereas *Millions Like Us* seeks to contain the contradictions raised by women's new (if 'temporary') gender roles through the invocation of a collective and democratic community and the reinstatement of a domesticity that will heal the wounds of wartime, *Dance Hall* offers up an invitation to inhabit a new space: not the space of pre-war containment and production, but that of post-war reconstruction and consumption. This film presents a differently emphasised autonomous role for women, as consumers rather than producers, and explores the contrary and the absonant through an examination of the disjunction between the characters' desires, ambitions and expectations of marriage and domesticity, and the uneasy relationship of this to a newly emphasised role for women.

Thus, *Dance Hall* outlines the lives and experiences of four women – Eve (Natasha Parry), Mary (Jane Hylton), Georgie (Petula Clark) and Carole (Diana Dors) – and through these characters it represents the contradictions between woman as worker, woman as 'homemaker' and woman as a consumer who is drawn into the rhetoric of 'affluence' and susceptible to 'Americanisation'. The opening sequence of the film transports us and the characters from the workplace into the cramped and crowded homes in which they live, and then to the Chiswick Palais: three sites which recur throughout the film.

The factory scenes recall images of women as wartime workers: overall-clad figures in headscarves on the production line surrounded by the trappings of factory life – oily rags, clutter and incessant noise, punctuated by the end-of-shift siren. These scenes are always juxtaposed against domestic scenes and thus rather than fixing women in the role of worker, they situate the characters more centrally in relations of consumption: these are 'modern' women who work in order to be able to play.

The home mediates between the women's involvement in the world of work and that of consumption and provides a space of transformation from worker to consumer. These homes are not 'private' places: bedrooms are always shared and siblings are always present, fathers are no more than shadowy figures behind the evening newspaper, mothers fulfil 'traditional' female roles – ironing, preparing dinner. This domesticity is something that Eve, Mary, Georgie and Carole believe they will escape from (they *don't* want to be 'like their mothers'), yet they also aspire to conventionality (they *do* want to be married). The bars on Eve's bedroom window echo the confinement she feels when she has a 'home of her own': the flat she shares with her husband (Phil) is dark and as she ties her apron strings she tries to conform to the domestic role she always wanted but she is no good at it; she breaks things, knocks things over. The distant strains of big-band music transport her away from the restraints of home life and into a world of fantasy. These domestic scenes represent the disjunction between the characters' desires and their experience: cramped living spaces over which they exercise only nominal control, places where they feel hemmed-in, as Eve's experience demonstrates. In *Dance Hall*, working-class domesticity represents an 'austerity' that is both real and imaginary, and contradictory; home life is functional but not necessarily comfortable, it is domestic and familial but not private or intimate. Yet at the same time, the home acts as a transitional space between work and leisure and therefore it is also a place wherein the imaginative possibilities of other experiences are contained and nurtured.

The location that embodies imagination and fantasy is the dance hall; it is here that the women want to be, it is here that they can be 'themselves' and it is here that they are exposed to, and seduced by, the glamour and promise signified by 'affluence' and 'Americanness'. From the grandeur of the décor (the columns, sweeping staircases, lights and balcony); to its inhabitants (men in bow ties who are smart, suave, polite and protective – even paternal, as the manager arranges for Georgie to have a 'real' ballroom dancing gown for the competition); to the thrill and abandonment of dancing itself ('I want to dance', says Eve; 'I want to go now', replies Phil; 'ladies, ladies, come out of that jungle' urges the manager to two young women who are jiving), the Palais represents all that is exciting and other. The milieu of the dance hall provides a transition from the forced closeness of council flats, where too many people live in too small a space, into an arena where a desired intimacy is legitimated.

This is also the site through which the characters enter into new patterns of consumption. Yet the desire to escape from a world bounded by 'austerity' is tempered by another boundedness: the lack of means ever to fully escape. This is most poignantly articulated when Georgie's parents come to watch her dance in the competition; she is not wearing the dress they made sacrifices to give her and they try to leave before she notices their presence. Georgie's guilt at betraying her parents is also that precipitated by her attempt to replace her working-class reality and its values with the fantasy offered by 'affluence'.

A central feature of the ideological configuration of the immediate post-war period is the evocation of America and 'Americanness' as a force both seductive and threatening to established Britishness and as a sign of aspiration and consuming power. In *Dance Hall* the danger and promise of 'Americanness' is located in the Palais itself, with its promise of riches and success (the dancing competition and prize money as well as the imaginative sphere it represents), and through the presence of a 'real' American, Bonar Colleano as Alec. It is through the character of Alec, a spiky and angular man, unconcerned with and detached from the human dramas that surround him and which he precipitates, that the glamour, insincerity, gloss and ultimately unfulfilling nature of Americanisation reveals itself. Alec owns his own flat, has an open-top sports car and the latest Benny Goodman record, and he shakes his cigarettes out of the packet. He is Eve's dancing partner for the competition (because Phil neither dances nor wants to). When Eve, already married, visits Alec in his flat the empty promise of 'Americanisation' is echoed by the words of a song Hy Hazel is singing, one she also sings at the Palais: 'You're only dreaming … What a fool you are … Why won't you understand, fairyland won't do … '. While Phil and Eve exist in a world where tins of food and steak are all 'on points', Alec has an excess of food – a flat full of Scottish kippers, more than he can eat or give away. And when Alec attempts to seduce Eve for a second time she refuses; recognising the shallowness of their affair she tells him that in retrospect their first encounter was insignificant. Similarly, Georgie does not dance well with Peter because she has fallen for the fantasy of the borrowed dress ('Its just like stepping into a cloud') over the more mundane virtues of the dress (plain and 'straight') that her parents gave her. Alec's last words in the film – 'I used to thank my lucky stars that I didn't care about anybody; now I know that nobody cares about me' – express the dichotomy and impossibility of the 'American dream' in post-war Britain: it may be a fantasy, it may be desired, but ultimately, it is hollow. It is the authentic world of 'austerity Britain' that is the only possibility for the women of *Dance Hall*, however much it is a life of hardship and even if they are 'bored, bored, bored!'

### 'Are those real pearls? They're not very big, are they? I like my jewellery to be noticed'

The possibilities for femininity in the mid-1950s are explored in *Turn the Key Softly* through the figures of three women who have transgressed the boundaries of acceptable femininity. Quilliam (Kathleen Harrison), Monica (Yvonne Mitchell) and Stella (Joan Collins) have been imprisoned for, respectively, shoplifting, burglary and soliciting. The film charts the women's first hours of freedom when they face situations that mirror these initial 'transgressions': tests that function to place the three women within 'proper' modes of feminine conduct and correct expressions of womanliness.

In prison, hidden from the outside world and from men, the individual identities of the characters in *Turn the Key Softly* have been lost; they have become women as defined by a bureaucratic and state-sanctioned system in which 'woman' is a single (damned and condemned) category – a failed femininity that has been put to improper use. *Turn the Key Softly* begins with a scene of transformation: about to be released, the characters are given back their own clothes and are transformed from shapeless and unrecognisable figures into distinctively feminine women. The reconstructed femininities of Quilliam, Monica and Stella are linked to class and sexuality: 'woman' is firmly located within hierarchical social relations and relations of consumption which are in turn expressed through appearance as the outward sign of sexuality.

Thus, *Turn the Key Softly* presents us with three models of femininity. The elderly Quilliam is a cypher for an outmoded and outdated working class. She is a subservient figure (offering to help Monica dress), a woman who recognises and accepts her place. Quilliam is marginalised by modernity, the power of the ideological call of 'affluence' and the new patterns of consumption it demands; her clothes are dirty, a little ragged and out-of-fashion, she looks like a woman from pre-war, depressed Britain. She has a neglected air and her 'working-classness' is of little significance in the 'affluent fifties'. But Quilliam is more than simply a signifier of a superfluous class position, hers is a femininity that is redundant – old and no longer appropriate or desired.

Monica, a signifier of bourgeois middle-classness, is also aware of her place in the social scale and assumes her role with a knowingness and self-composure. She is dignified and refined; her clothes are smart and of good quality, her pearl earrings are small, delicate and tasteful. You have to look closely to see them, but when you do, you realise that they are real; the pearls are not just an ornament or a piece of jewellery, they are over-determined signifiers of authentic 'middle-classness'.

Stella is the most problematic of the three and is antagonistic to the other figures; she despises the compliance of Quilliam, her values and out-modedness, and she envies Monica's authority and self-assurance. Stella recognises the quality of the pearls but she refuses it, she wants people to see her jewellery, she wants to be recognised for what she is: ambitious and modern. Hers is a newly determined position, that of the reconstructed, working-class female consumer. Stella despises yet aspires to the certainty of Monica's social position in the world, although she will never attain it.

As the women move from the inside of the prison towards the outside world, Stella rushes towards the open gate but she loses her nerve, she hesi-tates and cannot take the step, either to freedom or into the 'proper' femi-ninity that she believes she is about to enter (she is to be married). It is Monica, reserved but secure in her role, who in the end must lead the way. Quilliam follows to one side, admiring one woman, despairing of the other, and knowing that her own place is where it has always been – last, at the bottom.

Through its resolution of each character's dilemma *Turn the Key Softly* reconstructs acceptable femininity by closing off possible choices: Quilliam's death as she runs across a road to rescue her dog emphatically underscores the evacuation of an asexual, 'pre-modern' femininity; for Monica the assumption of correct femininity is predicated on her rediscovery of the principles that give her the courage to abandon her lover and her past, thus she assumes her 'rightful' place as the repository of moral values. Once again it is Stella who presents the biggest problem for *Turn the Key Softly*'s model of 'acceptable femininity'.

Having bought a pair of overblown and gaudy earrings with the money her fiancé gave her to find a room, it is only when she voluntarily relin-quishes them that she is redeemed. Her surrender of the earrings signifies her acceptance of her 'proper' place, a consumer, yes, but an honest and pru-dent consumer. Stella's appearance insists that she is seen as a subject in, and of, consumerism and 'affluence'. At the same time though, her position is uncertain, it is almost as if she – the signifier of aspirant working-class fem-ininity – cannot shake off the attitudes and values of her working-class ori-gins. Thus, a newly emerging femininity which is unstable but vigorous is placed in an uneasy alliance with a middle-class femininity. And whilst 'affluent' femininity may be in flux, the direction it will take is clear: judi-cious consumption and domesticity achieved at a cost. Although Stella apparently willingly accepts her new place as the suburban housewife whose spending power is central to the 'ideology of affluence', the spark of optimism and glamorous desire is extinguished; her re-formation does not appear to leave a viable space in which imagination or fantasy can sustain her vibrancy and energetic sexuality.

In its presentation of class-specific images of femininity *Turn the Key Softly* represents women in such a way that the visible signs of sexuality are also the signals through which class position is identified. In addition, the film articulates three elements that were central to 'affluence': the elevation of the working-class in material terms; the expectation that working-class prosperity would be accompanied by an adoption of supposedly middle-class values and decorum; and the proposition that women and female sexuality were crucial to the discourses surrounding 'the affluent fifties'.

The differently emphasised aspects of femininity represented in *Dance Hall* and *Turn the Key Softly* can be traced to a context in which a single – although shifting – notion of 'woman' was produced in the material and discursive structures associated with 'austerity' and 'affluence'. The films focus on the demands placed on women in the formation of a specifically British modernity. The tension created by such attempts to mould femininity delineates both a *problem of inadequacy* in those who are unable to take their place within a femininity which is premised upon and constructed around relations of consumption, and a *problem of an excess of desire*, as a femininity moving to the limits of consumption, artifice and glamour is physically and symbolically punished. *Dance Hall* and *Turn the Key Softly* exemplify the promise and foreboding that settled around 'affluence' and 'Americanisation' at this time, such that they articulate the fear of a modernised femininity exceeding the continuities and traditions of 'womanliness'.

## Notes

1 My own research into British cinema of the mid-1940s to the late 1950s suggests that from the late 1940s onwards, with the demise of Gainsborough melodramas in particular, representations of women and therefore possible alternatives for female audiences are considerably curtailed and by about 1953 have disappeared almost completely. It is also worth noting that this period also sees a shift in audience preferences from British 'quality film' to Hollywood productions.

# 17

## Two weddings and two funerals: the problem of the post-war woman

### TESSA PERKINS

What, you might ask, do a farmer, a highwayman, a ballet dancer who commits suicide, and a pianist who fails to commit suicide have in common with each other let alone with the Royal Commission on Equal Pay, the New Look, austerity and employment? The brief answer is 1945–48. The longer answer is the topic of this article in which I want to explore the ways in which four British films made and shown during this period addressed some of the contemporary concerns about the position of women, and men, in post-war Britain. The films I will be examining are *The Loves of Joanna Godden* (1947) (about a woman farmer), *The Wicked Lady* (1945) (about a woman highwayman), *The Red Shoes* (1948) (about a woman ballet dancer) and *The Seventh Veil* (1945) (about a woman pianist). All of these were popular films with some of the most popular British stars in the leading roles. *The Seventh Veil* (James Mason and Ann Todd) and *The Wicked Lady* (James Mason and Margaret Lockwood) were the top box-office films in Britain of 1945 and 1946 respectively.[1] *The Red Shoes* (a film which seems to figure in the film-going memories of a generation of women/girls, including myself, in a particularly powerful way) was also one of the most popular films of 1948. Of these films, two are costume melodramas (*The Wicked Lady* set in the eighteenth century and *The Loves of Joanna Godden* set in the early 1900s) while two are set in some indeterminate peacetime present (*The Red Shoes* and *The Seventh Veil*).[2] The two costume melodramas are about women who take on men's roles (as a highwayman and a farmer) while the other two are about women who have an exceptional talent in a more conventionally female role as artistic performers (a pianist and a ballet dancer). Hereinafter I will, for the sake of convenience rather than elegance, refer to the first two as 'men's roles' films and the second two as 'talent' films.

The period with which I will be dealing is one of those historical con-junctures of particular complexity and uncertainty and, perhaps for that reason, relatively under-researched. It falls uneasily between the more dra-matic crisis period of the Second World War and the conservatism and puri-tanism of the 'consensual' 1950s. Perhaps one of the dominant feelings of the period, both at the time and retrospectively, is one of disappointment: disappointment that life was, in some respects, even harder after the war than during it; retrospectively, for socialists and feminists alike, disappoint-ment that an opportunity was missed, that something 'went wrong'. It is not for nothing that the period has been dubbed 'the age of austerity'. The new Labour government was faced with the massive job of post-war reconstruc-tion, both economic and social.

In looking at films made during this transitional period of post-war reconstruction I wanted to see whether, and how, the contemporary debates about women's and men's roles were being registered dramatically and what position, if any, the films were taking on these debates. I found that while each of the films works towards a position which appears to confirm that the differences between the sexes are 'natural', that women's primary role is in the home and family, and affirms the importance of male strength and authority, they are all marked by uncertainty and ambivalence about gender.

The following section briefly identifies some key contemporary themes which are particularly relevant to understanding how these films registered women's experiences.

## Austerity

Austerity, the name given to the 'age', is an important context for under-standing the conditions under which women lived and in which they viewed these films, partly to appreciate the real privations they suffered and the dif-ficulties that they had to manage on the domestic front, and partly to under-stand the context in which they might, or might not, make demands. The escalating social and economic crisis of 1946–47 provided a climate in which demands from women whether for equal pay or consumer goods were dis-missed and were increasingly constructed as selfish and counter to the national interest.[3]

## Employment

Perhaps the greatest myth about the post-war period is that women returned to the home. Certainly, between 1945 and 1947, many women were either 'thrown out' of, or 'willingly left', the industries which they had joined during the war, although all of these industries employed considerably more women in 1947 than they did in 1939.[4] The skills which women had acquired in their wartime occupations were frequently insufficient to allow them to keep their new jobs and status and they were often returned to more lowly, womanly occupations, sometimes having to train returning men before vacating their posts.[5]

Nevertheless, women's employment increased in some areas as a range of 'peacetime' industries began to revive and women were urged to return to work in these industries to help the export drive. Contrary to received wisdom, the post-war period from 1947 and throughout the 1950s demonstrates a marked increase in married women in their mid-thirties returning to work, suggesting, in part at least, that the war did break the taboo on married women working. The other most significant feature of the post-war years has been the gradual shift of all women's employment into various service industries and the continuation, indeed re-establishment, of occupational segregation so that gender continued to define what are appropriate jobs for men and women.[6] To this extent the importance of the process of re-establishing the differences between the sexes, of which these films are a part, cannot be overestimated.

In the late 1940s things were not straightforward. At the same time that the government and industry were calling on women to enter the labour market to help solve the nation's acute labour shortage, day nurseries were being closed down and the 'working mother' was also being blamed for a whole host of problems, most particularly the perceived increase in juvenile delinquency and divorce, so there were competing pressures on women to remain at home. The conflicting pressures between home and work were explored sympathetically in one of the best-known books on women of that period, Myrdal and Klein's Women's Two Roles (1956).[7]

### Equal pay

In many respects the report of the Royal Commission on Equal Pay (October 1946) seems symptomatic of what happened to women after the war. Delaying their response until June 1947 the government affirmed, as a general principle, 'the justice of the claim for equal pay for equal work' but stated quite categorically that 'this principle could not be applied at the present time' because of the expense (which they estimated to be £24 million a year) which would not be 'in the national interest'. This betrayal did not go unremarked. Vera Brittain commented bitterly: 'The very administrations which make poverty their excuse for withholding equal pay have found no difficulty in budgeting additional millions for "defence" or conscription or even in raising the wages of well-organised male workers who would create trouble if an increase were refused'.[8] Women were once again at the back of the queue (but then they were used to queuing at the time!).

The report was much concerned to investigate and evaluate three types of explanations for unequal pay, namely those explanations which rest on legal, conventional or natural differences between the sexes. Of particular relevance here are the latter two since it is these that are articulated in the films under discussion. If the differences between the sexes are held to be 'natural' then this lends apparent legitimacy to inequalities (or 'differences') in social and economic arrangements. If the differences are held to be 'conventional' then the ideological grounds for inequality are undermined. During the war the 'natural' differences explanation had been seriously undermined but, as evidence submitted to the Commission shows, there was considerable debate about it. The report provides evidence of contemporary arguments about women's abilities, their attitudes to work (they were less committed because of the primary commitment as wives and mothers), their attendance records (which were worse than men's), and their lack of expertise and training. While the report generally conceded that during the war women had demonstrated equal ability to men in most of the jobs they had done, it equivocated about whether men's and women's abilities were 'naturally' the same. Significantly there was disagreement between the Commission's members which led to a dissenting minority report, written by three of the four women on the Commission, in which they took issue with some of the 'natural' differences described in the majority report.[9] However, even in this dissenting report housekeeping and childcare were referred to as not only the 'traditional' but also 'the natural' sphere of women's work and there was no suggestion that men should have responsibilities in those areas. Rather the solution to the excessive burden placed on women was seen to be the provision of more state facilities, home helps, etc.

### New Look

In 1947, the year that Dalton, the Chancellor of the Exchequer, described as *Annus Horrendous,* the controversy over the New Look broke. If a controversy over a fashion conventionally seems frivolous and trivial, it was nonetheless symptomatic of the time and indicative of disagreements and confusion about women's identities. The conflict has been described by Pearson Phillips in *The Age of Austerity*[10] as a conflict between the Amazons and the Nymphs. The Amazons were those women, including a number of Labour MPs, who were opposed to the New Look, feeling that it was not only grossly impractical and irresponsible at a time when clothing was rationed, but also that it represented a threat to women's equality: 'Women today are taking a larger part in the happenings of the world and the New Look is too reminiscent of a caged bird's attitude. I hope our fashion dictators will

[ 267 ]

realise the new *outlook* of women and will give the death blow to any attempt at curtailing women's freedom' wrote Mrs Mabel Ridealgh, one of the new Labour MPs, in *Reynold's News*. This was not simply a media event either; there were questions and answers about it in the House of Commons, and representations from the government to the clothing industry to discourage it. The Nymphs on the other hand were those who welcomed the New Look which encouraged 'them not only to be women, but "girls"'.[11] *Harper's Bazaar* described the New Look in the following sensuous terms:

> Paris swells with femininity ... a tight, slender bodice narrowing into a tiny wasp waist, below which the skirt bursts into fullness like a flower. Every line is rounded. There are no angles in this silhouette. Shoulders are gently curved. Bosoms are rounded out with padding ... Hips are very full, stiffened with padding or swelling with pleats stitched from waist to hips and then released.

Janey Ironside, the editor of *Vogue*, wrote later: 'It was like a new love affair, the first sight of Venice, a new chance, in fact a new look at life ... [Dior] held a mirror up to women, in which they saw themselves as they wished to be; no longer Amazons, but Nymphs; no longer Cinders, but Cinderella'.[12] According to Phillips, by the end of 1947 the battle was over and the New Look Nymphs had won – the fashion battle at least.

### Gender ideologies and gendered experiences

Clearly women were subject to a number of contradictory pressures both during and after the war and the question of women's position was a subject of debate, a site of struggle. While many of the changes women experienced during the war undermined gendered ideologies, the war had also reinforced gendered ideologies, foregrounding the ways in which women were the carers, mothers, girlfriends, etc. and the basic definitions of those roles didn't change.[13]

If war provides women with opportunities to break with convention and enter male domains, the reverse is not so clearly true for men. On the contrary war is the time when men are primarily asked to, and able to, demonstrate those aspects of masculinity which have conventionally been held to mark them off most particularly from women. Furthermore in order to maintain morale among the troops, considerable efforts were made to reassure men that the changes in women's roles were only for the duration, that there would be no fundamental change in their domestic arrangements, that the family and marriage were still viewed as women's primary responsibility and concern. But there are also, of course, ways in which war must undermine masculinity, not simply because women entered into what was previously men's domain, though this is an important reason, but also because faced with the realities of war some men must question precisely those masculine values that war embodies, and must find themselves in some sense 'lacking' what it took to 'be a man' and even feeling critical of it. It is significant that films about war are one of the few sites in which men are 'allowed' to show emotion, to touch each other, to express love, compassion, grief, and even a strong desire for wife and family. The view that many men returning from war were likely to face problems of 'adjustment' and would need compassion and understanding from the wives and girlfriends was common, as the pages of women's magazines demonstrate. But there was also some recognition that men would also need to make some adjustment to the fact that their wives, mothers, girlfriends had acquired more independence during the war and might not be willing to return to their previous role of unquestioning submission to male authority.

## The films

In the analysis that follows I will not be arguing that the films 'mirrored' society. Rather I offer a reading that identifies the ways in which the narratives, their characters, twists of plot, etc., articulate themes, ideas and feelings which had particular currency in both the public debates and everyday experiences outlined above. My reading also identifies areas which seem to be problematic – tensions which the narrative does not resolve, issues which are raised but not pursued – and argues that such problems are equally symptomatic of the time. The fact that I argue that the films do ultimately take a position in relation to such issues as whether the differences between the sexes is 'natural' or 'conventional' does not necessarily mean that individual members of the audience accepted these positions. Nonetheless it is these positions which provide 'explanations' that make sense of the narratives and provide opportunities for emotional satisfaction offered by the resolution. In so doing they played a role in re-constructing the 'normal'.

Each of these films works through the contemporary concern with defining women's 'difference' from men in a context when many of the markers of that difference had been erased and where women's wartime experience could not simply be ignored. In this respect the films participate in debates exemplified by the Equal Pay report's discussion of 'natural' and 'conventional' differences between the sexes, particularly those questions about women's lack of experience and expertise, their lack of (and perceived unwillingness to acquire) training and their lesser commitment to work because of their domestic responsibilities. Differences are examined primarily by focusing on women rather than men as the source of the problem – the women all desire something that men have rather than vice versa – indicating the fact that changes in men's roles were never on the agenda. The films do, however, register difficulties around masculinity, particularly around what it is men have to offer, but these difficulties do not get explicitly formulated in a way that renders masculinity problematic or which suggests the need for any change in men's roles. This inability (or unwillingness) to see masculinity as problematic at times produces a sort of incoherence in the text, most notably, I will argue, in the resolution of *The Seventh Veil*. Such an inability was not of course limited to films, but is one of the notable features of the period as suggested above and discussed elsewhere in this volume by Alison Oram.

### Desire and domesticity

The common narrative theme of all four films is that each woman desires something that places her in an occupational role outside the home, although none of these are the occupations of the 'typical' woman. Each film sets up an opposition between romance and domesticity on the one hand and the women's occupations on the other. It is only in *The Red Shoes* that this conflict turns out to be insoluble, so that Vicki (Moira Shearer) kills herself. In the other three films, the conflict is resolved by the women admitting their love for a man, though Barbara in *The Wicked Lady* is killed by the man she has fallen in love with at the end of the film.

### 'Talent films'

In *The Seventh Veil* and *The Red Shoes* both women have an exceptional talent which is essential to their life: for example, Francesca (Ann Todd), believing she can no longer play after an accident, says to Max 'Why didn't you kill me?' The women's talent is recognised by an authoritarian man in a position of power (Lermontoff (Anton Walbrook), the head of the ballet company, in *The Red Shoes* and Nicholas (James Mason), Francesca's guardian, in *The Seventh Veil*). While in their recognition of the characters' passionate commitment to their art the films acknowledge that women can be talented and successful, it takes a man to identify, nurture and develop the women's talents and to drive them on. The men have the expertise, the genius, the vision and ultimately the commitment. Moreover both Lermontoff and Nicholas seem to usurp the women's talent to the extent that the women become vehicles, mere performers rather than artists. In *The Red Shoes* it is Lermontoff who will 'make' Vicki into one of the best ballerinas of all time. The story of *The Red Shoes* is significant here too since it is an allegory, in which wearing the red shoes which she so desires causes the ballerina to lose all control. They take over. She can dance anywhere, but she cannot stop dancing even when she is exhausted, and so eventually she dies. What appears to be freedom is actually the result of a man's work (the shoemaker) and under his control and then turns out to be a death sentence. For both Francesca in *The Seventh Veil* and Vicki, the price of realising their desire, fulfilling their destiny, is to be subject to an extreme form of male control and to agree to submit themselves totally to these men's rule. Both women try to resist this control and in so doing incur the wrath and vengeance of their 'masters'. More importantly both women, in resisting their masters, lose their opportunity to realise their dream. They cannot do it alone. Both women's attempts to resist patriarchal control involve them going off with a younger, less authoritarian man who is also an artist. Significantly, neither of the men's artistic careers are threatened by romance nor are either of the men dependent on a 'master', thus subtly suggesting that it is not being an artist that is a problem, but being a *woman* artist. This is most clear in *The Red Shoes* when Lermontoff forces Vicki to choose between dancing and romance when she falls in love with Julian (Marius Goring). Lermontoff's view is that romance and a career are incompatible, for *women*. Indeed early on in the film he sacks Irina, the previous prima ballerina, because she is planning to marry.

The women's 'life-giving' talent places them in such an intolerable situation that both of them attempt suicide, Vicki successfully. Vicki's suicide may be read in many ways: that the two men, in trying to control her, destroy her; that she, unable to choose between career and romance, destroys herself; that freedom (represented by the red shoes and representing women's desire for liberty) is a dangerous illusion. Whatever one's reading, the ending is deeply shocking and leaves the conflict unresolved – and thus implies that it is unresolvable. The lesson of both films seems to be that whatever the apparent attractions for women of 'freedom' and independence they turn out to conflict with what is 'natural' – namely romance.

### 'Men's roles films'

*The Loves of Joanna Godden* and *The Wicked Lady* both invite the audience to identify with a woman who is defying convention by occupying a male role. The question they pose to the audience is whether the women will succeed, and thereby demonstrate that inequality is purely an effect of convention, or fail, thereby confirming the 'natural' differences between the sexes. As with the talent films, both women are involved with a man who also 'happens' to occupy the same role (a farmer and a highwayman) that the women aspire to, thus providing a model by which to measure the women's performance. Both Joanna (Googie Withers) and Barbara (Margaret Lockwood) relish their independence. Joanna's derives from the fact that she has inherited the farm. Her inheritance gives her access to money and consequently the power to make decisions about how money should be spent. Barbara seizes her independence by becoming a highwayman at night to escape from the claustrophobia and tedium of being a 'lady' during the day.

In both films women are seen to have *some* of the abilities necessary to the *performance* of such male roles as farmer and highwayman, but they lack the expertise and experience which is necessary and need to be trained and supervised by a man. Significantly the question of whether they could eventually become as expert as the men is not considered to be of narrative importance. As the film progresses various incidents and narrative themes suggest that these women's strengths and weaknesses are the result of certain 'naturally' feminine characteristics. By the end of the film each woman has realised the error of her ways, each of them end up 'confessing' she was wrong (Barbara) or that it was 'all her fault' (Joanna) and, in the end, both fall in love/find their man and in so doing 'dissolve' the problem. Male expertise is one theme in the films, particularly in *The Loves of Joanna Godden,* which has obvious connections with the sorts of debates circulating about women and work during and after the war. It is clear that women's *ability* to perform many men's jobs could not be disputed. The question then was were they just as able as men to perform these tasks, was it purely a matter of *convention* (and education and training) that men and women did different jobs (and that when they did the same jobs men were paid more than women), or did the different types of work men and women tended to do, and the different rates of pay they received, reflect a *natural* difference between the sexes?

In *The Loves of Joanna Godden* Joanna challenges convention by deciding to go it alone as a farmer, rather than marrying Arthur (John MacCullum). Throughout the early part of the film Joanna is frequently described as stubborn because she will not take advice from people (men) who have experience and expertise, but our sympathy is with Joanna. She defiantly hires a new 'looker' (as shepherds are known in Romney Marsh) and, against everyone's advice, attempts with his help to cross breed her flock in order to increase them. We hope, and in some genres could legitimately *expect*, that she will be successful. However it turns out to be a disaster and she loses nearly all the flock it had taken her father years to establish. This failure is important because it results not from an act of God, or of vengeance by a rival farmer, as it might have if the hero had been a man, but from ignorance. As it becomes evident that the experiment is a disaster, it also becomes evident that Joanna is sexually attracted to the looker which *now* suggests that her judgement in hiring the looker was influenced more by sexual attraction than by farming expertise. This attraction, and her need to repress it, shows her as vulnerable and undermines her outward show of strength and independence. Shortly after this there is an altercation between Arthur and the looker during which the latter chides Arthur with not being man enough for Joanna. This scene is not merely about a struggle to possess Joanna; more importantly it is about the need to control her – to 'be man enough'. Up until this point the looker has seemed to be the only one on her side; but we now discover that he is as keen to preserve male prerogatives as any of the other men. Her second plan – to turn over a lot of the pasture land to growing food to feed the sheep during the winter months – also receives a contemptuous reception from most of the local farmers. Interestingly, although it appears from the film that this plan was *probably* successful we are not explicitly told this; nothing is made of its success. This makes the film curiously unbalanced. After her first disaster we expect either another disaster, or a definite success. Instead the romantic theme takes over and the question of whether Joanna is capable of being a successful farmer is shelved. Instead the failures in other areas of her life, supposedly caused by her stubborn insistence on behaving like a man, take over as the central narrative problem, and it is these problems that are 'resolved' in the film's denouement when Joanna finally admits she loves Arthur and offers him help, in exchange for his expertise and brawn. As part of the resolution Joanna takes the blame for what has happened ('it was all my fault ... my stupid stubbornness'), thus confirming that Arthur's account of her was correct all along and that her own attempts to defy convention, and *our* sympathy with them, were misplaced.[14]

The theme of men having experience and expertise can also be seen in *The Wicked Lady*. On her second foray as a highwayman Barbara is helped out by Captain James Jackson (James Mason) and subsequently acknowledges how much she can learn from him. However, despite her enormous ability as a horsewoman and a highwayman, she gradually reveals her unsuitability for this occupation, first when she shoots and kills the guard, instead of the horse, thus ignoring Jackson's advice and demonstrating her excessive greed, and later when she betrays Jackson and then plots to kill her husband. Jackson, an honourable thief, realises too late that he was wrong to 'put his trust in a woman'. But Barbara is not an honourable thief. Barbara's motivation for being a highwayman does not come from financial necessity – she is Lady Skelton, the wife of a wealthy and respectable member of the local aristocracy. She robs, she tells Jackson, mainly for the excitement, and to escape the stifling boredom of domestic duties and her respectable marriage to the kind, just and good Ralph (a model of what the aristocracy should be in the new social democratic Britain). As an afterthought almost, she says that the money is also important. This account matches very well the view that women who work outside the home do so primarily for social rather than financial reasons, an argument which was supported by the Equal Pay Commission and has often been used to explain and justify women's weaker position in the labour market. Barbara's disregard for Jackson's expertise lands them both in trouble; she is the amateur, he the professional; she cannot be trusted (she betrays him), he refuses to betray her – until he discovers she plans to kill her husband, Ralph. It is this threat to the representative of patriarchal law and order that finally makes Jackson close ranks with his erstwhile antagonist, Ralph; as Jackson leaves to warn Ralph, Barbara kills him.

One surprising thing about all these films is the contempt they express for domesticity and housewifery. This functioned partly to emphasise the attractions of the women's various occupations, especially in the men's roles films, and most obviously in *The Wicked Lady*. Yet despite this contempt, the heroines end up 'embracing' domesticity and housewifely virtues. The films' contradictory attitudes to domesticity are interesting. The drudgery of housework was one of the 'discoveries' of wartime; there was much, no doubt genuine, sympathy expressed in various public discourses about this drudgery and it was also usefully mobilised in order to attract women out of the home and into the services and factories. After the war, however, women were once again encouraged to see the charms of 'homemaking'. Contempt for housework and domesticity, its triviality and the low level of intelligence it supposedly requires, is a central assumption of patriarchal ideology, and one accepted by many men, and one, I would suggest, which infiltrates these films. In *The Wicked Lady* Barbara's contempt and dislike of managing the house are wonderfully extreme and cathartic. She despises, and is mystified by, her cousin Caroline (Patricia Roc) who performs these tasks with infinite efficiency and patience. Barbara's lawlessness is an effect of this dislike, whereas for Caroline 'if you love someone' you subjugate your own desires to his – or rather what you desire *is* to satisfy his needs rather than to have any of your own. Barbara's 'problem' is that she dares to desire things on her own account. Only at the end of the film when she has finally met again the man she can love does she admit that now she wants those domestic pleasures, a home and children, which she had always despised. As with so many wayward women, the love of a good strong man is all they really need to discover their 'true' desires, namely to make a home. In films as different as *Double Indemnity* (1944) and *Calamity Jane* (1953) the ending is the same. However Barbara's revelation that she too wants a home and family comes too late – it is more or less her death speech. It is interesting to speculate whether the audiences who voted *The Wicked Lady* the most popular film of 1947 were responding to Barbara's wickedness, including her dislike of housework, or her conversion.

### Femininity and masculinity

While all of these films are marked by considerable uncertainty about gender roles, it is femininity which poses the greatest problem and around which there is the most ambivalence, wavering between appreciation and understanding of women to outright misogyny. While certain aspects of masculinity are presented as problematic, these are not foregrounded as problems of masculinity *per se*, but rather of a masculinity which has lost faith in itself. Ideas about femininity and masculinity in these films are most obvious at the level of plot and in the characterisation of the main characters, but these may be significantly amplified, modified or undermined at other levels, for example by the range of different male and female characters in the film, their relationships with each other and so on. It is striking, if not very unusual, that the majority of secondary female characters are represented negatively while male characters are more varied. The women's concerns and interests are shown to be mainly trivial and superficial; they are selfish and materialistic, interested in clothes, parties, social status and gossip; they are mainly stupid or, if not stupid, conniving; and are either unattractive and asexual or highly sexual and immoral. This is undoubtedly, in the films' terms, what women should not be, but typically are. Perhaps most interesting in the context of post-war austerity is not only the strength of these women's passionate desire for material comforts and pleasure but also the strength of the condemnation of it. Most of the women are also shown as lazy and reluctant to do any form of domestic work; they are in short parasites and their desire for glamour or the obsession with female trivia is frowned on severely. However, despite this morality lesson, the films do offer women in the audience the opportunity to escape from the rigours of austerity. All of the films offer spectacles of enormous abundance: for example the beautiful dresses with yards and yards of fabric in *The Red Shoes*, *The Wicked Lady* and *The Seventh Veil*; foreign travel in *The Red Shoes* and *The Seventh Veil* at a time when foreign travel for pleasure had been stopped and petrol was still rationed; and the banquet in *The Loves of Joanna Godden*. So while through the narrative the audience are being asked to condemn the women's (and perhaps their own) desire for material goods and their laziness/dislike of drudgery, through the *mise en scène* women in the audience can satisfy those same desires in themselves at least at the level of fantasy.[15] The contradictory attitudes to women registered here are dramatic enactments of the arguments used in debates about the 'New Look' and equal pay.

Of the main characters in these films Barbara is the only one who is depicted negatively. Caroline, her cousin, represents the conventional ideal woman. If Caroline has a fault it is that she is too willing to subjugate her own desires: she has too low an opinion of herself. Caroline has something in common with Francesca inasmuch as they are both a little too timid and shy and prone to influence; what both films suggest women have to learn is to be a little bit more assertive, to make it clearer what they want, and be less subject to domination. By contrast, Joanna shows us the dangers of being too independent; she must give up her autonomy (defined increasingly as stubbornness) and assertiveness and be less resistant to men's advice. The above discussion may suggest that femininity is always constructed negatively but in fact the films are all, in different ways, rather ambivalent about femininity. This ambivalence is perhaps most marked in *The Loves of Joanna Godden*.

Joanna's feminine qualities – constructed here as compassion, generosity and enthusiasm – *are* valued and are favourably contrasted to the stuffiness, prejudice and meanness of the men; but they are also shown to be incompatible with her occupancy of the male role of being a farmer. The audience is invited at the start to identify with Joanna's ambition to defy convention but we are gradually pulled away from this position, partly because we see her beginning to feel unsure of herself, and partly because it conflicts with our own 'good sense' which suggests, for example, that her generosity has been misplaced because she has lost £18,000 in a single year. We are thus put in the position of 'accepting' that she has been irresponsible and needs to make some hard decisions – 'as men must do'? The scene in which Arthur does her accounts and remonstrates with her about her extravagance (which we have been encouraged to see as generosity) and her 'manly' behaviour, captures the film's ambivalence about male and female values. The film's attempt to resolve the conflict between Arthur and Joanna is achieved rather awkwardly and seems to want to affirm the importance of both male and female values while implying that they cannot be held by one person, thus suggesting the 'natural' *complementarity* of men and women – equal but different.

In attempting to identify what these films have to say about masculinity it would be tempting to say that they all affirm a traditional view of the strong man, defined as authoritative, dominant, honourable and reasonable. However each film suggests that there are problems with this traditional view of masculinity.

In the two 'talent' films, as I've already indicated, the women's success depends on strong, dominant men although this is complicated by the fact that since neither is very likeable they seem hardly ideal. Alongside these strong dominant men, we have younger, more easy-going men (Julian in *The Red Shoes* and Peter and Max in *The Seventh Veil*). Although more likeable at the beginning they are eventually all shown to be lacking in some way, and none of the younger men get the woman at the end, suggesting that they have not got what it takes and that their attractions were superficial.

In the two 'men's roles' films there are also a range of male types. Interestingly, though perhaps not surprisingly, in these films, in which women enter and thereby threaten a male domain, the need for the men to become stronger and more dominant is a more explicit theme. Joanna and Barbara have to be brought into line, and in both cases it requires some assertive action by one or more of the men to achieve this. In *The Wicked Lady* all three men have finally to free themselves of Barbara's sexual charms and have to take a stand to bring her back under the patriarchal law. Although early on in the film they are constructed as rivals who represent different types of masculinity, in the end their antagonisms disappear and they stand together against Barbara, with James Jackson giving his life in his attempt to prevent her killing his erstwhile enemy, her husband Ralph. In *The Loves of Joanna Godden* Arthur has both to challenge Joanna, and to defy her by marrying her sister, in order for Joanna to see that she loves him. In this film also there are three central male characters who are not only rivals involved in a competitive struggle to 'possess' and control Joanna, but who also represent different aspects of masculinity. At this level then the films register confusion around masculinity when women occupy male roles, and work towards the view that men need to be 'real' men – authoritative, dominant and above all confident of their right to rule. The shift in the men's relationships with each other from animosity to some sort of comradeship represents an assertion of male solidarity, and of common interests. By contrast women's relationships with each other are characterised by jealousy, rivalry, betrayal, manipulation and social control. One aspect of women's wartime experience which is not registered in the films is their experiences of the pleasures of living in female communities. The possibility that women need to 'close ranks' or to identify their common interests is not on the agenda at all.

Three of the films register problems with masculinity which they are not able to resolve at the end, the exception being *The Wicked Lady*. In both *The Loves of Joanna Godden* and *The Seventh Veil* these problems stem partly from the strength of our identification with the central female character whose feminine qualities the films appear to value. In *The Red Shoes* Vicki's death must raise doubts about the behaviour of the two men whose struggle to control her causes her death. These doubts are not explicitly addressed by the film, and it is an open question how audiences responded. The shocking end of the film can be read not merely as suggesting that the conflict between a woman's career and marriage is unresolvable but also that men's attempt to control women ultimately destroys what it is they want to control.

Of all the films *The Seventh Veil* is the most disturbing and inconsistent in its treatment of masculinity. On the one hand it raises most starkly some of the most negative aspects of masculinity (including physical violence), but on the other it manages at the end to completely shelve those problems as if they had never been raised in the first place. This is facilitated by *The Seventh Veil*'s narrative structure about which a few words are necessary. The film opens with Francesca in a hospital bed, from which she 'escapes' and subsequently tries to commit suicide. From the start then we know that

[ 277 ]

Francesca is unstable. We soon discover she is no longer able to play the piano, and the objective of the hypnosis which she undergoes is to discover what psychological barrier is preventing this. Francesca's story is thus told by her, through flashback, while she is under hypnosis. Francesca's account of her life, which we see enacted, tells of how she was orphaned and sent to live with her misogynist, domineering and at times sadistic cousin, Nicholas (James Mason). Discovering Francesca's musical talent Nicholas takes over her musical education and later her career. Throughout her account of her life with Nicholas, Francesca makes it clear that she wanted to escape from his excessive control over her, wanted to be free, but both her attempts to escape from him fail. Francesca's account of Nicholas presents us, then, with the excesses of masculinity; throughout the film we have felt that her happiness depends on her being able to be free of Nicholas. Consequently, when at the end of the film she freely 'chooses' Nicholas, considerable 'work' has to done to make sense of this choice. This work is done, in the denouement, by the hypnotist Larsen (Herbert Lom), whose position as 'expert' enables him to give the final and *authoritative* explanation of Francesca's trauma. In his account Francesca's timidity and an early trauma at school (caused by women) become the key factors which explain her inability to play rather than, as in Francesca's account, Nicholas's sadistic and authoritarian control of her. Francesca's voice-over, which has mainly led the narrative up until now, is suppressed, and the male voice which takes over cannot explicitly acknowledge that there was anything problematic in Nicholas's behaviour. In so far as Nicholas (and men in general) has/have any changes to make, these are dealt with off-screen or by veiled references to what Francesca will be like when she comes out of this traumatic illness. She will, says Larsen, be completely different, more independent and less easily controlled. This seems to be some acknowledgement of a need to redefine gender relations, with a warning to men that they cannot expect to be able to exert unlimited control over women; but this is not explicitly stated in the way that Francesca's need to change is. The problem is the woman – the victim.

We have been offered, early on in the film, one tentative explanation for Nicholas's misogyny: it is implied that his contempt for women stems from his having been abandoned by his mother and his sadistic cruelty and coldness are the result of this obsessive (but completely uninvestigated) relationship. Nicholas's need to control Francesca may then be understood as resulting from his fear of being abandoned by women. Francesca only chooses him when she is free of his control and that is what he must learn; and it is only when she has freely chosen him that he can accept her affection and demonstrate his own. The love of a good woman heals the injury done by a bad one. Neither Francesca, nor the audience, is then allowed to see in Nicholas's behaviour any fundamental criticism of masculinity; rather we must be understanding and trust that with care and compassion the damage done (by the war) will be healed. Nicholas has a completely unexplained limp and walks with a stick, his physical disability mirroring his emotionally damaged personality. There is no suggestion that this is a war injury, but it is impossible not to read it as such and at some level to see Nicholas as representing on the one hand the injured men returning from the war, whose psychological injuries were more severe than their physical ones and who need love and understanding from women, and on the other hand the juvenile delinquent abandoned by his (working) mother.

### The family

And what of the family, that was to be the cornerstone of the nation? In none of these films do we see a 'typical', healthy, functional family. On the contrary, in three of the films, the lack of a properly functioning family provides, implicitly, the explanation for the problems faced by the characters. In *The Wicked Lady* Caroline's excessive gratitude and Barbara's lawlessness are both explained by their orphaned state, and in *The Loves of Joanna Godden* it is the death of Joanna's father that leaves her 'free' of patriarchal guidance so that she erroneously attempts to fill the role of the patriarch herself. The disruption of family life, and of appropriate role models, functions as the primary explanation for the deviant behaviour of the central characters and each film works towards a resolution which will form the basis of a new and functional family – the heterosexual couple. But though this is the goal, the films all demonstrate that marriage is by no means unproblematic. In two of the films, *The Wicked Lady* and *The Loves of Joanna Godden*, the heroes Ralph and Arthur have both married wicked (and adulterous) ladies (Barbara and Ellen) and are thus unable to marry the woman they really love (Caroline and Joanna); in both films divorce is actually proposed as a rational means of removing the barriers which stand in the way of 'true' romance. But the stark conclusion to *The Red Shoes* shows that even a marriage based on love does not necessarily lead to a happy ending.

### Conclusion

My interest in writing this article came from a desire to see in what ways popular films of this period addressed the question of women's position in society, whether they could be said to have participated in an ideological drive to 'return women to the home', and how, if at all, they articulated contemporary debates about the differences between the sexes. I hope I have shown how even though none of the films is explicitly about post-war adjustments, there was plenty to connect them to the audiences' wartime and post-war experiences: they drew on discourses familiar from debates about women's employment in the war and about equal pay; they related to the problems of returning husbands; to a period of austerity and women's experience of food and clothes rationing and to their desire for long promised consumer goods; and to the experience many of them had had of greater independence and autonomy during the war.

What is perhaps most notable about the films is the uncertainty of the terrain on which they operate, a feature that seems to mark them as transitional films. This is notable in the films' ambivalent attitude towards women – their combination of misogyny and admiration – and in the way each film shifts the focus of its narrative, and therefore also of potential audience satisfaction. The films all start by offering the audience one sort of pleasure (the women's success in their chosen careers) and end by offering a different one (romantic involvement). Each woman's desire for something which places her outside the home is transformed into a desire for a man and, by inference, domesticity. But it would be wrong to see these films as crudely returning women to the home: the two women who survive (Joanna and Francesca), and presumably marry the heroes, are not necessarily going to give up their occupations; by the end of the films the women's career interests have simply ceased to be of importance. I have argued that the narrative problems of these films were such as to articulate dramatically the debates about whether differences between the sexes were 'conventional' or 'natural'. As each woman's desire is transformed into the desire for a man and diverted from its original goal, the ground is taken away from the 'conventional difference' explanation and support for the 'natural differences' explanation grows.

## Notes

I want to thank Christine Gledhill, for being once again a most sympathetic and constructive editor; Gill Swanson for helpful comments; Jill McKenna for viewing the films with me and for her astute comments on both the films and an early draft of this article; and finally my mother, Crystal Hale, whose memories, and memorabilia, of this period I have plundered and to whom this article is dedicated.

1 Antonia Lant, *Blackout: Reinventing Women for Wartime British Cinema* (Princeton, Princeton University Press, 1991); Robert Murphy, *Realism and Tinsel* (London, Routledge, 1989); Jeffrey Truby (ed.), *Daily Mail Film Award Annual 1948* (Winchester Publications Ltd, 1948). See also: Sue Aspinall, 'Women, realism and reality in British films, 1943–53', in James Curran and Vincent Porter (eds), *British Cinema History* (London, Weidenfeld and Nicolson, 1983); George Perry, *The Great British Picture Show* (London, Michael Joseph, 1985).

2 Another film of the period which would obviously have been relevant is unfortunately unavailable and my memory of it is too dim to allow me to write anything of

it – *Annie Get Your Gun* (1950). *Annie Get Your Gun* was one of the top box-office films of 1950. Three of its most famous songs are worth mentioning in passing: 'Anything you can do I can do better … ', 'You can't get a man with a gun', and 'The girl that I marry will have to be, as soft and as pink as a nursery'.

3  David Marquand, 'Sir Stafford Cripps', in Michael Sissons and Philip French (eds), *Age of Austerity* (London, Hodder and Stoughton, 1963).

4  *British Labour Statistics – Historical Abstracts 1886–1968* (London, HMSO, 1971), Tables 112–13.

5  Gail Braybon and Penny Summerfield, *Out of the Cage* (London, Pandora, 1987); Penny Summerfield, *Women Workers in the Second World War* (London, Croom Helm, 1984).

6  Catherine Hakim, *Occupational Segregation*, Research Paper No. 9 (London, Department of Employment, 1979).

7  Alva Myrdal and Viola Klein, *Women's Two Roles – Home and Work* (London, Routledge and Kegan Paul, 1956). For an interesting discussion see Jane Lewis, 'Myrdal, Klein, *Women's Two Roles* and post-war feminism 1945–1960', in Harold L. Smith (ed.), *British Feminism in the Twentieth Century* (Aldershot, Edward Elgar, 1990).

8  Vera Brittain, *Lady into Woman* (London, Andrew Dakers Ltd, 1953).

9  Memorandum of Dissent, *Report of the Royal Commission on Equal Pay* (London, HMSO, 1946), p. 188. The memorandum was signed by Dame Anne Louglin, Dr Janet Vaughan and Miss L. F. Nettlefold. See also Hansard Vol. 438, 1946–47 (London, HMSO, 1947).

10  Sissons and French, *Age of Austerity*.

11  Pearson Phillips, 'The New Look', in Sissons and French, *Age of Austerity*, p. 130.

12  *Ibid.*

13  Raynes Minns, *Bombers and Mash* (London, Virago, 1980). In talking of women in this way, and at this period, it is important to remember the differences between women both in terms of age and class and the different ways in which war would have affected them.

14  *Calamity Jane* fans will recognise the similarity in the endings of these films about women who defy convention.

15  Richard Dyer, *Only Entertainment* (London, Routledge, 1992); Jackie Stacey, *Star Gazing* (London, Routledge, 1994).

# Filmography

Films listed are produced in the UK unless otherwise indicated.

*2000 Women*, 1944, Gainsborough, d. Frank Launder
*A Canterbury Tale*, 1944, The Archers, d. Michael Powell and Emeric Pressburger
*A Place of One's Own*, 1945, Gainsborough, d. Bernard Knowles
*All About Eve*, 1950, US, Twentieth Century Fox, d. Joseph L. Mankiewicz
*Annie Get Your Gun*, 1950, US, Metro Goldwyn Mayer, d. George Sidney
*Born Yesterday*, 1950, US, Columbia, d. George Cukor
*Brief Encounter*, 1945, Cineguild, d. David Lean
*British Pathé News*, British Pathé News Inc.
*Calamity Jane*, 1953, US, Warner Brothers, d. David Butler
*Captains of the Clouds*, 1942, US, Warner, d. Michael Curtiz
*Casablanca*, 1942, US, Warner, d. Michael Curtiz
*Convoy*, 1940, Ealing, d. Penrose Tennyson
*Dance Hall*, 1950, Ealing, d. Charles Crichton
*Desert Victory*, 1943, Army Film and Photographic Unit/Royal Air Force Film Production
    Unit, d. Captain Roy Boulting
*Double Indemnity*, 1944, US, Paramount, d. Billy Wilder
*Elizabeth: The Heart of a Nation*, 1990, Parkfield Publishing Video
*English Without Tears*, 1944, Two Cities, d. Harold French
*Escape Me Never*, 1935, British and Dominions, d. Paul Czinner
*Fanny By Gaslight*, 1944, Gainsborough, d. Anthony Asquith
*First Love*, 1939, US, Universal, d. Henry Koster
*Gert and Daisy's Weekend*, 1941, Butchers, d. Maclean Rogers
*Gilda*, 1946, US, Columbia, d. Charles Vidor
*Gone With the Wind*, 1939, US, Selznick/MGM, d. Victor Fleming
*Goodbye Mr Chips*, 1939, MGM British, d. Sam Wood
*Great Day*, 1945, RKO-Radio, d. Arthur Crabtree
*Hatter's Castle*, 1941, Paramount British, d. Lance Comfort
*Holiday Inn*, 1942, US, Paramount, d. Mark Sandrich
*How Green Was My Valley*, 1941, US, Twentieth Century Fox, d. John Ford
*I Know Where I'm Going*, 1945, The Archers, d. Michael Powell and Emeric Pressburger
*I Live in Grosvenor Square*, 1945, Associated British, d. Herbert Wilcox
*I See a Dark Stranger*, 1946, Independent Pictures, d. Frank Launder and Sidney Gilliat
*I Wanted Wings*, 1943, US, Paramount, d. Mitchell Leisen

*I'll Be Your Sweetheart*, 1945, Gainsborough, d. Val Guest
*In Which We Serve*, 1942, Two Cities, d. Noel Coward/David Lean
*It Always Rains on Sunday*, 1947, Ealing, d. Robert Hamer
*King's Row*, 1942, Warner Brothers, d. Sam Wood
*Lady Hamilton*, 1941, Alexander Korda Films, d. Alexander Korda
*Love Story*, 1945, Gainsborough, d. Leslie Arliss
*Madonna of the Seven Moons*, 1944, Gainsborough, d. Arthur Crabtree
*Mildred Pierce*, 1945, US, Warner, d. Michael Curtiz
*Millions Like Us*, 1943, Gainsborough, d. Frank Launder and Sidney Gilliat
*Miss Grant Goes to the Door*, 1940, Crown Film Unit, d. Brian Desmond Hurst
*Mrs Miniver*, 1942, US, Metro Goldwyn Mayer, d. William Wyler
*Night Train to Munich*, 1940, 20th Century Productions, d. Carol Reed
*Odette*, 1950, British Lion/Imperadio Pictures, d. Herbert Wilcox
*Old Mother Riley In Society*, 1940, British National, d. John Baxter
*Perfect Strangers*, 1945, MGM/London Films, d. Alexander Korda
*Piccadilly Incident*, 1946, Associated British, d. Herbert Wilcox
*Random Harvest*, 1942, US, Metro Goldwyn Mayer, d. Mervyn Le Roy
*Sally in Our Alley*, 1931, Associated Radio Pictures, d. Maurice Elvey
*Sergeant York*, 1941, US, Warner, d. Howard Hawks
*Ships With Wings*, 1941, Ealing, d. Sergei Nolbandov
*Sing As We Go*, 1934, Associated Talking Pictures, d. Basil Dean
*Sixty Glorious Years*, 1938, Imperator, d. Herbert Wilcox
*Spitfire*, 1942 (see *The First of the Few*)
*Sunshine Susie*, 1931, Gainsborough, d. Victor Saville
*Tawny Pipit*, 1944, Two Cities, d. Bernard Miles and Charles Saunders
*That Certain Age*, 1938, US, Universal, d. Edward Ludwig
*The 49th Parallel*, 1941, Ortus, d. Michael Powell
*The Bells Go Down*, 1943, Ealing, d. Basil Dearden
*The Black Swan*, 1942, US, Twentieth Century Fox, d. Henry King
*The Demi-Paradise*, 1943, Two Cities, d. Anthony Asquith
*The First of the Few*, 1942, Melbourne/British Aviation, d. Leslie Howard
*The Gentle Sex*, 1943, Two Cities, d. Leslie Howard
*The Lamp Still Burns*, 1943, Two Cities, d. Maurice Elvey
*The Life and Death of Colonel Blimp*, 1943, The Archers, d. Michael Powell and Emeric Pressburger
*The Love Parade*, 1929, US, Paramount, d. Ernst Lubitsch
*The Loves of Joanna Godden*, 1947, Ealing, d. Charles Frend
*The Man in Grey*, 1943, Gainsborough, d. Leslie Arliss
*The Next of Kin*, 1942, Ealing, d. Thorold Dickinson
*The Queen Mother: A Life of Our Times*, 1990, Independent Television News video
*The Red Shoes*, 1948, The Archers, d. Michael Powell and Emeric Pressburger
*The Scarlet Pimpernel*, 1934, London Films, d. Harold Young
*The Seventh Veil*, 1945, Theatrecraft/Ortus, d. Compton Bennet
*The Silver Fleet*, 1943, The Archers, d. Vernon Sewell and Gordon Wellesley
*The Way Ahead*, 1944, Two Cities, d. Carol Reed
*The Way to the Stars*, 1945, Two Cities, d. Anthony Asquith
*The Wicked Lady*, 1945, Gainsborough, d. Leslie Arliss
*The Young Mr Pitt*, 1942, 20th Century Productions, d. Carol Reed
*They Were Sisters*, 1945, Gainsborough, d. Arthur Crabtree
*This Happy Breed*, 1944, Two Cities/Cineguild, d. David Lean

*Three Smart Girls*, 1936, US, Universal, d. Henry Koster
*Three Smart Girls Grow Up*, 1939, US, Universal, d. Henry Koster
*Thunder Rock*, 1942, Charter Films, d. Roy Boulting
*Tudor Rose*, 1936, Gainsborough, d. Robert Stevenson
*Turn the Key Softly*, 1953, Chiltern, d. Jack Lee
*Victoria the Great*, 1937, Imperator, d. Herbert Wilcox
*Waterloo Road*, 1944, Gainsborough, d. Sidney Gilliat
*Western Approaches*, 1944, Crown Film Unit, d. Pat Jackson
*Went the Day Well?*, 1942, Ealing, d. Alberto Cavalcanti
*Yellow Canary*, 1943, Imperator Film Productions, d. Herbert Wilcox

# Bibliography

## Newspapers and magazines

BBC Year Book 1941
Daily Express
Daily Telegraph
Everybody's Weekly
Film Pictorial
Film Weekly
Girls' Cinema
Herald Tribune
Home Notes
International Women's News
Irish Independent
Kine Weekly
Kinematograph Weekly
Motion Picture Herald
My Weekly
New Statesman
New York Times
Night and Day
Picture Post
Picturegoer
Pictureshow
Punch
Radio Times
Sunday Times Magazine
The Lady
The Listener
The Observer
The Sheffield Star
The Spectator
The Standard
Time and Tide
Vogue
Woman
Woman and Beauty
Woman's Friend
Woman's Magazine
Woman's Own
Woman's Weekly
World Film News

## Archival sources

Bernard Miles Papers, British Film Institute Library.
*British Board of Film Censors Scenario Notes.*
British Film Producers' Association Executive Council Minutes.
Mass Observation File Reports, June 1942, No. 1316–7.
Mass Observation File Reports, October 1941, No. 919.
Mass Observation Box 2 File F.
Mass Observation Box 3 File F.
Mass Observation File Report 1083, 2 February 1942.
Mass Observation File Report 1238, 1 May 1942.
Mass Observation File Report 1567, 12 January 1943.

Mass Observation File Report 1980, August 1943.

Mass Observation File Report 2429, October 1946.

Mass Observation File Report 2464, March 1947.

Mass Observation File Report No. 458, *MoI Shorts*.

MRC MSS 66/1/1/2 (1940) and MSS 66/1/1/6 (1942), Proceedings in local conference between Coventry and District Engineering Employers' Association and Transport and General Workers' Union.

PRO BW 4/18.

PRO BW 4/21.

PRO BW 4/40.

PRO Cab 65/20 (1941), War Cabinet Conclusions.

PRO FO 371/22839.

PRO FO 371/24227.

PRO FO 371/34386.

PRO INF 1/196.

PRO INF 1/251.

PRO INF 1/318.

PRO INF 1/543.

PRO INF 1/615.

PRO INF 1/724, 1 June 1939.

PRO INF 1/867.

PRO LAB 26/35.

PRO Lab 8/623 (1942/3), Consultation with Trades Union Congress and British Employers' Federation about definition of part-time work for women.

PRO Lab 8/703 (1942–47), 'Development of part-time and spare-time employment and outwork' general policy.

PRO Lab 18/169 (1944).

PRO Lab 18/170 (1945).

PRO Lab 26/130 (1941), Meetings of the Women's Consultative Committee.

PRO Lab 26/63 (1942), Women's Services (Welfare and Amenities) Committee.

Publicity material, *Madonna of the Seven Moons*, British Film Institute Library.

## Government reports and publications

*British Labour Statistics – Historical Abstracts 1886–1968* (1971), London, HMSO.

Cantwell, J. D. (1989), *Images of War: British Posters 1939–45*, London, HMSO.

Denning, Mr Justice (1947), *Report of the Committee on Procedure in Matrimonial Causes*, Cmd 7024, London, HMSO.

Ferguson, Sheila and Fitzgerald, Hilde (1954), *Studies in the Social Services*, London, HMSO.

HM Government (1947), *Economic Survey for 1947*, Cmd 7046.

Hakim, Catherine (1979), *Occupational Segregation, Research Paper No. 9*, London, Department of Employment.

*Hansard* (1947), Vol. 438, 1946–47, London, HMSO.

Hargreaves, E. L. and Gowing, M. M. (1952), *The History of the Second World War: Civil Industry and Trade*, London, HMSO.

Hooks, J. M. (1944), *British Policies and Methods of Employing Women in Wartime*, Washington, U.S. Government.

Inman, P. (1957), *Labour in the Munitions Industries*, London, HMSO.

Ministry of Information Wartime Social Survey (1943), June/July, 'The cinema audience', London, Central Office of Information.

Ministry of Labour and National Service (1947), *Report for the Years 1939–1946*, Cmd 7225.

Morton, Lord (1956), *The Royal Commission on Marriage and Divorce*, London, HMSO.

Royal Commission on Equal Pay (1946), Memorandum of Dissent, London, HMSO.

Social Survey (1948), 'Women and industry: an inquiry into the problem of recruiting women to industry carried out for the Ministry of Labour and National Service' by Geoffrey Thomas, London, Central Office of Information.

*US Senate, 77th Congress* (1942), 1st Session, S. res. 152, 9–26 September 1941, US Govt. Printing Office.

Wartime Social Survey (1944), 'Women at work: the attitudes of working women towards post-war employment and some related problems' by Geoffrey Thomas, London, Central Office of Information.

## General bibliography

Abrams, Mark (1946), *The Condition of the British People, 1911–1945*, London, Victor Gollancz.

Addison, Paul (1977), *The Road to 1945: British Politics and the Second World War*, London, Quartet.

Aitken, I. (1990), *Film and Reform*, London, Routledge.

Alberti, J. (1989), *Beyond Suffrage: Feminists in War and Peace, 1914–28*, London, Macmillan.

Aldgate, Anthony and Richards, Jeffrey (1986), *Britain Can Take It*, Oxford, Blackwell.

Aldgate, Tony (1983), 'Comedy, class and containment: the British domestic cinema of the 1930s', in James Curran and Vincent Porter (eds), *British Cinema History*, London, Weidenfeld and Nicolson.

Allen, M. (1983), 'The domestic ideal and the mobilisation of woman power in World War II', *Women's Studies International Forum*, Vol. 6 No. 4.

Ang, Ien (1985), *Watching Dallas: Soap Opera and the Melodramatic Imagination*, London and New York, Methuen.

Anonymous (1944), *Ourselves in Wartime: An Illustrated Survey of the Home Front in the Second World War*, London, Odhams Press.

Ashelford, Jane (1974), *CC41 Utility Furniture and Fashion 1941–1951* (catalogue, Geoffreye Museum), London, ILEA.

Aspinall, Sue (1983), 'Sexuality in costume melodrama', in Sue Aspinall and Robert Murphy (eds), *Gainsborough Melodrama: BFI Dossier 18*, London, British Film Institute.

Aspinall, Sue (1983), 'Women, realism and reality in British films, 1943–53', in James Curran and Vincent Porter (eds), *British Cinema History*, London, Weidenfeld and Nicolson.

Aspinall, Sue and Murphy, Robert (eds) (1983), *Gainsborough Melodrama: BFI Dossier 18*, London, British Film Institute.

Attar, Dena (1990), *Wasting Girls' Time: The History and Politics of Home Economics*, London, Virago.

Barr, Charles (1986), 'Introduction: amnesia and schizophrenia', in Charles Barr (ed.), *All Our Yesterdays*, London, British Film Institute.

Bartlett, F. (1940), *Political Propaganda*, Cambridge, Cambridge University Press.

Beddoe, Deirdre (1989), *Back to Home and Duty: Women Between the Wars 1918–1939*, London, Pandora.

Beech, Joan (1989), *One WAAF's War*, Tunbridge Wells, D. J. Costello (Publishers) Ltd.

Bendit, Phoebe D. and Bendit, Laurence J. (1946), *Living Together Again*, London & Chesham, Gramol Publications Ltd.

Berrios, German E. (1991), 'British psychopathology since the early 20th century', in German E. Berrios and Hugh Freeman (eds), *150 Years of British Psychiatry, 1841–1991*, London, Gaskell.

Bhabha, Homi (1983), 'The other question … the stereotype and colonial discourse', *Screen*, Vol. 24 No. 6, November/December.

Biddle, Eric (1942), *The Mobilization of the Home Front: The British Experience and Its Significance for the United States*, Chicago, Public Administration Press.

Bishop, Alan and Bennett, Y. Alexandra (eds) (1989), *Wartime Chronicle: Vera Brittain's Diary 1939–1945*, London, Victor Gollancz Ltd.

Blacker, C. P. (ed.) (1952), *Problem Families: Five Inquiries*, London, Eugenics Society.

Bland, Lucy (1983), 'Purity, motherhood, pleasure or threat? Definitions of female sexuality 1900–1970s', in Sue Cartledge and Joanna Ryan (eds), *Sex and Love: New Thoughts on Old Contradictions*, London, Women's Press.

Boston, Anne (ed.) (1988), *Wave Me Goodbye: Stories of the Second World War*, London, Virago.

Bousquet, B. and Douglas, C. (1991), *West Indian Women at War*, London, Lawrence and Wishart.

Braithwaite, Brian, Walsh, Noelle, and Davies, Glyn (eds) (1987), *The Home Front: The Best of Good Housekeeping 1939–1945*, London, Ebury Press.

Braverman, Harry (1974), *Labor and Monopoly Capital: The Degradation of Work in the Twentieth Century*, New York, Monthly Review Press.

Braybon, Gail (1989), *Women Workers in the First World War*, London, Routledge.

Braybon, Gail and Summerfield, Penny (1987), *Out of the Cage: Women's Experiences in the Two World Wars*, London, Pandora.

Bridenthal, R. *et al.* (1984), *When Biology Became Destiny: Women in Weimar and Nazi Germany*, New York, Monthly Review Press.

Brittain, Vera (1941/1981), *England's Hour: An Autobiography 1939–1941*, London, Macmillan 1941, Futura 1981.

Brittain, Vera (1953), *Lady into Woman*, London, Andrew Dakers Ltd.

Brittain, Vera (1978), *Testament of Experience*, London, Virago.

Broad, Richard and Fleming, Suzie (eds) (1981), *Nella Last's War: A Mother's Diary 1939–45*, London, Sphere Books Ltd.

Brookes, P. (1967), *Women at Westminster: An Account of Women in the British Parliament 1918–1966*, London, Peter Davies.

Brooks, Peter (1976), *The Melodramatic Imagination*, New Haven, Yale University Press.

Brown, Geoff (1977), *Launder and Gilliat*, London, British Film Institute.

Burnett, John (1986), *A Social History of Housing 1815–1985*, London, Methuen.

Byars, Jackie (1988), 'Gazes, voices, power: expanding psychoanalysis for feminist film and television theory', in Deirdre Pribram (ed.), *Female Spectators: Looking at Film and Television*, London, Verso.

Calder, Angus (1982), *The People's War: Britain, 1939–1945*, London, Granada.

Calder, Angus (1991), *The Myth of the Blitz*, London, Jonathan Cape.

Chesser, Eustace (1952), *Love and Marriage*, London, Pan (originally published in 1946 under the title *Marriage and Freedom*).

Chesser, Eustace (1958), *Women: A Popular Edition of 'The Chesser Report'*, London, Jarrolds.

Clarke, J., Cochrane, A. and Smart C. (1987), *Ideologies of Welfare*, London, Hutchinson.

Cobb, Ruth (nd, 1941?), *The Village Story*, John Crowther Publications.

Coglan, W. N. (1936), *The Readership of Newspapers and Periodicals in Great Britain, 1936*, London, Incorporated Society of British Advertisers.

Colls, R. and Dodd, P. (1985), 'Representing the nation – British documentary film 1930–45', *Screen*, Vol. 26 No. 1, January–February.

Connell, R. W. (1987), *Gender and Power*, Cambridge, Polity Press.

Cook, Pam (1983), 'Melodrama and the women's picture', in Sue Aspinall and Robert Murphy (eds), *Gainsborough Melodrama: BFI Dossier 18*, London, British Film Institute.

Cooke, Douglas (ed.) (1944), *Youth Organisations of Great Britain 1944–45*, London, Jordan & Sons, Ltd.

Croucher, R. (1982), *Engineers at War*, London, Merlin.

Curran, James and Porter, Vincent (eds) (1983), *British Cinema History*, London, Weidenfeld and Nicolson.

Curran, James and Seaton, Jean (eds) (1991 4th edition), *Power Without Responsibility: The Press and Broadcasting in Britain*, London, Routledge.

Darian-Smith, Kate (1994), 'War stories: remembering the Australian home front during the Second World War', in Kate Darian-Smith and Paula Hamilton (eds), *Memory and History in Twentieth Century Australia*, Melbourne, Oxford University Press.

Darracott, Joseph and Loftus, Belinda (1972), *Second World War Posters*, London, Imperial War Museum.

Davidson, Caroline (1982), *A Woman's Work is Never Done: A History of Housework in the British Isles 1650–1950*, London, Chatto and Windus.

Davies, Jennifer (1993), *The Wartime Kitchen and Garden: The Home Front 1939–45*, London, BBC Books.

Dickinson, Margaret and Street, Sarah (1985), *Cinema and State: The Film Industry and Government, 1927–1934*, London, British Film Institute.

Donaldson, Frances (1974), *Edward VIII*, London, Weidenfeld and Nicolson.

Doule, Vera (1943), *The Lesser Half*, London, Women's Publicity Planning Association.

Duchess of Windsor (1956), *The Heart Has Its Reasons*, London, Michael Joseph.

Dyer, Richard (1979), *Stars*, London, British Film Institute.

Dyer, Richard (1992), *Only Entertainment*, London and New York, Routledge.

Ehrenreich, Barbara and English, Deidre (1979), *For Her Own Good: 150 Years of the Experts' Advice to Women*, London, Pluto.

Ellis, John (1978), 'Art, culture, quality: terms for a cinema in the forties and seventies', *Screen*, Vol. 19 No. 3.

Everson, William K. (1976), 'The career of Deanna Durbin', *Films in Review*, Vol. 27 No. 9.

Ewing, Elizabeth (1981), *Fur in Dress*, London, Batsford.

Ewing, Elizabeth (1986), *History of Twentieth Century Fashion*, London, Batsford.

Ferguson, Marjorie (1983), *Forever Feminine: Women's Magazines and the Cult of Femininity*, London, Heinemann.

Figes, Eva (ed.) (1994), *Women's Letters in Wartime, 1450–1945*, London, Pandora.

Flamini, Roland (1992), *Sovereign Elizabeth II*, London, Corgi.

Flugel, J. C. (1930), *The Psychology of Clothes*, London, Hogarth Press.

Forty, Adrian (1986), *Objects of Desire*, London, Thames and Hudson.

Friedan, Betty (1963), *The Feminine Mystique*, New York, Dell Publishing.

Fryer, P. (1984), *Staying Power*, London, Pluto Press.

Fussell, Paul (1989), *Wartime: Understanding and Behaviour in the Second World War*, Oxford, Oxford University Press.

Gibson, C. (1974), 'The association between divorce and social class in England and Wales', *British Journal of Sociology*, Vol. 25 No. 1.

Gill, D. (1977), *Illegitimacy, Sexuality and the Status of Women*, Oxford, Blackwell.

Gittens, Diana (1982) *Fair Sex: Family Size and Structure, 1900–39*, London, Hutchinson.

Gledhill, Christine (1987), 'Mapping the field', in Christine Gledhill (ed.), *Home Is Where the Heart Is: Studies in Melodrama and the Woman's Film*, London, British Film Institute.

Gledhill, Christine (1992), 'Between melodrama and realism: Anthony Asquith's *Underground*, and King Vidor's *The Crowd*', in Jane Gaines (ed.), *Classical Hollywood Narrative: The Paradigm Wars*, Durham, North Carolina, Duke University Press.

Gledhill, Christine (ed.) (1987), *Home Is Where the Heart Is: Studies in Melodrama and the Woman's Film*, London, British Film Institute.

Gledhill, Christine (ed.) (1991), *Stardom: Industry of Desire*, London, British Film Institute.

Gledhill, Christine and Swanson, Gillian (1984), 'Gender and sexuality in Second World War films – a feminist approach', in Geoff Hurd (ed.), *National Fiction: British World War Two in British Films and Television*, London, British Film Institute.

Glover, Edward (1940), 'Changes in psychic economy', *The Lancet*, 23 March.

Glover, Edward (1940), *The Psychology of Fear and Courage*, Harmondsworth, Penguin.

Gordon, Linda (1986), *Heroes of Their Own Lives*, London, Virago.

Gorer, Geoffrey (1971), *Sex and Marriage in Britain Today*, London, Nelson.

Grafton, Pete (1981), *You, You & You!: The People Out of Step with World War II*, London, Pluto Press.

Grieve, Mary (1964), *Millions Made My Story*, London, Victor Gollancz.

Griffith, Edward F. (1948), *Morals in the Melting Pot*, London, Methuen & Co Ltd.

Grove, Valerie (1989), 'Introduction' to Jan Struthers (1939/1989), *Mrs Miniver*, London, Virago.

Hall, Stuart (1972), 'The "social eye" of *Picture Post*', *Working Papers in Cultural Studies 2*, Centre for Contemporary Cultural Studies, University of Birmingham.

Hall, Stuart (1977), 'Culture, the media and the "ideological effect"', in James Curran *et al.* (eds), *Mass Communication and Society*, London, Edward Arnold.

Harper, Sue (1983), 'Art direction and costume design', in Sue Aspinall and Robert Murphy (eds.), *Gainsborough Melodrama: BFI Dossier 18*, London, British Film Institute.

Harper, Sue (1987), 'Historical pleasures: Gainsborough costume melodrama 1942–47', in Christine Gledhill (ed.), *Home Is Where the Heart Is: Studies in Melodrama and the Woman's Film*, London, British Film Institute.

Harper, Sue (1988), 'The representation of women in British feature film 1939–45', in P. Taylor (ed.), *Britain and the Cinema in the Second World War*, London, Macmillan.

Harper, Sue (1994), *Picturing the Past*, London, British Film Institute.

Harrisson, Tom (1976), *Living Through the Blitz*, London, William Collins.

Harrisson, Tom and Madge, Charles (1939/1986), *Britain, by Mass Observation*, London, Century Hutchinson.

Heath, Joan (1988), '"Fashion by government order": fact or fiction?', unpublished undergraduate thesis.

Hermes, Joke (1995), *Reading Women's Magazines: An Analysis of Everyday Media Use*, Cambridge, Polity.

Higgonet, Margaret *et al.* (1987), *Behind the Lines: Gender and the Two World Wars*, New Haven, Yale University Press.

Higson, Andrew (1986), 'Britain's outstanding contribution to the film', in Charles Barr (ed.), *All Our Yesterdays*, London, British Film Institute.

Hiley, Nick (1991), 'British cinema fan magazines in 1936', unpublished manuscript.

Holcombe, L. (1983), *Wives and Property: Reform of the Married Women's Property Law in Nineteenth Century England*, Oxford, Martin Robertson.

Holtby, Winifred (1934), *Women*, London, John Lane The Bodley Head.

Holtby, Winifred (1985), 'Black words for women only' (1934) and 'Shall I order a black blouse?' (1934), from *Women*, London, John Lane The Bodley Head, reprinted in P. Berry and A. Bishop (eds), *Testament of a Generation: The Journalism of Vera Brittain and Winifred Holtby*, London, Virago.

Hopkins, Eric (1991), *The Rise and Decline of the English Working Classes 1918–1990: A Social History*, London, Weidenfeld and Nicolson.

Hopkins, Harry (1964), *The New Look: A Social History of the Forties and Fifties in Britain*, London, Secker & Warburg.

Houston, Penelope (1963), 'The figure in the carpet', *Sight and Sound*, Autumn.

Howard, Ronald (1981), *In Search of My Father: A Portrait of Leslie Howard*, London, Kimber Press.

Igra, Samuel (1940), *Germany's National Vice*, London, Quality Press Ltd.

Jackson, Alan (1973), *Semi-detached London*, London, Allen and Unwin.

Jarrett-Macauley, Delia, 'Interviews with black British women', unpublished.

Jarrett-Macauley, Delia, 'The biography of Una Marston', unpublished manuscript.

Jeffrey, Truby (ed.) (1948), *Daily Mail Film Award Annual 1948*, Winchester Publications Ltd.

Jenson, Joli (1990), *Redeeming Modernity: Contradictions in Media Criticism*, Newbury Park, Sage.

Jerrold, Blanchard and Dore, Gustave (1872), *A London Pilgrimage*, London, Grant & Co.

Johnson, Lesley (1992), *The Modern Girl*, Sydney, Allen and Unwin.

Joshi, H. (1989), 'The changing form of women's economic dependency', in H. Joshi (ed.), *The Changing Population of Britain*, Oxford, Blackwell.

Kaplan, Ann (1987), 'Mothering, feminism and representation: the maternal in melodrama and the woman's film 1910–1940', in Christine Gledhill (ed.), *Home Is Where the Heart Is: Studies in Melodrama and the Woman's Film*, London, British Film Institute.

Keating, P. (ed.) (1976), *Into Unknown England*, London, Fontana.

Kirkham, Pat (1988), *Wedding Belles* (exhibition catalogue), Leicester, Leicester Polytechnic.

Kirkham, Pat (1995), 'Beauty and duty: keeping up the (home) front', in Pat Kirkham and David Thoms (eds), *War Culture: Social Change and Changing Experience in World War Two Britain*, London, Lawrence and Wishart.

Koven, S. and Michel, S. (eds) (1993), *Mothers of a New World: Maternalist Politics and the Origins of the Welfare State*, London, Routledge.

Kuhn, Annette (1994), 'Researching popular film fan culture in 1930s Britain', in J. Gripsrud and K. Skretting (eds), *History of Moving Images: Reports from a Norwegian Project*, Oslo, Research Council of Norway.

Laird, Sydney M. (1942), *Venereal Disease in Britain*, Harmondsworth, Penguin.

Lake, Marilyn (1990), 'Female desires: the meaning of World War II', *Australian Historical Studies*, Vol. 24 No. 5.

Lake, Marilyn (1993), 'The desire for a yank: sexual relations between Australian women and American servicemen during World War 2', in Patricia Grimshaw, Ruth Fincher and Marion Campbell (eds), *Studies in Gender: Essays in Honour of Norma Grieve*, University of Melbourne: Melbourne University Studies in Gender.

'Lance Comfort: Filmography', *Filme Cultura*, Vol. 4 No. 18, January/February 1971.

Land, H. (1985), 'The introduction of family allowances: an act of historic justice?', in C. Ungerson (ed.), *Women and Social Policy: A Reader*, London, Macmillan.

Landy, M. (1991), *British Cinema Genres: Cinema and Society, 1930–1960*, New Jersey, Princeton University Press.

Lang, Caroline (1989), *Keep Smiling Through: Women in the Second World War*, Cambridge, Cambridge University Press.

Lant, Antonia (1990), 'The female spy: gender, nationality and war in *I See a Dark Stranger*', in Robert Sklar and Charles Musser (eds), *Resisting Images: Essays on Cinema and History*, Philadelphia, Temple University Press.

Lant, Antonia (1991), *Blackout: Reinventing Women for Wartime British Cinema*, Princeton, Princeton University Press.

Leitch, M. (1975), *Great Songs of World War II*, London, Wise.

Leman, Joy (1980), '"The advice of a real friend": codes of intimacy and oppression in women's magazines 1937–1955', *Women's Studies International Quarterly*, Vol. 3, pp. 63–78.

Leser, C. E. V. (1952), 'Men and women in industry', *Economic Journal*, No. 62.

Levine, P. (1990), *Feminist Lives in Victorian England*, Oxford, Blackwell.

Lewis, Bernard (nd), 'Always and everywhere', unpublished manuscript.

Lewis, Jane (1983), 'Dealing with dependency: state practices and social realities, 1870–1945', in Jane Lewis (ed.), *Women's Welfare, Women's Rights*, London, Croom Helm.

Lewis, Jane (1984), *Women in England 1870–1950: Sexual Divisions and Social Change*, Sussex, Wheatsheaf.

Lewis, Jane (1990), 'Myrdal, Klein, women's two roles and postwar feminism 1945–1960', in H. Smith (ed.), *British Feminism in the Twentieth Century*, Aldershot, Edward Elgar.

Lewis, Jane (1992), *Women in Britain since 1945*, Oxford, Blackwell.

Lewis, Jane (ed.) (1986), *Labour and Love: Women's Experiences of Home and Family 1850–1940*, Oxford, Blackwell.

Light, Alison (1991), *Forever England: Femininity, Literature and Conservatism Between the Wars*, London and New York, Routledge.

Lovell, Terry (1980), *Pictures of Reality: Aesthetics, Politics and Pleasure*, London, British Film Institute.

MacAndrew, Rennie (1941), *The Red Light: Intimate Hygiene for Men and Women*, The Wales Publishing Co.

MacCabe, Colin (1974), 'Realism and the cinema: notes on some Brechtian theses', *Screen*, Vol. 15 No. 2.

MacKenzie, N. and J. (1985), *The Diary of Beatrice Webb, Vol. 4, 1924–43*, London, Virago.

Manvell, Roger (1945), 'Recent films', *Britain Today*, May.

Marquand, David (1963), 'Sir Stafford Cripps', in Michael Sissons and Philip French (eds), *Age of Austerity*, London, Hodder and Stoughton.

Marwick, Arthur (1976), *The Home Front: The British and the Second World War*, London, Thames and Hudson.

Mass Observation (1943/1987), *War Factory*, London, The Cresset Library.

Mass Observation (1944), *The Journey Home: A Mass-Observation Report on the Problems of Demobilisation*, London, John Murray.

Mayer, J. P. (1946), *Sociology of Film: Studies and Documents*, London: Faber and Faber.

Mayer, J. P. (1948), *British Cinemas and Their Audiences*, London, Dennis Dobson.

Mayhew, Henry (1851), *London Labour and the London Poor*, London, Frank Cass & Co.

McCooey, Chris (1994), *Despatches From the Home Front: The War Diaries of Joan Strange, 1939–45*, Tunbridge Wells, JAK Books.

McLaine, Ian (1979), *Ministry of Morale: Home Front Morale and the Ministry of Information in World War II*, London, George Allen & Unwin.

McNeil, Peter (1994), '"Put your best face forward": the impact of the Second World War on British Dress', *Journal of Design History*, Vol. 6 No. 4.

Medhurst, Andy (1991), 'That special thrill: *Brief Encounter*, homosexuality and authorship', *Screen*, Vol. 32 No. 2.

Miller, Emanuel (ed.) (1940), *The Neuroses in War*, London, Macmillan and Co. Ltd.

Minns, Raynes (1980), *Bombers and Mash: The Domestic Front 1939–45*, London, Virago Ltd.

Morgan, A. E. (1943), *Young Citizen*, Harmondsworth, Penguin.

Morgan, David and Evans, Mary (1993), *The Battle for Britain: Citizenship and Ideology in the Second World War*, London and New York, Routledge.

Morgan, Guy (1948), *Red Roses Every Night: An Account of London Cinemas Under Fire*, London, Quality Press.

Morris, Lynda and Radford, Robert (1983), *The Story of the Artists' International Association: 1933–1953*, Oxford, Holywell Press.

Mowat, C. L. (1955), *Britain Between the Wars, 1918–1940*, London, Methuen.

Mulvey, Laura (1984), ' "It will be a magnificent obsession": the melodrama's role in the development of contemporary film theory', in Jacky Bratton, Jim Cook and Christine Gledhill (eds), *Melodrama: Stage, Picture, Screen*, London, British Film Institute.

Mulvey, Laura (1989), 'Melodrama inside and outside the home', in *Visual and Other Pleasures*, Houndmills, Macmillan.

Murphy, Robert (1989), *Realism and Tinsel*, London and New York, Routledge.

Myrdal, Alva and Klein, Viola (1956), *Women's Two Roles – Home and Work*, London, Routledge and Kegan Paul.

Neale, Stephen (1993), 'Melotalk: on the meaning and use of the term melodrama in the American trade press', *The Velvet Light Trap*, No. 32, Autumn.

Nowell-Smith, Geoffrey (1987), 'Minnelli and melodrama', in Christine Gledhill (ed.), *Home Is Where the Heart Is: Studies in Melodrama and the Woman's Film*, London, British Film Institute.

Oakley, Ann (1974), *Housewife*, London, Allen Lane.

Ohmer, Susan (1990), 'Female spectatorship and women's magazines: Hollywood, *Good Housekeeping*, and World War II', *The Velvet Light Trap*, No. 25.

Olivier, Laurence (1982), *Confessions of an Actor*, London, Weidenfeld.

Orwell, George (1941), *The Lion and the Unicorn: Socialism and the English Genius*, London, Secker and Warburg.

Parkin, D. (1989), 'Women in the armed services, 1940–45', in Raphael Samuel (ed.), *Patriotism: The Making and Unmaking of British National Identity, Vol. 2: Minorities and Outsiders*, London, Routledge.

Pateman, Carol (1989), *The Disorder of Women*, Cambridge, Polity Press.

Perry, George (1985), *The Great British Picture Show*, London, Pavilion Books/Michael Joseph.

[ 293 ]

Petrie, Charles (1950), *Chapters of Life*, London, Eyre and Spottiswoode.

Phillips, A. (1993), *Democracy and Difference*, Cambridge, Polity Press.

Phillips, Pearson (1963), 'The New Look', in Michael Sissons and Philip French (eds), *Age of Austerity*, London, Hodder and Stoughton.

Pierotti, A. M. (1963), *The Story of the National Union of Women Teachers*, London, National Union of Women Teachers.

Pierson, R. R. (1991), 'Experience, difference, dominance and voice in the writing of Canadian women's history', in K. Offen, R. R. Pierson, and J. Rendall (eds), *Writing Women's History: International Perspectives*, London, Macmillan.

Pinchbeck, I. (1930), *Women Workers and the Industrial Revolution*, London, Routledge.

Pines, Jim (1992), *Black and White in Colour*, London, British Film Institute.

Pollock, Griselda (1988), 'Vicarious excitements: *London: a Pilgrimage* by Gustave Dore and Blanchard Jerrold, 1872', *New Formations*, No. 4, Spring.

Porter, Vincent and Litewski, Chaim (1981), '*The Way Ahead*: the case of a propaganda film', *Sight and Sound*, Spring.

Powell, Michael (1986), *A Life in Movies*, London, Heinemann.

Priestley, J. B. (1934), *English Journey*, London, William Heinemann.

Priestley, J. B. (1943), *British Women Go To War*, London, Collins.

Pronay, Nicholas (1980), 'Introduction' to Frances Thorpe and Nicholas Pronay, *British Official Films in the Second World War: A Descriptive Catalogue*, Oxford, Clio Press.

Pronay, Nicholas and Croft, Jeremy (1983), 'British film censorship and propaganda policy during the Second World War', in James Curran and Vincent Porter, *British Cinema History*, London, Weidenfeld and Nicolson.

Pugh, M. (1992), *Women and the Women's Movement in Britain 1914–1959*, London, Macmillan.

Ramdin, R. (1987), *The Making of the Black Working Class in Britain*, London, Gower.

Randall, V. (1987), *Women and Politics*, London, Macmillan Education.

Rhodes, Anthony (1983), *Propaganda. The Art of Persuasion: World War II, Vol. I*, New York and London, Chelsea House Publishers.

Rice, Marjorie Spring (1939/1981), *Working Class Wives*, London, Virago.

Richards, Jeffrey (1979), 'Gracie Fields: the Lancashire Britannia', *Focus on Film*, No. 33.

Richards, Jeffrey (1984), *Age of the Dream Palace: Cinema and Society in Britain 1930–39*, London, Routledge and Kegan Paul.

Richards, Jeffrey (1987), 'Wartime British cinema audiences and the class system: the case of *Ships With Wings* (1941)', *Historical Journal of Film, Radio and Television*, Vol. 2 No. 2.

Richards, Jeffrey and Sheridan, Dorothy (1987), *Mass-Observation at the Movies*, London, Routledge and Kegan Paul.

Riley, Denise (1981), 'The Free Mothers: pronatalism and working mothers in industry at the end of the last war in Britain', *History Workshop Journal*, No. 11.

Riley, Denise (1983), *War in the Nursery: Theories of the Child and Mother*, London, Virago.

Riley, Denise (1988), '*Am I That Name?*', London, Macmillan.

Rose, Nikolas (1986), *The Psychological Complex: Psychology, Politics and Society in England, 1869–1939*, London, Routledge.

Rose, Nikolas (1990), *Governing the Soul: The Shaping of the Private Self*, London and New York, Routledge.

Rosen, Philip (1993), 'Document and documentary: on the persistence of historical concepts', in M. Renov (ed.), *Theorizing Documentary*, New York and London, Routledge.

Routh, G. (1965), *Occupation and Pay in Great Britain 1906–1960*, Cambridge, Cambridge University Press.

Rowell, G. (ed.) (1971), *Victorian Dramatic Criticism*, London, Methuen.

Rowson, Simon (1936), 'A statistical survey of the cinema industry in Great Britain in 1934', *Journal of the Royal Statistical Society*, Vol. 99 No. 1.

Rowson, Simon (1939), *The Social and Political Aspects of Films*, London, British Kinematograph Society.

Rupp, L. J. (1978), *Mobilizing Women for War: German and American Propaganda 1939–1945*, Princeton, Princeton University Press.

Saunders, Kay and Bolton, Geoffrey (1992), 'Girdled for war: women's mobilisations in World War Two', in Kay Saunders and Ray Evans (eds), *Gender Relations in Australia: Domination and Negotiation*, Sydney, Harcourt Brace Jovanovich.

Schmideberg, Melitta (1942), 'Some observations on individual reactions to air raids', *International Journal of Psychoanalysis*, Vol. 23.

Scott, George Ryley (1940), *Sex Problems and Dangers in War-Time: A Book of Practical Advice for Men and Women on the Fighting and Home Fronts*, London, T. Werner Laurie.

Scott, P. (1940), *British Women in War*, London, Hutchinson.

Scott, P. (1944), *They Made Invasion Possible*, London, Hutchinson.

Sheridan, Dorothy (1990), 'Ambivalent memories: women and the 1939–45 war in Britain', *Oral History*, Vol. 18 No. 1.

Sheridan, Dorothy (ed.) (1991), *Wartime Women: An Anthology of Women's Wartime Writing for Mass-Observation, 1937–45*, London, Mandarin.

Short, K. R. M. (1991), '*That Hamilton Woman* (1941): propaganda, feminism and the production code', *Historical Journal of Film, Radio and Television*, Vol. 11 No. 1.

Silverman, Kaja (1988), *The Acoustic Mirror: The Female Voice in Psychoanalysis and the Cinema*, Bloomington, Indiana University Press.

Six Point Group (1945), *Dorothy Evans and the Six Point Group*, London, Six Point Group.

Slater, Eliot and Woodside, Moya (1951), *Patterns of Marriage*, London, Cassell & Company Ltd.

Smart, Carol (1984), *The Ties That Bind*, London, Routledge.

Smith, A. C. H. with Immirzi, E. and Blackwell, T. (1975), *Paper Voices: The Popular Press and Social Change 1935–1965*, London, Chatto and Windus.

Smith, H. (1981), 'The problem of "Equal Pay for Equal Work" in Great Britain during World War II', *Journal of Modern History*, Vol. 53 No. 4, December.

Smith, Harold L. (1986), *War and Social Change: British Society in the Second World War*, Manchester, Manchester University Press.

Smith, Harold L. (1986), 'The effect of war on the status of women', in Harold L. Smith (ed.), *War and Social Change: British Society in the Second World War*, Manchester, Manchester University Press.

Smith, Harold L. (1990), 'British feminism in the 1920s', in Harold L. Smith (ed.), *British Feminism in the Twentieth Century*, Aldershot, Edward Elgar.

Smith, J. H. (1961), 'Managers and married women workers', *British Journal of Sociology*, No. 12.

Smithies, Edward (1982), *Crime in Wartime: A Social History of Crime in World War II*, London, George Allen & Unwin.

Spence, Jo (1977), 'What did you do in the war mummy? Class and gender in images of women', *Photography/Politics One*, London, Photography Workshop.

Spensky, Martine (1992), 'Producers of legitimacy: homes for unmarried mothers in the

1950s', in Carol Smart (ed.), *Regulating Womanhood: Historical Essays on Marriage, Motherhood and Sexuality*, London and New York, Routledge.

Stacey, Jackie (1991), 'Feminine fascinations: forms of identification in star–audience relations', in Christine Gledhill (ed.), *Stardom: Industry of Desire*, London, Routledge.

Stacey, Jackie (1994), *Star Gazing: Hollywood Cinema and Female Spectatorship*, London and New York, Routledge.

Stanley, L. (1984), *The Diaries of Hannah Cullwick*, London, Virago.

Stott, M. (1978), *Organisation Woman: The Story of the National Union of Townswomen's Guilds*, London, Heinemann.

Struther, Jan (1939/1989), *Mrs Miniver*, London, Virago.

Summerfield, Penny (1984), *Women Workers in the Second World War*, London, Croom Helm.

Summerfield, Penny (1989), *Women Workers in the Second World War: Production and Patriarchy in Conflict*, London, Routledge.

Summerfield, Penny (1993), 'The patriarchal discourse of human capital: training women for war work 1939–1945', *Journal of Gender Studies*, Vol. 2 No. 2.

Taylor, Eric (1988), *Women Who Went to War 1938–1946*, London, Grafton.

Taylor, Helen (1989), *Scarlett's Women: Gone with the Wind and its Female Fans*, London, Routledge.

Taylor, Lou and Wilson, Elizabeth (1989), *Through the Looking Glass*, London, BBC Books.

*The Shorter Oxford English Dictionary* (1968), Oxford, Clarendon Press.

Theweleit, Klaus (1987), *Male Fantasies, Vol. I*, Cambridge, Polity Press.

Theweleit, Klaus (1989), *Male Fantasies, Vol. II*, Cambridge, Polity Press.

Thompson, Kirstin (1985), *Exporting Entertainment: America in the World Film Market, 1907–34*, London, British Film Institute.

Thorpe, Frances and Pronay, Nicholas (1980), *British Official Films in the Second World War*, Oxford, Clio Press.

Thumim, Janet (1991), 'The "popular", cash and culture in the post-war British cinema industry', *Screen*, Vol. 23 No 3.

Thumim, Janet (1992), *Celluloid Sisters: Women and Popular Cinema*, London, Macmillan.

Thumim, Janet (forthcoming), 'Film and female identity: questions of method in investigating representations of women in popular cinema', in Douglas Petrie (ed.), *New Scholarship Working Papers*, London, British Film Institute.

Tickner, Lisa (1976), 'Women and trousers: unisex clothing and sex role changes in the twentieth century', *Leisure in the Twentieth Century: Design History Conference Papers*, London: The Design Council.

Titmuss, Richard M. (1950), *Problems of Social Policy*, London, HMSO and Longmans, Green & Co.

Townsend, Colin and Eileen (1989), *War Wives: A Second World War Anthology*, London, Grafton Books.

Trist, G. and Murray, H. (eds) (1990), *The Social Engagement of Social Science: A Tavistock Anthology, Volume I: The Socio-Psychological Perspective*, Philadelphia, University of Pennsylvania Press.

Waller, Jane and Vaughan-Rees, Michael (1987), *Women in Wartime: The Role of Women's Magazines 1939–1945*, London, Macdonald Optima.

Watson, Elizabeth (1994), *Don't Wait For It, or Impressions of War 1939–41*, London, Imperial War Museum.

Wheeler-Bennett (1958), *King George VI*, London, Macmillan.

White, Cynthia (1970), *Women's Magazines 1693–1968*, London, Michael Joseph.

Willey, Bob (1989), *From All Sides: Memories of World War II*, Gloucester, Alan Sutton Publishing.

Williams, Christopher (1980), *Realism and the Cinema: A Reader*, London, Routledge and Kegan Paul.

Williamson, Judith (1986), 'Woman is an island: femininity and colonization', in Tania Modleski (ed.), *Studies in Entertainment: Critical Approaches to Mass Culture*, Bloomington and Indianapolis, Indiana University Press.

Wilson, Elizabeth (1977), *Women and the Welfare State*, London, Tavistock.

Wilson, Elizabeth (1980), *Only Halfway to Paradise: Women in Postwar Britain, 1945–1968*, London, Tavistock.

Wilson, Elizabeth (1985), *Adorned in Dreams: Fashion and Modernity*, London, Virago Press.

Wilson, Elizabeth, and Taylor, Lou (1989), *Through the Looking Glass: A History of Dress from 1860 to the Present Day*, London, BBC Books.

Winnicott, D. W. (1950), 'Thoughts on the meaning of the word democracy', in *Human Relations*, No. 4, reproduced in Eric Trist and Hugh Murray (eds) (1990), *The Social Engagement of Social Science: A Tavistock Anthology, Volume 1: The Socio-Psychological Perspective*, Philadelphia, University of Pennsylvania Press.

Winship, Janice (1981), 'Woman becomes an "individual": femininity and consumption in women's magazines 1954–69', Occasional Paper 65, Centre for Contemporary Cultural Studies, University of Birmingham.

Winship, Janice (1984), 'Nation before family: *Woman*, The National Home Weekly, 1945–53', in *Formations of Nation and People*, London, Routledge and Kegan Paul.

Wood, Heath and Maggie (1989), *'We Wore What We'd Got': Women's Clothes in World War II*, Warwickshire, Warwickshire Books.

Woolf, Virginia (1967), 'Royalty', in Virginia Woolf, *Collected Essays, Vol. 4*, London, Hogarth Press.

Worden, Suzette (1989), 'Powerful women: electricity in the home, 1919–40', in Judy Attfield and Pat Kirkham (eds), *A View from the Interior: Feminism, Women and Design*, London, Women's Press.

# Index

Page numbers in **bold** are main references to a subject, *italics* indicate page numbers for illustrations